CONTEMPORARY PUBLISHING
AND THE CULTURE OF BOOKS

Contemporary Publishing and the Culture of Books is a comprehensive resource that builds bridges between the traditional focus and methodologies of literary studies and the actualities of modern and contemporary literature, including the realities of professional writing, the conventions and practicalities of the publishing world, and its connections between literary publishing and other media. Focusing on the relationship between modern literature and the publishing industry, the volume enables students and academics to extend the text-based framework of modules on contemporary writing into detailed expositions of the culture and industry which bring these texts into existence; it brings economic considerations into line alongside creative issues, and examines how marketing strategies are employed to promote and sell books.

Chapters cover:

- The standard university-course specifications of contemporary writing, offering an extensive picture of the social, economic, and cultural contexts of these literary genres
- The impact and status of non-literary writing, and how this compares with certain literary genres as an index to contemporary culture and a reflection of the state of the publishing industry
- The practicalities and conventions of the publishing industry
- Contextual aspects of literary culture and the book industry, visiting the broader spheres of publishing, promotion, bookselling, and literary culture

Carefully linked chapters allow readers to tie key elements of the publishing industry to the particular demands and features of contemporary literary genres and writing, offering a detailed guide to the ways in which the three core areas of culture, economics, and pragmatics intersect in the world of publishing.

Further to being a valuable resource for those studying English or Creative Writing, the volume is a key text for degrees in which Publishing is a component, and is relevant to those aspects of Media Studies that look at interactions between the media and literature/publishing.

Alison Baverstock is Professor of Publishing within the Kingston School of Art, Kingston University, UK.

Richard Bradford is Professor of English and Senior Distinguished Research Fellow at the University of Ulster, Ireland.

Madelena Gonzalez is Professor of English Literature at Avignon University, France.

CONTEMPORARY PUBLISHING AND THE CULTURE OF BOOKS

Edited by Alison Baverstock, Richard Bradford, and Madelena Gonzalez

Routledge
Taylor & Francis Group

LONDON AND NEW YORK

First published 2020
by Routledge
2 Park Square, Milton Park, Abingdon, Oxon OX14 4RN

and by Routledge
52 Vanderbilt Avenue, New York, NY 10017

Routledge is an imprint of the Taylor & Francis Group, an informa business

British Library Cataloguing-in-Publication Data
A catalogue record for this book is available from the British Library

Library of Congress Cataloging-in-Publication Data
Names: Baverstock, Alison, editor. | Bradford, Richard, 1957- editor. |
Gonzalez, Madelena, editor.
Title: Contemporary publishing and the culture of books / edited by Alison
Baverstock, Richard Bradford, and Madelena Gonzalez.
Description: Milton Park, Abingdon, Oxon; New York,
NY: Routledge, 2020. | Includes bibliographical references and index.
Identifiers: LCCN 2019040708 | ISBN 9780415750226 (hardback) |
ISBN 9780367443153 (paperback) | ISBN 9781315778389 (ebook)
Subjects: LCSH: Book industries and trade—Great Britain. |
Publishers and publishing—Great Britain. |
Books and reading—Great Britain. |
Authors and publishers—Great Britain.
Classification: LCC Z323 .C75 2020 | DDC 070.50941—dc23
LC record available at https://lccn.loc.gov/2019040708

ISBN: 978-0-415-75022-6 (hbk)
ISBN: 978-0-367-44315-3 (pbk)
ISBN: 978-1-315-77838-9 (ebk)

Typeset in Bembo
by codeMantra

Printed in the United Kingdom
by Henry Ling Limited

CONTENTS

CONTRIBUTORS

David Barker is Senior Lecturer in Publishing at the University of Derby. Before this he worked in academic publishing for over 20 years – first at Cassell Academic, where he was Commissioning Editor for Business and Tourism books, and then at Continuum, where he was responsible for lists in Literary Studies, Film Studies, and Popular Culture. He was the founding editor of the 33 1/3 series of books about classic albums. He moved into managerial roles as Editorial Director (2006–2011) at Continuum Publishing in New York and then as Publishing Director (2011–2016) at Bloomsbury in London. He has been lecturing at the University of Derby since early 2017 and has been Programme Leader for MA Publishing since September 2018. His research interests focus on new areas for non-fiction publishing and on how publishers can better engage with adults who feel ignored by the publishing ecosystem.

Alison Baverstock is Professor of Publishing at Kingston University, where she jointly founded MA Publishing in 2006. A former publisher and now a publishing consultant, she is a regular commentator on the industry and the author of several key books, including *How to Market Books* (Routledge, 6th edition, with Susannah Bowen of the University of Melbourne) and *Is There a Book in You?* (Bloomsbury). She has a particular commitment to encouraging reading for pleasure and is the founder of www.readingforce.org.uk – shared-reading to encourage good communication between Services families – and *The Kingston University Big Read*, which won a *THE* Award for Widening Participation/Outreach (2017). She is a past winner of the Pandora Award and a National Teaching Fellow (2018).

Peter Bolan is a Senior Lecturer and Course Director for International Travel and Tourism Management at Ulster University, Northern Ireland. Dr. Bolan has published widely in the area of niche tourism and is a leading expert in film tourism. Peter's research interests and consultancy specialisms include digital tourism, film- and media-induced tourism, golf tourism, and food tourism. Peter writes for a number of business and industry trade publications, and is a regular speaker at tourism industry events, conferences, and workshops.

Ellie Bowker was born and raised in Cornwall, where she developed her obsession with stories, before moving to London. She has a degree in Publishing with English Literature from Kingston University, where she co-created *Forgotten Female Voices*, a series of eight books written by British women lost in history. She has researched and written about children's literacy, public libraries, and social diversity in the publishing industry. She now works at Hachette UK as Group Contracts Assistant. This is her first publication.

Richard Bradford is Research Professor at Ulster University and Visiting Professor at the University of Avignon. Previously, he held posts in Oxford; the University of Wales; and Trinity College, Dublin. He has published twenty academic monographs on topics as varied as stylistics, Russian Formalism, crime fiction, literary aesthetics, and eighteenth-century criticism. He has also published eight trade literary biographies, including on the lives of Kingsley Amis, Philip Larkin, Alan Sillitoe, Martin Amis, and John Milton, and, most recently, *The Man Who Wasn't There: A Life of Ernest Hemingway* (Tauris/Bloomsbury trade, 2019). His life of Orwell, *Orwell: A Man of Our Time* (Bloomsbury trade), will appear in January 2020 on the seventieth anniversary of the author's death. He is founder and general editor of a new Blackwell/Wiley series of literary biographies called 'The Life of the Author', and his Blackwell *Companion to Literary Biography* (ed.) was published in 2018.

Amy Burns completed a BSc in Nutritional Sciences at University College Cork (1996), MSc in Biomedical Sciences (1997), and a PhD at Ulster University (2001) before taking up a post in the Ulster Business School at the University of Ulster. Amy is the Course Director of the Consumer Management & Food Innovation programme and the Director of the Food and Consumer Sensory Testing Suite (FACTS). She is an expert in nutrition and sensory testing. She has published widely on aspects of nutrition and consumer issues. Her areas of expertise include nutrition, food innovation, and sensory science.

Lucie Ducarre was born in France in 1991. After completing a Graduate Diploma in Academic English and International Studies at King's College London, and a Master's degree in Law at Paris II Panthéon-Assas University, she pursued an MA in Publishing at Kingston University. In 2018, she received the national prize for the best Masters dissertation, awarded by the Association for Publishing Education, for her dissertation on French children's literature and autism. She had previously been awarded the 2013 Coordinators' prize for best essay of the year at King's College London for her essay on private-public partnerships and the crisis management of Hurricane Katrina. Her law Masters dissertation on the economic and cultural consequences of the funding of French cinema and series by television channels was also shortlisted for the 2015 'Law, media and Internet' national prize, awarded by Lagardère Active, Microsoft, and TF1. Along with publishing, children's rights, and autism, her main areas of study are the impact of socioeconomics and cultural factors, and the role played by the creative industries in the enforcement of laws and rights. She is currently working as a freelance writer.

Robert Fraser's life of the poet George Barker was a *Spectator* Book of the Year in 2002, and in May 2012 his life of the surrealist writer David Gascoyne topped the *Independent*'s chart of Best Ten New Biographies. He has also written books about Marcel Proust (1994), Sir James Frazer (1990), and international print history (2008). He has held academic posts in Ghana, Leeds, London, and Trinity College Cambridge, and is now Emeritus Professor of Literature at the Open University. He is a Fellow of the Royal Society of Literature, the English Association, and the Royal Asiatic Society. His latest book, *Ancient Biography and Its Afterlives: Plutarch & Co.*, will be published by Palgrave Macmillan in 2020.

Madelena Gonzalez studied at the universities of Birmingham, Aix-en-Provence, and Vienna before settling in France. She is currently Professor of Anglophone Literature at the University of Avignon and head of the multidisciplinary research group ICTT ('Identité culturelle, textes et théâtralité'). She is also in charge of the Master's programme in English Studies. She has published widely on Anglophone literature, theatre, and culture. Her most recent publications include *Aesthetics and Ideology in Contemporary Literature and Drama* and *Minority Theatre on the Global Stage: Challenging Paradigms from the Margins*.

Caroline Harris has lectured on publishing for more than a decade, most recently as Course Leader for BA Publishing (Combined) course at Bath Spa University. With over 25 years' experience in book publishing and journalism, she is co-founder and director, with Clive Wilson, of the book creation and consultancy business Harris + Wilson. The business works with world-leading publishers to propose and produce high-quality illustrated non-fiction titles, such as the popular Ella's Kitchen cookbook series. She is also a published fiction and non-fiction author (*Ms Harris's Book of Green Household Management*, John Murray 2009) and poet. Currently, she is studying for an interdisciplinary practice-based PhD in the English department at Royal Holloway, University of London.

Per Henningsgaard is a lecturer in professional writing and publishing at Curtin University in Perth, Western Australia. Prior to arriving in Perth, he was the director of the Master's degree in book publishing at Portland State University in Portland, Oregon. His most recent publications are 'Not Your Average Reader:

Interviewing Literary Agents, Editors, and Publishers' in *Participations: Journal of Audience and Reception Studies* and 'Ebooks, Book History, and Markers of Place' in *Logos: Journal of the World Publishing Community*. His research interests include editing, publishing, Australian studies, and regional literature. He is especially interested in the work of independent publishers located outside London and New York City, even though he used to work as an editor for a multinational, educational publisher in New York City.

Nicholas W. N. Jones is founder and Managing Director of Strathmore Publishing, which produces audio and printed books from studios in Clerkenwell, London. After reading science at the University of Oxford, he started his publishing career at Michael Joseph, then part of Thomson Publications. He subsequently published tie-ins, both printed and audio, for Thames Television, then produced books for architects at the Royal Institute of British Architects, where he was also responsible for the Royal Institute of British Architects (RIBA) Bookshops. He established Strathmore in 1995 and has recorded more than a thousand books with readers as diverse as Ian McKellen, Michael Palin, Richard Dawkins, and Bono. He has thus been aware of the importance of media beyond printed books throughout his career and has experience in every part of the publishing process, from concept, through editorial, production, and marketing, to bookselling. He regularly writes about audiobooks for *BookBrunch* and *Publishers Weekly Book Fair Dailies*, and speaks at industry events and to university publishing courses.

Jasmin Kirkbride is a writer and editor. She is currently undertaking a PhD Creative and Critical Writing at UEA, exploring climate change in science fiction. Previously, she worked in publishing in London as an editor, a book trade journalist with bylines at *BookBrunch* and *BookMachine*, and finally as the publishing director at Endeavour Media. On a freelance basis, she has worked with a range of book trade businesses, including big five publishers, Hay Festival, Galley Beggar Press, *Time Out*, and *Publishers Weekly*, among others. She has a background in digital engagement, market research, and paralegal consultancy, for clients including Motorola, CAKE, and AT&T. She also holds an MA Ancient History from King's College London and an MA Creative Writing from UEA. Her short stories and poetry have appeared in various magazines, and she wrote a successful four-book self-help series for Summersdale Publishers.

Alison Lawson is Head of the Discipline of Marketing and Operations in Derby Business School at the University of Derby in the UK. Her PhD examined the impact of information and communications technology in the UK book publishing industry at a time when ebooks, print-on-demand, and social media networks were just on the horizon. She teaches research methods, marketing communications, copywriting, and marketing for publishing. Before going into academia she worked for 20 years in the UK book publishing industry, mostly in the academic and professional sector, and her passion for books and publishing has not waned. Her research interests are in consumers' emotional response to products, especially books and other print products. Alison specialises in qualitative research and the use of interviewing, case study, and appreciative enquiry approaches, in particular.

Angus Phillips is Director of the Oxford International Centre for Publishing Studies at Oxford Brookes University. He formerly worked in the publishing industry as a trade editor at Oxford University Press. He has given talks and lectures about publishing all over the world, including across Europe and in China and South America, and has carried out consultancy and training work with international publishers. He is on the European Advisory Board of Princeton University Press and was a judge for *The Bookseller* industry awards for four years in a row. He is the author of *Turning the Page* and *Inside Book Publishing* (with Giles Clark); with Michael Bhaskar he is the editor of *The Oxford Handbook of Publishing*. He is the editor of the premier publishing journal *Logos* and published a book of selected articles from the journal's 25-year history: *The Cottage by the Highway and Other Essays on Publishing*.

R. Lyle Skains researches and teaches Creative Writing and Digital Media, conducting practice-based research into writing, reading/playing, and publishing digital and transmedia narratives. She has previously published articles in *Convergence, Digital Creativity, and Computers and Composition*, and her book *The Digital Author: Publishing in an Attention Economy* was published in 2019 by Cambridge University Press. She is currently a Senior Lecturer in Writing at Bangor University.

Clare Somerville is a lecturer in Publishing at Kingston University and a publishing industry consultant. She has held senior management positions in a number of major publishing houses in the UK and international sales, marketing, and operations. Most recently she has been project managing General Data Protection Regulation (GDPR) compliance for Hachette UK.

Claire Squires is the Director of the Stirling Centre for International Publishing and Communication at the University of Stirling, Scotland. Her research focusses on contemporary book cultures, including literary festivals and book prizes, editorial, marketing, and communication processes within publishing, and aspects of diversity and politics relating to book industries. Her publications include *Marketing Literature: The Making of Contemporary Writing in Britain* (2007) and, as co-editor with Andrew Nash and I. R. Willison, the *Cambridge History of the Book in Britain Volume 7: The Twentieth Century and Beyond* (2019).

INTRODUCTION

Alison Baverstock

Some of the mental pictures from books you read as a child live on for a long time. I've always loved the imagery of the pools in C.S. Lewis's *The Magician's Nephew*. In case you've yet to get beyond *The Lion, The Witch and the Wardrobe*, in the same way that I have yet to read any more Harry Potter than the first, the titles in the Narnia Series are different – not simply a continuation of the best-known volume. In *The Magician's Nephew*, two of the key protagonists, Polly and Diggory, find a series of pools, each one leading to a separate universe. They make their selection, jump in, and adventures follow.

It's not a bad analogy for this book. We offer a series of investigations, not exhaustive but pretty comprehensive – and consistently fascinating. Together the chapters interconnect, building our understanding of a landscape opportunity for publishers (and would-be publishers), librarians, retailers (of all sorts, as books no longer sell only through bookshops), authors, and others to ponder. Both challenges and opportunities are outlined.

The timing of this book is particularly apposite. Publishing arguably remained largely constant throughout the twentieth century. Some things are still the same – as an industry we want to make available material that readers want to read, and recommend to others, and to do so through communication channels and formats they find acceptable and collectible. But in the last 20 years we have also seen fundamental changes in how the industry is organised, as publishing has moved from being a self-contained industry ('book publishing') to being part of something far larger and wider ('the media industry'). The chapters in this book reflect these changes and that is why it forms both an important contribution and a catalyst to discussion.

Who is involved in discussing publishing is also important as there is a real need to get more people interested in the industry. While the chapters in this book chart how publishing is now starting to attract interest from wider media, there is still very little understanding about what the industry is and does, and an industry that cannot explain its operation sufficiently well to interest others may have difficulty in encouraging payment for what it produces. The recording industry has lived through this, and largely turned to live events and the sale of merchandise to create income – will the book industry go the same way?

It is of course fairer that there should be more open access to an industry that offers particularly pleasant employment. But given that the publishing industry plays such a significant role in what society has available to read, and has an important role within our culture, there is also an noteworthy commercial imperative for wider access. If publishing (as an industry or group of people) is largely unaware of the reading tastes of sectors of society of which it has little personal knowledge, how is it going to source and make available reading matter that is to their taste? Given that we know how beneficial to individual development the habit of reading can be, this is really important. This was echoed in a recent conversation[1] with Philip Connor of Unbound, the platform that seeks to develop material that readers want through crowd-funding (people pledging money to make something happen), and thus is inclined to take a broader look than the traditional industry at both content for which there is likely public appetite and how to make it available. He commented:

> I come from a bookish family but not a single one of them (nor any of my former classmates) to this day have a clue what publishers do. This is problematic on multiple levels - first, it prevents both authors and potential publishers even recognising it as a career possibility. This is, I believe, a huge contributory factor to the regrettable lack of diversity inside publishing; how few people even know the industry's existence and how many fewer people again see working in it as a realistic possibility. What comes up again and again through the course of my interviews for the podcast is that their getting into publishing was a result of a huge stroke of luck - well publishing is very much riding its luck if it hopes to still recruit dynamic people who will keep the industry relevant and evolving. If the public do not understand what publishers do, where we add value, what the work we do *is* - in short why it takes 12 months to publish a book - why then would they be willing to pay £10, £15, £20 for the product of that work?

The impetus for this book came from an overlap between academics and an academic publisher keen to develop their list of resources for what they spotted as a developing field. Over the past few years Routledge have been building their list within Publishing Studies, making available most of the texts and key resources for a field that also overlaps with Creative Writing, Literature Studies, Librarianship and Information Management, Creative Economy, and Business Studies.

Overall, although the chapters are consistently book-related, the variety of content is wide – just as the industry itself, and its surrounding context, provides ongoing change. New genres arrive, retailers think of different ways of displaying stock, events are planned to extend audiences; the publishing industry is a kaleidoscope of involvements. To chart this multiplicity of connections, all the authors offer significant experience of publishing, and the common factor is that all are aware of possibilities and lessons that can be learned from looking at other sectors. Publishing companies can be very insular, so at its most basic this volume will serve to increase understanding of areas other than the one in which readers work.

The material will be valuable to scholars, from the full range of disciplines with which Publishing Studies intersects, to practitioners, and some will (or at least should) be particularly meaningful to policy makers and others who make decisions on our behalf. Here is an introduction to what is on offer.

Dr David Barker from the University of Derby begins with an exploration of the make-up of a standard publishing house. He outlines early the states in which such organisations can operate: 'enormous or tiny; global in their reach or focused on a very local market; run efficiently or in a state of near chaos', and of course it's possible for several of these situational coordinates to apply at the same time. For example, there can be organisations with a particularly strong local connection that also have an international presence (e.g. Emerald Publishing, specialising in the dissemination of academic content, books, and journals, from a defiantly non-London base in Yorkshire, or Cicerone Press Ltd, producing guides for walkers, trekkers, mountaineers, and cyclists from their entirely appropriate starting point in the UK Lake District).

For the wider purposes of outlining the structure and functions of a publishing house, Barker creates his own, offering not only a way of displaying his subsequent serial analysis of structures and processes but at the same time revealing how relatively easy it is to establish yourself as a publisher, and the low risk/operation costs that can lie behind, depending on the outcomes sought. As Clay Shirky so memorably pointed out, publishing is no longer a job but a button (2008). Individual authors or campaigning groups seeking to make material or a message available can literally turn publisher at the flick of a button. That's not to say they always should.

Barker gives his sample publishing company a name – The Ludlow Press – and proceeds to outline the options available to it which extend far beyond the Welsh Marches. What follows is divided by functions rather than departments, and so his very useful analysis can be up- or down-scaled as appropriate, as markets are interested and products appeal.

For future development of this thinking, and analysis of the kinds of activity in which the book community are involved, I suspect events will become more significant. Already they are increasingly becoming a key platform through which titles are made available – and at which profits can really start to work, because consumers in general will pay more for an event (which usually counts as a 'leisure' or 'educational spend') than a book (which counts as a 'personal indulgence' and can therefore be deemed expensive). While this is frustrating to authors and their publishers, expansion into events is proving a lifeline for the industry, hence Stephen Page, MD of Faber (and given an honorary degree by the University of Derby in 2017) describing[2] the wide variety of involvements for his organisation, which is still seen as the quintessential UK publisher:

> Faber is a company concerned with reading and writing. Through most of our history, making and selling books based on limited licenses has been our only activity. Now, that has changed, as has the business of making books. Today we seek to be valuable and useful to writers and readers in any way we can that honours our identity and literary reputation. That means that we still mainly publish books, and that most of our income comes from making and selling print books. However, we also do other things. We run paying events through our Faber Members scheme. We run a creative writing school called Faber Academy out of our offices. We offer print, sales and digital services to fellow independent publishers, and both aggregate and fragment our copyrights into academic databases, or single poems as limited edition letterpress prints. So the panoply of opportunity has widened for publishers, and our imagination has widened as has our desire to reach and represent our societies more widely.

Dr Per Henningsgaard from Curtin University, Perth, Australia, explores publishing institutions further. He offers 'three distinct models for surveying the different types of publishing houses: a model based on funding source, a model based on market segment, and a model based on size'. He also considers how 'specific types of publishing houses within each model are favourably disposed towards the publication of particular genres'. His article is richly furnished with international examples that suit the different structures he has indicated. Again, however, the kaleidoscopic nature of involvements strikes one, and whereas he skilfully conveys the nuanced vocabulary used to describe self-publishing, this too is an area that is sub-dividing. Traditional publishing companies are increasingly influenced by what has been privately successful and can be henceforth made more commercially available, with evidence of the author's proactivity playing a key part in prompting decisions about whether or not it's a good investment.

Is final categorisation ever possible? About 20 years ago I worked with an international policy/practice organisation that was seeking to produce a system – to be expressed in a flow diagram – for its various contributing authors and editors, based all across the world, on how their publishing department ran and how they helped disseminate messages of vital importance to their sponsors and users. It got more and more complicated and we ended up with an informal (and until now unvoiced) conclusion that the publishing operation involved so many careful, and often discreet, considerations that perhaps the only effective summation of their contribution was 'we are really central to everything you do, and you'd really miss us if we weren't here'.

I am still not entirely sure where this particular organisation would sit within Henningsgaard's very well-explained structures, which could perhaps be turned into an algorithm of issues to consider before deciding what kind of publisher you the organisation seeks to be and hence what routes might best suit these purposes.

Dr Alison Lawson, again from the University of Derby, considers the UK's reading culture and consumers' emotional responses to books. She offers an exploration of the channels for reaching readers and encouraging them to take part in a range of initiatives that develop a reading culture, from book groups and festivals to prizes (and particularly their shortlists) and libraries, with some new options emerging through noted gaps (e.g. The Women's Prize for Fiction arising from the observation that women were less frequently featured on prize shortlists than men).[3] It's a rich and energising range of options.

The book industry relies on an underlying assumption that people who buy books will continue to do so, and many marketing trajectories are based on selling more books to people who may already have enough. There are however a couple of trends working against this, of which the publishing industry needs to be aware. The first is a trend towards minimalism, owning and desiring to own less; the second is politically enforced austerity.

The trend towards minimalism we can surely trace back to the influence of Dawna Walter, who first brought the idea of clutter consultancy to the UK from her native US and surely influenced the uber-tidier Marie Condo.[4] If the population who mainly buys books is ageing and female (as Nielsen have repeatedly pointed out), then they will soon be downsizing, and books are large objects to store.

Telegraph journalist Tom Cox interviewed Walter back in 2005, as the television series ('The Life Laundry') that featured her views, along with lots of working examples, came to an end. His personal reflection is significant:

> A few years ago, I did something that Walter would have been proud of: I stripped my house of items I'd been clinging to for no good reason: books I would never read; records I felt I ought to own; presents from relatives that stayed on the shelf out of a combination of guilt and sentimentality.

Interest in decluttering has however since spawned a genre of printed books about the effective management of clutter, now seemingly also including memoir – both personal and how to help others rationalise their possessions (e.g. Susannah Walker's *The Life of Stuff*, 2018).

Longer term, owning less, and writing about owning less in book form are perhaps on a collision course. Upcoming generations are vastly more environmentally aware than were their parents, and the attitude that too much clutter is not good seems to be growing. Our grown-up children are used to renting rather than owning (e.g. Spotify, Netflix, and the gym memberships and phone contracts they are lost without but surprisingly astute in negotiating). They may need to be persuaded to own more, as Molly Flatt remarked at the beginning of her introduction to the book industry assembled for the 2019 Futurebook:

> How do we make people care about what we do?
>
> The biggest disruption coming our way is people who just don't care about us anymore. People who just don't see the value in deep reading when they've grown up with the joy of the scroll. People who are more concerned with broadcasting their own stories than reading yours. People who default to easily addictive and socially-validated entertainment options such as Netflix and Call of Duty and Spotify. People who don't trust curators anymore and trust only what they can see their friends doing, which probably isn't what you're selling.

The second trend is austerity, and a growing lack of budget for books as a governmental or societal priority. As Lawson says, there are indeed many children in the UK who 'grow up with reading and books and, perhaps, take them for granted, as they are ubiquitous'. But there are growing numbers who don't and book poverty very much concerns Nick Poole, Chief Executive of the Chartered Institute for Librarians and Information Professionals (CILIP, formerly The Library Association), who fears that cuts to benefits and library opening hours, and library closures, may mean that books are simply off the radar for many.

Poole was a key interviewee for the chapter contributed by **Ellie Bowker and Clare Somerville**, and he was eloquent about the need for society to be on continuous lookout for pockets of deprivation where reading can be emphasised more – as both a means of personal development and a form of community cohesion. Bowker and Somerville have been resourceful in exploring how the value that libraries offer their communities can be best presented, but the figures of decline over the past ten years are stark:

- There are currently approximately 3,300 public libraries in the UK, an overall reduction of c. 10% since 2010
- Around 500 statutory library services have been transferred out into community ownership since 2010
- An estimated 10,000 professional public librarians have lost their jobs, also since 2010
- Public libraries in England, Wales, and Scotland received 233 million in-person visits in the year 2017–2018.

In addition to all the regular readers who access public libraries, there are discrete communities who can particularly benefit from access to the range of services on offer: parents/carers at home with small children, the long-term unemployed, those seeking to develop digital literacy but who lack internet access at home, welfare applicants, the lonely, the elderly, the unwell – all can be tempted into a library which so often works as a community centre. But without sufficient funding such institutions are under considerable pressure. And in a time of austerity, responsibility for funding libraries is being pushed backwards and forwards between local and national government. Government-commissioned reports (e.g. The Sieghart Report, 2014) consistently highlight the tremendous value that libraries offer within their communities. Policy makers, however, seem bizarrely unaware of the problem; they have reached a totally erroneous conclusion that because they don't use them themselves, preferring the instant access of Amazon, nor does anyone else.

One of the most memorable experiences for our BA Publishing students in recent years was a fieldtrip to a local library, in leafy Kingston-upon-Thames. Here students were genuinely shocked to see how the same librarians, who had been filling them in on the range of services they offer for readers, had to routinely break off and serve as front-line for gaps in social services, talking to the mentally ill and those with nowhere else to go. Their vulnerability but immense professionalism struck all.

Reading is such a key life skill and it is vital to ensure it is open to all. Research, within a wide range of disciplines from Neuroscience to Librarianship, from Early Years to Publishing Studies, has consistently confirmed this. Under new management, Ofsted have made it one of their key priorities. Bowker and Somerville have done a good job in summarising the problems and how libraries can address them in future, and the situation they outline should concern us all. A final word from Poole[5]:

> Public libraries are the most important infrastructure we have for learning and literacy beyond the classroom. Librarians play an incredibly important role not only in developing literacy and promoting readership, but in helping readers discover their next new favourite book. The loss of public libraries directly impacts on opportunities for discovery and readership, particularly in the most disadvantaged communities. Less access to high-quality, up-to-date reading materials has a direct impact on people's ability to learn, to develop empathy and to participate productively in our democracy.

Encouraging people to become regular readers and purchasers of books – to know about specific titles, and either buy or recommend them – will likely continue to underpin the marketing processes of most publishing houses. But in the same way that libraries promote the wider development of literacy and build local communities, there are new areas of marketing and market development activity which seek to use books as therapeutic items. The experience of reading can be variously beneficial: for example, enabling readers to gain an objective view of difficulties similar to their own, and so spot solutions without feeling personally criticised, or the deployment of guided reading as an activity that promotes personal progression or a sense of belonging. Collectively such activities have become known as bibliotherapy; the use of books and reading to treat psychological or mental disorders and encourage a sense of well-being. The UK is particularly well advanced in bibliotherapy and home to many reading and literacy charities.

The advantages of being a reader have been studied within a variety of disciplinary frameworks, are well established, and correlate with all sorts of good outcomes from greater articulacy to reduced likelihood of developing Alzheimer's. Books can also work well as items that represent belonging, and to this end have been widely used in the US as welcome gifts within higher education – or as 'common reads' as they are more generally known. My own chapter within this volume reports on a comparison between an established common reading programme at the University of Mississippi and a similar programme established at Kingston University, London. The processes of book choice, delivery, and associated activities were compared via the universities' respective monitoring procedures and then discussed via transatlantic Skype sessions during which practice and future plans were shared. We subsequently presented together at the First Year Experience Conference in San Antonio (2018).

There is an inherent irony in me reviewing **Professor Claire Squires**' review of the role and processes of 'The Review and the Reviewer'. She begins by quoting Gail Pool (2010) on the 'slippery nature of the word' – perhaps because of its Scrabble-handy over-concentration of vowels.

Squires starts by drawing our attention to the key distinction that a 'review is neither the literary feature nor the interview with the author' and takes us on a fascinating historical tour of the format, from its heyday in the 1970s–1990s to a decline in the twenty-first century. She draws a neat distinction between the review and the cover quote, referencing Michael Maguire in asserting that 'the solicited blurb makes no special claim to impartiality' and 'readers expect the review of a book not to have any conflicts of interest or relationship with the author'.

Seeking to understand the review's decline as a format of big influence, the issue of just how much space gets allocated to the opinions of others on what is being published has always been controversial. Those managing space/time within the media have long been conscious that while book reviews may be the reason readers committo/buy/watch a particular format, particularly the Sunday papers, they bring in very little advertising spend. But any association between high readership/low income and the allocation of space has been routinely denied.

When publications/formats are struggling, of course generating income matters. And review space has been particularly under pressure since the arrival of informal means of reviewing: for example, blogging and the rise of the (unpaid) citizen journalist. The reviewer's voice is no longer the authority it once was.

Why is this? Perhaps first because there are now so many other ways of gaining attention for new work. An MA Publishing student at Kingston (Roberts, 2019) recently came up with 32 different ways in which a consumer may hear about a new book, only some of which rely on securing formal opinions from others. Given that many of these operate pre-publication, and are designed to get an order before the title is actually available, the reader must be relying on information designed to make it sell rather than objective post-publication analysis.

Second, perhaps today's consumer is also less willing to wait to find out what those well qualified to judge make of new work. Extracts from reviews used to be the main way of authenticating what was between the covers; the tendency today is to secure advance quotations from other writers and commentators. Can readers tell the difference between what has been said about previous books and the new title by the same author in their hand; between feedback on pre-review 'reading' copies and post-publication thinking?

The consumer is also perhaps more suspicious and likely to check, having become used to double-checking the advice of those on whose opinion they are relying. Practices developed from assessing opinions on Airbnb or regulars on Mumsnet presumably spill over into how they assess whether reading material is worth their time. It's worth noting too that the market is increasingly cynical; a look through some of the reviews posted on Amazon's star ratings system will show occasional references to a title 'living up to the cover quote', which must mean they often don't. And does it add to the endorser's impressiveness – or simply imply a different motivation – if they offer a quote but also mention their own most recent title?

Whatever position is taken on the quality of current reviewing platforms, Squires makes clear that the spaces within which reviewing in the twenty-first century takes place are both changing and growing very fast.

Emeritus Professor Robert Fraser is preoccupied by what he outlines as a 'crisis of form' within life-writing. He identifies its antecedents back in the eighteenth century and explains how more recently it has become 'a convenient banner for a cluster of activities, genres or subgenres broadly affiliated to the task of narrating a life' offering us Zachary Leader's list of possible forms: 'memoir, biography, autobiographical fiction, and biographical fiction, but also letters, writs, wills, written anecdotes, court proceedings…marginalia, nonce writings, lyric poems, scientific and historical writing, and digital forms (including blogs, tweets, and Facebook entries)' (Leader, 2015).

Fraser considers how 'varieties of literary exercise [have had the effect of] encouraging them to merge', in the process often blurring the distinction between author and subject and drawing the conclusion that 'the more challenging the subject, the more versatile the shape tends to be'. He outlines the emergence of a new breed of biographers as serial offenders, looking at one life after another in great detail; authors such as Michael Holroyd, Clare Tomalin, and Victoria Glendenning are all producing very long books. New scholars have meanwhile injected a renewed vigour into the format with biographies of individual years (e.g. 1688 by John E. Wills), shorter periods of individuals' lives (e.g. Jenny Uglow on just ten years of the life of Charles II), or unexpected takes on over-analysed subjects (e.g. Shakespeare considered by James Shapiro through the context of public and political events rather than his plays). The canon was always replete with politicians, but a wider range of subjects for biography have emerged, notably of scientists (e.g. Andrew Hodges on Alan Turing, 1983, and Adrian Desmond and James Moore on Charles Darwin, 1991).

Fraser highlights another stream of literature with *eccentricity* as the 'fulcrum around which several of these English lives swung'. These include Jane Harrison, a classical scholar who 'remains indomitable, even if in her time she was largely ignored' and has since proven interesting to Professor Mary Beard (2000) and the Costa-prize-winning Helen Macdonald, whose 'self-prescribed course of convalescence took the unusual form of training a goshawk to fly in captivity' (2014).

Finally he turns to writing about family members, and the truism that writers often have strange or at least interesting family histories (e.g. Penelope Fitzgerald and Edmund de Waal). There is also a significant stream of books based on seeking to understand a parent, and not always emerging with the story you anticipated; examples here include Blake Morrison's sequential books about his parents (Morrison, 1993, 2002), Nigel Nicolson's view of his parents' marriage (1990), and Jackie Kay's 'absconding biological male parent' (2011).

The titles he references have all remained in print, or are known about, and he illustrates the variety of different lives for which there is an obvious market. But a general summary might be that if you are going to read a biography, it will generally be about someone who attracts approval rather than attention because you take it home and offer it shelf space. Goodrich's investigations (2019) into why it is that a political biography has received a big shot in the arm from the Trump presidency, with people who disagree profoundly on his politics and life choices buying books about President #45, set my research partner, economist Jackie Steinitz, and I thinking. Is it possible to come up with a list of criteria that must be present for a biographical subject to work and find a market? Our conclusions (Baverstock and Steinitz, 2019) offer a framework for thinking rather than an instant solution.

Although 'the dominant assumption of the creative writing workshop is that the students' goals are always to become published writers', how information on the publishing industry is imparted is seldom as well thought out, argues **Dr R. Lyle Skains** from Bangor University.

How much information to make available needs careful consideration. Provide too much detail on the processes and practices of the publishing industry, and the student may be tempted to spend time worrying about the market rather than concentrating on their writing. Having been in this position, involved with the establishment of a new degree in Creative Writing, I found the module I had developed on marketing for authors perhaps put too much pressure on them by requiring them to anticipate how they would present or market themselves before they were ready to do so. Nicholas W. N. Jones of Strathmore Publishing[6] commented that this reminded of the chief protagonist in Michael Frayn's 1960s satire *The Tin Men*, who spent his time writing and re-writing the blurb for the paperback edition of his book. He never gets around to writing the actual book. For my students, for the subsequent year I reworked the assignments into exercises so as to be focussed on the publishing industry rather than themselves.

In any case, deciding to write for a specific market opportunity or gap is a risky strategy; the market will almost certainly have moved on by the time they have finished. Publishers generally want what they don't yet know about; to be compelled and fascinated, but are reluctant to specify what about. Speaking in a podcast on 'What editors want' Louisa Joyner, Editorial Director of Faber, said she 'tried not to look for anything' although on further exploration the interviewer (Philip Connor) drew out a series of abstract concepts: 'a strength of voice, the quality of the story-telling, originality, something I haven't seen before or an insight into an experience you haven't had before' (2019).

It's a mysterious process and although Joyner identified trends that come around, 'like mumps, every seven years', writing that editors want to publish is often the product of a particular alchemy, at a particular time: a combination of a great idea and writing talent that come together at the right moment, hence for some authors it happens long after their first book, at which point the rest of their oeuvre can either be brought out for reconsideration (or not). For other authors, who have long been published, a particular title will suddenly take hold and their writing henceforth be given greater notice. Examples of a 'breakthrough' book are *About a Boy* for Nick Hornby, or *Wolf Hall* for now twice Booker-winning Hilary Mantel. She commented (Singh, 2012):

> My publishers were always announcing my 'breakthrough book' but it never really happened. It happened in terms of critical esteem, but it didn't happen in terms of sales or impact on the general public. My fortunes began to turn when I met Thomas Cromwell.

So rather than advising writers how to market themselves to the industry they hope will invest in them, sharing with them the processes of publishing may be more useful; pointing out the variety of means through which content can now be shared – and the valuable advice that approaching publishers should be put off until your work is ready, because you really can only make a first impression once.

The first creative writing courses, which can be traced back to the 1930s, offered an opportunity for writers not just to teach writing (it having been previously argued that writing cannot be taught) but to nurture both themselves as writers and their work; in the process to develop personal discipline and create writing worth the time of readers.

This is a journey Skains has taken herself. She began by teaching the options she had been taught, the existing genres and sub-genres within which authors can deposit their work. But to this she has added the first-hand experience of running a publishing company, which Barker has already shown us can be set up with relative ease, the history of publishing and other slots left open for further exploration of topics students find interesting – as well as practice in negotiation and thinking on the spot. Skains describes it as striving to 'scaffold our students with innovative, flexible and insightful practices that will benefit our classrooms, their careers and our culture as a whole'. The importance of understanding the basic requirements and the lines that are regularly crossed to reach a market is a useful framework for all involved in book creation.

Angus Phillips, Director of the Oxford International Centre for Publishing, explores the role of the literary agent in the current literary market place, beginning with their emergence in the late nineteenth century when the prime role was 'to recognise work that would sell' (Gillies, 2007) and continuing to Jonny Geller developing the role of literary manager, representing the author's interests in whatever format material can be made available.

Several particularly interesting themes emerge. The fact that there are literary agents in the UK and the US but much less within continental Europe, Phillips ascribes to 'the returns available to authors being higher (in the UK/US) than in other markets. Writing in the English language opens up a range of international markets whilst global exposure encourages sale in translation' but given that 'the two strongest world markets for the exploitation of copyrights are the USA and Germany', could there be other forces be at play?

An EU report of 2009 considered the operation of sports agents within Europe, with a view to possible closer collaboration and regulation, and found that

> France, Germany, Italy, Spain and the United Kingdom account alone for close to 75% of the 3,600 officially listed agents in the EU. Football is by far the sport with the largest number of official sports agents, followed by rugby, basketball and athletics. These four sports account for 95% of the total number of official sports agents in Europe.
>
> *EC Europa EU, p. 4*

So, maybe we could say that the emergence of agencies is the product of the combination of a mature market, a high box office, and strong export potential. Given that the basic financial structure for agencies is a percentage of the author's earnings, this seems appropriate. But the non-proliferation of agencies also correlates neatly with those countries where there is still resale price maintenance on books. Perhaps it can be concluded that agents are indeed the product of a mature market, a high box office, and strong export potential – but also a less tightly regulated economy. Neoliberalism will be further explored in Jasmin Kirkbride's chapter.

Another issue worthy of future investigation is the extent to which literary agents represent, and hence really understand, the markets for which they not only commission but to which they could extend. The issue of diversity within the publishing workforce is much discussed at the moment, and it may be interesting to enquire whether within the context of being able to meet the anticipated/actual needs of the full and diverse range of society, literary agents are themselves sufficiently diverse? Mostly drawn from the publishing industry and largely operating separately from agencies that represent other forms of talent such as sports or theatrical management, do they need to consider their own recruitment more carefully? The requirement to recognise work that would sell to a wider range of the public would certainly benefit their business model, given that it relies so heavily on what their clients earn.

For the future, Phillips thinks that the same forces that led to the amalgamation of publishing companies – notably the rise of self-publishing and the general erosion of authors' earnings – are likely to impact on agents as well. While larger firms will be able to diversify and find new sources of revenue – events management, writing tuition – smaller agencies may struggle to survive.

Caroline Harris begins with a bold statement that 'Some of the most exciting, innovative publishing is currently being developed outside the traditional publishing ecosystem'. She charts a world of amalgamating formats ('there is not print versus digital; no either/or – the two are companions and interconnected'), changing routes to sharing work and much wider involvement.

Her work is the result of broad research and consultation with more than 50 organisations and her chapter includes material from responses to an online survey and semi-structured interviews. She identifies four emerging publishing trends: magazine publishers who also create books; spoken word and live events generating book operations (a reversal of the book festival model); social enterprise and charitable publishing and tech-enabled businesses.

Given that publishing has long operated on the basis of being a quiet backwater where those who knew what to do got on and did it, this is a big change. Louisa Joyner referred in her previously referenced podcast to publishing being an 'opaque business' in which 'no bit of the process works without everyone else, which makes you deeply respectful of their expertise' (2019), but outside the confines of the book industry, these processes have traditionally been little understood.

The trends Harris identifies can be variously appreciated. Is this a collective shot in the arm for the industry, with books becoming more mainstream as culturally/socially significant objects, and therefore more relevant to society as a whole? Should we hail the ability of technology, effectively managed, to solve everything and provide links across our increasingly fractured society? Or should it just exercise everyone to think more deeply about how to service, fully effectively, markets that emerge and are identified by these new protagonists. Harris concludes optimistically: 'This may not be *the* future of book publishing, but (these trends) are indicative of how publishing is being transformed and remade in post-digital times'.

Dr Amy Burns takes a fascinating look at food writing in the UK, from its emergence in post-war Britain when it added colour to life, to its current status as part of celebrity culture. She highlights a significant gap between the British novel offering 'very few passages of any length in fiction (and virtually none in poetry) dedicated to eating and hardly any to cooking' and food being 'used as a symbolic transference mechanism, a way of focusing our attention to ensure we concentrate on something else'.

Early cook books were apparently 'food-grammars' listing what would go with what, and she charts the rise of cookery writing as entertainment, writing engagingly about the screen performances of the Craddocks, Jamie Oliver, and Nigella Lawson, and the emergence of food writing as a 'sub-genre of popular fiction'. She moves on to highlight the 'similarity between contemporary food writing and media presentations' and cookery writing as reflecting confusion over the modern woman's identity, with an ability to cook countable on a scale that ranges from practical evidence of female emancipation to a component within an individual's repertoire of likely male-pleasing accomplishments.

She looks at the publishing industry's tendency to make books on behalf of names made in other areas and whether this is either ethical or appropriate. It seems however that readers continue to want to buy into the lifestyle and personality of those they emulate, and this includes what they both eat themselves and serve to their family and friends. These may end up being books they own but never cook from; books as a form of soft porn, stroked rather than read, and which go nowhere near the kitchen.

Finally there is interesting guidance on how to publish food writing. It operates on the same financial basis as other sectors: what sells well serving to underpin more speculative ventures. But as the area is now as full of subdivisions and sub-genres as any other area of publishing, maybe it offers another example of how publishing is a reflection of contemporary society. Certainly within today's celebrity culture, the desire to see a lifestyle or cookery book that reflects a personal commitment or enthusiasm marks the book out as another form of brand extension (cue agents from outside publishing?).

Jasmin Kirkbride, a really experienced publisher who is currently undertaking a PhD in Creative and Critical Writing at the UEA, has a self-confessed 'broad overview of the industry', and this has enabled her to develop a theory of the 'reading ecosystem; a network of book production and consumption, of which publishing is part, and (offers) a helpful tool to look at how the culture of reading is maintained'.

She begins with tracking the book at its most basic, from author to publishing and review processes and then on to being read. To this basic model she adds all the individuals involved and their various motivations, and sets this unpredictability in the context of post-war neoliberalism or the development of an economy that encourages a freer spirit in how things are regulated, allowing privatisation, unregulated free trade, and reductions in government spending. But growth in a country's GDP, which tends to be the way of measuring outcomes of neoliberalism, is not necessarily to the long-term benefit, if assets which can only be sold/used once are squandered in the process (e.g. destroying trees which are not replaced and mean future generations lack the resources they provide – as arguably happened on Easter Island). Kirkbride outlines the processes of too many books; insufficient reading habits/tendencies to buy; and, in the process, a decline in the income of authors.

The concept that 'too many books get published' greeted me on my arrival in the industry and has been much quoted ever since, but still the number produced each year rises. What is more, new options to create content have arisen, largely through self- or independent publishing, and the amount of reading material today is greater than ever. Kirkbride concludes by advocating 'the need for tension between commercialism and intellectual idealism – one sells books and the other keeps them alive'.

The difficulty however is working out which is which. It is notoriously difficult to predict the tastes of the reading public, and publishing can be compared to horse-racing: watch with interest; back the winners but keep an eye out for what's creeping up on the outside – or going on in the paddock. What is more, we all need different books at different times, to match our interests, moods, and physical states. Someone new to reading will not head straight for *War and Peace* if a range of more accessible fiction, derided by some, is taken away.

Dr. Peter Bolan outlines the history and influence of travel writing, from ancient Greece (e.g. Homer's *Odyssey*) to today's travel blogger. On the way, he addresses sub-genres (e.g. like writing on the homes of writers, often dubbed 'literary tourism'), consumer trends which fuelled the genre (e.g. the grand tour), and the impact of systematising volumes such as Baedeker and Bradshaw's Railway Guides, which went on to have much wider societal impact through standardising timing and spelling – as well as resulting in commissions for popular television such as the programmes presented by former MP Michael Portillo.

Bolan ends with consideration of the informality of much modern travel writing and the various ways in which it can be spread. Underpinning all this are the curious and contradictory responsibilities of the travel writer. An effective travel writer will record for posterity how a place looks and feels, but the very act of making such places more interesting to a wider population may carry the risk of destroying their charm through wider access and exploitation.

From the point of view of the publishing industry remaining in business, the issues of brand recognisability and brand loyalty are particularly significant within travel writing. One views the backpacker generation, whose belongings have been slimmed down to the barest of essentials, still finding room for a weighty guide-book to where they are going. What is more, they tend to hang on to the, by then battered, volume once they get home – as a long-term souvenir of a really influential period of their lives. So, perhaps the key thing for travel publishers is to concentrate their efforts on becoming the first volume that potential future travellers buy, as this will likely influence their purchasing (and display) habits for the rest of their lives.

Nicholas W. N. Jones, Founder and MD of Strathmore Publishing, charts the 30-year overnight success of audiobooks. The rise has been sudden; until the late 1990s in the UK audiobooks were seen as a specialist niche in publishing industry a substitute, for those who were unable to manage a book, either physically or because visually impaired. Loaned through libraries in large, unwieldy cases from which a key disk or reel always seemed to be missing, they were cumbersome and not particularly attractive. Yet by 2018 the market was worth about £100 million in the UK, where consumer digital sales rose 43%; the US market is estimated at $1 billion at retail, up 24% year-on-year. Audiobooks now stand as a fourth format alongside hardback, paperback, and e-book.

Jones relates the rise of this format including the techniques involved. Particularly interesting is the rise of recorded books as a social trend, notably the needs of the significant number of those blinded during the First World War. In fact those blinded through combat was a small percentage of those with poor sight (less than 1% in the US, 10% in the UK), but their plight served as the catalyst for the wider development of talking books, and publishers making their work available royalty-free for such editions.

We are fortunate that Jones is also well informed on the technologies involved; fascinating details emerge, like the early recordings which had to be made in one go and could not be edited, requiring the speaker to keep going for at least 20 minutes. There are also key rites of passage in the development of the audiobook, like the founding of Audible in 1995 with its portable player to which about two hours of audiobook could be downloaded in a file format that protected content from piracy. The BBC broadcast of Stephen Fry's unabridged reading of the first Harry Potter on Boxing Day 2000 introduced many to the pleasure of being read to. The development of the internet made downloadable files possible; audiobooks needed no longer be constrained in length by physical media, cassette, or CD. And when Amazon purchased Audible in 2008, many more people became aware of what was available. More recently, the widespread consumption of podcasts has encouraged listeners to move on to longer-form content. Some podcasts, Jones suggests, are 'audiobooks for which there happens to be no book', and they have become a habit for many.

The issue remains about whether or not this is 'real reading', one that sufficiently practices phonetics and improves the reader's literacy. It's certainly a different form of reading – slower, one that permits you to do other things at the same time, and which allows what author Michael Morpurgo refers to as 'room to imagine', unlike television and cinema which provide all the images and characters the story needs to progress. It can also add new dimensions to a book, in particular when read by the author. As a family, none of us have ever forgotten the experience of listening to a former President of the US describe directly to us his relationship with Monica Lewinksy, as we travelled through France one summer!

As a discipline, Publishing Studies combines academic understanding with professional practice at the highest level, leaving students well placed to bring both theory and practical solutions to the future solving of problems we do not as yet even anticipate. One of the advantages of this blend of knowledge, understanding, and skills is an ability to respond effectively to societal issues that matter particularly to the individual. In this context the final chapter in this volume, offered by **Lucie Ducarre**, is a significant (and prize-winning[7]) piece of work.

It was her experience of working with an autistic child that drew Ducarre's attention to the very limited range of books available in support; both titles featuring autistic children and those offering guidance and information on the condition seemed very few in number. This is significant because, as Ducarre points out early on in her chapter, 'narrative fiction positively impacts empathy and behaviour towards one another (Johnson et al., 2013). Reading books with look-alike characters also helps children develop their sense of belonging and their self-esteem (Shedlosky-Shoemaker et al., 2014)'. Similarly,

> Disabled characters offer non-disabled children a way to engage with disability and thus to develop empathy, entrancement and connectedness with disabled children (Brenna, 2009)...Although books alone cannot fight against discrimination, they are indeed effective tools for parents and teachers to promote tolerance, prevent bullying and educate children on human diversity.
>
> *Artman-Meeker et al., 2016*

Autism is a neurodevelopmental disorder, impairing the sensory, cognitive, communicative, and social skills of an individual and affecting around 1% of the world's population. Within France however, while autism falls within the general legislative framework for those with special needs, the country is regularly accused of violating autistic children's right to education. Ducarre points out that since 2004, 'France has been condemned five times by the Council of Europe for discrimination against autistic people, including violations of their educational rights', principally because they were not allowing autistic children to be educated primarily in mainstream schools.

Her research involved establishing the number of such titles available (just 64 were published from 1993 to 2017), surveying the parents of both autistic and non-autistic children about their readiness to purchase and use resources that offer relevant support and then interviewing librarians about the extent of relevant information available.

What emerges is both socially and economically significant. Ducarre highlights an opportunity for the support of a specific community and for reading to play a part in building a more diverse and mutually respectful society. But she also draws attention to a market opportunity for publishers, within a special category of publications for which those interested would likely pay more for relevant resources.

In addition to highlighting a significant gap, Ducarre offers practical strategies for ensuring that autistic children, and those interested in the condition, can draw maximum benefit from any future associated published resources. These include offering a few blank pages at the end of a book where the child could apply the story or lesson to their own situation, perhaps personalising through the inclusion of pictures or photographs. Similarly, to deal with the autistic child's tendency to appreciate information being offered in one format at a time, she suggests it might be worth 'systematically separating text pages from illustration pages so the oral/narrative and visual information are not offered at the same time'.

This is a significant study, not least in its demonstration of the value Publishing Studies, and the value its disciplinary framework of theory and practice can offer in highlighting and supporting a market that has been significantly neglected. Her combination of theory and practical solutions offers potential for longer-term significant change, the effective management of social change through developing expert and specialist resources for previously unappreciated but highly specific market sectors with particular needs.

Conclusion

> Reading books about writing is, in my experience, like reading books about sex. I'd rather be doing it.
>
> *Brubach, 2005*

Famously cross-connected – there is a long-established joke about the sex workers of Frankfurt leaving during the book fair as the publishers all sleep with each other – the publishing industry's longstanding practice has been to get on with publishing rather than think about how to get on with publishing. The fact that Unwin's famous exposé (Unwin, 1926) lasted so long without challenge shows how little minded publishers were to discuss or analyse what they were up to. Necessarily collaborative, inclined to mutual respect and the personal validation of all involved – and above all optimistic – this most polite and considerate of employment environments has come late to self-analysis.

Of course, there is the fundamental difficulty that underpins the entire industry; that there already are enough books. Were no more books to be published ever, there would still be no shortage – because of what is available already. Louisa Joyner (2019) expressed it more lyrically: 'This weird, strange and mechanical business, is the process of disrupting busy people with a book you would like them to read'. We are consistently told that today time is the most precious commodity, so by asking them to read what we have selected is asking them for more of what it seems they have least.

So why the tendency, over the past ten years, for more reflecting within the creative economy? I would argue that the arrival of Publishing Studies as a discipline within higher education has led to the growth of consciousness about what publishing means – the responsibilities it brings, as well as the opportunities. University courses have offered publishers the opportunity to reflect on their roles and influences/influencers, and I am regularly told by those I ask to come and talk at Kingston that preparing for such opportunities brings the chance for personal development – along with professional affirmation. And being publishers, these reflections are starting to find homes in a printed output. There is a growing range of studies, of which this is one, where the value of reflecting on what we do is palpable. Looking forward, there are a range of other publishing-related issues that are surely ripe for analysis, from the way our industry works (we have a very flat management structure in comparison with others, and in particular contrast to higher education) to the way we manage collaboration (really effectively and – surely significantly – it's a key trait looked for by recruiters across the whole field of employment).

In her chapter on publishing in the neoliberal culture, Jasmin Kirkbride talks about the problems arising *because society was insufficiently self-aware*. Perhaps the growing tendency to think about the industry, analyse its processes, and really explore what benefits we can offer betokens a better future for us all: publishers, authors, retailers, readers – and out into the wider community. Certainly, all involved have much in common. Throughout all the chapters in this book we are reminded that books and the culture of books are fighting a defensive battle against the new age of social media and AI; messages rapidly composed and consumed – and often responded before they have been fully thought about. For reassurance we might turn back to CS Lewis and his prediction of great adventures – and presumably stories – yet to come:

> All their life in this world and all their adventures in Narnia had only been the cover and the title page: now at last they were beginning Chapter One of the Great Story which no one on earth has read: which goes on for ever: in which every chapter is better than the one before.
>
> *The Last Battle (1956, final paragraph)*

I will close with a word of sincere thanks to my fellow commissioning editors, Richard Bradford and Madelena Gonzalez – together we have assembled a most interesting range of views; to our commissioning editors at Routledge, Zoe Meyer, Polly Dodson, and Jeanine Furino, and finally to Tanuja Shelar and Kelly Squires who have kept us all in order.

Professor Alison Baverstock
Kingston-upon-Thames
December 2019

Notes

1 Personal conversation.
2 Private conversation.
3 The prize's archive is held at Kingston University.
4 https://konmari.com.
5 Personal communication.
6 Personal conversation.
7 The 2018 Association for Publishing Education Best MA Publishing Dissertation, presented at the London International Book Fair.

References

Artman-Meeker, K., Grant, T. O. and Yang, X. (2016). 'By the book: Using literature to discuss disability with children and teens'. *TEACHING Exceptional Children*, 48(3): pp. 151–158.

Baverstock, A., Morris, W., Dewey-Knight, R. and Dennis, M. R. (2018). 'What *The Kingston University Big Read* and *The University of Mississippi Common Reading Experience* learned from each other'. Conference of the First Year Experience, San Antonio, Texas. February 2018.

Baverstock, A. and Steinitz, J. (2019). 'What President Trump has shown us about choosing a subject for political biography'. *Logos*, 30(2): pp. 7–11.

Beard, M. (2000). *The invention of Jane Harrison*. Boston, MA: Harvard University Press.

Brenna, B. (2009). 'Creating characters with diversity in mind: Two Canadian authors discuss social constructs of disability in literature for children'. *Language and Literacy*, 11(1): pp. 1–18.

Brubach, H. (2005). Reviewing Lynne Freed's 'Reading, writing and leaving home', *New York Times*, 9th October 2005.

Cox, T. (2005). 'Junk male: It's time for Dawna'. *Daily Telegraph*, 10th May 2005. www. telegraph.co.uk/culture/books/3641841/Junk-male-Its-time-for-Dawna.html.

de Waal, E. (2011). *The hare with the amber eyes: A Hidden Inheritance*. London: Vintage.

EC Europa EU. Directorate-General for Education and Culture: KEA, CDES, EOSE (2009). Study on sports agents in the European Union. *The European Union*. http:// ec.europa.eu/assets/eac/sport/library/studies/study-sports-agents-in-eu.pdf.

Fitzgerald, P. (1977). *The Knox brothers*. London: Macmillan.

Frayn, M. (1965). *The Tin Men*. London: Faber.

Gillies, M. A. (2007). *The professional literary agent in Britain, 1880–1920*. Toronto: The University of Toronto Press.

Goodrich, J. (2019). *How Trump came to dominate the political book market*, CGTN, 13th February 2019. https://news.cgtn.com/news/3d3d514e7a496a4e32457a6333566d54/ index.html

Johnson, D. R., Cushman, G. K., Broden, L. A. and McCune, M. S. (2013). 'Potentiating empathic growth: Generating imagery while reading fiction increase empathy and prosocial behavior'. *Psychology of Aesthetics, Creativity & the Arts*, 7(3): pp. 306–312.

Joyner, L. (2019). *What editors want*. Podcast with Philip Connor of Unbound, 19th July 2019. https://podcasts.apple.com/gb/podcast/season-1-teaser/id1471548345?i= 1000443630153

Kay, J. (2011). *Red dust road*. London: Picador.

Leader, R. (2015). 'On life-writing'. *Oxford History of Life-Writing*. Oxford: Oxford University Press.

Macdonald, H. (2014). *H is for hawk*. London: Vintage.

Maguire, M. (2018). *The literary blurb economy*, 11th November 2018. http://post45. research.yale.edu/2018/11/the-literary-blurb-economy/

Morrison, B. (1993). *And when did you last see your father?* London: Granta.

Morrison, B. (2002). *Things my mother never told me*. London: Chatto and Windus.

Nicolson, N. (1990). *Portrait of a marriage*. London: Weidenfeld and Nicolson.

Pool, G. (2010). *Faint praise: The plight of book reviewing in the US*. Colombia: University of Missouri Press.

Roberts, H. (2019). *The relationship between marketing materials and reader behaviour*. Kingston University Library, available on request.

Shapiro, J. (2005). *1599: A year in the life of William Shakespeare*. London: Faber.

Shedlosky-Shoemaker, R., Costabile, K. A. and Arkin, R. M. (2014). 'Self-Expansion through Fictional Characters'. *Self and Identity*, 13(5): pp. 556–578.

Shirky, C. (2008). *Here comes everybody*. New York: The Penguin Press.

Sieghart, W. (2014). *The Sieghart report*. HMSO: www.gov.uk/government/publications/ independent-library-report-for-england

Singh, A. (2012) 'Hilary Mantel's Booker novels get stage treatment' *The Telegraph*, 17th October 2012, www.telegraph.co.uk/culture/books/booker-prize/9614679/Hilary-Mantels-Booker-novels-get-stage-treatment.html

Uglow, J. (2009). *A gambling man; Charles II and the restoration*. London: Faber.

Unwin, S. (1926). *The truth about publishing*. London: George Allen and Unwin.

Walker, S. (2018). *The life of stuff: A memoir about the mess we leave behind*. London: John Murray.Walter, D. (2019). *De-junk your mind: simple steps for positive living*. London: Penguin.

Walter, D. and Chislett, H. (1997). *Organised living*. London: Conran Octopus.

Wills, J. E. (2002). *1688: A global history*. New York: Norton.

1

THE STRUCTURE AND WORKINGS OF A PUBLISHING HOUSE

David Barker

Introduction

The title of this essay, of course, implies that there exists, somewhere, such a thing as a standard publishing house. There doesn't. Publishing houses (I'll use that term throughout this essay, rather than the less precise 'publishers') vary tremendously. They can be enormous or tiny; profitable, loss-making, or not-for profit; they can be fully digital or almost entirely print-based; global in their reach or focussed on a very local market; and they can be run efficiently or in a state of near chaos. For the purposes of this essay, which is designed to outline briefly the structure and functions of a publishing house, let's create our own.

We'll call our publishing house, 'The Ludlow Press'. Although founded in the Shropshire town of that name in the late nineteenth century, it long ago moved its headquarters to London and now has offices there as well as in New York, Sydney, and Toronto. The Ludlow Press prides itself on publishing a wide range of content. For much of the twentieth century it was seen as a slightly staid publisher of serious non-fiction but following an overhaul in the mid-1980s, the Press expanded into more commercial non-fiction as well as fiction, children's books, and academic books and journals. Much of this growth came via acquisition.

As we near the end of the second decade of this century, The Ludlow Press is seen as a well-run business that has adapted nimbly to the shifts of recent years. As with all publishing houses it has its strengths and vulnerabilities, but it's a Press that many authors would be happy to publish with and that a decent number of readers recognise.

In this essay, we'll work through – in no particular order – the various departments and teams that can exist at a publishing house like 'The Ludlow Press'. Bear in mind that other medium-sized or large publishing houses will not mirror these departments and structures exactly, and that at many small presses all of these functions are handled by just one or two staff members.

Senior Management

The Ludlow Press has a Board of Directors as well as a Senior Management team – it's the latter we'll concentrate on here. The team consists of seven people: the Chief Executive Officer (CEO) who is a descendant of the Press's founder, and six other senior staff members. The make-up of those six is interesting: three occupy editorial positions (the heads of Trade, Children's, and Academic publishing, respectively), while the other three are drawn from Sales, Production, and Finance. This imbalance in a senior team isn't unusual: of the 16 members of Hachette Book Group's US leadership team in 2017, for example, 8 have worked their way up through editorial careers (Hachette website, 2017) and reflects a belief system in the industry that very experienced, senior editorial staff are more likely to have a clear overview of the business and its strategic needs than senior staff who have risen through the ranks of other departments.

The key function of the Senior Management team at The Ludlow Press is to provide a strategic vision for the company – and to communicate that vision to all staff. On top of that, the team is responsible for setting overall (for the Press as a whole) and specific (for each Division of the Press) targets for each financial year. The team meets on a monthly basis to monitor progress against those targets, and to discuss longer-term projects or initiatives which could range from ideas for possible acquisitions (of other publishers or imprints) to plans for a major overhaul of the Press's online presence.

Across the industry, Senior Management teams vary considerably in terms of how they convey their goals, vision, and corporate ethos to staff. In some publishing houses there is transparency around financial performance; in others, much less so. Some houses arrange regular 'all staff' meetings at which Senior Management teams offer short presentations on developments in their areas – others leave this up to individual teams. Either way, it's imperative for staff morale that a publishing house's Senior Management team is seen to be accessible, communicative, and strategically ambitious.

Audio

Given the steady rise in popularity of audiobooks and the increasing desire of publishing houses to fill their social media channels with high-quality, well-produced content, including book trailers and author interviews, there is a trend to invest in audio/video facilities. Such an investment is under consideration at The Ludlow Press. Currently, though, the Press makes do by licencing its content to specialist audiobook companies **(see the section on *Subsidiary Rights*)** and by asking staff (usually in Publicity or Marketing) to use phones or tablets to create other audio and video content in-house.

Marketing

> Marketing plays a full role in the development of new projects, from coming up with new ideas and commenting on editors' proposals to market testing new projects during their development. Marketing will also be involved in commenting on the book's title (including any subtitle) and other textual elements to maximize search engine optimization (SEO) and discoverability; its genre or subject classification; cross-marketing opportunities with other titles; and the cover design and how it works with the target market.
>
> *Clark and Phillips, p. 227*

The Marketing department is a core team in any publishing house. Put crudely, there's no point in publishing a book unless you're able to back it up with parallel activity designed to alert potential customers to that book's existence. (Note the use of the word 'customers': in some types of academic publishing in particular, marketing efforts may be focussed upon institutions like libraries rather than on individual 'readers'.)

For any Marketing team, the first job is to identify key audiences for a book and then to create appropriate communications to get the book ready presentation to those audiences, who can include: the Press's own sales reps, booksellers, librarians, and individual consumers. Successful marketing develops collaborations and partnerships with a range of influencers and other brands, through paid placement (including advertising) and by getting books into non-traditional outlets.

Every publishing house is different, of course. At The Ludlow Press, the Marketing teams build and implement social media campaigns, while in other houses that's the role of the Publicity team (**see the section on *Publicity***). The work of marketers and publicists is connected in many ways – perhaps the simplest way of thinking about them is this: marketing is what *publishing houses* say about their books and authors, while publicity is what *others* say.

There are stark differences between how trade and academic sides of publishing conceive of and carry out marketing activities. On the trade side, the overall aim is to produce campaigns that will grab the attention of consumers, drive sales, and build upon an author's profile. This means developing long-term strategies for existing brands and creating plans for newer authors and brands. Marketing activity doesn't kick off around the time of publication, of course: often it starts months earlier with 'pre-awareness' campaigns designed to maximise sales in the first few days and weeks of a book's published life.

In their study of publishing houses' use of social media, Criswell and Canty observe just how early this marketing activity can begin. With regard to the Stephen King novel *The Wind Through the Keyhole*, for example, the first mention of the book was in 2009, while King's UK publisher Hodder announced the book's publication in June 2011, a full ten months before its publication date of April 2012.

The first mention of the book's potential existence was on the 9th November 2009 on Twitter. From this point on Hodder & Stoughton methodically released pieces of information about the upcoming title, including extracts and information on the 'StephenKingFaces' campaign, whetting fans' appetites right up to the publication date. This generated hype on social media, and influenced 2,457 tweets before the release of the Hardback on the 24th April 2012. This is an incredible achievement for Hodder & Stoughton, as they resurrected conversation about a finished series, and gathered a large, active social media audience awaiting the release of the book.

Criswell and Canty, p. 369

There is pressure on marketing staff to be innovative, given the noise that bombards consumers on a daily basis. Marketers are also expected to evaluate their campaigns to ascertain what has worked well and what hasn't. (Although, of course, if it were that simple, publishing houses would execute successful marketing campaigns every time. They don't.)

This leads to an intriguing question: who to blame when a book's performance doesn't meet expectations? The standard responses, in my experience, are for editorial staff to blame the marketing team (for failing to alert enough readers to a book's existence) or the sales team (for failing to get a book into retail outlets in big enough quantities to be visible); while marketing and sales staff tend to blame the editorial team (because a book simply wasn't good or distinctive enough, or for failing to provide good quality supporting information about the book in a timely manner, or for signing up an author who proved to be unhelpful in terms of promotional effort). If left unchecked, these attitudes can be problematic. It's important, therefore, for a publishing house to run regular post-mortem exercises on key titles – at The Ludlow Press, this doesn't happen, leading to occasional flare-ups between the teams.

In scholarly and professional publishing, marketing activities need to be more precisely defined. In the Academic Division of The Ludlow Press, for example, much of this focus stems from a database of customer contacts which has been built up over several years and requires considerable maintenance to ensure its currency. The names, email addresses, and subject specialisms of tens of thousands of scholars around the world are stored, enabling marketing staff to alert academics to the publication of a new book or series in their field. Some academic publishing houses are more aggressive in their pursuit of new contacts, using data-mining techniques (either in-house or freelanced out) to add scholars to their databases. (The vast majority of academics display this information on their institution's website so the data is not hard to find.) Other publishing houses are more careful – wary of data protection laws – and ask people to 'opt in' to mailing lists via pop-ups on their website and via conversations at conferences or on campus.

Two other key tasks for marketing staff in academic publishing are to send books out for review and to attend specialist scholarly conferences. Finding suitable review outlets for academic books can be challenging – textbooks, for example, rarely get reviewed anywhere. While there are potentially dozens of journals in any given subject area, there are still more books being published than can be reviewed, and even when a review is assigned by a journal it can often be a year or two before it's published. (By which time everyone at the publishing house has moved on to hundreds of newer titles.) Academic books with higher-profile authors do get reviewed though, and a positive review in the *New York Review of Books* or *Times Literary Supplement* can drive sales, so marketing staff work hard to foster good relationships with such outlets. In terms of academic conferences, these can range from very small affairs with just a couple of hundred attendees to huge meetings at which 10,000 scholars converge on a city to network, present papers, and browse the book exhibit. It's the role of marketing staff (and sometimes editorial colleagues too) to work on the publishing house's booth selling books, meeting with scholars, developing contacts, and listening to book ideas, and to be seen as a serious publisher in that field.

Publicity

> Media outlets need content, and books, authors and writing provides good copy and material for book and culture programmes. Small publishers often fail to take advantage of this, or don't know how to exploit it, while big publishers have departments dedicated to chasing down every promotional opportunity.
>
> *Guthrie, p. 177*

The goal of the Publicity team is to persuade people outside of the publishing house to generate noise about its books and authors – and ideally to modulate that noise so it conveys an upbeat and positive message. (The old adage 'all publicity is good publicity' may well be true, but negative publicity is never good for an author's ego.) Publicity staff, either in-house or external – there are a large number of talented and experienced freelance book publicists who do a lot of work for smaller and medium-sized houses – set up author events at bookshops and other venues including libraries, museums, and book festivals. They send out – either physically or electronically – advance proof copies, letters, and lists of talking points to print, online, and broadcast media. There is a great deal of follow-up work involved. Publicists must strike a difficult balance, being dogged and thorough without irritating their media contacts.

Publicity staff need good social skills. They organise lunches and parties where media contacts can meet authors, and sometimes set up drinks to talk through forthcoming lists with their contacts. (The quality of those contacts is, of course, crucial to the success and value of any book publicist.)

The publicity team works very closely with authors, helping them find effective ways to talk about their books. Some authors need a lot of help with this, others none at all. Either way, it's fair to say that on the trade side of publishing, the relationship between publicist and author can be a close one, especially during the frenzied month or two around publication. It's a publicist who'll accompany an author to do a major radio interview, and a publicist who can offer support (or sympathetically absorb an author's diatribe) when a bookshop event only attracts four customers.

Operations

In some publishing houses, the Operations Department is closely intertwined with the Production team, while in others it's less so. Fundamentally, the staff who work in Operations lubricate the machinery of the publishing engine, to ensure that systems are working efficiently and smoothly. A lot of Operations effort takes place behind the scenes: it's one of the least glamorous departments in a publishing house and yet, without it the whole enterprise would collapse.

Senior staff in Operations liaise with colleagues in Sales and Production on a regular basis and are also the key point of contact with warehouses and distributors. It's their role to keep on top of even the most mundane items (for example, keeping shipping policies up to date), to maximise efficiencies around stock turnover – and it is normal practice to have several very large projects running concurrently in this department. Senior Operations staff need to have a deep knowledge of the publishing process across all market sectors, and good knowledge of the full range of systems used by the Press and its distribution partners.

One of the central roles with an Operations team is that of inventory manager. This is a core function at any publishing house – from the smallest (where it would be one part of a much broader role) to the largest (where there might be several inventory managers, each dedicated to a different imprint or division of the company). Any inventory manager needs a sharp mind and exceptional attention to detail. On any given day, an inventory manager might be: monitoring customer orders against estimates and making any necessary adjustments to print quantities; studying daily or weekly sales data from key accounts to ascertain if inventory levels are sufficient to meet demand for more stock; recommending reprints of frontlist titles as required; checking stock of hundreds (or thousands) of backlist titles; prompting reprint discussions for weekly or monthly reprint meetings; pulling together remainder and overstock lists for distribution to colleagues in Sales and Editorial departments; or acting as the primary point of contact for warehouse personnel. When this role is performed well it can make a real difference to the bottom line, and prevent key titles from being unavailable for a few days – which can then lead to irate editors, authors, agents, and more.

Subsidiary Rights

Being part of a publishing house's Rights team typically requires very strong communication and negotiation skills and a sensitivity to both customer and author care. Even at more junior levels, there can be considerable overseas travel involved and the ability to speak more than one language is seen as a desirable skill. Some of the biggest book fairs in the world are, in no particular order:

Abu Dhabi International Book Fair
London Book Fair
Frankfurt Book Fair
Book Expo America
The Hong Kong Book Fair
Guadalajara International Book Fair
Cairo International Book Fair
Bologna Children's Book Fair
Tehran International Book Fair
Book Expo Australia
Shanghai Book Fair

As Lynette Owen observes in her classic text *Selling Rights*, the necessity of attending book fairs (with their attendant preparatory and follow-up work) can create additional pressures which are unique to the Rights Department in a publishing house:

> Rights work usually involves seasonal pressure, with the majority of book fairs concentrated in the spring and autumn each year. Considerable patience, diplomacy, physical and mental stamina, and adaptability will allow the same rights person to move from the comparatively leisurely pace and gastronomic delights of Bologna in March to the less than perfect physical conditions of Moscow or Beijing in September, closely followed by the rigours of Frankfurt in October. The working conditions may vary but the role of the rights person is the same – to achieve rights sales on the best possible terms to appropriate partners.
>
> *Owen, p. 66*

The goal of the dozens of meetings that a Rights Manager can have at a big book fair is to sell translation rights to overseas publishers – who could be based in South Korea, Poland, Brazil, Sweden, the UAE, Thailand, Italy, Lithuania, or almost any other nation that has its own thriving publishing industry. But the selling of translation rights is only one aspect of a Rights team's function. Particularly in the area of trade publishing – although some of these can occasionally apply to academic and professional books – staff are also looking to sell:

- English language territorial rights – for a UK publisher, this could mean selling the rights to another publisher in the US, Canada, South Africa, or Australia. If the book is agented, it's likely that the agent will retain those rights to sell herself; if the publishing house owns world rights and has its own international distribution networks then the calculation needs to be made as to whether more profit will be generated by publishing the work in those territories itself or by selling the rights to a publishing house which may be better suited to exploiting the book in that country or region. The agented American writer Colson Whitehead's multi-award-winning 2016 novel *The Underground Railroad*, for example, was published in the US by Penguin Random House and in the UK by Hachette.
- Serial rights – this involves selling excerpts from a book to a newspaper or magazine. Rights staff need to maintain good contacts with their counterparts at those media outlets in order to increase the publishing house's chances of securing such a deal – which can be lucrative in terms of both revenue and publicity.
- Anthology and quotation rights – otherwise known as 'permissions', this is where another publisher asks to reproduce material from one of the Press's books. Particularly in academic publishing and with poetry, this can generate decent additional income. Change is beginning to be felt now in scholarly publishing as increasing numbers of authors want their work to be freely available online (Open Access publishing) – so many permissions queries now come from a press's own authors, asking if they can upload the complete text of their work to an institutional repository or other online platform. Editorial and Rights staff are having to construct clear policies around this.
- Audio rights – as the audiobook market continues to grow, there is more revenue to be made from selling audio rights. Some bigger publishing houses have developed their own audio imprints. In the US, Audible is the biggest player in the audiobook market and has been a subsidiary of Amazon since 2008.
- TV, film, radio, and stage rights – these rights are much more likely to be retained by the author's agent. If the author doesn't have an agent and didn't kick up a fuss at contract stage, then they will belong to the publishing house. There is serious money to be made, of course, in selling film or TV rights, not to mention the boost in sales which can accompany any eventual release. (Think *Game of Thrones* or *The Martian*.) Very often, film rights to a book will be optioned – perhaps several times – only for the proposed film to fall into production limbo and never see the light of day. Jonathan Franzen's *The Corrections*, for example, has been optioned for both film and television since 2002 but hasn't yet been made.

- Book club rights – since their peak in the late twentieth century, book clubs have now diminished significantly in terms of their market share due to increasingly competitive retail discounting and online sales. Many publishing houses now view sales to book clubs as an opportunity to be handled by the Sales Department instead of by Rights.
- Paperback rights – as with book club rights deals, this is an area which has seen a decline since the 1980s when many publishing houses consolidated and most specialist paperback presses became divisions or imprints of larger companies. It is now typical, then, for a book that's published in hardcover initially to be published the following year in paperback by the same company. So Jesse Ball's 2016 novel *How to Set a Fire and Why* was published in hardcover in the US by Pantheon Books, then in paperback in 2017 by Vintage: both are imprints of Penguin Random House.

Given all of this potential activity, it's imperative that members of the Rights team communicate both internally (with colleagues) and externally (with agents and authors). Selling rights well can be an excellent way of boosting revenues for the company and the author, and can play a vital role in persuading the author that he should stick with the publishing house for future books.

Finance

In very basic terms, the role of the Finance department is to keep track of the money being spent by the business and the money coming into the business. Ideally there will be more of the latter and the numbers will show an increase over the prior year – if that's not the case, the Finance team will then be expected to come up with creative ways of making those disappointing numbers look as positive as possible.

To be more precise, the purchase ledger team deals with incoming invoices and payments from printers, booksellers, distributors, and so on, while the royalties team deals with payments to authors and agents. If an advance against future royalties has been paid (standard practice in trade publishing, much less so in academic and professional publishing), the royalties team needs to monitor sales so that if the advance is ever earned out – and there are many, many books where this never happens – then the correct remuneration is paid to the author. Bear in mind that an author can earn money not only from book sales but from the sale of serial rights, translation rights, film rights, and more. There are vast numbers of transactions needing to be tracked in order to ensure authors are paid accurately, hence larger publishing houses need to invest in robust and complex royalties and sales reporting systems and in the staff to deal with the resulting work. It's worth mentioning, perhaps, that this work can often be thankless: at The Ludlow Press, it's rare for an author (or her editor or agent) to contact the royalties team to express gratitude for a prompt and accurate payment; while it's not unusual for an author (or her editor or agent) to complain – often vigorously and repeatedly – about a late, inaccurate, or confusing payment.

Other key functions of the Finance team are budgeting and evaluating performance against those forecasts. As publishing houses have grown, the task of setting budgets and monitoring performance has become increasingly complex. At The Ludlow Press, there is an overall budget created for the financial year and within that it's possible to see quarterly, monthly, weekly, and even daily forecasts for each Division. The role of the Finance team isn't simply to provide that data to management staff but also to analyse and interpret the data. Working with colleagues in Sales, Marketing, Editorial, and Production, the Finance team could be asked to explain why the backlist numbers in children's picture books are down by 14% compared to prior year, or why revenues from academic monographs are up by 7% in North America despite lower USD prices having been implemented (by the Operations team) due to a shift in the exchange rate. Key staff in the Finance team need to have sharp analytical skills and a deep understanding of how the broader publishing industry works. They may also be asked to produce monthly written reports for senior management – reports which outline the numbers against budget and previous years and which pick up on anomalies and trends, helping management to predict financial performance over the rest of the financial year.

Editorial

The Editorial departments at The Ludlow Press are responsible for bringing in the books that the Press will publish. Whether it's a new cookbook or a new YA detective fiction series or a new economics textbook, all of this content is first discovered, assessed, and then brought to a Publishing Meeting by individual editors. All editors at the Press have targets to hit each year: these vary by Division and by the relative seniority of the staff member but are based on the number of new projects each editor brings in and the projected value of those projects.

The typical hierarchy of an Editorial department looks like this, in order of descending seniority:

Publishing Director – Editorial Director – Senior Publisher – Publisher – Senior Editor – Editor – Assistant Editor – Editorial Assistant

Each team of editors and assistants reports in to an Editorial Director, and those Editorial Directors report to a Publishing Director. At The Ludlow Press, the three Publishing Directors (for Adult books, Children's books, and Academic books) sit on the Senior Management team.

Acquiring or commissioning books (acquiring being the term used more commonly in the US than the UK and implying a financial transaction on the part of the publishing house which isn't always the case – not all books have a royalty advance attached to them) isn't the only function of the Editorial Department. Once any new title has been commissioned and the contract signed, editors and their assistants are also responsible for what is broadly termed 'author care' – keeping in touch with the author during the writing process, which could be a few weeks, a few months, or a few years. (Some projects are acquired when the manuscript is already completed, of course.) All authors are different and while some are happy to write with no assistance or support from the publishing house at all, others prefer plenty of hand-holding. This is where assistant-level staff, in particular, can learn the key skills of cajoling, motivating, and guiding authors through what can be a challenging time. The aim of author care is twofold: first, it's to provide the author with an impressive level of service so that she'll tell her friends and peers how wonderful the publishing house is; second, it's to encourage the author to deliver his manuscript on time. Any such delays can have profound impacts upon a publishing house's financial performance.

Once the manuscript is delivered by the author, it is the role of the Editorial team to read it and then propose any structural changes to the author. Authors respond in many different ways to such edits – while some are happy to have their work altered by publishers in this way, others are less so. (And there are occasional interjections from literary agents to complicate / ameliorate matters.) Structural editing varies from publisher to publisher and even internally. While editors on the trade side have more time to do this type of work, their counterparts in academic publishing typically don't. (Academic books on the whole generate less revenue per title so editors need to publish many more of them to justify their existence – and if an editor is working on 30–50 titles per year, then there's not the time to edit each manuscript.)

When the final version of the manuscript is agreed upon by editor and author, it's the role of the Editorial team to hand it over to colleagues in Production or Managing Editorial for copy-editing, typesetting, proofreading, and indexing. At The Ludlow Press, editors are required to 'transmit' each manuscript to the Production team in a formal meeting. Detailed forms need to be filled out and conversations need to be had about text design, the quality of any images to be used in the book, the level of copy-editing required, schedules, author availability to answer questions, and much more. These meetings are generally collegial and constructive although if the editor is unprepared or the manuscript appears sloppy or to be missing some elements they can break down – it's an unspoken rule at The Ludlow Press that Production has the right to 'abandon' any such meeting in which case the editor must retreat to his desk, do some more preparation, and request another meeting. The point of this is not so that editors can be put in their place (although this is sometimes how the Editorial team sees it) but so that Production staff have the precise information they need in order to shepherd each book through the process as efficiently as possible.

All of this is for one individual title. Editors need to work on that level, of course – but they also need to commission books more strategically. Many would argue that the true measure of any editor or Editorial team is in *list building* – the idea that, over a period of years, it's possible to build up a portfolio of books with its own identity, its own innate sense of quality, so that readers in a particular market segment come to trust that publisher or imprint, and the best authors in that field will want to work with the editor or team in question.

> A set of titles that presents a defined genre or subject to a specific audience will have a greater value than one which simply aggregates disparate titles. Successful lists attract both authors and readers, and marketing a list is often more cost-effective with cross-marketing opportunities between titles.
>
> *Clark and Phillips, p. 139*

Contracts

The work of the Contracts department (note that many smaller publishing houses don't have a dedicated team for this and typically rely on editors, rights staff, and senior management to ensure that contracts are handled correctly) seems simple at first glance but can often be complicated. It is important work: a publishing house's future financial health is dependent on the robustness of the contracts by which its Intellectual Property has been secured.

At The Ludlow Press, once an editor has made a broad offer for a book and that offer is accepted by the author/agent, a member of the Contracts team will pull together a contract – almost always based on one of many templates stored by the Press. (If the book is represented by an agency with which the publishing house does a lot of business, there will be a template for this, too, with agency-specific language that may have been agreed years ago.) These templates are important and are regularly checked and updated to ensure that they reflect the most recent industry developments.

The Contracts team sends a draft of the contract to the agent or author – if it's based on a template the agent has seen before, of course, there shouldn't be much to argue about. This draft comes back with comments and suggested changes, and the process goes back and forth. As a rule, any questions or disputes are handled by the Contracts team. Occasionally, issues arise that need to be referred (perhaps to a senior member of the Editorial team, for a second opinion) or escalated (to the Legal team or senior management).

The next phase, once the contract has been fully agreed, is to get it signed. (Often this is done via email but some publishing houses still prefer mailing out hard copies.) An agented book requires three signing copies: one for the author, one for the agent, and one for the publisher. It's the job of the Contracts team to send these out to the appropriate party, tracking them to make sure none fall through the cracks, and chasing up where necessary. Most publishing houses still ask for handwritten signatures instead of digital, for legal reasons. Once the signed copies come back, they are checked (for any last-minute tweaks) and then counter-signed – usually by an authorised signer, such as a Publishing Director, Finance Director, or member of the Senior Management team. After that's been done, the fine detail of the contract (particular sub-rights, royalties, delivery schedules, etc.) needs to be confirmed and checked on the relevant internal database so that staff from all other departments can quickly access the relevant information on each book. Many publishing systems now allow for the scanning and uploading of the signed contract, too.

It can take two days or several months to shepherd one book contract through to completion. The Contracts department needs staff who are skilled negotiators, good communicators, knowledgeable about the industry, and meticulously organised.

With the proliferation of digital content, a newer role is now becoming standard at larger publishing houses – that of anti-piracy manager or controller. This can fall under the remit of the Rights team, or the Legal team, or Contracts. The role involves monitoring file-sharing and social media sites and following up on instances of piracy reported by authors or their agents. The internet is awash with illegally posted book content and there's clearly an audience looking for it (try typing into Google the title of almost any book and see how popular the search for a PDF of that title is) – although there has been little research so far around the actual negative impact of this pirated content on publishing houses' revenues.

Human Resources

Rarely discussed but crucial to the success of any publishing house is the Human Resources team. This can, of course, range from one person (or even half a person) at a small company to a team of several dedicated HR staff at a large publishing house. The key responsibilities of the HR team – as in many other industries – are in helping with the recruitment of staff; ensuring that wages are paid in an orderly and reliable manner; making sure that the correct legal processes are followed when staff leave the company, voluntarily or otherwise; and helping to provide training and career development guidance wherever possible.

Publishing houses vary tremendously in the types and levels of training they offer their staff. In the past, this has perhaps been seen as an unnecessary expense, based on an assumption that if staff are bright enough (which, of course, they all are, since they work in publishing) then they can learn on the job. Given that publishing now is more complex and more competitive than it has ever been, senior management have realised that commercial advantages can be gained by allocating time and money to enabling staff to reach their full potential.

In terms of recruitment, the HR team has a key role to play. At The Ludlow Press, entry-level positions in Marketing, Editorial, or Production may receive hundreds of applications – no matter how stringent the criteria listed in the job ad. Typically, the HR team will have the task of whittling these applications down to a handful of candidates to be interviewed, and those interviews will either be conducted by HR or by the relevant department, or by a combination of the two. The whittling process, as innocent as it sounds, can have a key impact on the eventual demographic make-up of the publishing house and the industry more widely. The publishing industry has started to make a lot of noise over the last ten years about its desire to increase diversity, and it is HR teams who are in pole position to turn these words into actions. Although, as we can see from a 2016 article in *Publishers Weekly*, pole position doesn't necessarily equate to full control:

> One alternative, according to a Big Five [in terms of US publishing] HR exec, is for companies to create internal targets around diversity hiring. Acknowledging that people "get very nervous talking about quotas," she said a company can instead "set internal targets it aspires to hit." To implement these targets, she thinks big publishers should rely on their key executives to see to it that the hiring plan is "enforceable." Employees can even be incentivized to hit certain goals with things like bonuses.
>
> "Human resources can't do this in a vacuum," the HR exec said, adding that it can be particularly difficult to bring up the issue of diversity to executives who are successfully overseeing their corners of the business. "They'll say, 'Everything is running smoothly, so why are you telling me diversity is a problem?'"
>
> *PublishersWeekly.com, accessed Aug 2 2017*

In the UK, organisations such as Creative Access are working to address the issue of diversity and have partnered with several of the biggest publishing houses specifically by placing Black, Asian and minority ethnic (BAME) interns across these companies. Internships are still one of the key routes into a publishing career, and these are often organised by the HR team. A typical internship lasts between three and six months, and it is fairly standard practice now for interns to be paid something close to an entry-level salary. Work placements, however, tend to last for a couple of weeks and often cover only travel expenses. Given that publishing is such a competitive industry to break into, work placements and internships are seen as important ways of gaining experience and making connections.

Information Technology

The Information Technology (IT) department is one of the core teams of any modern publishing house. IT now permeates every aspect of the book publishing process. Even as recently as the mid-1990s it was common to find some staff working on typewriters or primitive word processors, to see profit and loss sheets being filled in by hand, and to see a line of staff waiting to use the fax machine. Now, even the slightest glitch in a company's IT performance can cause staff meltdowns and potentially serious issues for the business – so publishing houses invest considerable resources in their IT systems, making sure they are as robust, flexible, responsive, and resilient as possible.

The staff who make up an IT department are unusual in the book publishing world, as the majority of them know little about the publishing industry itself. They are hired instead for their expertise in specific systems, problem-solving, coding, and so on. Staff at the higher levels of the IT department do tend to know more about publishing-specific issues (often by osmosis over the years) but even there, it's not unusual for a publishing house to recruit a Head of IT from a different industry entirely.

There are many functions performed by an IT department, some of which are too specific (not to mention too technical!) to detail here. One of the most important is to provide an over-arching IT service strategy for the business – because technology in this sector is so fast-moving, there is a perpetual need to identify opportunities for improvements across the organisation. The best IT teams establish a culture of continual improvement, communicating with staff in all other departments what is being done, and why. (The 'why' is particularly key here, as some other staff in publishing are not the smartest when it comes to technology.) Best practice can involve organising monthly catch-up sessions to ensure dialogue, and ensuring that issues are followed up quickly, as well as being clear about service levels across the company – senior staff need to know, for example, that if the main sales reporting system goes down overnight, dedicated efforts will be made to get it fixed within a certain time scale. Major technology issues can happen outside of regular work hours, of course, so plans must be in place to cover any such eventualities.

Security is an increasingly important issue for IT teams to consider and be prepared for. Despite regular reminders (both inside and outside of the workplace), it's always possible that one member of staff will open a link sent in an unsolicited email – thus exposing the company to viruses and malware. Publishing houses store a lot of sensitive data electronically, from intellectual property itself (tens of thousands of manuscripts) to private email discussions and authors' bank details. It's true that there are more tempting targets for hackers and cyber criminals (see the Sony Pictures hack of 2014, or the British Airways frequent flyers data breach of the following year) but a publishing house's IT team needs to be aware of the potential issues.

For many presses, the key is to work with technology suppliers to create IT systems and processes that match up with the company's specific publishing profile. (A Canadian university press publishing around 100 titles a year has very different IT requirements from a large, global commercial press or a not-for-profit poetry press based in Michigan.) If IT can be intelligently applied to the submission of book proposals, the academic peer review process, production workflows and schedules, business analytics, royalties processing and payment, author care, internal and external communication, and more – then the business in question gains a competitive advantage and the costs invested in implementing and sustaining that technology can be justified.

Art and Design

The Design department at The Ludlow Press is perhaps the most creative of all the teams. Its function, put crudely, is to make every book look as good as possible in order to maximise sales. Despite the enormous emphasis placed on editorial quality, research consistently shows that in terms of consumer purchasing decisions, an appealing cover design – and, for many segments of the non-fiction market, an appealing interior design as well – is one of the key factors and can make the difference between browsing and buying.

Motives for book purchasing

Subject	25%
Author	25%
Price/offer	20%
Series	17%
Characters	11%
Cover appeal	10%

Source: *Books & Consumers* (April 2014).

(Some surveys show higher figures for cover design being a key driver, others slightly lower – but 10% seems the average. It is possible that the real figure is higher, as some of those people surveyed might not want to admit that they're so easily swayed by a cover design.)

At The Ludlow Press, the design team is divided across Adult, Children's, and Academic publishing: designers are considered specialists in one of these areas and are paired with certain editors or lists as a result.

In theory, the work of designing a book cover for a romance novel or a business textbook is the same; in practice, the two are rather different. In trade publishing – and with fiction in particular – it is assumed that a great cover design often stems from reading the manuscript itself.

> The design process usually involves reading the brief and maybe the book and coming up with a few ideas, which are then sent to the publisher. Sometimes all the ideas I've come up with are hated and sometimes one idea is accepted exactly as it is, but usually it's somewhere between the two and it's a case of knocking into shape whichever idea went down best until everyone's happy. 'Everyone' being quite a few people at the publishing company and possibly authors, agents, bookshops and even supermarkets.
>
> **Jamie Keenan**, *book cover designer*
> *shinynewbooks.co.uk, accessed July 17 2017*

In academic publishing, the cover is often designed in advance of the manuscript being delivered. (Does a designer really need to read and understand a dense manuscript of contemporary philosophy, for example, in order to conjure up a look for it?)

It is the responsibility of the editorial team to write a cover brief for each book and this forms the basis for what the Design team creates. Cover briefs vary tremendously: some are detailed, full of concrete ideas and suggestions for images; while others are vague and leave much more to the Design team. (There's an implicit assumption behind this process that all Editorial staff are visually literate enough to convey useful ideas in a cover brief. It isn't always the case, and some briefs are considerably better than others.) Upon receiving the brief from the Editorial team, a designer usually has three to four weeks to come up with a range of possible visuals for the book's front cover. These are then shared with the relevant editor. This tends to be done more informally for academic books where the cover design isn't deemed to be quite so essential to the book's success but more formally in trade publishing. At The Ludlow Press, for example, designers are required to present a board of visuals to a publishing meeting. There, colleagues from Editorial, Production, Sales, and Marketing teams will respond to those visuals. Designers need to have the resilience to withstand some fairly sharp critiques of their work. Sometimes, all initial designs are rejected; or, one is deemed to be promising and then sent away for further work. Eventually – after input from the author as well, although this can be fraught with difficulty – a final design is agreed upon and the design team's work is then nearly done.

At The Ludlow Press, designers are required to upload several versions of the final front cover onto the central system. Different sizes and formats of the same image are needed – for use in marketing catalogues, or to be sent to online retailers and wholesalers. These vary in size from large to very small data files for the thumbnail image versions. Cover designers have tended towards using larger type on book covers since the rise of Amazon: if you're viewing a book cover on your phone it can often be less than one inch tall, so legibility can be a real issue. Some publishing houses are now creating different cover designs for print and electronic editions as a way of circumventing this problem, as noted in this blog post by Phoebe Morgan of HarperCollins in London:

> Sometimes, we'll even do a different cover for the ebook, because what might look great on a shelf could easily get lost in an Amazon line-up – tiny details can be missed online.
>
> *BookMachine.org, accessed 26 July 2017*

The spine and back cover are finished later in the process, as confirmed spine width and endorsements for the back cover sometimes aren't received until shortly before the files are sent to press.

Production

The Production department at any publishing house is the engine that makes the entire machine tick over. Through their own endeavours and through working closely with a wide network of printers, binders, distributors, designers, typesetters, copy-editors, indexers, and more, the production team strives to turn each and every manuscript into a finished book (print or digital) that – all being well – is free of errors and has the look and feel to serve the content perfectly and justify its retail price.

At many larger publishing houses (The Ludlow Press in 2016, for example, published over 1,200 new books), there are intense demands placed upon the production department to deliver a constant flow of product efficiently and reliably. To help with this, most production teams have developed intricate systems of scheduling which ideally are adhered to by every title – although exceptions always need to be made for last-minute projects which hold out the promise of quick revenues.

> Schedules…are a vital tool in project and production management because they allow a publisher to manage the time it takes to produce a product. But schedules do more than that. They make it necessary for Production to think through and test the logic of the entire project in terms of all its components and how they fit together before it even starts.
>
> *Bullock, p. 53*

In a very basic sense, a typical schedule follows this path (Figure 1.1):

In reality, each stage can have several potential phases of its own and the unexpected can occur at any point: the author could object to copy-edits causing a delay; the editorial team may have inadvertently handed over to production a previous draft of the manuscript, causing the whole process to start again; the author could fall ill during the time she's been allocated to check the first proofs; the index may not be up to scratch; a percentage of the books might be printed with one signature upside down; whole pallets of books could disappear *en route* from the printers to the distributor's warehouse. All of these are rare, but all can and do happen. It's the job of the production team to intervene at any such points, to fix the issue and keep the project on schedule wherever possible.

For senior staff in a production department, aside from overseeing the day-to-day business of running their teams, considerable time goes into communicating with external suppliers – particularly printers and (where used) project management companies. Publishing houses with consistently large outputs are able to leverage that critical mass of work to negotiate advantageous rates with printing companies. Some publishing houses use one dedicated printer for almost all their work; others prefer to use a range of printers either for geographical reasons or because those printers have different specialist skills. There is constant pressure to keep print costs as low as possible – at The Ludlow Press, printers are used in Hong Kong, India, and Poland as well as in the US and the UK, and senior production staff pay regular visits to these facilities to see their latest technology and negotiate the best prices. There is always a balance to be struck between

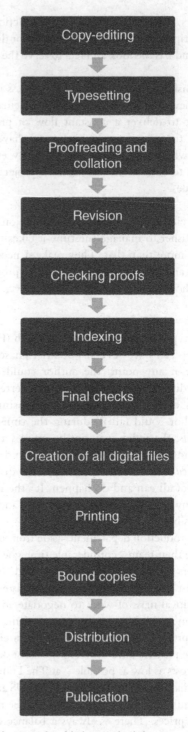

FIGURE 1.1 Example of a typical publishing schedule

obtaining the lowest print prices and ensuring that print quantities are kept at sensible levels to minimise the risk of overstock:

> With lower sales of print books, manufacturers report that publishers have become more willing to take advantages of short print runs. Publishers understand that while unit costs may be higher, producing only what they need cuts warehousing costs and lowers the risk of larger print runs not selling through. Bolstered by the latest IT systems and printing technology, book manufacturers continue to invest in ways to improve and broaden their services by offering warehousing, distribution, and even editorial and other publishing services. Digital printing is now fully incorporated among printers, especially for small-to-midsize players.
>
> *PublishersWeekly.com, accessed July 26 2017*

Senior production staff at The Ludlow Press have similar working relationships with the project management companies used by the Press: companies which will oversee the entire process from final manuscript to the creation of digital files ready for printing or for distribution as e-books.

Project management companies are used much more heavily in academic publishing than in trade publishing. Trade books typically have a broader readership, therefore it's seen as more important that more time and money is spent on having them shaped, designed, and edited. Academic publishing houses would never express it in these terms, of course, but there is a direct correlation between the smaller readership of scholarly books and the desire – some would say necessity – to cut costs in producing them. And as dedicated and thorough as many of the project management companies are, they are able to offer cheaper rates because their staff are, on the whole, less likely to be specialists in the field. Not all scholarly publishing houses outsource their Production processes – it's less common at university presses, many of whom try to attract the best authors by touting their more 'traditional' editing processes.

Digital Production

Some larger publishing houses have an entirely separate Digital Production department, reflecting the increasing importance over the last decade of e-books and the revenues they generate. Other publishing houses, like The Ludlow Press, have dedicated Digital Production staff within the main Production department and it is the responsibility of those staff to ensure that e-book editions are produced on time and in the correct formats required by the market. If any minor errors are spotted in a book after publication, it's also industry standard now for those to be corrected immediately in the e-book edition, whereas the physical edition has to wait for a second printing.

In some publishing houses these functions are performed by an e-book 'Operations' team. And that team tends to own the responsibility for liaising with key e-book vendors to ensure the smooth flow of product to market. This is just for new content, of course. Many publishing houses – particularly in the academic sector – have been working for years now to digitise thousands of backlist titles so they can be offered as e-book editions to libraries and individual consumers. This has created a lot of extra work – from making sure that rights have been cleared on older titles where electronic editions may not even have been mentioned in the original contract, to creating records and metadata for each new edition – and at many publishing houses, new roles have been created and new teams developed as a result.

For those publishing houses which have moved into the world of book-related apps, such work could also fall under the remit of a Digital Production team, unless it is farmed out to specialist app developers. UK-based children's publishing house Nosy Crow, for example, is well known for its work with apps such as *Cinderella* and *Jack and the Beanstalk* – although the number of apps Nosy Crow has released is tiny compared to the number of books it has published. Nosy Crow has a small Apps Development team which falls under the wing of its Digital Project team. The challenge with apps, of course, is that typically consumers are prepared to pay even less than for a paperback book:

> Nosy Crow did well from Apple's Kids category: many of its apps were featured by Apple when it went live last year. [Managing Director Kate] Wilson doesn't shirk questions about children's apps as a business though, admitting that it remains hard work for any publisher focusing on paid book-apps rather than games with in-app purchases. 'The tough thing is that a lot of people expect everything for nothing, or at least for very little. At the moment, it's hard to say that the price these apps are commanding is a reflection for the effort, expertise and thought that goes into them,' she says.
>
> *TheGuardian.com/uk, accessed July 21 2017*

Other publishing houses have chosen to work with app developers on more premium level content – Faber and Bloomsbury, for example, worked with Touch Press to develop the apps for *The Wasteland* and *Shakespeare's Sonnets*, respectively, which retail at prices that are more in line with a full-priced paperback book.

Sales

The primary goal of the Sales department in any publishing house is to ensure that beneficial relationships are created and maintained with a vast array of potential customers for the company's content: from a global giant like Amazon to national chains such as Barnes & Noble or Waterstones, and from a small independent bookshop in Colorado to a supermarket chain in New Zealand, a museum gift store in the Lake District or an academic library supplier in Japan.

It is through these relationships that sales opportunities can be developed, explored, and built upon. A career in Sales is not for the faint-hearted: there is constant pressure for growth and results are scrutinised on a daily basis at many publishing houses – but for those who thrive under pressure, like to negotiate and enjoy being the public face of an organisation, working in Sales can be highly rewarding.

An early career role in a Sales department often has a particular focus, which could mean supporting sales efforts to the key accounts in the publishing house's 'home' territory, or working to increase digital sales efforts, or supporting commission reps or sales agents in export territories.

A lot of time is spent obtaining and collating the relevant information needed to sell to customers, and on the flipside it's vital for sales staff to respond quickly to any queries from those customers. Sales kits and customer presentations need to be pulled together – at The Ludlow Press, various sales teams and international partners work on different selling schedules; a large part of the department's work involves keeping on top of who needs which information on which titles at any given time. Centralised database systems help with this, of course, but there is always plenty of detailed, bespoke sales material to create and provide.

Further up the ladder in a Sales department, staff can have a great deal of influence over much more than sales numbers. Senior staff are involved in publishing strategy and often work closely with colleagues from other teams including Marketing and Editorial in particular. At The Ludlow Press it's often the sales team who have the strongest opinions in the weekly publishing meetings. While it's the job of editors to present each new project with passion, conviction, and enthusiasm, it's easy for that positivity to spiral out of control. (Some editors are very experienced and skilled at presenting a new project backed up by carefully selected evidence.) Senior Sales staff act as a counterpoint – not by criticising proposals so vigorously that they get rejected (although that does and occasionally should happen) but by asking the right questions and checking the project from every angle: does the author have a sales track record that can be analysed? Has the editor included the most relevant and recent competing titles from other publishers – and if so, how did they perform in the market? Even if the topic and author are ideal, is the project in an area where the publishing house has the right sales and marketing profile to do it justice? Is the editor's suggested title and subtitle sharp enough? Does the project's sales-potential justify the advance that's needed to acquire the book from the agent? All of these questions are key to effective publishing decisions being made, and it is often Sales staff who drive those discussions forward.

In a larger publishing house, a great many Sales staff spend the majority of their time outside of the main office. Sales reps are a very important part of the mix. Smaller publishing houses often don't have the resources to employ full-time field reps, so instead they hire commission reps to do this work on their behalf. Either way, sales reps can offer not only the dynamism and geographical coverage to get more books into the marketplace but also valuable feedback on forthcoming titles.

> The final factor that helps [publishers] come up with their priority titles is feedback from the sales reps. The sales reps are not just selling: they are also the eyes and ears of the corporation in the world of the publisher's most immediate customers, the bookstores and the retail chains. 'We have an electronic bulletin board,' continued Tom. 'We've got all these reps out there meeting buyers and giving manuscripts and galleys to booksellers and things bubble up to the surface. All of a sudden we may get a sense that the buyers and booksellers like a particular book and that we should make it a priority.'
>
> *Thomson, pp. 190–191*

There are many other functions performed by members of a Sales department – too many to mention here in detail. They would include the pursuit of 'special sales' (bulk sales to organisations, usually at a very high discount) and the monitoring and negotiation of discounts with a range of retailers – negotiations which can be fraught and combative.

Conclusion

These 15 departments or teams, as noted at the start of this essay, vary across the industry. They all describe functions that any publishing house needs to perform – or at the very least consider – if it is to succeed. Some of the teams work closely together on a daily basis (Production and Operations, or Sales and Publicity) while others are more separate in their objectives. Either way, I hope this essay provides a quick grounding in the structure of a publishing house and the sometimes complex relationships that enable it to operate.

References

Bullock, A. (2012). *Book Production*, Abingdon: Routledge, 2012.
Clark, G. and Phillips, A. (2014). *Inside Book Publishing*, 5th Edition. Abingdon: Oxford.
Criswell, J. and Canty, N. (2014). 'Deconstructing Social Media: An Analysis of Twitter and Facebook Use in the Publishing Industry' in *Publishing Research Quarterly*, December 2014, Volume 30, 352–376.
Guthrie, R. (2011). *Publishing: Principles and Practice: Publishing*. London: Sage.
Owen, L. (2010). *Selling Rights*, 6th Edition, Abingdon: Routledge.
Thomson, J.B. (2012). *Merchants of Culture*, 2nd Edition, Cambridge: Polity Press.

Web

"Interview with cover designer Jamie Keenan", *shinynewbooks.co.uk*, accessed July 17 2017.
"The Importance of Covers in Commercial Fiction", *BookMachine.org*, accessed 26 July 2017.

"How Big Printers Are Changing to Stay Competitive", *PublishersWeekly.com*, accessed July 26 2017.

"Nosy Crow talks fairytales, reluctant readers and game-like apps for kids", *TheGuardian.com/uk*, accessed July 21 2017.

"Why Publishing Is So White" *PublishersWeekly.com*, accessed Aug 2 2017.

Web reference

http://www.hachettebookgroup.com/about/leadership/, accessed Aug 2 2017.

2

TYPES OF PUBLISHING HOUSES

Per Henningsgaard

The phrases 'all types of publishing' and 'different types of publishing' regularly appear in authoritative sources on the subject of publishing, such as textbooks about publishing and industry newsletters. Every publishing house is different, of course, but what makes one *type* of publishing different from another? Unfortunately, these sources rarely bother to elaborate. In those rare instances in which they offer examples of 'different types of publishing', the implicit criteria by which difference is judged seems to vary from source to source – for example, one source might contrast multinational corporations and independent publishing houses, while another might contrast traditional publishing and self-publishing.

This essay offers three distinct models for surveying the different types of publishing houses: a model based on funding sources, a model based on market segment, and a model based on size. It also considers how specific types of publishing houses within each model are favourably disposed towards the publication of particular genres.

Using a model based on funding sources to survey the different types of publishing houses reveals just three main sources of funding that support the activities of the book publishing industry. These funding sources can be designated as traditional publishing, dependent publishing, and self-publishing. Traditional publishing gets the most attention – or, more precisely, books published using the funding sources typical of traditional publishing get the most attention. For example, the vast majority of the books mentioned in this essay collection were published using the funding sources typical of traditional publishing.

The distinguishing feature of traditional publishing is that all of the upfront costs are paid by the publishing house. The author is usually expected to contribute time and energy to the book's promotion, but the author does not pay for services like editing and design, nor does the author pay for printing or the production of an e-book. Of course, the author has probably laboured for many months or even years to write the book, and only in limited circumstances would the publishing house directly compensate the author for this time. The author may hope, however, to receive some financial return on this investment of time in the form of a royalty on sales of the book. Not all traditional publishing houses offer royalty arrangements (more on this later, in the part of this essay that discusses a model based on market segment), but for the ones that do, the amount is usually calculated as a percentage of either gross or net sales. The most commonly mentioned royalty rate is 10% of the book's retail price, but the frequency with which this rate is mentioned has more to do with mathematical convenience than reality. Royalty rates vary considerably based on a variety of factors including genre, publication format, author platform, and so forth; in recent years, for example, 25% has become the standard royalty rate for e-books at some traditional publishing houses (Deahl, 2016). In some cases, an author will be paid an advance against royalties, which is money paid in advance of book sales that must then be 'earned out' through book sales before the author is paid any further royalties. This is yet another example of that distinguishing feature of traditional publishing: upfront costs are paid by the publishing house.

Traditional publishing is a financially risky business because of this requirement that the publishing house assume all of the upfront costs. The main income source for traditional publishing is book sales, which cannot, of course, occur until after the money has been spent and the book has been published. There are, however, ancillary sources of income available to traditional publishing houses, such as licensing the rights to foreign editions, translations, and film and television. Other ancillary sources of income involve segmenting the book for distribution through online databases, licensing serial rights, and so forth. If any of these can be arranged prior to a book's publication, it helps reduce the financial risks assumed by the traditional publishing house.

When using a model based on funding sources to survey the different types of publishing houses, dependent publishing is arguably the second-most visible type of publishing after traditional publishing. Indeed, for certain kinds of books, a dependent publishing house might actually offer the greatest visibility. The distinguishing feature of dependent publishing is that the publishing house is supported by an institution, so compared to traditional publishing it is not nearly so reliant on book sales as an income source.

Dependent publishing comes in a lot of different shapes and sizes. For example, many university presses are examples of dependent publishing because their publishing activities are underwritten (through direct subsidy, the provision of space or administrative resources, payment of salaries, or some other arrangement) by their named university. Nonprofit publishing houses are another example of dependent publishing because they are reliant on donations or grants to plug the gap between their expenses and their income from book sales. Examples of nonprofit publishing houses include The Feminist Press in New York City, New York; Graywolf Press in Minneapolis, Minnesota; McSweeney's in

San Francisco, California; and Comma Press in Manchester, England. A slightly different type of dependent publishing can be found in organisations where publishing is a subsidiary activity – in other words, it is not their main business activity. Many professional, educational, governmental, religious, sports, and other organisations, as well as companies of all stripes, regularly publish books (or book-length documents) about their histories, strategies, and performance. For these organisations and companies, like other examples of dependent publishing, sales comprise only part of the funding model supporting their publishing activities.

Dependent publishing houses are favourably disposed towards the publication of particular genres and against others, such as popular fiction and how-to books. The reason for this is that dependent publishing houses tend to be mission-driven, serving an audience or subject matter that (for one reason or another) they believe is underserved. University presses publish scholarly monographs for this reason. Some university presses have also, in recent years, diversified their output to include regional titles, such as regional fiction, guides to local plants and wildlife, and nonfiction about regional history and culture (Givler, 2002, pp. 113–114). Many nonprofit publishing houses specialise in literary fiction, literary nonfiction (including life writing), and poetry. In organisations where publishing is a subsidiary activity, the books they publish tend to be about the organisations themselves, which means they are of interest only to individuals with an existing connection to these organisations; in this way, they are serving both a subject matter and an audience that would otherwise be underserved.

In contrast to dependent publishing, self-publishing is a type of publishing that crosses *all* genres. Indeed, the only thing that self-published books have in common is their source of funding – the author funds all aspects of the publication, including services like editing and design, as well as printing or the production of an e-book. The author may later recoup some of these expenses through book sales, just as the traditional publishing house hopes for a return on its upfront investment.

Within the self-publishing community, however, there is a tendency to distinguish between types of self-publishing. For example, the terms 'subsidy publishing' and 'vanity publishing' can be used interchangeably to refer to a type of self-publishing in which the author pays a company to publish a book. Companies specialising in subsidy publishing typically offer an array of services that can be packaged to suit the author's needs, such as editing, cover design, marketing, e-book production, printing, and so forth. Subsidy publishing is often contrasted with 'true self-publishing', which refers to an author who takes primary responsibility for a book's publication. The author may, however, contract out certain aspects of the publishing process, such as hiring a freelance editor or cover designer, or utilising an e-book distributor (like Smashwords, Draft2Digital, IngramSpark, and PublishDrive) that takes a cut of profits in return for placing a book in a variety of retail channels (like Amazon's Kindle, Google Play, Apple's iBooks, Barnes and Noble's Nook, and Kobo). Nonetheless, the true self-published author ultimately acts as the publishing house. There is also an emerging self-publishing category known as 'hybrid publishing', which refers to a set of business practices that fall on a spectrum between self-publishing and traditional publishing.

Of the three types of publishing identified using a model based on funding source, self-publishing is the easiest type to overlook or discount. Most of the books mentioned in this essay collection were not published using the funding sources typical of self-publishing. However, bear in mind that in 2016, in the US alone, 229 million self-published books were purchased, totalling more than $867 million in book sales (Data Guy, 2017). Just over one billion traditionally published books were purchased in the same period, so obviously traditionally published books outsell self-published books, but most people would expect an even greater disparity (Data Guy, 2017). If for every four traditionally published books that are purchased, one self-published book is purchased, self-published books do not seem to occupy a commensurate amount of the public imagination about book publishing.

This essay now proceeds to offer a second distinct model for surveying the different types of publishing houses: a model based on market segment. Market segmentation refers to the process of dividing the market into smaller segments of customers that share characteristics. Accordingly, the organisations targeting these market segments tend to share business practices. In the case of the book publishing industry, it is possible to divide the market for books into three smaller segments representing customers with shared characteristics and publishing houses with shared business models. These three market segments are trade publishing, educational publishing, and academic and professional publishing. It is worth noting, however, that while these three terms are certainly recognisable to anyone working in publishing, there is no general agreement about how exactly the industry is best segmented – or, to put it another way, what segments most accurately represent industry dynamics. Indeed, there is not even general agreement about the term 'market segment'; industry observers variously use the terms 'market sector', 'industry sector', 'category', and even just 'types of publishing' to refer to this same basic concept. Nonetheless, these three market segments – trade publishing, educational publishing, and academic and professional publishing – represent a particularly useful, internally coherent model for surveying the different types of publishing houses.

Trade publishing is so called because it publishes books that are sold 'to the book trade' – that is, to bookstores. When the term was coined, there were only brick-and-mortar bookstores; online bookselling is a more recent invention. Online booksellers do not suffer from the same pressures around shelf space as brick-and-mortar bookstores. So, when the term 'trade publishing' was coined, it was designed to refer to the kinds of books that a brick-and-mortar bookstore would stock – that is, books for a general audience, rather than specialist or obscure books. Of course, online booksellers also sell trade books, but they tend to stock books for specialist audiences, as well. Nonetheless, the term 'trade publishing' has stuck and is used to refer to most works of adult fiction; general interest adult nonfiction including life writing, popular history, and current affairs; how-to books including cookbooks, travel guides, and self-help books; poetry; children's books; and much more. In other words, trade publishing covers most of the books and genres discussed in this essay collection.

Trade publishing is also sometimes referred to as 'consumer publishing' because it is meant for the ordinary consumer. The customers with shared characteristics that constitute this market segment are people who shop at brick-and-mortar bookstores, online bookstores, and other general retailers that stock books (such as supermarkets and mass merchandisers). Accordingly, the publishing houses that target this market segment share business practices. This should not be confused, however, with shared funding models. After all, trade publishing can employ any of the three main sources of funding (traditional publishing, dependent publishing, and self-publishing) that support the activities of the book publishing industry. Rather, to say that the publishing houses that target this market segment share business practices is to highlight the importance of intermediaries in these practices. It is the rare consumer who can name the publishing house responsible for a given trade book, and that is because trade publishing does not have a direct relationship with the end consumer. Instead, trade publishing (as a general rule) sells to bookstores and other general retailers, which then sell to the consumer. This business practice is a hallmark of trade publishing that is driven by the market segment or customer they are targeting.

The ordinary consumer or a general audience might seem like an incredibly unspecific market segment, making it difficult to understand how this market segment could beget an entire set of business practices. However, this sequence of cause and effect can be brought into clearer focus by examining the remaining two market segments: educational publishing, and academic and professional publishing. The shared characteristic of the customers for educational publishing is that they are all students, whether in primary school, secondary school, or university. Students are the end users for books published by educational publishing houses; however, teachers, educational administrators, and others make most of the purchasing decisions, with considerable input from governments, examination boards, local education authorities, and so forth. Industry observers will sometimes further divide educational publishing into smaller market segments, such as schools publishing and tertiary publishing, in order to distinguish who or what influences the purchasing decision, which can inform business practices. Nonetheless, for the purposes of this essay, 'educational publishing' is an adequate term representing customers with shared characteristics and publishing houses with shared business models.

The most notable feature of educational publishing's shared business model is its responsiveness to regulatory control and content prescription (Clark & Phillips, 2014, p. 60). Of course, when a business's customer base is students (which is to say, mostly young people), responsiveness to regulatory control should be expected. Every time educational regulations change at the national, state, regional, or local level, publishing houses must adapt the books they publish. In recent years, an increase in the overall number of these regulations has produced a narrowing in the range of acceptable educational materials, which increases the likelihood of competition between publishing houses; this competition favours large publishing houses (with more resources) over small publishing houses (with fewer resources). Educational publishing houses also need to be able to explain – to anyone who asks, but especially to those who make purchasing decisions – how exactly they have adapted their books in response to regulatory changes, as well as how their books are different from the competition. Educational publishing houses rely on sales representatives to fulfil this important function; sales representatives regularly meet with teachers, educational administrators, examination boards, local education authorities, and so forth. Once again, this arrangement favours large publishing houses (which can afford to employ armies of sales representatives around the nation or even the world) over small publishing houses. Consequently, most educational publishing is an example of traditional publishing, where the most money and the largest publishing houses can be found, rather than dependent publishing or self-publishing.

The educational publishing business model, which relies on sales representatives hand-selling books to those directly responsible for making any purchasing decisions, is clearly very different from the trade publishing business model, which is defined by the importance of intermediaries. Compared to the ordinary consumer or a general audience – which must be targeted by trade publishing houses through intermediaries like brick-and-mortar bookstores, online bookstores, and other general retailers that stock books – students and educational decision-makers are much more readily identifiable and, thus, more easily and directly targeted as members of the educational publishing market segment.

On the topic of comparing educational publishing and trade publishing, it is important to clarify that many books and genres taught to university students are considered products of trade publishing rather than educational publishing. The reason for this is that students are a secondary audience for the novels studied in a literature class, for example; their primary audience at the time of publication was the ordinary consumer or a general audience.

Academic and professional publishing is the third and final entry in the market segment model for surveying the different types of publishing houses. Like educational publishing, academic and professional publishing represents a market segment that is readily identifiable and, thus, more easily targeted than trade publishing. First, though, it is important to understand why the 'academic' part of 'academic and professional publishing' is *not* included in the educational publishing market segment. Educational publishing targets students, while academic publishing targets experts, including teachers of the aforementioned students. Of course, professional publishing also targets experts in a variety of professional fields, such as humanities and social sciences (HSS publishing); scientific, technical, and medical (STM publishing); law; business; and so forth. Whereas educational publishing is defined by regulatory control and content prescription – in order to protect the young students who are its target customers, or to rationalise their educational trajectory – academic and professional publishing is not subject to such influences. It is assumed that the expert customers targeted by academic and professional publishing houses are capable of making their own judgements about the value of a given book.

The trend in academic and professional publishing is towards online content and services – a business practice informed by the customers of this market segment. Due to their expertise in their respective fields, these customers know what they are looking for in their reading material. Consequently, academic and professional publishing houses can sell directly to the end user, cutting out almost all intermediaries. Online is the easiest and best way to accomplish this. Trade publishing and educational publishing worry about discoverability in an online environment where all books can be accessed at the touch of a button, hence their reliance on brick-and-mortar retail and sales representatives, respectively. Academic and professional publishing does not, however, have this same problem with discoverability; the content is highly specialised, the market segment is readily identifiable, and the customers have a defined need they seek to meet.

This trend towards online content and services has also facilitated a shift away from one-time product sales (as is the case with print books) and towards site licences, subscription models, content aggregation, linked data, and so forth. In other words, academic and professional publishing is moving towards online content and services that require regular payments by the purchaser in order to continue to access the most up-to-date material. Sometimes the purchaser of a site licence, for example, is a university library rather than the end user, but even in this case the purchasing decision is typically driven by the end user's request for the content.

While discoverability might not be a problem for academic and professional publishing, it remains largely invisible to the average consumer. The size of this market sector is unknown even to industry observers because many academic and professional publishing houses sell directly to their own communities. This ignorance perhaps explains why, among the books mentioned in this essay collection, very few of them are examples of academic and professional publishing. It is worth noting, however, that academic and professional publishing can employ any of the three main sources of funding (in other words, traditional publishing, dependent publishing, and self-publishing) that support the activities of the book publishing industry, with dependent publishing responsible for an especially large gap between the number of books produced and the visibility of those books to industry observers. Examples of academic and professional publishing that have been produced using funding sources typical of dependent publishing are also the most likely not to pay the author a royalty; instead, the author might take a one-time payment (or no payment at all), ostensibly because their reason for publishing is in order to establish and share their expertise, rather than for personal financial gain (Table 2.1).

TABLE 2.1 Each category in the three models for surveying the different types of publishing houses can intersect with any category in another model, resulting in a smaller set of publishing houses that represent this new 'type' and share a more specific business model

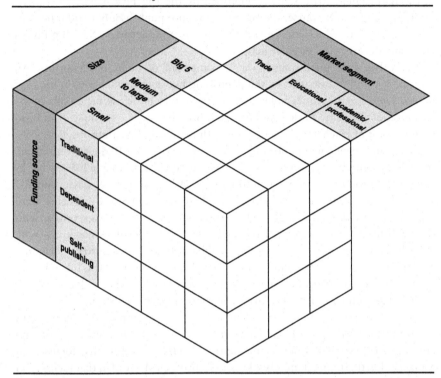

A model based on size represents the third and final model for surveying the different types of publishing houses. As was evident in the previously discussed model based on market segment, each of the three models for surveying the different types of publishing houses overlaps with the other models. For example, trade publishing can employ any of the three main sources of funding (in other words, traditional publishing, dependent publishing, and self-publishing). The same is true for a model based on size – academic and professional publishing houses come in a variety of sizes, for example, as do dependent publishing houses. However, the language of size is most commonly used in the publishing industry when discussing traditional trade publishing, perhaps because there is the greatest range of publishing house size in this category, from the very largest publishing houses in the world with thousands of staff to one-person operations.

In a model based on size, 'Big Five' is the name given to the largest type of publishing house. The Big Five is the result of a 'phase of mergers and acquisitions in trade publishing, which began in the early 1980s and has continued to the present' (Thompson, 2012, p. 108). Indeed, this number was the Big Six up until just a handful of years ago when Penguin and Random House merged. The Big Five is made up of Penguin Random House, HarperCollins, Macmillan, Simon & Schuster, and Hachette. According to some sources, as much as 90% of the fiction market by value is published by the Big Five (Clark & Phillips, 2014, pp. 52–53). Of course, the Big Five does not publish only fiction, but this is the category in which its size and influence is most apparent. The Big Five is especially dominant in popular fiction.

Every Big Five publishing house is comprised of numerous imprints. An imprint is a trade name used by the publishing house to market certain kinds of books. These are the names and logos that appear on a book's spine, usually to the exclusion of the name of the Big Five publishing house. For example, Seal Press is an imprint of Hachette. As is the case with many Big Five imprints, Seal Press started as an independent publishing house – in this case, in Berkeley, California, in 1976. From the beginning, Seal Press was dedicated to publishing books by women writers and about feminist issues. When Seal Press was eventually acquired by Hachette, the decision was made to keep the Seal Press name as an imprint because this name suggested a certain type of book to those familiar with the publishing house's history. Even if the average reader does not know who published the book he or she is reading, members of the book industry – including book reviewers, booksellers, and so forth – are keen observers of this information. Thus, the imprint's name becomes part of the way in which the book is marketed to the huge number of intermediaries that support trade publishing.

Many imprints focus on particular genres. For example, Del Rey Books is an imprint of Penguin Random House that focusses on science fiction and fantasy, while Mills & Boon is an imprint of HarperCollins that focusses on romance. Furthermore, Times Books is an imprint of Macmillan that focusses on nonfiction about politics and current events, and the Simon & Schuster imprint Margaret K. McElderry specialises in children's books.

Imprints have varying degrees of autonomy from their parent companies, so they also serve a practical function of dividing large organisations into manageable parts. Typically, imprints have editorial autonomy (in other words, the ability to make their own editorial and acquisitions decisions), but they often use back-office services provided by the parent company. By sharing these services – including distribution services, sales forces, warehouses, and more – imprints and their parent publishing houses achieve economies of scale that would not otherwise be possible.

The term 'Big Five' is used almost exclusively with reference to trade publishing; however, the Big Five publishing houses are themselves owned by larger media companies that also own non-trade publishing houses. For example, Hachette is owned by Hachette Livre, which is based in France and has a substantial presence in educational publishing. Macmillan is owned by the German company Holtzbrinck, which is especially well represented in academic and professional publishing through publishing houses like Springer. Penguin Random House is also owned by a German company, Bertelsmann, which owns Pearson, one of the world's largest educational publishing houses. Meanwhile, HarperCollins is owned by News Corporation, which is based in New York City and has a much more substantial presence in newspapers, magazines, and television than it does in book publishing. Simon & Schuster's parent company, CBS Corporation, is also based in New York City with a more substantial presence in television than book publishing.

One of the implications of large, multinational corporations owning the Big Five is what is known as the 'growth conundrum'. John B. Thompson (2012), author of arguably the most influential book about contemporary trade publishing, *Merchants of Culture: The Publishing Business in the Twenty-First Century*, describes the growth conundrum in the following way:

> The conundrum arises because every corporation needs to grow and to generate a good level of profitability. ... The problem with trade publishing in the US and UK is that these are very mature markets which have been largely static for many years; total sales of trade books in these markets tend to increase by about the rate of inflation year on year, but not much more.
>
> *p. 110*

Of course, one strategy for continued growth in the face of a stagnant market is to acquire your competition – in other words, buy out small, independent publishing houses and turn them into imprints. Another strategy employed by all members of the Big Five in order to combat the growth conundrum is to try and take market share from their competitors by publishing more bestsellers. This strategy disposes Big Five publishing houses towards the publication of certain types of books, including specific genres and authors with established track records. Conversely, it becomes harder for editors at Big Five publishing houses to justify the publication of genres and authors that don't tend to sell well, such as poetry, literary fiction, and authors whose earlier publications failed to distinguish themselves.

A publishing house that is not part of the Big Five but has a lot in common with the Big Five is Amazon Publishing. Founded in 2009, Amazon Publishing has many imprints with a variety of specialisations: 47North specialises in science fiction and fantasy, AmazonCrossing publishes more books in translation for the US market than any other publishing house (Abrams, 2015), Waterfall Press specialises in Christian fiction, and so forth. Amazon Publishing is a traditional publishing house, completely separate from Amazon's self-publishing services. It is estimated that in 2016, in the US alone, Amazon Publishing sold more than 68 million copies of their own books (Data Guy, 2017). These were mostly e-books with an average price of US\$4.30, but still these kinds of numbers would seem to merit the expansion of the Big Five into the Big Six (Data Guy, 2017). Furthermore, the Amazon Publishing business model is remarkably similar to the Big Five business model – consider, for example, the presence of imprints, parent companies, and the focus on bestselling genres. However, there does not seem to be a consensus among industry observers for this kind of expansion, so for the time being Amazon Publishing exists in a kind of limbo state – not Big Five but also not a good fit for the other types of publishing houses that comprise a model based on size.

It is necessary, when surveying the different types of publishing houses using a model based on size, to divide up all of the remaining publishing houses outside of the Big Five. For the purposes of this essay, these have been roughly divided into just two categories: medium to large independent publishing houses, and small independent publishing houses. How exactly to distinguish a medium to large publishing house from a small publishing house is, of course, subject to debate. For example, *BookStats* – a now-defunct joint venture between the Association of American Publishers (AAP) and the Book Industry Study Group (BISG) that annually attempted a comprehensive study of the US publishing industry – defined a large publishing house as having over US$100 million in annual sales revenue, while a medium publishing house had between US$5 and US$99.9 million in annual sales revenue (Association of American Publishers and Book Industry Study Group, 2014, p. 56). A small publishing house, of course, had less than US$5 million in annual sales revenue. Using sales revenue to determine the placement of a particular publishing house within a model based on size makes a lot of sense, though it must be remembered that different sources draw different lines in the financial sand – that is, specify a different figure distinguishing small from medium publishing houses, and medium from large publishing houses. Also, the sales revenue of a particular publishing house is rarely public knowledge, making a determination difficult.

Another feature that distinguishes most medium to large publishing houses from small publishing houses – and which is easier to identify – is that most medium to large publishing houses have imprints, while relatively few small publishing houses have imprints. Medium to large independent publishing houses use these imprints in a manner similar to Big Five publishing houses – as a home for their efforts in particular genres. For example, Bloomsbury Publishing fits within the category of medium to large independent publishing houses, and its imprints include Absolute Press (specialising in food and drink), Fairchild Books (specialising in fashion and interior design), and Continuum (specialising in nonfiction). Another medium to large independent publishing house, Grove Atlantic, has several imprints including The Mysterious Press (focussed on mystery, crime, and suspense fiction), as well as less-focussed imprints like Grove Press ('a hardcover and paperback imprint … publishing fiction, drama, poetry, literature in translation, and general nonfiction') and Atlantic Monthly Press ('one of two hardcover imprints of Grove Atlantic, publishing fiction, history, biography, and narrative nonfiction') (Grove Atlantic, n.d.).

Small independent publishing houses generally do not have imprints because there is no need to divide their workload; they do not publish enough books to necessitate divisions within the company, and the books that they do publish tend to share a specific focus. For example, you can find small independent publishing houses that are exclusively dedicated to the publication of poetry – Five Islands Press in Melbourne, Victoria, and Tavern Books in Portland, Oregon, are just two examples. It was mentioned earlier that dependent publishing houses tend to be mission-driven, serving an audience or subject matter that for one reason or another they feel is underserved, and the same is true for many small independent publishing houses. Indeed, virtually all dependent publishing houses would fit within the category of small independent publishing houses, though the latter category includes a lot of traditional publishing houses, too.

Clearly, the casual use of a phrase such as 'different types of publishing' to refer to only corporate-owned publishing versus independent publishing, or traditional publishing versus self-publishing, conceals the true diversity of the publishing industry. Indeed, this essay has offered three distinct models for surveying the different types of publishing houses: a model based on funding source, a model based on market segment, and a model based on size. Each model contains three categories, and any category from one model could intersect with virtually any category in the other two models. Even self-publishing, for example, which is a category in the model based on funding source, intersects with the Big Five, which is category in the model based on size. Or, at least, these two categories intersected up until recently; Penguin Random House owned and operated the self-publishing service Author Solutions up until 2016, while Macmillan owned and operated Pronoun up until 2017. By offering for the first time a set of internally coherent (rather than anecdotal) models for surveying the different types of publishing houses, this essay highlights how specific types of publishing houses within each model are favourably disposed towards the publication of particular genres. It also points to the extraordinary number of ways in which literature and the written word are shaped by the industry that brings these texts into existence. In other words, economics inform culture – and vice versa.

References

Abrams, D. (2015), 'AmazonCrossing still biggest publisher of translated lit in US', *Publishing Perspectives*, 7 May. Available from: https://publishingperspectives.com/. [31 January 2019].

Association of American Publishers and Book Industry Study Group (2014), *BookStats*, vol. 4.

Clark, G. & Phillips, A. (2014), *Inside book publishing*, 5th edn, Abingdon: Routledge.

Data Guy (2017), 'Print vs. digital, traditional vs. non-traditional, bookstore vs. online: 2016 trade publishing by the numbers', *Author Earnings*, 20 January. Available from: http://authorearnings.com/. [31 January 2019].

Deahl, R. (2016), 'Could publishers and agents agree on a flat royalty rate?', *Publishers Weekly*, 3 June. Available from: https://www.publishersweekly.com. [31 January 2019].

Givler, P. (2002), 'University press publishing in the United States' in R.E. Abel & L.W. Newlin (eds), *Scholarly publishing: books, journals, publishers, and libraries in the twentieth century*, pp. 107–120. New York: Wiley.

Grove Atlantic (n.d.), *Imprints*. Available from: http://groveatlantic.com/imprints/. [31 January 2019].

Thompson, J.B. (2012), *Merchants of culture: the publishing business in the twenty-first century*, 2nd edn, New York: Plume.

3

THE UK'S READING CULTURE AND CONSUMERS' EMOTIONAL RESPONSE TO BOOKS

Alison Lawson

Introduction

Why are books so popular in UK society and what has contributed to their popularity? This essay begins by discussing the UK's reading culture and how it has arisen, is supported, and is encouraged. As part of the discussion, the link between reading and literacy is considered, alongside the role played by book clubs, best-sellers, reviews, literary prizes, book festivals, and public libraries. Following this discussion, readers are considered as consumers and their relationships with books are viewed through the lenses of attachment theory and involvement, aligned to a typology of consumers developed to describe the market for books.

Reading culture

A few years ago, I prepared a teaching session for a group of undergraduates on a publishing degree at a UK higher education institute. The session was about the big challenges facing the industry at the time, which included the threat to smaller, independent booksellers from larger bookselling chains, supermarkets, and the internet; the rise of electronic books; and the competition for people's leisure time, in which reading vied with cinema, music, playing outdoors, computer games, and so on. Having planned my session, I began by posing the students a question. What did they think were the big challenges facing the industry today? When they answered, I was dumbstruck. 'Censorship from the government', they said. The group were largely from African nations and the issues I had identified were very UK-centric. I learnt a lot in that session – not only about being much more aware of the students' needs and planning my teaching more carefully, but about how extraordinarily lucky we are in the UK to have no censorship of publishing or reading. We can publish and read on virtually any subject in any genre and be safe from criticism, prejudice, and criminal proceedings as long as we respect the laws of privacy, libel, obscenity, and copyright.

We can read for pleasure, leisure, professional interest, information, instructions, learning, excitement, escape, or thrills. We can read at home, at work, during study, in public, in private, in the garden, in the park, on the train or bus, wherever we like. Reading matter of some sort is available for sale or for free at almost every retail outlet, as well as in libraries, doctors' surgeries, churches, restaurants, and other places. And in recent years, we have had new options about whether to read print or electronic versions of some titles. We take all this for granted and don't stop to wonder at how lucky we are. What we have is a very strong and well-embedded culture of reading that we should cherish. Recent research has shown that more than six out of ten had read a physical printed book in the 12 months up to June 2018, with smaller numbers reading other formats or using audiobooks (Mintel, 2018a). This research was conducted using a survey of 2,000 internet users aged 16 and over, and is generalisable to the wider population, but with the caveat that the respondents were all internet users.

How did this come about? Books are part of the UK's heritage. Books and reading in general are popular leisure pursuits as well as providers of educational or professional information. Although initially the circulation of reading matter was restricted to the wealthy and better-educated people of the UK (Feather, 2006), the importance of books as cultural objects or as vehicles for political messages was clear from the outset. As publishing grew and the variety of books published expanded from religious and government texts to include law, fiction, natural history, science, medicine, and so on, the number of groups of people for whom published books were appropriate increased. Similarly, as education improved, books became accessible to a larger number of people, both in terms of literacy and in terms of economics. Essentially, for books to be successful in any given society, the people must have both the reading ability and the desire to read, coupled with the economic ability to buy the books and the opportunity to read them.

Hence, as the nation prospered, education was made more widely available and books became an accepted part of society. As general levels of literacy in the population rose and books became available more readily, a 'reading culture' became established (Sutherland, 2002).

The publishing industry has fuelled the reading culture and its desire for books, but it also benefits from it. Books are acceptable, desirable products with an enormously broad range. The reading public is spoilt for choice and spoilt by good quality at reasonable prices. The advantages for publishers are that there is little, if any, consumer resistance to the industry's products and that there are very well-established routes to the market. The disadvantage of such a strong and deeply entrenched reading culture is that consumers' expectations are very high and are likely to become higher, as books compete not only with each other for the consumers' money, but also with many alternative products that offer entertainment, information, education, and so on in different formats. We shall return to consumers later in the essay. First we shall consider links between reading and literacy and some of the events, activities, and services that promote reading and or literacy in the UK.

Reading and literacy

There is a strong emphasis on reading and literacy in the National Curriculum for England and Wales, and in other educational systems, too. Literacy is seen as a major stepping stone to independence in society. Children in the UK grow up with reading and books and, perhaps, take them for granted, as they are ubiquitous. There is some evidence that those who enjoy reading are better at it and that it is also beneficial for wider learning outcomes (Clark and Teravainen, 2017). The Progress for International Reading Literacy Study (PIRLS) is conducted every five years with children aged 9 across 50 participating countries. In 2017 England was ranked joint 8th, which was a big improvement on England's previous position in the survey. UK government sources attribute this to an increased focus on phonics in the curriculum. This puts children in England amongst the highest performing European countries and above the USA, Australia, and Canada in terms of reading literacy.

In addition to government support for reading initiatives, there is support from charities such as World Book Day, funded by various publishers and National Book Tokens Limited. In research to celebrate World Book Day's 20th anniversary in 2017, a survey of over 9,000 pupils aged 8–11 revealed that 9 out of 10 pupils in this age group were aware of the initiative and it inspired nearly 6 out of 10 to read more (World Book Day, 2017). The charity sells books to children for only £1 on the day, making them well within pocket money budgets and encouraging those children (and others) who would not normally buy books to give them a try. Lots of other events are organised by schools to accompany World Book Day, such as authors doing readings or allowing the children and staff to come in dressed as their favourite character. Despite the initiative's clear success and popularity, it has come under some fire recently for the selection of titles to be promoted in 2018, which featured several books written by celebrities (Flood, 2017). Some children's authors have described the inclusion of books written by celebrities as 'patronising and demeaning' and feel that more could have been done to promote diversity of authorship. The organisers stated that the list of £1 books for 2018 was a good mix of authors children will recognise and some that will be new to them.

Reading is, therefore, encouraged and supported in schools, inspiring many to carry on reading for pleasure and for other reasons after it has ceased to be compulsory for school work. We don't all read and we don't all enjoy reading – the UK Government's Taking Part survey reports that 36% of adults don't read for pleasure and in the 16–24 age group this rises to 44%. Yet reading is the 8th most popular free-time activity indulged in by adults (watching television and spending time with friends and family were the most popular activities) (DCMS, 2015a).

More recently, the Taking Part survey of 2017/18 has shown that 'reading and writing' is the most common form of engagement in the arts for those aged 5–10 (83.2% having engaged in the 12 months prior to the survey) and those aged 11–15 (87.8% engaged in the same period) (DDCMS, 2018a). The Office for National Statistics reported in 2015 that accessing mass media, which included activities such as reading, watching television, and listening to music, was the most popular leisure pursuit for men (more than 16 hours a week) and women (more than 14 hours a week). Unfortunately, this survey, which is generalisable to the whole population, did not split out reading from other activities, although it is the most up-to-date information available (ONS, 2017).

Taking inspiration from World Book Day, the Reading Agency, a UK charity, runs World Book Night on 23 April each year. Working in collaboration with publishers, libraries, booksellers, printers, private donors, trusts, and foundations, the Reading Agency gives books away for free in a number of places, including care homes, prisons, and public libraries in an attempt to encourage people to read (World Book Night, 2017).

The drive to improve literacy and promote reading as an activity is not all to do with education (and selling books), but is also about social understanding, social mobility, democratisation of the people who have access to a range of views and, it has been shown, self-esteem. Research reported in *The Bookseller* (Shaffi, 2015) showed that 'people who read regularly for pleasure have greater levels of self-esteem, are less stressed and can cope better with difficult situations than lapsed or non-readers'. The research was conducted for The Reading Agency's Quick Reads – an initiative to help adult readers. While we may be surrounded by reading material of all sorts and have a strong reading culture, as many as 16 million adults in the UK are 'lapsed readers'. This may be for a variety of reasons, and not least because leisure time is limited and there is so much choice now for consumers, especially in the digital arena.

The impact of book clubs

Evidence of our reading culture is also seen in the rise and proliferation of book clubs and reading groups, especially online, where readers can review titles, read reviews, share their thoughts, and discuss issues arising from the books they have read. One very popular bookclub is the Richard and Judy book club – two popular television presenters, Richard Madeley and Judy Finnegan, teamed up with bookselling chain WHSmith to create a hugely successful book club in 2010. The evolution of social media has also helped to spread word about the book club and increased involvement by the reading public. Book clubs are not new, but the internet has allowed them to be global, interactive fora for sharing views and reviews, recommending books and, importantly, for book readers to feel part of a community that welcomes them. Richard and Judy's bookclub is now encouraging new writers, too, though a competition being run with publisher Bonnier Zaffre (Onwuemezi, 2016).

Other celebrities have also set up or been linked to book clubs and/or reading initiatives, such as well-known vlogger Zoella, who also works with WHSmith but for an entirely different market – young adult fiction. Pairing the vlogger with YA fiction in an online bookclub was a stroke of genius, as the appeal to Zoella's followers is so strong that the books she recommends see their sales soar (Eyre, 2016).

Another recent example of a book club linked with a celebrity is the club set up by David Bowie's son in tribute to his father, following the artist's untimely death in 2016 (Onwuemezi, 2018). Bowie's son announced the new club on Twitter and the titles selected are based on Bowie's 2013 list of 'must read' books.

A similar pattern was seen in America. Popular television presenter and personality Oprah Winfrey launched an online version of her book club, followed by Facebook founder Mark Zuckerberg launching his take on an online book club, A Year of Books. In 2015 he challenged himself and others to read a book every two weeks. A hundred thousand Facebook users 'liked' the page within the first two days (Buhr, 2015) and at the time of writing the Facebook page has over 682,000 'likes'. Such is the power of celebrity teamed with enthusiasm for reading. Although A Year of Books ran for only one year, its impact on Facebook users led to increased sales for the titles reviewed.

Book clubs linked with celebrities of all kinds have a good chance of reaching a wide audience and, although not all the celebrities' followers may be keen readers, a club linked to their favourite star may encourage reading, as the books come as a recommendation from a trusted and respected source. Readers may then go on to recommend the books, further increasing their popularity with the celebrity's followers. Celebrity endorsement is by no means a new concept in marketing and is known to work well for a range of products and services. To use the concept to encourage reading and discussion about books seems an obvious step to take. The use of social media in online book clubs also helps readers to feel a more personal connection with the books that are recommended – when using social media, consumers can feel as if the communications are directed personally to them. The medium is informal and personal, allowing users to feel at ease, and is well targeted and tailored, offering users products that seem to be exactly what they need or want.

Of course, there are book clubs and reading groups that do not rely on celebrities to attract interested readers. The online book club Goodreads, for example, was launched in 2007 and has over 50 million unique visitors each month. The website boasts 90 million members and 90 million reviews, and has featured 2.6 billion books (Goodreads, 2019). For readers everywhere, here is a club where they feel they can truly belong, accessible at their fingertips, regardless of whether they read books in print or as e-books, sharing with people they are never likely to meet. This is also a community for authors – whether published or aspiring. Goodreads lists more than 270,000 authors on its website.

The most 'popular' is Stephen King, with 21,120,607 member reviews and 646,924 followers. Readers who enjoy his work can find his works listed here with reviews by people they trust – people like them.

While books have long been discussed and reviewed and read on radio, with programmes such as *A Book At Bedtime* and *Book of the Week*, this kind of programme is rarer on television, perhaps because it is perceived to be too 'highbrow'. This seems odd, and a great shame, for a country that has such a strongly embedded culture of reading. However, a new daytime television programme presented by Zoe Ball, a popular broadcaster and television presenter, was launched in April 2018 and included a discussion and review of books over ten weeks in the summer of 2018. The allied Zoe Ball Book Club, run in association with SpecSavers, promotes the reviewed titles.

Book clubs are certainly one proven way of bringing titles to potential readers' attention, but they are by no means the only way, as we shall see in the next section.

Bestsellers, reviews, literary prizes, and festivals

As my teaching specialism is marketing, I can't help but see book clubs, bestseller lists, book reviews, and literary prizes as promotional tools in the marketing professional's toolkit. These not only inform booksellers of which books are or will be popular and should therefore be stocked, but they also inform potential readers of their readability, credibility, worthiness, relative merits, and popularity. Use of a bestsellers list may help guide readers' choices, which is both good and bad – it's good that readers are guided to books about which they feel informed, but bad that they may then miss the many hundreds of books that don't make it onto a bestseller list, a review, or the shortlist for a prize. So, what is a bestseller? And how do books get reviewed and nominated for literary prizes?

'Best-seller' is a relative term. When I worked in science, technical, and medical publishing, a bestseller on our lists might have been a title that had been reprinted more quickly than anticipated, having only had an initial print run of 800 copies. I used to joke with one of the commissioning editors on the physics list that he should slip in a couple of essays of bodice-ripping romance into his next text on semi-conductors to see if we could surprise the publisher with record sales (not to mention the surprise of the 800 academics/librarians who purchased a copy).

Generally, however, a bestseller is considered by the trade to be a title that sells in huge volume. *The Bookseller* publishes lists of bestsellers by category each week, based on data gathered by Nielsen BookScan. Many factors may contribute to a book becoming a bestseller, including exposure in reviews, being shortlisted (and winning!) literary prizes, and promotion at literary festivals.

In the past, books have been reviewed in the print and broadcast press, including newspapers, magazines such as the *London Review of Books*, genre-specific magazines and radio programmes such as *A Good Read* on BBC Radio 4 (winner of the Best Radio Music and Arts Programme at the Listener and Viewer Awards for Excellence in Broadcasting 2015), and *Open Book* (also on BBC Radio 4). The rise of the internet and in particular of social media broadened the field of reviews to include star ratings, blogs, comments on websites such as Amazon, discussion in online groups, and so on. Consumers no longer have to listen only to the opinion of 'experts', but can now submit their own opinions and hear the opinions of other consumers. Having one's book talked about online creates a 'buzz' that helps to promote the book and the author. While the short *Meet the Author* programme is broadcast on the BBC News channel, for many years there has been no mainstream television programme about books until the advent of the previously mentioned Zoe Ball Book Club. This has been lamented by some as a sad state of affairs for arts coverage in the UK (Lister, 2016).

There are too many literary prizes to mention here, although most of the reading public may never have heard of them, with the exception of the Man Booker Prize for Fiction. Even being shortlisted for this prize is a guarantee of huge publicity and concomitantly huge sales. The Man Booker is for literary fiction, rather than mass-market fiction, and pulls media attention (even coverage on television) in ways that other prizes do not. The prize for the author is considerable at £50,000, but it is the kudos and publicity that goes with the win that is longer lasting and can have a profound effect on sales of the author's other titles as well as titles published by the same publisher. Proliferation of literary prizes has led to prizes for a large range of genres. Examples include:

- the Gold Dagger Award for crime fiction, awarded annually by the Crime Writers ' Association (£2,500 prize)
- the Ted Hughes Award for new work in poetry awarded by the Poetry Society and the Poetry Book Society (£5,000 prize)
- the TS Eliot Prize for the best new collection of poetry published in the UK and Ireland, awarded by the TS Eliot Foundation (£20,000 prize)
- the Bailey's Women's Prize for Fiction (formerly known as the Orange Prize for Women's Fiction), awarded each year for the best full-length novel published in English (£30,000 prize)
- the Costa Book Awards in five categories – best novel, best first novel, best children's book, best poetry, best biography (£5,000 prize in each category), and best short story (£3,500)
- the Hugo Awards – for the best science fiction and/or fantasy in several categories (no prize money).

The British Book Awards are run by *The Bookseller*, the trade magazine for the publishing and bookselling industries. Awards are made not only for books but also to publishers and booksellers, recognising excellence throughout the trade. In 2018 some new awards were included (Bookseller, 2018) to recognise the best audiobook, author of the year, and illustrator of the year. These awards allow the industry to celebrate its own success and highlight exceptional achievement, giving inspiration to many and setting the bar for competition.

While the good effects of book prizes are clear in terms of increased publicity and increased sales, some feel that the effects are not all good and that the prizes are actually causing harm. Kean (2017) writes that the cost of entering the three biggest awards (the Man Booker, the Costas, and the Bailey's Prize for Women's Fiction) can be prohibitive for smaller publishers. The entry fee, if shortlisted, is £5,000 for each of these awards. This represents a significant investment for smaller publishers, but the increase in sales due to appearing on the shortlist may cover the cost. It may not. Once shortlisted, the book will be reviewed, written about, and commented on – and to make the best capital out of this interest, publishers may wish to organise author promotional events, which add an extra layer of cost. And then there's the attendance at the ceremony itself – the author is likely to need overnight accommodation, staff will be needed at the ceremony, public relations work will need to be done, and so on. Investing in a shortlisted title can pay dividends, but must be weighed up against a potentially significant investment up front.

Aside from the costs associated with the awards, Kean (2017) also notes that some feel that publishers are reluctant to take risks on unusual titles. She quotes Jonny Geller of successful literary agency Curtis Brown, who said 'Literary fiction is under threat in this country due to a combination of factors – reluctance by major houses to take risks; a bottleneck in the distribution chain [and] diverse voices being ignored by a predominantly white, middle-class industry'. There are some serious points here. If publishers do not have the financial cushion to take risks with authors and titles that may be out of the ordinary, do we run the risk of narrowing the spectrum of literature that is recognised by awards? The question of diversity (or lack of it) is recognised in the industry and initiatives are under way to improve this, including the launch of the BAME (Black and Minority Ethnic) in Publishing network in 2016 (Onwuemezi, 2016) and HarperCollins tackling the problem through their BAME traineeship programme (Wood, 2018).

Literary and other book festivals are another well-established vehicle for promoting books while also giving readers the opportunity to meet their favourite authors (or at least hear them speak) and to mingle with fellow book lovers. Well-known festivals such as the annual Hay Festival in Hay-on-Wye in Wales, which celebrated its 30th year in 2017, attract huge crowds every year. The festival includes special events for school children, encouraging reading not only of fiction but also of a broad range of subjects across the National Curriculum. The festival attracts a considerable amount of media attention, both locally and nationally. The 2017 festival had more than 2,100 press mentions between January and June 2017, featured in 24 articles in *The Bookseller* and had a media reach of 1.8 billion (calculated by multiplying the number of press mentions by the circulation of each outlet) (Hay Festival Report, 2017).

Book clubs, prizes, and festivals all contribute to the buzz about books, they feed into our culture whether high-brow or low-brow and become part of our reading culture, fuelling it and shaping it, and thereby involving the reader/ consumer, who may join a book club, read about prizes, choose to read the book that won the prize, and attend the local literary festival.

The role of libraries

For those not inclined towards online book clubs and literary festivals there are, of course, traditional libraries, although public lending libraries in the UK are facing very difficult times as funding is squeezed remorselessly. Libraries are available in all sorts of communities – schools, universities, prisons, care homes, hospitals, hotels, churches, homeless hostels, and mobile libraries. The Public Libraries and Museums Act 1964 gave local authorities the duty to 'provide a comprehensive and efficient library service to all persons' in their communities (DCMS, 2015b).

UK public lending and reference libraries are in a period of transition. Books were traditionally their mainstay, and as media evolved, so did the libraries, taking to stocking video, then CDs, computer games, DVDs, and internet access for visitors. Simultaneously, these media became cheaper and more easily accessible for the public, who no longer rely on a library for borrowing, but can now buy their own copies. Public libraries have become much more than repositories of books and other media, offering a range of other services, such as training, reading groups/clubs, access to wider arts, parent and toddler groups, and being a hub for community activities.

Over the years, active borrower numbers have declined. 'Reading and writing' is still the most common form of engagement with the arts for children aged 5–15 (DDCMS, 2018a). In the 12 months leading up to the DDCMS Taking Part survey in 2018, nearly 60% of children aged 5–10 and just over 70% of those aged 11–15 had visited a library outside of school (not only for reading). However, the proportion of adults using public libraries dropped from 17% in 2016/17 to only 15.3% in 2017/18, with more than 64% of people reporting that they had not used a library at all (DDCMS, 2018b), despite the broadening of services and expertise offered by the library staff. The most common reason for not using a public library, given by 40% of those surveyed, was lack of need. The services and their buildings, being a calculable cost to local authorities, became targets for spending cuts, particularly in the austerity years since the financial crisis hit the UK in 2008.

As borrower numbers have declined, the number of public libraries has also fallen steadily from over 4,600 in 2003–2004 (CIPFA, quoted in Shaffi, 2015) to 3,618 (including mobile libraries) in 2017–2018 (Page, 2018), representing a significant decrease in service since 2003. It may be that the loss of visitors to libraries is due in no small part to the affordability of books in comparison to other leisure activities and the competition from other leisure pursuits. We know from recent research that people – especially young people – are spending ever more time online (Mintel, 2018b), and the traditional library may just have lost some of its appeal.

One crucial factor when considering our reading culture and how this is affected and supported by libraries, reading schemes, literary awards, and so on, is the reader herself/himself. Reading as an activity is symbiotic – the reader and the reading material must work together to result in the reading activity. This leads us to consider readers as consumers of books; how they interact with books, how they feel about books, and what books mean to them. The rest of this essay will consider readers as consumers.

Readers as consumers

Recent figures show that 56% of those aged 16 and over bought a print book in the year April 2018–May 2019, representing an increase on the previous year, and 26% bought a digital book (this includes audio downloads and digital subscriptions) representing no growth or decline in this product category (Mintel, 2019). Women generally buy more books than men do and more fiction is bought than non-fiction. Reassuringly for publishers and for drives to improve literacy and reading, the consumer book market is predicted to grow steadily over the next five years.

The growth may be stimulated by a number of factors, such as the general affordability of books; popularity of some genres, characters, and authors; coverage of literary prizes and bestsellers in the media; and the ease with which books can be purchased, whether in store or online.

Back in 2001, with the internet and e-books looming large on the horizon, Overdorf and Barragree suggested that the publishing market could be divided into five Tiers, according to readers' needs:

1. **Information seekers**, who need access to sources purely for information and do not wish to keep that information for posterity – this could include, for example, consumers looking for the weather forecast, news headlines, sports scores, or cinema reviews. These needs are easily met by online sources, and electronic distribution of this information will be met with enthusiasm.
2. **Professional users** – consumers who need to find research reports, technical documents, and work-related information. This category need reliable information quickly for reference only and may not need to keep it for long, but would need it to be up-to-date. This category therefore also welcomes online distribution of information and could include academic libraries and the medical and legal professions, for example (Baverstock, 2015).
3. **Students**, who need information to support their learning – online and/or digital sources are useful to this group, who need up-to-date and relevant information, but they also need portability and some of the traditional features of print media, such as space to annotate texts, the comfort and convenience of reading when and where they wish, and the opportunity to do so away from a computer.
4. **People who just enjoy reading** – these are people who enjoy the look and feel of a book; who enjoy the tactile nature of the product; who admire the cover, enjoy the back cover, and see the product as part of the experience of reading. Immediate availability is not as much of a concern to this group and there is no problem here that needs a digital solution.

5. **Book lovers** – this group value books intrinsically as objects in their own right, whether or not the books are actually read. This group cherishes the printed product and cannot conceive of a digital alternative, as the aesthetics of the product are just as important as the content. Books are owned and kept as loved objects.

Of course, technology has changed considerably since 2001 and consumers' needs (and wants) have changed considerably, too. Yet the categories observed by Overdorf and Barragree still work to a large degree today, with a little alteration. The information needs of Tier 1 are now met with online resources (although much of this information is still also available in print) and these are regularly and frequently updated. The professional needs of those needing technical information are also met online as well as in print. Students at all levels have a wide range of needs and wants that are met in a range of ways, including digital and online resources that are regularly updated as well as printed sources. The portability issue predicted by Overdorf and Barragree has been solved with laptops, notebooks, and mobile phones, making online and other digital resources available wherever there is a suitable connection. Annotation of online and electronic resources is also now available, so students no longer need a printed book with a wide margin for taking notes. Tier 4 readers still enjoy reading for pleasure and still enjoy the look and feel of a printed book. Perhaps the evidence for this is in the persistent refusal of the sales of print books to decline and the slowing of the popularity of e-book readers. And for those consumers in Tier 5, the book lovers, it remains today as difficult as it was envisaged in 2001 to 'sell an aesthetic buyer a digital Dickens' (Overdorf and Barragree, 2001, p. 15).

What Overdorf and Barragree and other researchers and writers of the early 2000s could not predict was the rise of social media and how this would affect both the dissemination of information and the behaviour of readers as consumers, such as using online book clubs to share experiences and views and to post about these to social networks.

While it is appealing and feels very neat and tidy to categorise the market and its readers into five Tiers, it is true that we are all individuals and that this kind of segmentation does not really take into account all our personal differences. It is necessarily a broad brush approach. At an individual level, readers as consumers may have some similar needs and wants but are also likely to have as many differences. While it may be possible to understand and predict readers' rational needs for information (particularly in Overdorf and Barragree's Tiers 1 and 2), it is more difficult to understand and predict the emotional drivers behind readers' motivation and behaviour as consumers. It is this emotional side of consumer behaviour that we shall consider next.

Consumers' emotional response to products

There are several theories that help us to understand how consumers respond to products: the theory of uses and gratification, attachment theory, and the theory of self-concept.

TABLE 3.1 Uses and gratifications of social media (abridged from Whiting and Williams, 2013)

Theme	% of research participants who mentioned this theme
Social interaction	88
Information seeking	80
To pass the time	76
Entertainment	64
Relaxation	60
To express opinions	56
To communicate with others	56
For convenience	52
To share information	40
Surveillance of others	32

The theory of uses and gratification, originated by Blumler and McQuail (1969) in the realm of mass media, is still used today to help explain how consumers relate to products. The theory states that consumers choose media (or in the case of publishing, published products) that fulfil their needs and lead to gratification. This is not far removed from the traditional consumer decision-making process taught in marketing, that a consumer recognises a need; searches for information and investigates the options; selects the best option to fulfil the need; makes a purchase; evaluates the product; and, if appropriate, discards or recycles the product and offers feedback. Uses and gratifications theory cuts straight to how well the product satisfies the needs and accepts that the product has been specifically purchased to fulfil those needs. Whiting and Williams (2013) applied the theory to consumers' use of social media using seven themes derived from several previously published frameworks of uses and gratifications. Their results are summarised in Table 3.1.

It is not surprising in the case of social media that the most commonly mentioned use/gratification was to interact with others. Were this research to be repeated with consumers' uses and gratifications with regard to books, the results may not be very dissimilar. There are clear links to the Tiers of the publishing market proposed by Overdorf and Barragree, from simple seeking of information up to relaxation and entertainment.

So this theory tells us that consumers buy books to fulfil specific needs and wants and/or to experience gratification, but does not explain in any depth what those needs and gratifications are, which emotions are involved in the process and how this relates to each individual. For this we need to look at attachment theory.

Emotional response to products

The psychological theory of emotional attachment was proposed by Bowlby (1979) to explain the way that infants form attachments with those who care for them (and also considers the consequences of the lack of such an attachment forming). Transferring this theory to consumers' emotional response to products and services is not new, particularly with regard to building brand loyalty through emotional connections or storytelling (Papadatos, 2006) or exploiting those emotions in advertising appeals (Yeshin, 2011). Emotional attachment or involvement with products, services, or brands has been demonstrated to have an effect on long-term usage. Wakefield and Bush (1998) found that consumers who were more highly involved in a category (in the case of their research, a service category) are more likely to be involved with an organisation offering that product/service. A similar effect could hold true for books – those who describe themselves as 'book lovers' may be more likely to be involved with a particular genre, author, or character. Patwardhan and Balasubramanian (2011) posit that if consumers' primary motives for attachment to brands are to seek security and safety, a particular kind of attachment will form, while a different kind of attachment will form if the primary motivation is stimulation. This second type of attachment is applicable when consumers long for particular products or services or obtain pleasure from their use. Patwardhan and Balasubramanian call this 'brand romance' and, while their work is based on brands, it may be a concept that is transferable to consumers' emotional response to books. Emotional attachment and involvement has similarities to uses and gratifications and can also be demonstrated to link to the five Tiers of the publishing market (see Table 3.2).

Table 3.2 proposes a theoretical hierarchy of the uses and gratification themes noted by Whiting and Williams (2013) with regard to how these might relate to the consumers in each of the publishing Tiers, with 'information seeking' matched to the lowest tier and the lowest level of involvement or emotional attachment to the product and 'entertainment' and 'relaxation' matched to the highest tier and the highest level of involvement. This is only a theory, but it seems to fit what we know of consumers in the book market.

This helps to illuminate who the consumers are and why they may buy the books they do, but still does not treat them as individuals. For this we need to turn to the theory of self-concept.

TABLE 3.2 Relationship between theories for consumers of books

Tiers of the publishing market	Emotional attachment	Uses and gratification themes
1. Information seekers	Low involvement ↑	Information seeking
		Sharing information
2. Professional users		Expressing opinions
		Convenience
3. Students		Surveillance
		Communication with others
4. People who enjoy reading		Social interaction
		Passing time
5. Book lovers	↓	Entertainment
	High involvement	Relaxation

The theory of self-concept

Self-concept is how we see ourselves – our feelings and ideas about ourselves. This comprises several different components. The real self is the most objective view, as we are seen by others, while the looking-glass (social) self is how we think we are viewed by others. The self-image is our own view of ourselves and our ideal self is how we wish we were. We each have possible selves, which are the selves we would like to be or could become (Blythe, 2013). Szmigin and Piacentini (2014) also describe a negative self (what we are not and do not want to be), the situational self (self-concept depends on the situation), and extended self (in which our belongings come to represent our sense of self).

Much research in the area of self-concept concerns fashion, as this is a clear way of presenting yourself to others using very visible signs, such as designer labels, colours, style, and so on (see, for example, Millan and Reynolds, 2011; Peters *et al.*, 2011) or how consumers use products to help construct identity and achieve self-actualisation, as in the purchase of counterfeit luxury goods (Perez *et al.*, 2010).

Some brands also make use of self-concept to construct an ideal self or alternative self that attracts consumers and reinforces an emotional attachment. Papadatos (2006) gives the example of Harley Davidson, which allows people to become someone different when they ride their Harley. In this way consumers wear a specific brand of clothes or perfume or buy a particular brand of car or fly with a particular airline – the bond that has been made with the brand is part emotional attachment and part realisation of self, whether that is a real, ideal, or alternative self.

Books may be a less obvious product through which consumers reflect and construct their identity, as book-reading habits are not displayed as obviously as clothes. Yet books are often displayed on shelves and in bookcases (Toman, 2009) rather than hidden away in drawers and cupboards as are clothes. Some people believe that the books on our bookshelves are 'an intimate physical representation of your accomplishments ... aspirations ... associations ... personal development ... guilty pleasures ... escapes ... memories ... interests and other tells' that give insight into who we are (Knox, 2012).

In order to explore these ideas of attachment and self-concept a small research project was conducted with six young people. The research aimed to examine consumers' emotional response to books in order to determine whether there is a connection to consumers' construction of self. The objectives were first, to determine the reasons why consumers identify with particular books (with potential links to uses and gratification theory and Overdorf and Barragree's Tiers) and second, to analyse the deeper motivators and meanings for those consumers in order to improve understanding of their behaviour (with potential links to emotional attachment and self-concept). The results will help publishers understand their consumers at a deeper level and could help to inform future commissioning and marketing strategies.

The research used an interpretivist, qualitative approach in order to obtain deeper insights than could be achieved with a survey, which although more widely disseminated would yield only superficial results. Participants were volunteers who had responded to a local poster campaign to recruit for the study, so were likely to be at least interested in books, reading and publishing, and reading for pleasure (Tier 4) or self-confessed book lovers (Tier 5). Each participant was asked to bring three books with them to the interview. These books were to be 'special' to the participant in some way. The research was exploratory, using semi-structured depth interviews about the participants and about their chosen books. The interviews investigated the importance of the participants' three books, participants' emotional response to the books, and how they felt the books affected aspects of their sense of self. Questions were designed around real, social, and ideal self; emotional involvement; and Overdorf and Barragree's 5 Tiers.

The results showed that consumers in Overdorf and Barragree's Tiers 4 and 5 have strong emotional attachment to and involvement in books that are special to them. Books were shown to invoke childhood and other memories and the experience of reading a book was shown to be involving and emotional. In terms of self-concept, interesting results emerged about how readers see themselves and how others see them, with some clear discrepancies between self-image and real self. A 'fantasy self' also emerged as a new construct. The fantasy self exists when the reader immerses himself/herself in a story to such an extent that he/she 'becomes' a character that he/she could never be in real life. This is similar to the alternative self shown in the Harley Davidson example, except that this is achievable through owning and riding the Harley, whereas the book self is pure fantasy. Books were shown to be more than just products for Overdorf and Barragree's Tiers 4 and 5 – they can be magical, create/enable fantasy selves, and encompass memories and parts of consumers' lives.

The results of the interviews could not be amalgamated as each individual's response was owned only by them. Instead, a number of profiles were generated to demonstrate the link between books and self-concept for individuals and to show the emotional responses invoked by books. These profiles showed a range of responses. For example, for one participant reading was a very private matter – he did not like to discuss his reading with others as he was afraid of 'spoilers' or of having his own views challenged or changed. Falling into Overdorf and Barragree's Tier 4, he felt a very personal attachment to his books and described reading as his equivalent of 'a good night out'. He used fiction for escapism and identified strongly with key characters, while also describing memories of reading as a child that were fuelled with warm emotions. He described not only an ideal self, but alternative selves, a negative self and a future ideal self, all linked to his reading and how he felt about his reading.

Another participant also identified a range of selves through her reading and said she feels happy and comfortable when reading, transported to her 'own little world', demonstrating a clear positive emotional attachment to books. Stating that she could never throw any books away, even if she had not enjoyed them, this participant also fell into Tier 4.

A further participant said that people were 'sick to death' of hearing him talk about books. His family have a box for books that no-one ever intends to read again, but that no-one can bear to part with. When discussing his favourite books he admitted that he had several copies of some of them and could not bear to part with any of them. Clearly falling into Tier 5, this participant said that paperbacks are 'proper' books and he would be 'lost without them'. Books for this participant mean so much more than the paper on which they are printed. They are bound up in memories and emotions so strong that it is not possible for him to contemplate parting with them. When reading he felt so engrossed that he felt he had actually become the characters in the novels.

Based on such a small sample it is impossible to generalise the results of this study to the book-buying population, but the results do demonstrate that Tier 4 and 5 readers definitely have an emotional involvement with books and they do choose books that help them to express their self-concept or a fantasy self. The participants' uses and gratifications from their book-reading experiences also fell into the categories associated with higher involvement (attachment) with the product.

The theory (and the small research project) supports what publishers know in their bones, from decades of experience of readers and books. Consumers are complex, with a range of different needs, and are within a continuum of readers that ranges from pure information seekers through to genuine book lovers. This diversity could not be better for the publishing industry, as there are so many nuanced markets to serve, so many uses and gratifications to offer, so many levels of involvement requiring different types of products on different platforms, and so much for readers to express about themselves through their reading.

Concluding thoughts

The UK is blessed with a strong and vibrant reading culture that is supported and evidenced through the vast number and variety of retail outlets that offer books and other reading material, the many book clubs and reviewing websites, festivals, prizes, and various celebrations of reading and literacy. While libraries may be struggling at the moment, the majority of UK consumers still read printed books whether for pleasure, leisure, entertainment, or professional purposes. Books have the power to provoke strong emotions and through the power of the reader's imagination, can allow readers to explore parts of themselves that do not normally come to the surface. Books are an important part of our cultural heritage but are also part of each reader's own life experience. Publishers therefore play an influential and important role in our culture and society and are extraordinarily lucky to be able to publish in such a wide range of genres and on such a diverse range of topics, serving the needs and desires of the reading public.

References

Baverstock, A. (2015). *How to market books*, 5th edition, Abingdon: Routledge.

Blumler, J. G., & McQuail, D. (1969). *Television in politics: Its uses and influence*, Chicago: University of Chicago Press.

Blythe, J. (2013). *Consumer behaviour*, 2nd edition. London: Sage, 87–94.

Bookseller News Team (2018). British Book Awards launch for 2018 with three new categories, *The Bookseller* [online], available: www.thebookseller.com/news/british-book-awards-launch-2018-three-new-categories-703801 (accessed 12 January 2018).

Bowlby, J. (1979). *The making and breaking of affectional bonds*. London: Tavistock.

Buhr, S. (2015). Mark Zuckerberg starts a book club, becomes this generation's Oprah, *Tech Crunch* [online], available: https://techcrunch.com/2015/01/04/mark-zuckerberg-starts-a-book-club-becomes-this-generations-oprah/ (accessed 14 December 2017).

Clark, C., & Teravainen, A. (2017). Celebrating reading for enjoyment: Findings from our Annual Literacy Survey 2016, National Literacy Trust Research Report [online], available: file:///C:/Users/781549/Downloads/2017_06_01_free_research_-celebrating_reading_enjoyment_final_4uGtNrp.pdf (accessed 14 December 2017).

Department for Culture, Media and Sport (2015a). Taking part 2014/15, focus on: Free time activities, statistical release November 2015 [online], available: www.gov.uk/government/uploads/system/uploads/attachment_data/file/476095/Taking_Part_201415_Focus_on_Free_time_activities.pdf (accessed 14 December 2017).

Department for Culture, Media and Sport (2015b). Libraries as a statutory service [online], 16 December 2015, available: www.gov.uk/government/publications/guidance-on-libraries-as-a-statutory-service/libraries-as-a-statutory-service (accessed 10 September 2018).

Department for Digital, Culture, Media and Sport (2018a). *Taking Part Survey: England, Child Report 2017/18* [online], 30 August 2018, available: https://assets.publishing.service.gov.uk/government/uploads/system/uploads/attachment_data/file/736939/Taking_Part_Child_Annual_Report.pdf (accessed 20 July 2019).

Department for Digital, Culture, Media and Sport (2018b). *Taking Part Survey: England, Adult Report 2017/18* [online], 30 August 2018, available: https://assets.publishing.service.gov.uk/government/uploads/system/uploads/attachment_data/file/740242/180911_Taking_Part_Adult_Annual_Report_-_Revised.pdf (accessed 20 July 2019).

Eyre, C. (2016). Sales of Zoella book club titles surge on Amazon, *The Bookseller* [online], available: www.thebookseller.com/news/sales-zoella-bookclub-titles-surge-amazon-333416 (accessed 14 December 2017).

Feather, J. (2006). *A history of British publishing*, 2nd edition, Abingdon: Routledge.

Flood, A. (2017). Children's authors slam celebrity-heavy World Book Day line up, *The Guardian* [online], Monday 2 October 2017, available: www.theguardian.com/books/2017/oct/02/childrens-authors-slam-celebrity-heavy-world-book-day-lineup (accessed 14 December 2017).

Goodreads (2019). About us, Goodreads [online], available: www.goodreads.com/about/us (accessed 30 July 2019).

Kean, D. (2017). On eve of Costa awards, experts warn that top books prizes are harming fiction, *The Guardian* [online], available: www.theguardian.com/books/2017/jan/02/on-eve-of-costa-awards-experts-warn-that-top-books-prizes-are-harming-fiction (accessed 31 December 2017).

Hay Festival (2017). *Hay Festival Report: Imagine the world, 25 May–4 June 2017* [online] available: hayfestival.com/portal/documents/Hay-Festival-2017-Report.pdf (accessed 10 September 2018).

Knox, P. (2012). What does your bookshelf say about you? *The Guardian*, 7 September, available: www.theguardian.com/commentisfree/2012/sep/07/bookshelf-say-about-you.

Lister, D. (2016). It's mad not to have a single books programme on mainstream TV, *The Independent* [online], available: www.independent.co.uk/voices/comment/it-s-mad-not-to-have-a-single-books-programme-on-mainstream-tv-a6799451.html (accessed 31 December 2017).

Millan, E., & Reynolds, J. (2011). Independent and interdependent self-views and their influence on clothing consumption, *International Journal of Retail & Distribution Management*, 39(3), 162–182.

Mintel (2018a). *Books and E-books – UK – June 2018* [online], Mintel.

Mintel (2018b). *Social and Media Networks – UK – May 2018* [online], Mintel.

Mintel (2019). *Books and E-books – UK – July 2019* [online], Mintel.

Office for National Statistics (2017). *Leisure time in the UK: 2015*, 24 October 2017, available: www.ons.gov.uk/economy/nationalaccounts/satelliteaccounts/articles/leisuretimeintheuk/2015 (accessed 20 July 2019).

Onwuemezi, N. (2016). Launch of BAME in Publishing network, *The Bookseller* [online], 6 May 2016, available: www.thebookseller.com/news/bame-publishing-launches-328482 (accessed 10 September 2018).

Onwuemezi, N. (2016). Richard and Judy on their 'search for a bestseller', *The Bookseller* [online], available: www.thebookseller.com/news/richard-and-judy-325570 (accessed 14 December 2017).

Onwuemezi, N. (2018). David Bowie's son launches book club in his honour, *The Bookseller* [online], available: www.thebookseller.com/news/david-bowies-son-launches-book-club-his-honour-698971 (accessed 12 January 2018).

Overdorf, M., & Barragree, A. (2001). The impending disruption of the publishing industry, *Publishing Research Quarterly*, 17(3), 3–19.

Page, B. (2018). Latest CIPFA stats reveal yet more library closures and book loan falls, *The Bookseller* [online], 7 December 2018, available: www.thebookseller.com/news/cipfa-records-yet-more-library-closures-and-book-loan-falls-911061 (accessed 25 July 2019).

Papadatos, C. (2006). The art of storytelling: How loyalty marketers can build emotional connections to their brands, *Journal of Consumer Marketing*, 23(7), 382–384.

Patwardhan, H., & Balasubramanian, S.K. (2011). Brand romance: A complementary approach to explain emotional attachment toward brands, *Journal of Product and Brand Management*, 20(4), 297–308.

Perez, M.E., Castano, R., & Quintanilla, C. (2010). Constructing identity through the consumption of counterfeit luxury goods, *Qualitative Market Research: An International Journal*, 13(3), 219–235.

Peters, C., Shelton, J.A., & Thomas, J.B. (2011). Self-concept and the fashion behavior of women over 50, *Journal of Fashion Marketing and Management: An International Journal*, 15(3), 291–305.

Shaffi, S. (2015). Reading for pleasure boosts self-esteem, The Bookseller [online], available: www.thebookseller.com/news/reading-pleasure-boosts-self-esteem (accessed 14 December 2017).

Sutherland, J. (2002). *Reading the decades: Fifty years of British history through the nation's bestsellers*, London: BBC Books.

Szmigin, I., & Piacentini, M. (2014). *Consumer behaviour*. Oxford: Oxford University Press, 242.

The Zoe Ball Book Club [online] available: www.thezoeballbookclub.com/ (accessed 10 September 2018).

Toman, S. (2009, 25 September). What does your bookcase say about you? *BBC News Magazine*, available: http://news.bbc.co.uk/1/hi/8264572.stm.

Wakefield, K.L., & Bush, V.D. (1998). Promoting leisure services: Economic and emotional aspects of consumer response, *Journal of Services Marketing*, 12(3), 209–222.

Whiting, A., & Williams, D. (2013). Why people use social media: A uses and gratifications approach, *Qualitative Market Research: An International Journal*, 16(4), 362–369, doi:10.1108/QMR-06-2013-0041.

Wood, H. (2018). HarperCollins' BAME traineeship programme opens for 2018, *The Bookseller* [online], 28 March 2018, available: www.thebookseller.com/news/harpercollins-re-opens-bame-traineeship-757971 (accessed 10 September 2018).

World Book Day (2017). New research on reading: a quarter of the UK's 8 to 11 year-old children would not own a book without World Book Day [online], available: www.worldbookday.com/2017/03/new-research-on-reading/ (accessed 14 December 2017).

World Book Night (2017). About World Book Night [online], available: http://worldbooknight.org/ (accessed 14 December 2017).

Yeshin, T. (2011). *Advertising*. Andover: Cengage Learning EMEA.

4

SUNK TREASURE

Can the traditional public library service survive in contemporary Britain?

Ellie Bowker and Clare Somerville

In the last ten years, research has consistently reported on the dire situation of the public library service in the UK, many making recommendations for what action needs to be taken in order to save them. Libraries offer reading material and information but also form a very important part of both community and culture within the areas they serve. Libraries have been heavily involved in rectifying the demise in the standard of literacy in the UK, which has been linked with intergenerational poverty, poor public health, and unemployment. Research has consistently shown that access to books can help improve literacy levels and libraries provide this at no cost to the user. It is in the interest of everyone, publishers, policymakers, educators, and the public, that libraries remain an open resource. This essay will identify the key challenges facing the public library service; explore the methods being adopted to combat them; and, finally, evaluate the sustainability of the current library service.

Let's begin by defining terms and exploring historical context. The Oxford English Dictionary defines a library as 'a place set apart to contain books for reading, study or reference'. At its most basic level and during their initial establishment, this was certainly true. Before the invention of the printing press, books were rare, treasured items. Even after the introduction of printing, books remained expensive items, unavailable to those without means and irrelevant to the illiterate. Local benefactors might purchase volumes to create libraries to share with their communities – known as 'endowed libraries' – and other forms of library included parish libraries, subscription libraries, and those belonging to guilds and professional institutes. At the heart of all these models was the opportunity to develop literacy, raise educational attainment, and create a culture of reading and learning (McMenemy, 2018).

The need to create a formal public library system in the UK correlates with the Industrial Revolution which transformed British society to one 'where working class communities sprung up to support the major evolving industries' (McMenemy, 2018). Supporting social transformation and opportunities for social development and self-improvement, the Public Libraries Bill became part of the 1850 Act of Parliament, which introduced a tax in English and Welsh towns for the maintenance of a public library. The 1850 Act was extended to Scotland and Ireland three years later.

It was quickly evident that the tax was not working, especially for smaller towns and villages that did not have the population or resources to maintain their local library. This was exposed in a report by Lionel R. McColvin (1942). *The Public Library System of Great Britain*, also known as The McColvin Report, exposed the inequalities and inconsistencies of the service across the country. McColvin highlighted that 'only large structures could deliver the range of services modern libraries required to provide for their users' (McColvin, 1942). He called for central government to provide grants to fund the libraries and outlined the potential benefits of a well-delivered library service within local communities and national effectiveness.

The Public Libraries and Museums Act was adopted in 1964 and remains legislation in England and Wales to this day. The Act made local authorities statutorily obligated 'to provide a comprehensive and efficient library service for all persons desiring to make use thereof' (Public Libraries and Museums Act, 1964) and has shaped the five key principles of public libraries:

1. That public libraries should be publicly funded
2. That they should be administered by public bodies and not private organisations or individuals
3. That they should be freely available to all members of its community
4. That they should embrace the needs and interests of all members of the community
5. That they should be free both financially and intellectually, and provide access to materials without bias or interference (McColvin, 1942)

Libraries are so much broader than just buildings for books. They are free and accessible institutions serving their communities, without restriction or bias.

This essay aims to identify the challenges facing the UK's public library system in order to build understanding of both the current situation and the measures being used to combat them. Interviews with those working in the library service will provide broader understanding of the likely sustainability of the UK's public library service.

This investigation matters because, while as CEO of CILIP,[1] Nick Poole has said 'a modern library is the Common Room at the heart of its community' (CILIP, 2018), and the impact libraries can have within their local communities is highly beneficial, there are policymakers and those implementing policy at national level who overlook the library service because they do not use it themselves. Research and reports have consistently made recommendations that action should be taken to improve the service, and this essay will explore some of the findings and how implementable they are in order to secure the future of libraries in the UK.

Much of the literature relating to the position and role of libraries in the UK can be found in government publications and research reports by prominent bodies and figures in the public sector and from trusted news sources.

Understanding the values of public libraries is a significant start. One of the core values of public libraries is 'providing equity of access to their resources for all' (McMenemy, 2018). David McMenemy defines equity of access as 'the right to use the information and books [you] need regardless of [your] ability to afford them or without undue influence or prejudice from others who may wish them not to have access' (2018). Librarians are the frontline of defence for a community's right to access materials. This stems from responsibilities like including a selection of material that is popular and high quality, but this can be challenging for several reasons:

- Financial – libraries do not always have the budget to purchase new material.
- Censorship – special interest groups, individuals, or campaigns pressure librarians not to stock certain material that deviates from their own personal value system.
- Selection – in contrast to the above, the librarian needs to consider the interests of the entire community when selecting material to stock (McMenemy, 2018).

McMenemy further explains that libraries act as a social equaliser because everyone using a library, irrespective of their social demographic, is accessing information, books, and additional services free from cost and, importantly, prejudice. It was established previously that one of the key principles of public libraries is that they should provide access to resources without bias or interference, and, in particular, social exclusion. Typically, this can apply to users who are at risk of social exclusion, defined by central government as

> what can happen when people or areas have a combination of linked problems, such as unemployment, discrimination, poor skills, low incomes, poor housing, high crime and family breakdown [...] an extreme consequence of what happens when people don't get a fair deal throughout their lives.
> *Cabinet Office, 2006*

Libraries were encouraged to facilitate recruitment, training and to partner with local organisations to reach out to those who were at risk of being excluded (McMenemy, 2018). Alongside the adaptation of services, these methods ensured attention to the needs of every member of the community from all different age groups, demographics, genders, ethnicities, and sexual orientation.

In 2014, William Sieghart published the report on his investigation into the public library system (The Independent Library Report, 2014 also commonly known as *The Sieghart Report*). The report came to two major conclusions. First that 'there have already been far too many library reviews in recent years which have come to nothing'. Second that 'not enough decision makers at national and local level [appearing] sufficiently aware of the remarkable and vital value that a good library service can offer modern communities'. Sieghart recommended that a taskforce should be set up to work in partnership with the library sector that would provide a strategic framework to help local authorities to 'improve, revitalise and if necessary, change their local library service, while encouraging, appropriate to each library, increased community involvement' (Sieghart, 2014). The Libraries Taskforce was set up to deliver the recommendations laid out by Sieghart's report. *Libraries Deliver: Ambition for Public Libraries in England 2016 to 2021* (Department for Digital, Culture, Media and Sport, 2016) is a five-year action plan, generally known as 'Ambition', for 'libraries to be more resilient and better equipped to weather future challenges'.

Since 2010, nearly 600 public libraries have closed in the UK (Harris, 2017) with 130 of those shutting down in 2018 alone (Cain, 2018). This is due to a decrease in spending by local authority on public libraries with pressure from central government to minimise the public sector budget. Latest figures from the Chartered Institute of Public Finance and Accountancy (CIPFA), the UK's professional accountancy body specialising in public services, revealed that spending by local authorities on public libraries fell by a further £30 million in 2017/2018 with spending just over £740 million (CIPFA, 2018). Public libraries are just one of the many public services to be the victim of shrinking budgets, along with the National Health Service (NHS), child social care, and waste collection, but many believe that libraries are seen 'as an easy austerity target when government has demanded they make cuts' (UNISON, 2014). In response to the global financial crisis in 2008, austerity cuts were introduced in the UK by the Conservative–Liberal Democrat coalition of 2010 'sold to the country as a desperate measure to fix out-of-control spending, fuelled also by an ideological desire to shrink the size of the state' (Ball, 2018). Almost a decade on from the first of these cuts, the slashed library service budget is threatened by further stripping of funding that would be irreparably damaging. 'Libraries are vital community hubs–bringing people together, and giving them access to the services and support they need to help them live better' (Department for Digital, Culture, Media and Sport, 2016). Lack of funding has led to libraries having to think creatively about how they can continue to deliver their services. Librarian Ian Anstice explains that 'councils learnt early on how unpopular simply closing libraries is so they have had to cut the vital service in other, less obvious ways' (BBC, 2016). In response to funding problems, the Libraries Taskforce recommended that 'library leaders need to make a compelling case to local and national decision makers, articulating benefits, impact and cost savings' (DCMS, 2016). Interestingly, seeking funding through alternative channels such as fundraising and sector partnerships was implicitly prioritised. The Taskforce does not directly state that the public library service requires more money from central government, rather the implication is that alternative revenue streams and funding models will be accessed in order to support the survival of public libraries.

The disappearance of around 8,000 UK library jobs is one of the consequences of shrinking budgets. To continue to be able to deliver the service, libraries have had to rely heavily on volunteers. There are now over twice as many volunteers in libraries than there was almost ten years ago, roughly 31,000 compared to the 15,000 in 2010 (BBC, 2016). This suggests that people feel strongly about keeping their local library open and are consequently willing to donate their own time.

While appreciating their motivations, the use of volunteers in libraries is not universally appreciated. Sir Philip Pullman, President of the Society of Authors, argued that 'relying on volunteers to provide a service that ought to be statutory is not a good policy' (BBC, 2016). Local authorities are statutorily obligated to provide a 'comprehensive and efficient' library service, and volunteers are not generally quipped to do that. Lauren Smith, librarian and campaigner for Voices for the Library, explains that 'librarians adhere to a code of professional conduct in the same way that doctors, lawyers and accountants do' (BBC, 2016). Without the proper training, volunteers compromise those ethics and the very principles of the public library. Librarians commit to the upholding and promotion of a set of ethical principles which covers equity of access, avoidance of bias or prejudice, and user confidentiality (CILIP, 2018). Central and local government may see volunteers as a solution to the library staffing issue, but it begs the question whether volunteers can maintain a high-level library service. In the Independent Library Report (2014), Sieghart identified localism as 'a library's greatest strength' but highlighted the danger of it becoming a library's weakness. Localism has the ability to empower and benefit communities in a unique way but estranging public services too far from a government who is supposed to provide them may introduce more risks than benefits.

Volunteers are at the heart of community-managed libraries. David Barnett (2018) reported that '500 of the UK's 3,800 libraries are operated by ordinary people, working for free in a role once regarded as a profession'. When a library authority can no longer afford to maintain the service, it can be handed over to members of the community to manage rather than opting for complete closure. There are many successful cases of community-managed libraries in the UK. Burley Library in Bradford has seen usage of the library grow steadily since it was handed over to the community in 2017 and has secured £150,000 of funding for refurbishments (Barnett, 2018). Unfortunately, this is not the case for every community-managed library in the country. Laura Swaffield (2017) argues that the problem with community-managed libraries is that they vary wildly when it comes to staffing, funding, and quality of service. As a result, there is arguably no longer a national standard of library service. Swaffield's argument was based on the research report from the Libraries Taskforce exploring the effectiveness and sustainability of community-managed libraries which concluded that 'due to the variable nature of the [community library] models, it is challenging to recommend a set of support mechanisms that will address all the issues that [community libraries] face' (Department of Digital, Culture, Media and Sport, 2017). Every community has different needs to be met, which means that every library differs in its services in order to best serve their community. Debatably, it is the role of the local librarian to anticipate these needs and tailor the local library to work for those needs. However, the overriding feeling is that community-managed libraries are covering up drastic downturn in the library service diverting the pressure away from councils who have a statutory duty to deliver the service in the first place. Anstice (Flood, 2017) highlights that library closures 'would be double if volunteer libraries were not taken into account [...] a trend that will only continue while there's no effective statutory protection for libraries'.

The Libraries Taskforce (Department for Digital, Culture, Media and Sport, 2016) aims to promote 'positive messages about libraries and the outcomes they support, and reflect these consistently throughout interviews, placed editorial and other media'. This is particularly important when the media's attention may be focussed on negative aspects of library provision: closures, lack of staff, and poor funding which can impact on public willingness to go into libraries.

UNISON (2014) argues that 'too many politicians are stuck with the outdated and stereotypical view of libraries being solely about books where members of the public are told to "shhh"'. This promotes the notion that libraries are not welcoming spaces, they are buildings that are old and unappealing and so are the books they contain. In the digital age, the book as a source of entertainment or information has a lot of competition. Instant, or 'on-demand', entertainment such as Netflix, text messaging, and social media posting has 'created a reading style hierarchy that positions immediacy over everything else that makes the ability to immerse oneself in to a lengthy novel challenging' (Carr, 2008). But despite these changes in reading culture, statistics from Nielsen Books can report that the UK print book market is growing, selling 190.9 million books in 2018, a 0.3% increase on statistics from 2017 (Flood, 2019). Building on this, Simon Jenkins (2016) suggests that the issue lies not with the books but with the library itself; '[libraries] must rediscover their specialness [...] This strength lies not in books as such, but in its readers, in their desire to congregate, share with each other, hear writers and experience books in the context of their community'.

Libraries have certainly embedded themselves within their communities by expanding their services. For example, National Libraries Week 2018 focussed on how libraries benefit health and well-being. Many libraries across the country have expanded their services to offer NHS drop-in sessions, mindfulness sessions, and mental health and well-being check-ups (Dudman, 2018). Library usage is associated with numerous health and well-being factors, including 'higher life satisfaction, higher happiness and a higher sense of purpose', all of which contributes to good general health (Fujiwara et al., 2015). This same report estimated that regular library usage by the English population would save the NHS £27.7

million a year. Beyond health services, libraries across the country offer job-seeking support, IT, and business classes. The problem is that many of these important initiatives are saving money, amalgamating service delivery to the whole individual as well as their wider community, but are largely unknown and hence unappreciated by politicians and policymakers.

The success of a library is measured yearly by two major strands, the number of book issues and the number of visitors (McMenemy, 2018). Arguably, these are flawed measures of success as they do not account for the impact the library has on the community. Sector librarian for GLL Martin Stone said that 'the secret to [a library's] success is simple – an attractive building in a central location, plenty of computers, reliable Wi-Fi access, and a steady supply of new books' (Morton, 2018). Increased visitor numbers at Woolwich Centre Library and Chester's Storyhouse as a result of renovation of the library building confirm Stone's theory. Many libraries in central city locations such as London, Manchester, and Newcastle have gone through extensive renovations funded by Arts Council England. The newly designed libraries have encouraged more visitors and, by extension, have seen an increase in the number of book issues.

However, in more deprived areas of the country there are many rural libraries that do not get the same kind of funding and support. This inequality in services echoes the McColvin Report that funding from organisations to large structure libraries strengthens the inconsistencies in the national service.

Arts Council England's *Envisioning the Library of the Future Report* (2017) identified innovative methods libraries had adopted to deliver their services. This included exploring library spaces, developing the role of the librarian and digital distribution. One of the major themes throughout the report was funding models and how libraries were cutting costs to keep up with relentless budgetary cuts. The following innovative funding models being actively used by libraries were identified:

- Independent library services funded by a community levy
- Charitable fundraising trusts
- External trusts
- Merging or sharing library services with neighbouring councils
- High-performing library services adopting smaller library services not necessarily in the same region
- Online sponsorship and crowdfunding (Arts Council England, 2017).

The report uses case studies of a variety of 'flagship' libraries (libraries that are considered the best), explaining that 'flagship library projects [are] usually in city centres, and usually connected to a bigger construction and physical renewal project'. The report elaborates that the kind of innovation of flagship libraries 'can only happen in particular circumstances, take years of planning and cannot happen everywhere' (2017). The shortcoming of this report is that the research does not consider rural libraries and the report's recommendations may not therefore work for rural libraries.

The addition of digital services has been the cause of particular debate within the creative economy. Remote e-lending, the ability to borrow e-books and audiobooks from libraries without having to visit a library, allows libraries to fulfil one of their key principles of freely supplying books to those who may not be able to leave their homes.

Interviews with three key individuals within the library service shed interesting light on developments. The views of Ray Dyer (Managing Director of Peters, a library supplier specialising in children's books and furniture), Nicholas Poole (CEO of CILIP), and Alison Townsend (Team Leader of Adult Services and Acquisitions at Kingston Library) combine to offer valuable reflections for determining the future of public libraries in the UK and their longer term sustainability.

As a member of the Libraries Taskforce, Nick Poole co-authored *Libraries Deliver: Ambition* (Department for Digital, Culture, Media and Sport, 2016). He reinforced the purpose of the taskforce which was to provide leadership at a national level for public libraries. Poole explains how the action plan was in response to Seighart's Independent Libraries Report (2014) and elaborates that 'there was a big difference between what [Seighart] wanted to recommend and what he was allowed to recommend'. What was originally supposed to be a plan for a complete transformation of the library service and investment at a national level but 'what it ended up being was a sort of portfolio of fairly low level practical things'. Poole refers to the rolling out of free internet access at every library and e-book lending as examples arguing that, whilst these things are important, 'they're not fundamental to the future of the network'. The addition of digital services has become an important part of library culture; however, it is arguable as to whether it was detrimental to the survival of libraries, particularly in the face of other challenges identified in this essay. Alison Townsend however argues that digital and online resources have been very important in encouraging more people to use the library service. The offer of e-books and e-audio can be appealing to library users who are unable to physically visit the library. She reiterates that this 'idea of a 24/7 library becomes more important because libraries aren't just bricks and mortar'.

Regarding combatting the central challenges facing libraries, Poole explains that the Taskforce has been limited in their actions as 'no government-convened taskforce is going to contradict the government policies of the evolution of austerity [...] which means it has focused on a programme of activity around the edges'. Poole admitted to differing opinions between CILIP and the Taskforce, particularly on key challenges such as funding, local authorities' understanding of libraries, and literacy skills. CILIP were putting pressure on the Taskforce to release a statement that public libraries needed more funding however the Taskforce would not on the basis that 'we should be more efficient with the money we have already'. Supported by the research findings in the literature review, Poole explains 'half of the local authorities are actually pretty good at maintaining investment in their libraries, the other half vary from threatened cuts due to reduced budgets to permanently-damaging reductions in the service'. All areas of local government spending are under pressure, but political leaders need to be alerted to the challenges that uniquely affect libraries.

Referring to CIPFA figures (2018), Poole acknowledges the shrinking budget of public libraries, 'if you go back to 2006, we got £1.67 billion worth of investment from government for investment in public libraries, this year (2019) that's down to £760 million'. The criticism from national leadership of the public sector for being inefficient with their budget resurfaces. In Victoria, Australia, government are spending roughly $40 (c£72 at time of writing) a head on their libraries and seeing significant growth in literacy and educational attainment. In comparison, the UK have halved their spending, going from spending £18 a head to 'just over £10'. When Nick Poole presented these figures to Michael Ellis MP, the Minister for Public Libraries, he appeared unconcerned with the reduction in spending, 'his response was 'well, there's an awful lot you can do with £8 a head''. When asked about the Libraries Taskforce's anticipated outcome that by 2020, councils will fund public libraries from local revenue, such as council tax, business rates, and New Homes Bonus (2016), Poole argued this would significantly disadvantage communities in areas of deprivation. He elaborates that areas with 'multiple deprivation and lack of taxes and just people [mean] that the local authority can't run a library service from local revenue so then you do need top-up development support'. CILIP and the Taskforce advocate for a 'three-tiered library system'. On the bottom tier is public sector-led development including reinstating library standards which can be achieved through organisations like CILIP and Arts Council England. The central tier is about securing the funding into public libraries by local government. Consistent with Swaffield's article (2017), Poole acknowledges that the standard of libraries across the country is 'a very mixed picture [...] there's a piece of work to be done both to secure the good ones and convince the less good ones'. The top tier focusses on national action for fair development funding of libraries, which supports libraries in deprived areas of the country. This tier system cannot work entirely if just one tier is not fulfilling its own responsibility. There needs to be better collaboration between each level to deliver the library service defined in the 1964 Public Libraries Act.

As suppliers of content and resources, collaborating directly with publishers to source books would be an arguably plausible option for libraries attempting to reduce their costs. It's an option that would however significantly disrupt the publishers' current business model. For Dominic Smith, Group Field Sales Director at Hachette UK, publishers haven't changed their approach to libraries despite the challenges the service faces. The expectation is that libraries will continue to experience decline unless they begin majorly diversifying through repositioning, innovation, and securing new funding models. Publishers value the library sector immensely, and in addition to a previously relied upon market for sales, it has offered ongoing opportunities to boost debut authors and connect readers to new voices, but the involvement of wholesalers arguably reduces publishers' net receipts from library sales. But while cutting out the mediator would certainly reduce costs for the library authority, library suppliers have a level of expertise and understanding of the uniqueness of the individual libraries which most publishers would not have the capacity to replace. Peters is the UK's leading children's books and furniture supplier for libraries '[providing] book processing for the library customers to make the books "shelf-ready", direct delivery to library branches, electronic trading to aid efficiency'. While removing library suppliers from the supply chain could impact positively on the prices at which libraries are able to purchase, the service provided by library suppliers would need to be replicated, and neither libraries nor publishers are arguably well placed to offer a replacement.

Whilst funding has been identified as a core challenge facing libraries, Poole says this is due to 'a layered set of challenges that added up to further reduced funding'. When the UK went into the economic crisis of 2008, every public service had to defend their funding with evidence of return on investment, 'we had absolutely no evidence of return on investment which is absurd because the public library in a town affects literally every aspect of life in that town'. Ten years into a harsh austerity government, Poole compares the government's reduced investment into libraries to Margaret Thatcher's removal of free milk from schools, a political move that caused huge backlash, 'she took milk away from the hands of children and this government is taking libraries away from communities who have been left behind'. Agreeing with UNISON's reporting (2014), Poole reveals that government has previously described public libraries as being 'politically toxic'. Politicising the issue of library provision compromises their ability to provide services and support to those who need it most. A shrinking budget risks the reduction of support to job seekers, community, connectivity and the opportunities for improvement through self-directed learning.

Recently, CILIP received two-years' worth of funding to bring US political action group EveryLibrary over to the UK. In the US, EveryLibrary secured $500 million of US governmental funding for public libraries by building a campaign of library support around the voices of local users rather than aligning themselves with the state and debating with the senate, 'what [EveryLibrary] want to leave is a legacy of the UK doing library advocacy differently because [...] what we're doing right now isn't working'. The fundamental principle of EveryLibrary is that library support is non-political and library use is not an indicator of political support. There are more people who support libraries but do not use them than there are people who use the library. EveryLibrary aims to change the narrative from one about wanting to keep the library open just because people think it's a good thing to a narrative 'more about [wanting] to live in a world where people have the chance to read and get on and get online and the library does that for you'. The partnership between EveryLibrary and CILIP will offer leadership at a national level for public libraries which has proven to be an ongoing problem, Poole: 'I think we had a bunch of organisations at national level that preferred to spend time jockeying for status and position than actually doing stuff for the sector'. Many policymakers are under the impression that libraries are a soft target for stripping of funding and resources. Poole acknowledges that 'librarians aren't gifted at boasting [...] that's why you have national organisations to boast on your behalf, I think we just didn't do that job right'. Libraries need continuing advocacy to shine light on the important work they do that policymakers often overlook.

Community-managed libraries and volunteers have become an integral part of library culture. There are a variety of benefits that come from libraries that are led by the local users. 'Ambition' presented community-managed libraries in a way that suggests giving control back to the communities is a better alternative. Whilst the Libraries Taskforce remains in support of community-managed libraries, and in some instances encouraging communities to take over their local library, Nick Poole argues that 'we wouldn't be having this conversation about hyper-localism and community support and volunteerism if it wasn't for the dominant agenda to take [public libraries] out of the state of public service'. Separating libraries from government seems to be difficult when debating any aspect of the public library service as it all ties back to the impact of austerity within the public sector. Poole believes that localism tends to be a symptom of an austerity government, 'whenever you get a state-reducing government, part of it is local organisations springing up saying "you know what, big government is bad, small government and localism is good". It's not true'. Poole believes that a successful library service comes from cohesive collaboration between local, regional, and national governments.

Poole explains that, to an extent, CILIP not only protects professional jobs, meaning librarians, and other information professional but also protects the quality and accessibility of library and information services. Consistent with Lauren Smith (BBC, 2016), Poole agrees that, whilst volunteers are important and valued, community-led volunteerism makes national leadership complicit in the diminishment of the service. Community-managed libraries are however becoming one of the main organisational models for the service. Alison Townsend agrees that the introduction of the many different models has 'really changed the environment of libraries'. Kingston Library remains under the jurisdiction of the local authority so it has its own library management team and librarians on the frontline but also uses volunteers to help run their additional activities and events. Poole and Townsend agree that volunteers bring extra value to the library service. Poole acknowledges that volunteers bring 'broad perspectives and a flux of new energy and skills'. Townsend agrees and elaborates that volunteers are valuable as library staff do not always have the capacity to deliver certain services or activities so recruiting volunteers aids in championing the library service; particularly important in ensuring that Kingston Library has a voice and presence at community events in the borough. Townsend:

> it can be a challenge if you haven't got the staff to do that [...] we would look at where we can get volunteers so we can get the message out there as long as it isn't impacting on the actual running of the libraries themselves.

Kingston Library also relies on volunteers from other professions to run activities. Townsend explains a monthly reading group for adults with learning disabilities called Build Works, is run by externals 'they are volunteers but they're specialists; they're clinical psychologists'. Volunteers, in professional and non-professional capacities, add value to the library service but effective operation of such services comes from collaboration.

A trained librarian is however at the core of any library. Poole again: 'The best person to design a local library around local needs is a local librarian because we've got expertise and we know how to do it in a way that keeps people safe and fairly dealt with'. Librarians are trained to a set of ethical principles that volunteers or those without formal library training do not necessarily appreciate. Poole believes that 'libraries are trusted because they are trustworthy and the reason that they are trustworthy is because they are trained, ethical professionals working in the library'. With the increase in volunteerism and localism, the slip of these ethical principles has largely gone unacknowledged. Those who come into the library as a second career or voluntary role may lack this understanding. Poole again: 'while they've got a feel for the ethics of librarianship, they don't have a full grounding in the regulations'. CILIP are encouraging library employers to invest in on-the-job training and continue professional development to provide that grounding in information science and services. But it has become increasingly difficult for libraries to do this due to relentless budgetary pressure; investment in skills and staff has been minimised. The public sector has prioritised keeping the library building open, but the cost has been the undermining of the professional base of the workforce. This may compromise the library further, as a fully trained and qualified library staff could arguably 'accelerate out of the downturn' (Poole) when faced with the challenge of having to present a return on investment or evidence of value to the community. Referring to the 1964 Public Libraries Act, where there is a clear definition of the stewardship that should be provided to public libraries at a national level, Poole argues that 'we need to get back to running the library service in the way that it was designed to be run'.

Ambition (2016) planned to develop positive messages in the media to build a more consistent narrative and raise awareness about public libraries. Poole and Townsend both agree that libraries were the unfortunate victims of coverage that could be 'a bit cheap'. In line with UNISON's reporting, Townsend addressed the common misconception that libraries are places of strict silence when the truth is so far from that. She believes that 'there is slightly more coverage about some of the things that go on in libraries but I don't think there's enough generally'. Townsend refers to campaigns run by CILIP that have 'hit the radar' alongside other notable library events put together by organisations like The Reading Agency and Arts Council England such as World Book Night and the Summer Reading Challenge. When asked specifically about the negative stories associated with libraries such as closures and staffing issues, Townsend believes that the reporting 'could be more informed but I don't necessarily think coverage of libraries closing is a bad thing'. Media coverage of library closures generates awareness of what is happening in the public sector, especially as there is still a significant percentage of people who do not use public libraries and therefore would not be as informed about the struggle they are facing. Townsend sees that 'there is a growing awareness now that libraries aren't as they were 30 years ago'.

Poole argues that public libraries are 'one of the most emotive tools' for exhibiting the consequences that a harsh austerity government has had on the public sector and holding them to account for it. The aforementioned EveryLibrary build their campaign through social media, video content, and other digital media in order to reshape the public perception of public libraries. Regarding the current representation of libraries, Poole believes that they have been positioned in the public mind 'in precisely the wrong place'.

After research found that the fastest growing audience in public library use was 18–25 year olds, Poole explained how he began to think about the identity and marketing of public libraries for this user and concluded that libraries were not delivering an attractive message. He argued that libraries 'should be aspirational, experiential, quite design-led, they should be about time well spent, they should be about places to relax and recharge, places to engage with reading and books and literacy and places to be social'. They should have universal offers and be a welcoming, inviting, and safe space for everyone in the community to use at their own leisure. Instead, libraries are unappealingly positioned as a 'municipally architected part of a council offer, usually in places that look more like an office block than a place of creativity and relaxation and reading'. Poole makes an interesting that point that, when you have a core audience that is younger and more attuned to sharing experiences on social media as this age group is, libraries have 'no Instagram moments'. He suggests that to change this perception, public libraries could be following the lead of independent bookshops.

Independent bookshops too were increasingly facing a crisis, with many going out of business, closing or seeing reduced profits as customers used them for 'showrooming' – the opportunity to view titles they were thinking of buying, before ordering on line. In the Bookseller Association's Annual Report for 2012, booksellers identified the importance of positioning themselves in the heart of culture, reaching beyond bookselling to create an enriching experience. Poole recognised how independent bookshops rather morphed into places 'that book bugs really want to spend time and sit down with a coffee and share their love of reading'. Public libraries need to have a similar pivot; perhaps beginning in flagship libraries but building from this to be a national effort. Bookshops and libraries are both distributors of books, they connect books to readers; it would therefore make sense for the public library to adopt a similar method of transformation to appeal to a broader, or perhaps a new, audience.

There is also room for innovation in the library's offer. For example, Kingston Library hosts many events and activities in order to encourage visitors and library users such as monthly reading groups for adults and children, writers' groups, knitting circles, and Scrabble clubs. Curating events and activities with users in mind, and thus benefitting different age groups and demographics, enables contact with a wide range of different communities than other organisations could potentially reach. For example, offering some health services (such as blood pressure tests, some vaccinations, and non-intrusive tests) in libraries is beneficial in that not only do they provide a convenient location, they also widen awareness of the range of services libraries can offer. Stocking health-related collections such as The Reading Agency's 'Books on Prescription', dementia collections, and a long-term health conditions collection creates a strong partnership between public libraries and public health. Townsend explains that 'the directorate that the library sits in is "Communities" and Public Health is part of that same directorate [...] if [public health are] working with groups they can promote the fact that we've got these collections'. There is, however, the ongoing balance over the allocation of library space, maintaining a balance between the additional services they can offer without distracting from their core offer of books and reading.

All interviewees agreed that a library is so much more than a dictionary definition of a building that houses books. Townsend argues that 'you have books in a waiting room in a station, that doesn't make a waiting room a library because there are so many strands that go in to making a library'. Ray Dyer argues that the space a library occupies has influence over its visitor numbers and usage. He believes that 'creating warm, safe, inviting spaces can really enhance the whole experience'. The environment a child reads in is an important factor in their development of a love of reading. When children make positive connections and associations with reading from an early age, they are more likely to carry those beliefs and habits throughout their life. Nick Poole revealed that CILIP's big campaign for 2020 is the promotion of books and reading after '[being] totally startled coming in to libraries to find out there are a lot of people in library leadership who think that that's sort of a dead proposition'. All interviewees have agreed that public libraries' core offer is books and reading. Poole: 'Fundamentally, a library can do tons of [activities] such as "Rhyme Time", "Baby Bounce" and all the rest of it but if the books are not in a good state, people won't come back'. He refers to the collapse in library-user figures correlating with the decline in spending on books by public libraries. If there are fewer books available in the library, due to a lack of spending or budget, then it is likely that there will be fewer book issues as people will not be able to access the books that they want. Townsend agrees that a library needs to stock a wide range of books that are relevant to the community and individual user. Kingston Library has standing orders for popular bestselling books as they can be sure that they will be issued. The community influences the stock of a library based on what is being borrowed or requested. For children and young people, Townsend explains how the library has partnered with local schools by giving them a sum of money so students can choose the stock themselves; a key part of instilling reading habits. Dyer explains that Peters specialises in the distribution of children's books, 'our librarians read and review every children's title that is published each year that will be suitable for a school and public library'. Dyer agrees it is vital for a librarian to curate their collection so that it is relevant to the library user and Townsend agrees that in community-managed libraries advice on stocking is particularly valuable. A unique feature of Peters is their showroom which hosts 38,000 individual children's titles which allows librarians to experience books in the same way that a library user would. Understanding the needs of the library user is key to delivering a library service that they will want to use.

Conclusions

It can be concluded that central government has a large share of responsibility in the preservation of the public library service. Library authorities have been the victims of harsh government policies of minimising the costs of the public sector. Policymakers have overlooked the support that libraries offer the most vulnerable in our society and who risk social exclusion. What is funded within a library service – trained and qualified staff; a selection of activities and services and, arguably most importantly, a comprehensive range of books in a variety of formats – can be overlooked as insufficiently glamorous to compete for public spending.

While all these aspects of library provision were laid out in the 1964 Public Libraries and Museums Act, the service cannot be delivered to the required level without appropriate funding. The roughly £900 million decrease in the public libraries budget has risked permanent damage to the library service and, in turn, public health and educational attainment, especially in some of the most deprived areas of the country. While the restoration of the public library service requires funding from central government, it seems that governments consistently need to be reminded of their responsibility to advocate and ensure a national standard of library service. What is more, government-convened taskforces have been blocked by the governments they are supposed to be serving, which has resulted in what Poole has referred to as 'activity around the edges'.

Localism and volunteerism have become trends in regional authorities; pushing responsibility for running public services to the community for whom they should be provided. Constituents have already paid for these services through their council tax and are then expected to pay with their time by running them. It needs to be recognised that localism is the consequence of an austerity government. When a government neglects those who are most vulnerable in society by decreasing support for job seekers and slashing the budgets of schools and the NHS, so often the role of teacher, advisor, and support worker falls to librarian. Whilst localism and community-managed libraries allow for the configuration of services that are going to benefit the surrounding community the most, volunteerism compromises the confidentiality and equity that a professional librarian is able to provide. There needs to be greater investment into the training of librarians and information professionals including on-the-job training and career development. A librarian is the frontline of a library service and is no longer the outdated stereotype of someone who restocks shelves and berates users for being too noisy.

Libraries' abilities to think creatively have been integral in their survival so far. Innovation can be used as an umbrella term for any type of non-traditional aspect of the library service such as additional services, digital resources, renovation, events, and organisational models. Community-management is just one example of innovative organisational models. Reading initiatives are used as tools to promote reading for enjoyment, which in turn boosts health and well-being. Health services and collections are used as outreach techniques to connect with members of the community who struggle with accessing and understanding health information. These services are most important to those who have suffered from the consequences of social exclusion.

It is important to note that libraries are unique to each community they serve. Whilst national standards need to be made, such as stock, staff, and facilities, what works for one library will not necessarily work in another due to geographical specific factors such as unemployment rates, housing, average income, and crime rates. It needs to be recognised that these areas of opportunity areas require variable levels of involvement to achieve equity of access.

Libraries need to be redesigned and marketed in a way that will appeal to their main user group, 18–24 year olds, and the presentation of some independent bookshops can be used as a source of inspiration for this. People are investing more time and money into books and reading so the library, whose main function is the provision of books and reading, needs to be pitched as a relaxing and inviting space where they can do just that. This cannot be specific just to urban libraries. Arguably, those in rural areas of the country are those most reliant on their local library which is why rural libraries need top-up development funding in order to support reinvigorating their library services.

The public sector needs to remember and refocus on the library's core offer which is books, reading, and literacy. There have been countless studies into the benefits of reading. A wide selection of books in different formats, genres, and reading ability levels is vital in encouraging people to reading for enjoyment. More can be done at local and national levels to ensure the prioritisation of improving literacy and a love of reading across the nation.

Looking to the future, and how to extend the thinking within this chapter, it would be useful to continue the discussion with management within the public sector, or the UK's Minister for Libraries – and to make comparisons beyond the UK. This would give a greater understanding of the perspective of central government on the importance of sustaining libraries and improving literacy across the country and the actions being taken to ensure that. Case study research into a wide range of libraries, both rural and urban, in the UK would be beneficial to seek out opportunities for development and repositioning in public opinion. It would also aid in evaluating whether their current organisational method is sustainable. Additionally, interviewing librarians, volunteers, and informational professionals would be interested in gaining a greater understanding of the different routes into librarianship and the responsibilities they have of working on the frontline in the library service.

Whilst e-lending has been briefly mentioned, future research could effectively explore the effect that e-books and remote lending (being able to access e-books online away from the library) have on the library service. On the one hand, remote lending is a great tool for libraries to reach new demographics. Young people more attuned to technology as well as vulnerable people such as the elderly or people with disabilities, who can't always make the trip to the local library, are able to access a wide catalogue of titles from any location. Libraries can fulfil their goal of diminishing social exclusion whilst simultaneously aligning their service with the trend of on-demand entertainment that other subscription services provide and increasing lending numbers. On the other hand, remote lending puts the traditional bricks and mortar library at further risk of declining visitor numbers; one of the key metrics for their evaluation. Despite having identified the vast range of services beyond books that libraries offer, footfall is still a key, but identifiably flawed, measurement of a library's success. Further research into remote lending in relation to UK/EU law, authors and publishers would be recommended to understand the impact it has on public libraries.

Concluding overall, there are numerous current barriers to the survival of public libraries in the UK, including funding, misrepresentation, austerity, and the undermining of the librarian profession through localism, barriers that are connected and build connected difficulties. Generally, there is a lack of awareness about what a library, and by extension a librarian, is or does for a community. Arguably due to this lack of awareness, central government has overlooked the importance of public libraries and therefore deemed them an unworthy investment.

Two major conclusions can be drawn. The first is that the responsibility does not solely rest on central government but they have a bigger share of the responsibility for funding a service to allow local government to fulfil their statutory obligation.

By extension, the second is that public libraries need to undergo major transformation of public image. National organisations, such as CILIP or Arts Council England, can continue to advocate for libraries; however, this should be done separately from a government that is arguably working against them. Until funding is secured, individually, libraries need to think of cost-effective ways that they can rebrand themselves to become these hot spots where readers want to come and spend time. Refocussing on their core value of providing books and spaces for reading will support the publishing industry that is continuing to see increases in book sales. If the popularity of the book is growing then there is no reason why libraries should not see the same results.

Note

1 The Chartered Institute of Librarians and Information Professionals, formerly The Library Association, is the professional and representative organisation for librarians and information professionals.

References

Arts Council England (2017). Envisioning the library of the future Phase 1: A review of innovations in library. [online] Available at: www.artscouncil.org.uk/sites/default/files/download-file/Envisioning_the_library_of_the_future_phase_1_a_review_of_innovations_in_library_services.pdf [Accessed: 25th January 2019]

Ball, J. (2018). This is how eight years of spending cuts have affected the welfare state. *Huffington Post* [online] Available at: www.huffingtonpost.co.uk/entry/austerity-bites-public-sector-cuts_uk_5b8c48e9e4b0cf7b0037608f?guccounter=1&guce_referrer=aHR0cHM6Ly93d3cuZ29vZ2xlLmNvbvbS8&guce_referrer_sig=AQAAAFH-rb5_WuK92hJec1Iko0xaJjRmdANksfsFYTyv1SM1DhWhO7fmPwBtITltAP_5qsmyPrt79sfZukCrs6lDlxCzzvsne4hQGVHnponBEKR9OI3EMRwip--rLk_kLLQPiu-aFFq-YVKTDSh4AgzFR5G-LcV14npy2VUR9pJd3lEN [Accessed: 13th February 2019]

Barnett, D. (2018). Do libraries run by volunteers check out? *The Guardian* [online] Available at: www.theguardian.com/books/2018/jun/25/do-libraries-run-by-volunteers-check-out [Accessed: 13th February 2019]

BBC News. (2016). Book borrowing figures show library habits are changing. *BBC News* [online] Available at: www.bbc.co.uk/news/uk-england-35788332 [Accessed: 13th February 2019]

BBC News. (2016). Libraries lose a quarter of staff as hundreds close. *BBC News* [online] Available at: www.bbc.co.uk/news/uk-england-35707956 [Accessed: 25th January 2019]

BBC News. (2016). Libraries: The decline of a profession? *BBC News* [online] Available at: www.bbc.co.uk/news/uk-england-35724957 [Accessed: 13th February 2019]

Booksellers Association. (2012). Bookselling and the BA 2012: The Annual Report from the BA [online] Available at: www.flipsnack.com/FF6A8D5C5A8/annual-report-2012.html [Accessed: 13th February 2019]

Cabinet Office. (2006). *Context for social exclusion work.* Available at: https://web archive.nationalarchives.gov.uk/20061211103855/www.cabinetoffice.gov.uk/social_exclusion_task_force/context/ [Accessed: 13th February 2019]

Cain, S. (2018). Nearly 130 public libraries closed across Britain in the last year. *The Guardian* [online] Available at: www.theguardian.com/books/2018/dec/07/nearly-130-public-libraries-closed-across-britain-in-the-last-year [Accessed: 13th February 2019]

Carr, N. (2008). Is Google making us stupid? *The Atlantic* [online] Available at: www.theatlantic.com/magazine/archive/2008/07/is-google-making-us-stupid/306868/ [Accessed: 13th February 2019]

CILIP. (2018). Commitment to professional ethics by CILIP members. Available at: https://cdn.ymaws.com/www.cilip.org.uk/resource/resmgr/cilip/policy/new_ethical_framework/cilip_s_ethical_framework.pdf [Accessed: 13th February 2019]

CILIP. (2018). Libraries for the many, not the few. *Labour Party Conference* [online] Available at: www.cilip.org.uk/page/Librariesforthemany [Accessed: 13th February 2019]

CIPFA. (2018). Libraries lose branches and staff as spending continues to drop. *CIPFA.org* [online] Available at: www.cipfa.org/about-cipfa/press-office/latest-press-releases/libraries-lose-branches-and-staff-as-spending-continues-to-drop [Accessed: 13th February 2019]

Department for Digital, Culture, Media and Sport. (2016). Libraries deliver: Ambition for public libraries in England 2016 to 2021 [online] Available at: www.gov.uk/government/publications/libraries-deliver-ambition-for-public-libraries-in-england-2016-to-2021/libraries-deliver-ambition-for-public-libraries-in-england-2016-to-2021#the-outcomes-libraries-deliver-for-their-communities [Accessed: 13th February 2019]

Department for Digital, Culture, Media and Sport. (2017). Research and analysis to explore the service effectiveness and sustainability of community managed libraries in England [online] Available at: www.gov.uk/government/publications/research-

and-analysis-to-explore-the-service-effectiveness-and-sustainability-of-community-managed-libraries-in-england/research-and-analysis-to-explore-the-service-effective ness-and-sustainability-of-community-managed-libraries-in-england#conclusions-and-recommendations [Accessed: 13th February 2019]

Dudman, J (2018) Books are the best medicine: how libraries boost our wellbeing. *The Guardian* [online] Available here: www.theguardian.com/society/2018/oct/10/books-best-medicine-how-libraries-boost-wellbeing [Accessed: 29th October 2018]

Flood, A. (2017). Save your local! Should volunteers help keep our public libraries open? *The Guardian* [online] Available at: www.theguardian.com/books/2017/aug/08/public-libraries-at-the-crossroads-should-volunteers-be-keeping-them-open [Accessed: 13th February 2019]

Flood, A. (2019). 'Leading the entertainment pack': UK print book sales rise again. *The Guardian* [online] Available at: www.theguardian.com/books/2019/jan/03/leading-the-entertainment-pack-uk-print-book-sales-rise-again [Accessed: 13th February 2019]Fujiwara et al. (2015). The health and wellbeing benefits of public libraries. *Arts Council England* [online] Available at: www.artscouncil.org.uk/sites/default/files/download-file/The%20health%20and%20wellbeing%20benefits%20of%20public%20libraries.pdf [Accessed: 13th February 2019]

Harris, J. (2017). The Tories are savaging libraries – And closing the book on social mobility. *The Guardian* [online] Available at: www.theguardian.com/commentisfree/2017/dec/15/tories-libraries-social-mobility-conservative [Accessed: 29th October 2018]

Jenkins, S. (2016). Libraries are dying – But it's not about the books. *The Guardian* [online] Available at: www.theguardian.com/commentisfree/2016/dec/22/libraries-dying-books-internet [Accessed: 25th January 2019]

McColvin, L. (1942). *The public library system in Great Britain*. London: The Library Association.

McMenemy, D. (2018). Public libraries in the UK – History and values: Historical development of public libraries and library 'faith'. *University of Strathclyde*. Available at: https://cdn.ymaws.com/www.cilip.org.uk/resource/resmgr/cilip_new_website/plss/l1_and_l2_ethics.pdf [Accessed: 13th February 2019]

McMenemy, D. (2018). Public libraries in the UK – History and values: Public libraries – Service for all? *University of Strathclyde*. Available at: https://cdn.ymaws.com/www.cilip.org.uk/resource/resmgr/cilip_new_website/plss/l1_and_l2_ethics.pdf [Accessed: 13th February 2019]

Morton, B. (2018). Why more people are using these libraries. *BBC News* [online] Available at: www.bbc.co.uk/news/uk-46504759 [Accessed: 13th February 2019]

Public Libraries and Museums Act 1964, c. 75. Available at: www.legislation.gov.uk/ukpga/1964/75/section/7 [Accessed: 13th February 2019]

Sieghart, W. (2014). Independent library report for England. *Department for Culture, Media and Sport* [online] Available at: https://assets.publishing.service.gov.uk/government/uploads/system/uploads/attachment_data/file/388989/Independent_Library_Report-_18_December.pdf [Accessed: 13th February 2019]

Swaffield, J. (2017) The UK no longer has a national public library system. *The Guardian* [online] Available at: www.theguardian.com/voluntary-sector-network/2017/oct/19/uk-national-public-library-system-community [Accessed: 29th October 2018]

Unknown. (1961). *The Oxford English Dictionary*. Volume VI L-M. London: Oxford University Press.

UNISON National (2014). Cuts to local services. *UNISON.org.uk* [online] Available at: www.unison.org.uk/at-work/local-government/key-issues/cuts-to-local-services/#heading-9 [Accessed: 13th February 2019]

5

HOW CAN SHARED-READING CREATE A COMMUNITY?

What *The Kingston University Big Read* and *The University of Mississippi Common Reading Experience* have in common, and learned from each other

Alison Baverstock

Introduction

Kingston University (KU) and The University of Mississippi (UM) run pre-arrival shared-reading for their new students: *The Kingston University Big Read* (KUBR) and *The University of Mississippi Common Reading Experience* (UMCRE). Both are designed to ease student transition between school and university education through an institution-wide initiative, and help new arrivals settle in.

Literature review

Pre-arrival shared-reading is relatively common within US universities, but more described than analysed, perhaps because generally orchestrated within departments of marketing or communications rather than academic. UK involvement is much rarer, although the University of Hertfordshire has created *Connect*, a common reading experience for first years (University of Hertfordshire, 2017) developed in partnership with a US collaborator (The University of North Carolina, Wilmington) and UK universities have been encouraged by The ManBooker Foundation to read and subsequently host visits to university campuses of previously shortlisted authors (Man Booker Foundation, 2017).

Associated aims are generally lofty and broad-ranging. Michael Ferguson carried out a study of US colleges involved and commented 'common reading programs of all types are helping bridge divides on campus: between disciplines, between student life and academic affairs, between the orientation period and the first semester' (Ferguson, 2006, p.10). Similarly, The *Go Big Read* run by the University of Wisconsin-Madison aims to 'engage members of the campus community and beyond in a shared, academically focussed reading experience. Students, faculty, staff, and community members are invited to participate by reading the book, and taking part in classroom discussions and campus events' (University of Wisconsin-Madison, 2017). Lavine Laufgraben (2006) describes how in the US, programmes like these promote 'discussion and respect for diverse viewpoints'. Tienda (2013, p.470) argues that a shared read can mitigate the tendency to 'sort into islands of comfortable consensus' that can develop within institutions that have diverse populations but do not necessarily mix. R. Mark Hall (2003, p.659) promotes the idea that such schemes should be fun rather than purely academic, drawing people into their new community. Help with settling in can be particularly appreciated by mature students, who may be nervous about reengaging with education (ORA Prep, 2014).

How the book is chosen varies, with a panel usually involved. At Gustavus Adolphus College in Minnesota the shared title for their *Reading-in-Common* programme is 'selected the year before by a panel made up of faculty, staff, and students' (Twiton, 2007). Washington State University (WSU) explains that their 'Common Reading Selection Committee typically accepts many nominations from the community and beyond in fall semester, and then its members begin carefully reviewing each nominated book' (Washington State University, 2017). Ferguson noted that 'many campuses pick books that enable discussion of US and global diversity' (ibid, p.8), citing Albion College's using shared-reading to 'begin student understanding of differences' and 'provide an entry for students into the ideas of global citizenship'. Otterbein involves students in the choice: 'A committee of faculty, staff, and students select from over fifty books each year in an effort to find a significant contemporary work to read the next year'.

How the book is used also varies. Some US colleges integrate the book into a year-long programme, relating its themes to all aspects of the incoming student's experience and embedding the book within a 'year-long discussion of an academic theme derived from common book issues by exploring it in classes, residence halls, and co-curricular programming. This common reading experience involves all incoming first-year students, faculty, many staff members, and student leaders' (Otterbein University, 2017). Others concentrate on events around orientation and enrolment, encouraging more informal discussion, such as through online forums and welcome week events and in this context Ferguson cites Ball State University (ibid, p.9). Many US colleges give out the book during the summer orientation week for the incoming students, an opportunity not generally available to US universities. In the UK, the University of Hertfordshire embeds *Connect* events on campus throughout the first semester, encouraging academics to 'incorporate the text into a course you teach or programme you work with' and 'share expertise as a guest speaker in another class or for a *Connect* event'.

How long ahead of book circulation the planning should begin is a significant question. One Book, One Community (2003) recommends at least six months, if not more, and emphasises the importance of generating a variety of different marketing materials to reach the full range of individuals and departments who could be involved and encourage participation.

In both the US and the UK, information on the planning and outcomes of shared-reading schemes within wider media, particularly broadcast, may be relevant. The television book clubs delivered by Oprah Winfrey (1996–2011) and Richard and Judy (2004 onwards, from 2011 run as a website after the programme ended in 2010) have drawn strong levels of audience participation and arguably boosted a sense of community, and hence may have relevance for those organising pre-arrival shared-reading within universities (Rooney, 2005; Cooke, 2009).

Methodology

The link between those running the schemes in Mississippi and Kingston was made by Associate Professor Debora Wenger, Head of Undergraduate Journalism Program at The University of Mississippi who did her PhD at Kingston University. Her supervisor there was Associate Professor Alison Baverstock, from Kingston's Department of Journalism and Publishing, but also Director of *The Kingston University Big Read*. On a visit to the US in April 2017, Baverstock sought an opportunity to talk to her counterparts at the University of Mississippi and this was established through a Skype conference call on 25 April 2017, involving colleagues in the UK and the US.

Those taking part were:

UK colleagues: Alison Baverstock (Director, KUBR), Laura Bryars (Administrator, KUBR), Wendy Morris (Library Champion, KUBR), Fay Keegan and Jenny May (Library Information Advisors, KU), and Joanne Moulton (Director of Libraries, Museums and Archives, Royal Borough of Kingston).

US colleagues: Leslie Banahan (Assistant Vice Chancellor for Student Affairs), Melissa Dennis (Head of Research and Instruction in the UM Library and the librarian who spearheaded the One Book project), and Dewey Knight (Associate Director of the First-Year Experience).

During the conference call, colleagues from Kingston and Mississippi exchanged ideas on how shared-reading worked in their two institutions and found it reassuring to see how much the two schemes had in common, and particularly how many of the features of the respective projects and associated ethos had been arrived at independently. This paper reports on overlaps, differences, and what was learned in the process for future development.

Project origins

The University of Mississippi's Common Reading Experience (UMCRE) began with the 2011–2012 school year; the Kingston University Big Read (KUBR) in 2015–2016. Both of these programmes were developed out of extensive research conducted prior to implementation. For the UMCRE, various units within the university were developing independent programming, without pursuing a larger collaborative effort. The library instituted a 'One Book, One Community' project in 2010 that touched on all areas of the UMCRE that formed later that year.

Dr Baverstock, co-founder of MA Publishing at Kingston, had a long-term interest in the value and role of shared community reading. She had first heard of pre-arrival shared-reading within universities at a US conference – the International Conference of the Book in Boston where the practice was so well established that papers were offered on aspects of the process (e.g. Grenier, 2006). Since then she had looked for a way to organise something similar at Kingston, raising the idea at boards of study in several faculties. An opportunity for associated research arose through a student-staff research project as part of a wider initiative to improve the outcomes within higher education (HE) of students who have not traditionally thrived.

In Kingston the funding for the initial research project came from the Student Academic Development Research Associate Scheme (SADRAS), which has its origins in a successful proposal to the Higher Education Academy in 2012 to implement a Students as Partners programme, and is funded through the Access Working Group. The scheme is jointly managed by the Centre for Higher Education Research and Practice (CHERP) and the Kingston University Students Union (KUSU).

SADRAS aims to encourage students and staff, in equal partnership, to undertake educational research with the purpose of improving the academic experience of students at the university, particularly those from under-represented groups. It facilitates, in part, the enactment of the university's strategy of *Led by Learning* by enabling Kingston students to actively contribute to course development as part of a learning community. It is intended that such work will encourage collaboration between students and staff, enabling students to both provide a perspective on how the student experience might be improved and undertake paid research in an academic environment.

Both students and staff are invited to submit a project proposal that has a focus covered by the overarching themes of progression, attainment, and employability of Kingston University students. It is expected that the majority of successfully funded projects will focus on students who have not traditionally thrived within HE, notably BAME (black, Asian, minority ethnic), first-generation students, carers, or those from a care background, mature students, commuters, and parents.

The associated SADRAS research (reported in Baverstock et al., 2016) confirmed a strong appetite for pre-arrival shared-reading within the 2014–2015 cohort and the decision to launch a scheme of pre-arrival shared-reading was made for the following year. This was however to involve the entire university population, so as not to further marginalise the intended beneficiaries; The Kingston University Big Read (KUBR) was launched in 2015.

Project leadership

A planning committee drives the UMCRE project, with faculty and staff volunteering time to develop and implement the scheme with bi-weekly meetings each year, backed by funding from the Office of the Provost (a member of the university's senior management team). The collaborative team consists of

Leslie Banahan (Assistant Vice Chancellor for Student Affairs); Melissa Dennis (Head of Research & Instruction in the library and the librarian who spearheaded the One Book project); Kirk Johnson (Associate Professor of Sociology & African American Studies); Dewey Knight (Associate Director of the First-Year Experience); Stephen Monroe (Assistant Dean of College of Liberal Arts and Assistant Professor of Writing and Rhetoric); and the committee's chair, Robert Cummings (Chair of the Department of Writing and Rhetoric). The planning committee coordinates the event committee, resource guide committee, and the book selection committee, which is a separate larger committee with student, faculty, and staff voices helping decide on a new book each year. A Kingston colleague commented:

> There is clearly a dedicated team on Mississippi's end, all of whom seem to be completely on board with making the most of the project. This seems to be a huge benefit for them and allows them to get more done in the way of really engaging events. There are one or more events every month starting in August – some of these can also go towards students' grades if they attend.

At Kingston, the project was initially backed by the University Vice Chancellor (VC) Julius Weinberg and corresponding funding awarded by the VC's Department. The initial project was developed by the Course Leader for MA Publishing (Dr. Alison Baverstock) working with five students on a voluntary basis. As the project grew, her increasing involvement gained official funding through a half-time leadership role from January 2016 as Project Director, with a half-time fractional role in support, this position initially occupied by Laura Bryars, one of the students who had worked on the initial project. Support from the University Learning Resource Centre (LRC) was allocated in the form of an LRC KUBR Champion, Wendy Morris with other support on a voluntary basis.

After the departure of Professor Weinberg as VC in September 2016 the project's somewhat fluid siting was transferred from the VC's Department and formally located within the Faculty of Arts and Social Sciences under the sponsorship of the faculty Dean, Professor Simon Morgan-Wortham. While this fitted with the project's status as a research project, and with the location of the Director of the KU Big Read within the Department of Journalism and Publishing, it was perhaps not ideal in terms of representing a project that reaches across the whole university.

At Kingston the processes of choosing the book were reported on through organisational emails and featured on both staff and student intranets. The sponsoring dean and VC were informed of the panel's final choice, and offered the opportunity to intervene, but the proposed choice progressed without intervention.

> The Provost (higher management) has final approval on the book choice at Mississippi and could potentially veto it (though hasn't done so yet).
> I really like that at KU we don't do this – the Selection Committee's choice has so far been final.
>
> *Kingston colleague*

Project status

At Mississippi University, the project is a shared initiative across several departments, through which every first-year student receives a copy of the selected text during 'Orientation' (when prospective new students visit to find out about their upcoming studies) for them to read before the school year begins the following August. Instructors from the Department of Writing and Rhetoric, First-Year Experience, and others utilise the text in their classes. The programme aspires to achieve an enriched sense of academic community through a communal reading of the text.

At Kingston University, the KUBR is classified as a research project, seeking to monitor delivery and the effectiveness of outcomes. This was deliberate, as the project developed on the basis of observing pre-arrival shared-reading in the US (and to a very limited extent in the UK) and such schemes were generally *described* within marketing literature rather than *analysed*. In addition to wanting to use shared-reading to promote positive outcomes, the team spotted a research gap. It is also anticipated that the project, which began with research, could form a potential Impact Case Study for the forthcoming Research Excellence Framework (REF), which seeks to monitor the quality of research in the UK's HE system.[1]

Choosing a book to share

Both universities ask staff and students from across the institution to nominate titles and receive similar numbers of suggestions (around 140 per institution). The populations of the two institutions are similar in size (Kingston: 20,000 students and 2,000 staff; Mississippi: 24,000 students and 4,000 staff). Both institutions had appointed a cross-organisational selection committee of around 20 members to select the book.

The process at UM was rigorously organised, based on a structured representation from across the organisation within a three-year term, with rolling membership so only a third of the panel is new at any one time, where co-chairs and a senior member are permanent, and three students rotate with a one-year appointment. The committee strives to balance current representation of its members to assure diverse views from students, faculty, staff, alumni, schools, and disciplines within the University, as well as instructors from courses and programmes that incorporate the common read into their curricula.

The decision to go ahead with the launch of a reading scheme at Kingston was based on SADRAS research into the attitudes of first-year students in 2014–2015 through a survey asking about their involvement in reading and likely attitudes towards taking part in pre-arrival shared-reading. Receiving very positive responses, a decision was made to go ahead – and a book to read hence needed at very short notice. Kingston's VC chose *About a Boy* by Nick Hornby, a Kingston graduate. Since then Kingston has sought to involve the entire institution in choosing the book and made progress in widening staff involvement in book selection.

Having asked for suggested titles from across the university, in both 2015 and 2016 Kingston reduced those suggested down to a shortlist of six through a specially created algorithm, noting the criteria that would make a significant institutional choice (e.g. availability of author; length of book; gender-neutral cover) and then weighting these according to importance. This produced a shortlist that could be read by the selection panel – and there were two meetings at which books were presented, discussed, and a choice made.

There had been determined attempts to ensure broad involvement in this panel: for example, inviting colleagues from catering, delivery, reception, and facilities management. So far however, the panel had been created on a year-by-year basis, asking for volunteers and building up a waiting list of those who would like to be involved. This was a lot of work, and while it never achieved full organisational representation, it did enable the inclusion of students and staff members eager to be involved in the programme.

> I rather like the idea of a formal steering committee – we do in a sense have this in that we have key figures (Alison, Laura, Wendy) who determine most next steps but I agree it would be great to have it formalised, perhaps with a Dean on board for regular meetings to decide future plans.
>
> *Kingston colleague*

Within UM the committee meets weekly from mid-October to mid-January. Members divide up every nomination received through the website, deciding as a group when to close nominations and prepare brief reports on each nomination in order to consider the merits of all reported books so that a narrow list of five to six acceptable books emerges through discussion and deliberation based on suitability, author availability, and costs of books and speaking fees. This process requires significantly more meeting time and commitment from the volunteers than the KU model.

> This results in a long (three-year) Selection Committee term. This means it would be difficult to include the student voice in the same way, as in general they volunteer towards the end of their time at the university.
>
> *UM colleague*

Selection criteria

UM has established the following guidelines for the selection panel when choosing a text:

- Less than 400 pages
- Available in paperback format
- Accessible to students at all levels
- Accessible to community readers

- Multiple themes that are applicable to many disciplines
- Published in the last five years
- Written by a living author
- Written by an author available to speak on campus in the fall of the year of selection
- Written by an author available to interact with students on campus in the fall of the year of selection

> 400 pages seems to be the magic number in Mississippi – this I found interesting as we have found ours to be shorter (250–350 pages) by comparison.
>
> *Kingston colleague*

The criteria for Kingston's algorithm were more numerous, and were established through another SADRAS research project, again working as student-staff collaborators. A range of criteria were established, nominations sought, and the highlighted books were graded. However books that did not meet the criteria were not excluded, rather titles were graded according to the extent to which they met the criteria (so a book of 400 pages would receive a lower score than a book of 300 pages), and weighted so the most important criteria had a more significant impact on the outcome (so 'ability to attend' would be more important than 'other titles in print'). The criteria established were:

- An author able to attend
- Author diversity (Kingston is one of the most diverse universities in the world; the student and staff body includes representatives from over 150 different nationalities with a considerable population of international students)
- A well-known author
- An author with several titles available (so a reading journey could be begun)
- A recent title
- Currency of title (time in which the story is set; books describing years from 2000 onwards were given the highest score as it was within the living memory of students involved)
- Page count (optimum extent would be 250–350 pages, but a shorter book would still be preferable to a long one)
- Page size as expected (variation between publishers and their standard paperback sizes was allowed for)
- Gender-neutral cover (although this could have been worked around, by creating Kingston's own cover, it was thought important for students to see that a *real* book had been purchased for them that was also available in shops, enhancing their perception of a saleable/valuable item, that they were being given for nothing)

- Genre (findings to the pre-project research had shown that the specific appeal of fantasy, science fiction, romance, and thrillers had all drawn lower support than a more mainstream title that might appeal more broadly across the community)
- Location of plot (Kingston coded positively for a book set in an urban environment in order to instil a sense of geographical familiarity in the arrivals)
- Period in which the book is set (findings of the pre-research project had indicated that a modern setting would resonate more with incoming students)
- Reviews (recognising the likelihood of subjectivity, positive reviews on Amazon given that there was insufficient time to read all the books before grading them)
- Not a book on the school curriculum
- A 'general comments' section (enabling Kingston colleagues to address areas of difficulty for 18-year-olds' first move away from home or the specific issues of their student demographics). There was a unanimous view that the book should be the basis of an ice-breaking conversation that students could have with each other, and for this to be sufficiently deep to motivate conversation but without becoming too controversial, sad, dark, or depressive).

Establishing criteria for scoring the suitability of potential titles; weighting them for importance

At Kingston the various criteria for choice were discussed within a research group (a second student-staff research project conducted through SADRAS) and then each member ranked them in importance, the figures were then averaged out to establish which issues the group considered most important.

The second stage was to weight the criteria into three bands so the titles that achieved the strongest scoring for the factors considered most important would receive the highest scores. After more discussion, the group separated out the important criteria (ability to attend; length of book) from those of middle importance (gender-neutral cover; author well known) to those of least importance (location, currency). They then coded the full range of titles suggested (106 in total). Before finalising the list, the 2015 title *About a Boy* was added in, to see how this fared against others. This was how the shortlist was generated, and it is understood that this is the first computer-based shortlist for a literary prize.

At the two meetings of the Kingston selection panel these factors were briefly reprised, but the main point was the requirement to choose a book that could be read with interest by 18–19-year-olds arriving at their university for the first time. It was accepted that it was not necessary (or indeed possible) to find a book that everyone would approve of, rather those involved were seeking a book that could be universally shared; read with interest and provide themes for wider discussion. For more information see Baverstock et al. (2017b).

Comments on previous book choices

UM found that a few of the previous books used in the scheme had not been particularly successful because they were not accessible to students. Their thoughts on the best kind of book choice are as follows:

- Authors who are also great speakers really help promote involvement
- Authors who not only give a talk but also stay on to interact with classes and staff really encourage involvement
- Short story collections work well, because staff can pick stories that work for them to use in related activities (and do not have to commit to the effort of reading the whole book)
- Memoirs also prove popular in Mississippi if the right person is chosen
- The book presented as their students' first piece of 'coursework' when they come for orientation at the university and at that stage; when both students and parents are very keen!

Kingston have only made three book selections so far – the first was chosen quickly to enable the project to proceed, the next two by means of an organisational algorithm. The reactions to the books have been varied, mostly considered a good choice but with a small minority of vociferous complainers each time. Kingston have consistently sought to emphasise, in all project communications, that the university is seeking a book that can be read with confidence and enjoyment, targeting 18–19-year-olds about to begin university. General acceptance that the title is for them has helped offset some academic criticism about the book being less challenging than some of the critics would prefer.

Working with publishers

Once Kingston University had reached its shortlist, the Project Director contacted the associated publishers to find out if (a) their author was available to come to the university and talk to staff and students, (b) they would be willing to make a special edition of the book available at a reasonable price, this to be based on purchasing a significant number of copies but including the payment of the author royalty. If the publishers were willing to collaborate, then they were confirmed as part of the shortlist for reading by the cross-university panel.

The University of Mississippi's Common Reading Experience Group did not negotiate with publishers before short-listing, but rather reached out to publishers and agents when titles were shortlisted to let them know of potential interest and to try to discover any pertinent conflicts before making the final choice. Some books could therefore be excluded at the short-listing stage because a viable deal with the publishers could not be made/the author's fee was too large, and one year a popular short-listed title did not make it to the final cut because the author refused to come to the campus to speak. Mississippi colleagues admired the Kingston model of finding out whether all the titles/authors were available before announcing the shortlist as they had found it stressful trying to negotiate with publishers after the shortlist had been announced. Kingston colleagues' comments included:

> I do think we have a better system of approaching the publishers (prior to announcing the shortlist rather than after). So far, no publisher has come back to us saying they can't do it and I feel all parties go in knowing exactly what is expected early on our way. Approaching after could result in disappointment.
>
> In our first year, it took a while before we heard back from some of the publishers that they would like to take part, even though we were wanting to buy large quantities of books. Now we have publishers contacting us to ask if they can submit titles for consideration, and publishing services companies offering to produce our book for us.
>
> US universities pay their authors generously to attend and speak to students. I admit, I felt very lucky when they mentioned the high author fees ($20k-$80k) they have to pay in Mississippi – largely due to market expectations and the high expense of long-distance travel. In the UK, authors have been well entertained and their travel and accommodation funded but not otherwise remunerated.

It should however be born in mind that in the US flights, tiring journeys and longer distances would be required to support any author visit. Pre-arrival shared-reading is much less established in the UK and so not seen as a standard cost; had large fees been required it is very likely the project would not have taken place. The view also taken in the UK was that with a guaranteed large sale of books, and with the author royalty assured, the author was being effectively remunerated already, although their (first class) travelling expenses were all covered and they were hospitably entertained throughout. Kingston has also so far awarded an honorary degree to the author of each of their first three Kingston University Big Reads.

Specific editions of the chosen book

Both Kingston and UM produce special editions of the books. The UM edition has a cover and spine logo and a letter from the organisational head, but no other additional features. Kingston produced a bespoke edition featuring a letter from the Vice Chancellor; information on the scheme; feedback from previous participants; and, in the back of the book, reading group style questions. Kingston thought the addition of the university logo to the spine a very good idea and planned to incorporate next time.

Creating a bespoke edition has also prompted Kingston colleagues to develop their own associated value propositions, for example one librarian repeatedly presented it to students as valuable because it was a 'limited edition' and another pointed out that copies were never seen lying around, in waste-bins or being used as coffee mats.

Creating a bespoke edition, which cannot be returned to the publishers if it fails to sell, is a positive to the UK publishing industry, which routinely effectively loans stock to book retailers as it can be returned if it does not sell. The 'firm sale' nature of the transaction supporting shared-reading is a useful basis on which to negotiate an advantageous price, and the potential for incremental sales on the other titles by the same author is also an inducement to cooperate; in 2015 Penguin reported a spike in sales for Nick Hornby's other titles, which they felt was related to his choice that year as the first KU Big Read.

How the book is distributed/associated cost

The University of Mississippi hands out books to students for the forthcoming academic year at orientation events in May, when students for the next academic year visit the campus to prepare for their arrival the following September. Thus they do not incur a postage charge, gain the approval of parents, and get the book to students quickly.

Lacking this general opportunity (Kingston University does not run Orientation events for all forthcoming students), Kingston liaises with the University's Data Management Team to despatch the data for prospective students to a mailing house and then mails the book to students who meet the entry criteria for a place. There are three mailings: to those with unconditional places, to those who have met their entry grades (this taking place as soon as the grades for 'A' level are announced in August), and to those who gain a place after Clearing. The free book is thus the first communication received from the university they plan to join and receipt has the potential to make a significant impression on recipients and impact on their decision to both enrol and turn up:

> I could not believe it when my new university sent a book all the way to me in Brazil.
>
> *2016–17 Kingston Master's student*

Mailing the book in a polylope (plastic envelope) ensures the jacket is visible and the attractive contents can be seen by all, thus functioning as wider marketing of the university. Several students reported that their parents had been unable to resist their curiosity about the contents, and opened the package before they were home. While certainly annoying, this also demonstrated the attractive nature of the package.

Kingston hands the books out within pre-arrival orientation schemes for specific groups (e.g. Compact Scheme[2] attendees, International student orientation) and makes them available to existing students and staff through personal collection from libraries and reception desks throughout the institution.

Cost of books

At UM, the committee was able to add a $15 sum to the Orientation fee to cover book costs and help maintain a sustainable programme going forward. This allows a substantial book order of about 6,000–7,000 copies at less than market cost, where all faculties receive a customised version of the text and all incoming students. Staff may request copies as needed. Funds left over can support events and roll over into next year's book budget. Kingston makes it available free to all. But book costs are lower in the UK – a paperback novel in the US generally has a cover price of about $10. Kingston colleagues commented:

> Great idea raised by Mississippi which they have been doing recently – embedding a $15 fee into their already existing orientation fee (final fee total unknown) which will easily cover the cost of the books and some, if not all, of the events.
>
> Free books handed to students when they arrive (parents who come can also purchase, alumni also able to purchase – made available in campus bookshops which obviously we don't have). Though different method of getting books to the students, both ours and theirs seems to work best for the type of campus we have.

At Kingston the book is free to recipients. While student responders to post-project surveys were adamant that the book should remain free, they are unlikely to say it should not be. Free also means that the project is vulnerable and subject to political instability depending on changing faculty/organisational priorities. Kingston staff have worked hard to ensure the project both is and feels owned across the institution, especially by colleagues in marketing and communications. When the project was nominated within the University Staff Awards, the nomination included a colleague from every department that had supported (e.g. data management, delivery, communications, catering, reception, library, administrative, and academic staff). The project won 'Best University Project of the Year' in 2016.

The impact of the title being free on overall perceptions of both book and project quality, and on the overall effectiveness of the scheme, has been explored in a paper (Baverstock and Somerville, 2018a).

How the book gets used

Both universities seek to establish the book within welcome activities and academic programmes. For UM, the Common Read is consistently incorporated into first-year writing classes and first-year transition classes, as well as a few others depending on the themes of the book chosen that year. The goal of the programme is to support student learning outcomes. The Resource Guide produced by UM states that 'by reading, writing, and learning together through the shared experience of the UMCRE, students:

- Expand critical thinking, reading, writing, and research skills
- Build an emerging sense of confidence as learners, thinkers, readers, and writers
- Develop a sense of community among peers, neighbours, and instructors
- Establish connections among ideas, experiences, disciplines, and academics
- Relate the issues raised by the common book to their lives as students'.

A small sub-committee develops a Resource Guide each summer to distribute to fall instructors. This helpful teaching tool describes useful activities and approaches to teaching themes from the book, and lists supporting events that writing and first-year transition instructors use to incorporate the Common Read into assignments without overlapping into areas taught by other classes.

At Kingston regular emails are sent out to all who have expressed interest in the project, and information is included in staff training days and featured on both staff and student intranet, on screen-messaging, and within other opportunities. Discussion of the book is used within Kingston's Written and Oral Skills Workshops and within a STEM academic writing class in 2016. There are also many academics using the project in a personal way (e.g. within tutor meetings and to get to know tutorial students); this is a significant area for development. Having secured the inclusion of messaging about the Big Read included in email outreach to arriving students, they arrive expecting to discuss the book – and getting academics to include it is still quite patchy. As illustration, here are some Kingston staff comments from the post-delivery survey:

Question: Did you decide *not* to include activities/discussion related to The KU Big Read within your early contact with students? If so it would be helpful if you could tell us why.

Answer: 'because I wasn't informed about what or how to use it...'

(In fact regular emails had gone out and links had been provided to resources on the intranet accessed by all staff making suggestions for how the title could be used. Meetings had been organised to support staff seeking to include the scheme within welcome activities, and an outline power-point had been provided to further support project inclusion).

Answer: 'My early contact with them was limited to an individual tutorial, in which I tended to focus on their transition to HE. I know this project is aimed at enabling that, but it felt alien to me, partly because I had not read the book and partly because I had to address other issues in that time and could not relate the book to any other learning or teaching I had done with them'.

(Feedback from Kingston's post-project surveys consistently showed that academic responders underestimated student enthusiasm for the scheme.)

For the future, more effort to persuade academics of the value of taking part is clearly needed. Kingston staff subsequently followed the UM example and have produced a Resource Guide each year.

Level of internal support

Both universities had found that perhaps the most natural anticipated disciplinary allies for the project had not necessarily been keen on involvement. In both institutions colleagues from disciplines where study of literature is a fundamental activity were willing to choose the book on behalf of the project, or curate its selection, and quick to recommend their own/departmental colleagues' titles as the book to be chosen for shared-reading, but were not particularly willing to be part of negotiations with other departments for whom evaluating the respective merits of literature was not their primary concern.

At Kingston, staff surveys captured mostly very positive responses to both project and book choice. A few responses however were negative, mentioning that it was not a book they would otherwise have chosen to read and was not to their taste. In the case of colleagues subsequently finding that not all their new students had either read or finished the book, some felt that their time in reading it had been wasted. There were a couple of references to a book being chosen for the university as compromising the important principle of academic independence over the selection of resources for study, and there were also a few comments that it would have been more appropriate to choose a book by a member of Kingston University staff (although in fact Nick Hornby, author of the first KU Big Read, was a Kingston graduate). Negative comments on the scheme were however a consistently small minority within the overall feedback gained (see Baverstock, Steinitz and Bryars, 2017a).

It was also notable from responses to the staff survey that *not* approving the choice of book correlated with not having read it/read much of it. Similar findings appeared at UM, where student and instructor surveys were given to those involved in a class that used the book. The minority of students with the most negative comments were typically those who did not read all of the text.

At UM, book selection committee members who disagreed with a short-list selection that was not a book they personally advocated for sometimes felt disappointed with the process or direction of the programme. This was a rare occurrence, but always involved faculty who did not teach students using the book in first-year classes and preferred more rigor in the content. Like colleagues at Kingston, UM found that not everyone was always pleased with the book selection, and some voiced their disapproval through surveys, departmental/faculty emails or anecdotal feedback. Overall, the programme has been very well received, with many instructors, administrators, and students responding with positive feedback.

At Kingston post-project interviewing also made it clear that there was strong enthusiasm for the project from administrative and professional staff who reported feeling more 'joined up' and 'connected' after the first KU Big Read. The book had been used for team-building and informal discussion in a variety of departments including Finance and Estates, and Human Resources and Staff Engagement had used the book as an incentive. The reception team felt that involvement in handing out the book had drawn attention to their pan-university role and the library too felt that their profile had been significantly raised. Certainly the surveys revealed that the project and book were widely discussed – even if the book was not always read. At Kingston the project played a significant part in institutional connectedness, particularly significant at a time of big change.

Key library role

In both institutions the library played a key part in project dissemination and success.

Kingston was very quick to appreciate and acknowledge the key role played by librarians in spreading both information and enthusiasm about KUBR. Their involvement helped get the project on the agenda at institutional meetings from which packed or pre-agreed agendas meant the project could otherwise have been excluded, and contributed significantly to the project's internal/external profile.

Library involvement at UM was similarly extensive, but rather directed into organising a lot of the events supporting the Common Read Experience (CRE). For example, to support *Ten Little Indians* the library organised a lot of diverse and unusual events such as a social dance hosted by local Choctaw Indians. Kingston thought this a model of librarian proactivity that could be built on, with their Learning Resource Centre staff organising more. For example, the book has since been included in all campus events during Libraries Week, Mental Health Awareness Week, and various themed teaching weeks.

The UM library produce an accompanying online Resource Guide that connects with the teaching guide, but also helps anyone interested in the Common Read to find similar books, articles that explore themes from the book, local events, and websites connected to the book.

> The resource guides are a great idea on the Mississippi side and something we hoped to have available for the students given more time/staff to implement. However, for staff it may be more useful than the presentations we send out which I hadn't considered (having looked through one – it is full of information and guidance which may really benefit the staff in implementing the scheme within classes).
>
> *Kingston colleague*

At Kingston the Director/administrator produced a PowerPoint to support teaching, and the library colleagues added a list of resources in the LRCs that would support study, but this information and resourcing could clearly be developed and managed and more widely. Wendy Morris, Kingston LRC champion for the KU Big Read commented:

> The library could produce a LibGuide[3] – as Edinburgh Napier did.

Alumni involvement

Kingston transferred 1,000 copies to the alumni support department (DARE, which stands for development, alumni relations and engagement) for general distribution, believing there was a strong value to alumni in having a book with their university badge on the cover. UM invites alumni to events but does not provide customised copies of the book. Anyone wanting to make a purchase is directed to local retailers. Wendy Morris of Kingston's LRC commented:

> UM actively involves alumni in their scheme and they seem genuinely flattered to retain an academic connection with their alma mater. I think Kingston could do the same – possibly selling customized copies at an appealingly reduced rate from the retail price, which would still provide a modest profit to support the continued work of the project.

Developing a project to involve alumni became a significant focus for the project. A scheme was subsequently developed – *Big Read Alumni Chapter*[4] – whereby alumni could support the project financially (hopefully with an additional donation) and attend associated events. Advertised by email, it proved extremely attractive with a rapid sign up rate. As many students stay on in Kingston after graduation,[5] the option for local alumni to attend Big Read author events has proven particularly popular.

Project sharing and wider community involvement

Kingston ran the project on its own in 2015 but in 2016 collaborated with Edinburgh Napier University, a university in Scotland with a similar profile and disciplinary range but very different spread of ethnicity. Kingston included them in the process of choosing the book, produced a separate branded edition for their university, and shared press and communications strategies. Subsequently the project expanded to include the University of Wolverhampton, Edge Hill University, and the University of the West of Scotland.

Within their local community, Kingston has shared the project widely, making copies available copies to the local administrative authority (Royal Borough of Kingston) and building a significant alliance with the Director of Libraries, Museums and Archives, which has included dissemination through local libraries and associated events. Kingston also worked with the University of the Third Age[6] and a shelter for the homeless.[7] This won considerable approval within the institution, and led to staff and student volunteering opportunities and placements – as well as a wider range of populations within which to study outcomes.

This has met the civic engagement ambitions for all the organisations involved and helped the Kingston Big Read team maintain the profile of their project (because if external organisations are buying into it, it's arguably esteem-worthy). It also led to a significant opportunity to present the project on a national stage as an example of good practice within a seminar about the future development of libraries (Baverstock and Moulton, 2016; DCMS, 2016).

Along similar lines, seminars have been established between library colleagues in the university and borough, sharing good practice and improving professional connectivity. Kingston had also gained press coverage on the scheme, partly through inviting HE specialists to review the scheme (Frostick, 2015) and also through contributing to sector blogs (Baverstock, 2016a, 2017b).

UM was very interested in the collaborative community efforts as they have seen their own connections with the community at large decrease. Initially, the committee held an essay contest and the winner received a monetary award and a group dinner. Contest winners consisted of a UM student, local high school student, and a community member. The public library and the university library also tried a few times to coordinate a few events at each location, but various changes have widened the gap between the university and the local community more than the UMCRE group would like.

Associated opportunities for wider institutional acknowledgement

The Director of the KU Big Read has provided several references for staff and students involved in KUBR for professional development profiling: for example, the Higher Education Academy Awards and the Kingston Student Award as well as a range of professional awards. This was done for both Kingston University and our collaborative partner in 2016, Edinburgh Napier University.

UM were interested to hear of this and determined to pursue similar opportunities for staff support and institutional acknowledgement.

Working out if it has been successful

At Mississippi, the committee is working towards more assessment of the programme and its impact on the community. Instructors and students using the book in a class are surveyed annually, and enrolment and retention are monitored.

At Kingston the team have used a variety of different metrics, from counting the number of those attending related events and monitoring related traffic on social media to surveying staff and students at the end of the first semester, after the project was over for that year. Kingston have so far published six academic papers in peer-reviewed journals (Baverstock et al., 2016, 2017a, 2017b, 2018a, 2018b, 2019) as well as a range of blogs in professional and book trade publications/ forums (for example, Baverstock, 2016a, 2016b, 2017b; Morris, 2016a, 2016b; Morris and Ennis, 2016). Academic papers have been co-written by the staff and students involved, thus the project continues as a developmental opportunity for research involvement and means that several students and staff members now have a publications section on their CV.

Concluding and looking forward

While the idea behind Kingston's KU Big Read was gained in the US it was developed in an entirely UK context, bearing in mind the particular structures of the UK publishing industry and wider creative economy. The UM scheme had looked to other US universities in how to develop its Common Read, and their programme is a relatively recent arrival within the wider North American shared-reading landscape. Making comparisons between the mechanics and implementation of schemes in the UK and the US proved valuable to both parties – and it was hoped that this relationship would continue in future.

Within both institutions there was clear evidence that a community spirit had developed through involvement in shared-reading, and this resulted from involvement in project development, and wider community engagement as well as reading and discussing the book. In particular, it was the experience of both institutions that in addition to engaging students the projects created lateral links across the institution, building connections between staff from a wide variety of roles and responsibilities.

Finally, the shared involvement resulted in sharing with a wider community of academic practice. Common themes aired in this essay were shared at a joint presentation during the annual First-Year Experience Conference, in San Antonio, Texas, in 2018. Here US delegates were keen to learn how common reading had been developed 'across the pond', and in particular how analysis could be more fully embedded. Penguin's US company featured a blog on the process of what had been learned by the UK from the US, and what could be offered back in return, to the mutual benefit of the communities involved and their likely closer connectivity in future (Baverstock, 2018).

This paper relies on close collaboration with UK and international colleagues: Jackie Steinitz, Laura Bryars, Wendy Morris, Jenny May (Kingston University); Joanne Moulton (Royal Borough of Kingston); Leslie Banahan, Melissa Dennis, Dewey Knight (University of Mississippi).

Notes

1 www.ref.ac.uk/
2 The Compact Scheme at Kingston University aims to support the access, transition, and success of individuals from groups under-represented in higher education. It is available for mature learners, care leavers, students with a disability or specific learning difference, first-generation applicants (i.e. those whose parents have not been to university), and those who have a household income below £25,000. www.kingston.ac.uk/undergraduate/fair-access/compact-scheme/
3 A Libguide is an online resource, commonly used in academic libraries to provide an easy introduction to a specific topic. They are lists of resources in multiple formats, usually short and tailored to a particular audience. As well as books and journals, they might include videos, podcasts, and interactive polls.
4 www.kingston.ac.uk/alumni/get-involved/big-read-alumni-chapter/
5 Kingston's Estates Department estimated in 2015 that 1:8 Kingston homes has someone with a connection to the university (student, staff, or alumnus).
6 www.kingstonu3a.org.uk/
7 www.joelcommunitytrust.org.uk/

References

Baverstock, A. (2016a). '12 tips on how to work across a university.' *Times Higher Education*, 9th February 2016. Available at: www.timeshighereducation.com/blog/12-tips-how-work-across-university

Baverstock, A. (2016b). *Measuring the success of The KU Big Read*. Available at: www.unialliance.ac.uk/blog/2016/06/29/measuring-the-success-of-the-ku-big-read/

Baverstock, A. and Moulton, J. (2016). The KU Big Read, CILIP Conference, 8th December 2016.

Baverstock, A., Steinitz, J., Bryars, L., Kerin, M., Peel, N., Stohler, R. and Waddington, E. (2016). 'The implementation of a shared reading programme within a university: A case study'. *Logos* 2, pp. 48–61. ISSN (print) 0957–9656.

Baverstock, A. (2017a). 'How the book can become a badge of belonging in higher education.' HEPI blog. Available at: www.hepi.ac.uk/2017/07/21/4490/

Baverstock, A. (2017b) 'Librarians as partners – Engaging and effective', *CILIP Update* (June 2017), pp. 38–40.

Bavestock, A., Steinitz, J. and Bryars L. (2017a). 'What were the process and response of university staff and students to the availability of a shared reading scheme of those embarking on a university education. A case study.' *Logos* 28 (2), pp. 29–44.

Baverstock, A. et al. (2017b) 'How do you choose a book for a pre-arrival shared-reading scheme in a University?' *Logos* 28 (3), pp. 41–56.

Baverstock, A. (2018). 'On a shared reading scheme'. Penguin blog. Available at: https://penguinrandomhouseeducation.com/2018/03/26/on-a-shared-reading-scheme-by-dr-alison-baverstock-kingston-university/

Baverstock, A. and Somerville, C. (2018a). 'Does free mean without value? And is free ever worth stealing? The process, outcomes and learnings from a practice as research project encouraging recipients of books for pre-arrival shared-reading at a university to value what they receive'. *Logos* 29 (1), pp. 38–54.

Baverstock, A., Steinitz, J., Morris, J. and Fenwick, C. (2018b). 'What were the processes and outcomes of involving secondary school pupils transitioning from primary to secondary school in pre-arrival shared-reading? A case study', *Education 3–13*, doi:10.1080/03004279.2018.1541922

Baverstock, A. et al. (2019). 'Pre-arrival shared-reading to promote a sense of community: A case study across two institutions'. *Logos* 29 (4), pp. 37–52.

Reference within government minutes

Baverstock, A. and Somerville, C. (2018). 'Does free mean without value? And is free ever worth stealing? The process, outcomes and learnings from a practice as research project encouraging recipients of a free book to value what they received'. *Logos* 29 (1), pp. 38–55.

Cooke, D. (2009). 'How Richard and Judy changed what we read'. BBC News. Available at: http://news.bbc.co.uk/1/hi/magazine/8128436.stm [Accessed 12th November 2010].

Department for Culture, Media and Sport. (2016) 'Minutes of the eleventh meeting of the Libraries Taskforce' (December 2016). Available at: www.gov.uk/government/publictions/eleventh-meeting-of-the-leadership-for-libraries-taskforce/minutes-of-the-eleventh-meeting-of-the-ilbraries-taskforce

Ferguson, M. (2006). Creating common ground: Common reading and the first year of college. *Peer Review Summer* 8 (3), pp. 8–10.

Frostick, T. (2015). *Kingston University's big read*. Available at: www.unialliance.ac.uk/blog/2015/09/29/kingston-universitys-big-read/

Grenier, C. (2006). School of social work, Louisiana State University, USA. 'Which one book would you recommend to entering college freshmen?'. International Conference of the Book, Boston, US.

Reference to paper at 2006 conference

Lavine Laufgraben, J. (2006). *Common reading programs: Going beyond the book*. National Resource Center for First-Year Experience and Students in Transition.

ManBooker Foundation. (2017). The Booker Prize Foundation—Home Page. Available at: http://themanbookerprize.com/foundation [Accessed 3rd November 2017].

Mark Hall, R. (2003). 'The "Oprahfication" of literacy: Reading "Oprah's Book Club"'. *College English* 65 (6), pp. 646–667.

Morris, W. (2016a). 'Reading fellows', *UKSG eNews*, Issue no.373, June. Available at: www.jisc-collections.ac.uk/UKSGFiles/373/UKSGeNews373.pdf [Accessed 6th December 2016].

Morris, W. (2016b). 'The big read: How shared reading transforms lives', *CILIP Update*, November, pp. 32–34.

Morris, W. and Ennis, L. (2016). 'Getting some reading in – A collaboration between capital cities', *Taking Stock*, Winter issue.

One Book, One Community (OBOC). (2003). American library association. [Online] Available at: www.ala.org/programming/onebook [Accessed 3rd November 2017].

ORA Prep. (2014). *A guide to life as a mature student*. [Online] Available at: www.oraprep.com/guide-life-mature-student/ [Accessed 3rd November 2017].

Otterbein University. 2017. About common book. (Online) Available at: www.otterbein.edu/public/Academics/EnrichmentPrograms/CommonBook/AboutCommonBook.aspx [Accessed 3rd November 2017].

Rooney, K. (2005). *Reading with Oprah: The book club that changed America*. 1st Edition. Arkansas: The University of Arkansas Press.

Tienda, M, (2013). 'Diversity not equal to inclusion: Promoting integration in higher education.' *Educational Researcher* 42 (9), pp. 467–475.

Twiton, A. (2007). *Common reading programs in higher education*. [Online] Available at: https://gustavus.edu/library/Pubs/Lindell2007.html [Accessed 3rd November 2017].

University of Hertfordshire. (2017). *Connect: The common reading programme*. [Online] Available at: www.herts.ac.uk/connect/common-reading-programme [Accessed 3rd November 2017].

University of Wisconsin-Madison. (2017). *Go big read*. [Online] Available at: https://gobigread.wisc.edu/ [Accessed 3rd November 2017].

Washington State University. (2017). *WSU common reading: Overview*. [Online] Available at: http://commonreading.wsu.edu/overview/ [Accessed 3rd November 2017].

6

THE REVIEW AND THE REVIEWER

Claire Squires

Introduction

'Reviewing', writes Gail Pool in *Faint Praise*, one of the few extended studies on the review and the reviewer in the contemporary period, 'is a slippery subject. It's even a slippery word. The term reviewing refers at once to a literary field and a business, a system and an individual endeavour, a process and a multitude of very different products' (2007, p. 7). The slipperiness identified by Pool is furthered in Graham Law's overview of the process of reviewing, which places the multi-faceted subject in historical context. 'The long history of relations between volume and serial publication', comments Law, 'has produced no more complex and conflicted area than that of critical intervention in patterns of book consumption through the medium of the periodical' (2010, p. 1092).

This essay sets out to address the role of both the review and the reviewer within the wider framework of the circulation of books, assessing their roles and relationships to publishers, authors, and (prospective) readers. It does so both within the context of an historical overview, but also concentrates upon the review and the reviewers in the twenty-first century, including in the now thoroughly digital period.

In so doing, it examines key themes and aspects of the historical development of reviewing, its role in the circulation and reception of books in a variety of market sectors, and in gatekeeping and constructing cultural value. It also considers the economics of reviewing, the review as form, and its role in the marketing and publicity of books. In addition, the essay addresses the sometimes problematic positioning of reviewing with regard to a range of identities (both of the reviewer and of the reviewed). There is a concluding examination of the changes being brought to reviewing by digital technologies in their enabling of widespread, 'amateur' reviewing across a range of platforms, and their concomitant role in building communities around reading practices, and in creating data for algorithmically-led marketing processes. The essay's focus is predominantly upon the reviewing environment in the UK, though it brings in examples from across the Anglophone world.

Definitions

Before turning to a history of reviewing, and given the 'slippery' nature of the reviewing that Pool identifies, this essay begins with some definitions. These definitions are further amplified in the sections which follow, including through its historical development and current transmogrifications.

Pool begins her definitions by contemplating the purpose of the review for the (potential) book reader. As she outlines:

> Many of us – even reviewers – turn to reviewers both to help us decide what to read and to find out what is out there to be read: we read reviews in our areas of interest, looking for recommendations, and we read reviews of books we have no intention of reading, whether to arm ourselves for the cocktail party circuit or because we truly want to be informed. We may also of course read reviewers because we take pleasure in the play of ideas, or in reading about reading, or in the well-written review as a literary form. But essentially we want consumer advice and cultural guidance.
>
> *2007, p. 4*

In a few sentences, she sketches a variety of purposes: 'recommendations'; shorthand descriptions; for entertainment or edification; and, primarily, for 'consumer advice and cultural guidance'. The role of the review, she therefore states, is first and foremost one which is simultaneously linked to the business of publishing, and to its aesthetic output. Immediately, then, the review is placed in a potentially conflicted position, with a role in the weighing up of the cultural worth of books, but also in their marketing and promotion. Reviews 'influence reading', she also remarks (2007, p. 3); this is reading in both cultural and economic formations.

A key distinction to be made, at least with regard to the pages of newspapers, is that the review is neither the literary feature nor the interview with an author. Book review space is under pressure, Edna Longley describes with regard to the end of the twentieth century, as 'The preview and the interview try to usurp the review' (1998, p. 200). Stefan Collini is even more concerned about a potential loss of space, as '"features people" increasingly replace "literary people" as editors of the books pages, so the proportion of space devoted to self-advertising "personalities" and show-biz ephemera rises' (1998, p. 174). The focus of the review is thus on the contents of the book itself, rather than on details of the author's biography.

The book review's mode is also predominantly contemporary, focussing on new titles, or even, in pre-publication reviews, on titles soon to be released.

For Pool this is a key distinction between literary journalism and criticism, with the former concentrating on new books (and hence more clearly linking to immediate marketing and promotion of frontlist titles). Pool derives her distinction at least in part from Virginia Woolf, who places in historical context a 'split in the field of criticism' at the end of the eighteenth century, whereby, '"The critics," [Woolf...] wrote, "dealt with the past and with principles; the reviewer took the measure of new books as they fell from the press"' (2007, p. 9).

It might seem that the roles of reviewer and critic fall, respectively, to the (literary) journalist and academic, but in a volume of essays devoted to the inter-relationships between literary journalism and literary criticism (or *Grub Street and the Ivory Tower*, as the book title puts it (Treglown and Bennett 1998)), Collini nuances such a 'conventional distinction' (1998, p. 151). He notes the predominant focus of academic critics on 'literature' (thereby excluding general works of, for example, economics and philosophy, which the book reviewer might address). However, while recognising that '"Literary scholarship" refers to the disciplined study of a particular subject-matter', he does so by pointing out the frequency with which academics have also (and continue) to act as book reviewers in the newspapers and mainstream media, as well as non-academics contributing to 'literary scholarship' (1998, p. 152). Indeed, there are frequent examples, some of which are discussed later in this essay, of academics who have acted as book reviewers, as well as reviewers who are related to other aspects of bookish life; quintessentially, writers of books themselves.

The mid-century editor and literary critic Cyril Connolly paints a picture of the professional literary journalist in contrast to the salaried university academic. The literary journalist, writes Connolly:

> 'cannot afford to be obscure; he is not subsidised [unlike the "university teacher"]; he has to compress his views into a few hundred words; he must grade, explain and entertain all at once, and his work is immediately forgotten, totally ignored except for those who write in to correct a name or a date'.
>
> *Connolly, cited in Taylor 2016, p. 212*

Beyond the obvious mid-twentieth-century gendering of this generic professional book reviewer (gender and other forms of identity in the reviewing process are addressed later), Connolly hints at the economics of professional book reviewing – a recurring theme throughout this essay – as well as to the form of the review itself. It is brief but also, as with Pool's comments above on what readers turn to reviews for, it suggests the multiplicity of roles that the effective review must perform – to 'grade, explain and entertain all at once'. The explicatory role relates to the review's focus on new books, and the broad distinction between journalistic and academic criticism. Pool supports Collini's statement that it is largely (but not always) the case that reviewing focusses on 'new books and a lack of theory' (at least an explicit one), arguing that reviewers are:

> working not with a canon but with unknown quantities and need to find ways to discern which titles might have value. Because reviewers are dealing with new books, they're writing for an audience that hasn't yet read the books they're discussing, which is why not only an evaluation, but also an accurate description is such a necessary part of the review; without description, no assessment can make sense.
>
> *2007, p. 10*

That said, because of the assumption that a reader of academic criticism might have already read the book under consideration, an academic essay might well reveal key twists of a novel and its ending in a way that a reviewer of a new book would not be able to do without warning of major 'plot-spoilers'. Reviews which risk giving away key aspects of the story relate particularly to the novel (or perhaps a narrative-driven non-fiction title), whereas reviews of other forms of non-fiction might more thoroughly explain the contents of the title at hand. Such a digested version in itself means that the reader of the review has a strong sense of the contents of the book without needing to read it. (A range of additional strategies are put forward by Pierre Bayard in his book *How To Talk About Books You Haven't Read*, which starts with an epigraph from Oscar Wilde, *'I never read a book I must review; it prejudices you so'* (2007, p. v).)

Beyond the tantalising challenge presented by Bayard's book to reviewers, a less cynical approach to the form of the book review should also take into consideration the two other roles in Connolly's tripartite, that of grading and entertaining. The entertainment role, states Collini, is one which makes 'requirements of brevity, "liveliness", and "punchiness"' because of both 'commercialism and of the properties of the media themselves' which, he argues, 'make it extremely difficult to present a case that is complex, extended and nuanced' (1998, p. 173).

A more positive account than Collini's jeremiad on the need to entertain is to be found in Lorna Sage's chapter in the same volume. As both an academic and a regular book reviewer, Sage writes evocatively of the commercial art of book reviewing. Regular reviewers, she says:

> write on the run, in the present tense [...] You swap words for money, you reprocess reading into writing and commentary. You describe, paraphrase, quote, reperform, 'place' and help sell (or not) the books you're reviewing [...] What literary editors like is an excited, vivid, dramatized response, whether it is positive or negative is less important than its power to arouse interest, to make the book in question twitch and show signs of life [...] To write reading you must spot and exaggerate and semaphore all the signs,

insert yourself between author and real reader, make over long texts into short alliterative sentences, perform reading as surrogate and advocate, and at all costs help to keep the trade in words alive.

1998, pp. 262–263

Sage's commentary constructs the book review both as a piece of writing in its own right, which operates within particular conditions and constraints (including those of the publication it sits within, and the directives of its literary editor), and as that which performs a vital communicative function between author – or their book – and reader. In addition, the review sustains the literary world, in both its aesthetic and market orientations ('to keep the trade in words alive'). She encapsulates the need to entertain but also the review's potential role in book sales – if it makes the 'grade' (to make a noun from Connolly's verb). For, as Pool also asserts, the 'central ingredients of a review [are…] description and an assessment' (2007, p. 138).

Reviews have their role, then, in both judging literary quality and selling books. The former role sees it as one of the early points of (potential) canon formation. Pool argues that 'Reviewers' assessments indirectly help determine which books will win awards and which authors will be published' (2007, p. 3). Literary awards are themselves a proxy for literary value, and their decision-making processes frequently contested (see, for example, English 2005). However, they also have a role in canon formation, with their winners frequently finding their way onto university literature or school curricula (Allan and Driscoll 2013). Indeed, in the situation where literary editors seem to have overlooked a title and not elicited a review for it, it can cause consternation when it then goes onto prize success, as McDowell (2016) illuminates in the case of Graeme Macrae Burnet's Man Booker shortlisted *His Bloody Project* (2016). However, favourable reviews from key publications and reviewers such as the *New Yorker's* James Wood or the *New York Times Book Review's* Michiko Kakutani can set agenda for books, opening their pathway to critical success (Taylor 2016, p. 409).

Yet reviewers also react to publishers' marketing and promotion. This might take the form of a gatekeeping or sieving activity, in which heavily promoted titles are reviewed, so readers know whether to invest their time and money in them (Pool 2007, p. 22). In this sense, the reviewer sits both in literary judgement, but also as a buyer's guide, particularly in an age of proliferating numbers of titles available. Their role is one of recommendation: to value, or not; to buy, or not. Although it is hard to determine their precise effect, Pool reports on publishers' publicists who see certain '"selling review[s]"' which kickstart word-of-mouth success and '"buzz"' around a book, from which other reviews flow as well as 'interviews, profiles, and television appearances' (2007, pp. 114, 113).

Reviewers – and in particular literary editors – also react to publishers' marketing and promotion, and existing literary judgements, by upholding conventional patterns. This might occur in terms of according space to authors who already have significant marketplace presence, or by, as Pool puts it, 'sustain[ing] artificial cultural divisions' which privilege some publishers (particularly larger ones), authors, identities, and genres over others. As multiple review platforms focus on the same titles from a narrow band of publishers, rather than 'expand[ing...] not only readers' awareness but the cultural mainstream itself', Pool argues that '[w]hat is confirmed is not the value of the books but the consistency of the system and the discouraging conformity of the trade' (2007, pp. 31–32).

The implications of these concentrations are addressed in more detail later in this essay. After this preliminary scoping of key principles in the work of the review and the reviewer, the next section addresses their history and development.

The history and development of reviewing

Ending his short introduction to the subject of book reviewing in the *Oxford Companion to the Book*, Law comments that new reviewing platforms brought about by twenty-first-century digital developments 'seem no more likely to succeed in passing unscathed between the Scylla of ideological prejudice and the Charybdis of economic self-interest' than the centuries of reviewing that preceded them (2010, p. 1092). These contemporary digital manifestations of reviewing are explored later in this essay. But how did the book review and the role of the book reviewer develop historically?

As Law describes, within a British context, literary reviewing – beyond the mere listing of new titles available – was a mid-eighteenth-century development, in line with the expansion of the publishing industry, and was spearheaded by the *Monthly Review* (1749) and *Critical Review* (1756) (2010, pp. 1091–1092). It was in this period that, as Antonia Forster puts it, 'the business of criticism and its place in the history of the book was established' (2009, p. 631). The founder of the *Monthly Review* articulated the role of the reviewer in 1749 'in simple, practical terms to a reading public unused to the phenomenon of purchasing literary judgements or descriptions of books', meaning that the *Review* was placed 'in a mediating position between the booksellers and the reading public' (Forster 2009, pp. 632, 633). As such, from the early days of the review, it was a contested site: was its purpose to provide readers with notification and information of new titles, or to be more selective and evaluative?

As the number of such periodicals grew at the turn of the nineteenth century with the emergence of quarterlies such as the *Edinburgh Review* (1802) and *Quarterly Review* (1809), the relationship between booksellers and periodical publishers was close. Publishers would 'puff' their own books, particularly through the use of anonymous reviewers, and included paid advertisements for new titles alongside reviews. A move was also made from any attempt to review comprehensively, to a mode of selection, embedding 'considerable intellectual prestige over several generations' in the quarterly (Law 2010, pp. 1091–1092). The reviews were lengthy, and functioned as substantial paraphrases of titles, meaning that readers could 'keep up to date with the key arguments of new books without necessarily reading the books for themselves' (Fyfe 2009, p. 591). The review later spread into the general periodical in publications such as *Blackwood's Edinburgh Magazine* (1802), as well as with new literary reviews such as the *Athenaeum* (1828), which focussed on shorter, less essayistic reviews.

As the nineteenth century proceeded, with its increasing professionalisation of authorship, its growing publishing output (both books and periodicals), and rising levels of readership, so did the forums for book reviews, to the degree that reviews of reviews such as *Tit-Bits* (1881) and *Review of Reviews* (1890) began to be published (McKitterick 2009, p. 563; Fyfe 2009, p. 592). A parallel set of publications oriented at both the book trade and librarians was established (e.g. *Publishers' Circular* (1837), the *Bookseller* (1858), *The Best Books* (1887), the *Bookman* (1891), and the *Library Review* (1892)), emphasising both the principles of newness and selection (McKitterick 2009, p. 562, pp. 564–565). By the end of the nineteenth century, *The Times* published the weekly *Literature* (1896), a pre-cursor to the *Times Literary Supplement* (1902). *Literature*'s editor H.D. Traill did much in the announcement in *The Times,* and via *Literature*'s leaders, to establish what he saw as the role of the book review and the literary critic. These opinion pieces insisted on 'authoritative neutrality' which was deemed crucial in a 'marketplace of culture', and as Kijinski further argues:

> construct[ed] a case for the indispensable, and utilitarian, cultural function of the professional man of letters who guides the reading of a public that has an unprecedented number of books available to them but who are also beset by the commercial machinery of mass culture which would degrade standards of literary judgment in the interests of profit.
>
> *2010, pp. 359, 358*

The rise of the professional literary critic, however – seemingly autonomous from the burgeoning literary marketplace – was, in fact, intimately connected to it. The disinterested stance of the critic did not occlude the fact that such a role was dependent on the need to make distinctions in a period of mass-market production.

Into the twentieth century, literary reviewing was an important supplement to many authors' incomes, who could not live on income from their book-length writing alone. Aldous Huxley made money from reviewing for the *New Statesman* and *Nation*, and in 1919 joined the *Athenaeum* as a staff writer. For Virginia Woolf, until 1925, 'literary journalism was [her...] main source of income' (Nash and Squires 2019, p. 101). Indeed, the numbers of literary and cultural magazines grew again between the two world wars, providing opportunities both for authors to earn money by writing literary reviews and for them and their publishers to receive reviews of their output. The interwar period also saw the development of positive reviews being integrated into book cover design, not least via Victor Gollancz's typographic covers (Nash, Squires and Willison 2019, p. 23). Such (excerpted) reviews in the paratexts of books made evident the role of the review in the marketing and promotion of books, leading historian D. J. Taylor to typify the period as:

> the era of the light essay, of the overexcitable dust jacket with its constant intimations of 'genius'; of the 'puff' or over-the-top review in which all pretence of objective standards went out of the window and the potential reader was assured that his soul would 'scream with delight'.

Gollancz's company also 'extracted and arranged reviews' in advertisements, in order '"to create the suggestion that no one could afford not to read this book"' (Taylor 2016, pp. 83, 84). The link between the review and book sales was cemented.

Another development – or at least intensification of earlier practice – is noted by Taylor in the 1920s: that of '"star reviewer"', named as author of the article rather than being 'clothed in decent anonymity', which then became 'an essential part of the literary culture of the day' (2016, pp. 84, 85). Named reviewers were frequently novelists: Arnold Bennett (*Evening Standard*); J. B. Priestley, Frank Swinnerton (both at the *Evening News*); Compton McKenzie (*Daily Mail*); and Hugh Walpole (*Daily Sketch*). Big-name reviewers were trusted by book buyers and borrowers, creating a direct impact on sales and onward publicity for titles. Other publications, however, clung to a principle of anonymity, most notably the *Times Literary Supplement* (*TLS*), which retained it from its first publication in 1902 until as late as 1974. Articles were subsequently '"deanonymised"' as part of a digitisation project, revealing patterns which were discussed in the publication's 5000th issue in 1999, as Ruth Scurr later commented on the *TLS*'s website:

> Calculating the number of female reviewers in the paper's first thousand issues from 1902–21, McVea and Treglown wrote: 'It is of interest, though it is not a surprise, that of 1,036 contributions in these early years, the number of women (seventy-six) was exceeded by the number of clergymen (eighty-one) and almost matched by those of men educated at a single Oxford college, Balliol (sixty-seven)'.

2018

The issue of gendered reviewing is one to which this essay later returns. The named (and largely male), star reviewers in the interwar period attracted concomitant pay. Arnold Bennett, reveals Taylor, had the 'phenomenal' income in 1929 of £22,000, including 'journalism paid at a rate of two shillings a word', and an annual payment of £3,000 a year for his weekly *Evening Standard* page. Not all reviewers were so healthily recompensed, however, with fees for 600 to 700-word reviews cited between £1 and £5 (Taylor, pp. 138, 145). For the literary journalist John Hayward in the 1930s, he 'calculated [...] he wrote a review at the rate of one every two days' (Taylor 2016, p. 140). Taylor links such conditions to George Orwell's penning of one of the most quoted essays on the book review,

'Confessions of a Book Reviewer' (1946). 'In twenty years of reviewing', notes Peter Davison in a note to Orwell's essay, Orwell 'reviewed just over 700 books, plays, and films. His busiest year was 1940 when he reviewed 135 books, plays and films in 67 reviews' (1946).

In his essay Orwell draws a picture of the book reviewer as a desperate hack, for whom 'the prolonged, indiscriminate reviewing of books is a quite exceptionally thankless, irritating and exhausting job'. His portrait of the reviewer opens:

> In a cold but stuffy bed-sitting room littered with cigarette ends and half-empty cups of tea, a man in a moth-eaten dressing-grown sits at a rickety table, trying to find room for his typewriter among the piles of dusty papers that surround it.
>
> *1946*

Orwell continues to enumerate satirically the financial pressures on the freelance literary journalist, the small amount of time the world-weary reviewer has for each book, the press of the deadline, the limited scrutiny accorded to each title, and the stock phrases used to describe them.

Indeed, after the Second World War, there was a decline in the number of 'traditional literary and political weeklies', meaning fewer opportunities for paid reviewing, with many of the highest profile reviews undertaken by salaried academics rather than freelance writers (Nash and Squires 2019, p. 125). Taylor saw this shift as a direct response to 'the collapse of the middlebrow literary magazine' meaning that 'the world of belles-lettres was growing more restricted, more likely to be colonised by moonlighting academics on institutional salaries' than freelance literary journalists. Although fees for star reviewers were to some degree sustained, in the post-war period circumstances became yet more difficult for writers in terms of the number of books necessary to be read and reviewed to make decent money, with the novelist Anthony Burgess calculating 'he had read 350 new novels in the space of two years' for the *Yorkshire Post* (Taylor 2016, pp. 247, 255).

The immediate post-war period of austerity, paper-rationing, and limited page space eventually gave way to a regrowth in book reviewing in the 1960s and 1970s. It was 'metropolitan in character', a 'professional golden age', and saw the rise and rise of the newspaper and magazine staff literary editor, who oversaw the work of the freelance literary journalists and reviewers. Such roles were increasingly taken on by women, too: Claire Tomalin at the *New Stateman* and Miriam Gross, who moved on from a role at the books pages of the *Observer* to become literary editor of the *Sunday Telegraph* (Taylor 2016, pp. 305, 307, 308). A coterie of younger reviewers in the 1970s formed a 'distinctive literary scene', comprised of novelists and academics including Martin Amis, Julian Barnes, Ian McEwan, and Lorna Sage (Taylor 2016, pp. 324–325). This 'golden age' was economic in character as much as intellectual; as in the 1920s and 1930s it provided some writers with steady salaries which continued into the final decades of the twentieth century. Taylor comments that in the final two decades of the twentieth century, a freelance with an annual contract from one newspaper, plus commissions from others, could potentially gain £15,000–£20,000 a year. In this 'boom' period of multiple broadsheet newspapers, a star reviewer such as novelist Anthony Burgess earned £600 a review for the *Independent* in the late 1980s (2016, p. 426). However, as Nash and Squires explain, 'the slump of newspaper sales thereafter curtailed a once steady source of income', as the ongoing story of the review, and the reviewer, unfolds in its twenty-first-century manifestations (2019, p. 133).

Landscapes of twenty-first-century book reviewing

One narrative of book reviewing as it reaches the twenty-first century, then, is of decline, challenge, and loss of space. From an economic heyday in the 1970–1990s and the interwar period, book reviewing became a less and less lucrative profession, with Taylor reporting in 2014 that the *Independent* was offering only £100 for a book review – an amount which was less than what was offered when the newspaper was established in 1986 (2016, p. 430). For writers reliant on book reviewing as an additional source of finance to supplement that from book advances and royalties, the fall in reviewing fees was only one strand in an overall picture of worsening revenue derived from the writing life (Marsden 2018).

The rapidly developing digital environment would be cruel to the traditional newspaper, with plummeting sales and, therefore, depleting advertising revenue. The space allocated to book reviews in traditional, mainstream printed media particularly suffered, as discussed in the 'Definitions' section earlier, and found itself competing with other forms of exposure given to writers, through biographically led approaches. Already by the end of the twentieth century in the Irish context, Longley noted that 'crude slices of book-life now get on to the literary pages of the *Irish Times*', with the 'space for "reviews" […] shrinking' (1998, p. 217). Within a small-nation context such as Ireland's, Longley describes how this shrinkage presents particular challenges: to what extent the small number of editors (including the novelist John Banville) and their tastes then focus on Irish writers, or even books published in Ireland (as many of the more critically and commercially successful Irish writers are published via London publishers); or on writers from elsewhere in the world; or on new or established writers. To what extent, the argument continues, should the Irish newspapers be promoting the small-scale publishing industry in Ireland and showcasing its products; to what extent focussing on the established voices of Irish literature; and to what extent should it act as a window onto the wider world of literature? Limited page space throws such questions into sharp relief. The choices made are then heavily scrutinised, as Longley describes Banville 'accused of devoting both too much and too little space to Irish, and especially Irish-published, books' (1998, p. 216).

Limited space also means that sieving decisions taken by literary editors have further political and ideological ramifications. Pool's description of literary editors' gatekeeping decisions, described earlier in the essay, showed how they reinforce cultural hierarchies, often prioritising larger publishers at the expense of smaller presses. The fight for review coverage for smaller publishers is particularly acute. The retrospective lifting of the *TLS*'s anonymity discussed earlier in the essay revealed the overwhelming bias towards male reviewers over its lifetime. Such patterns did not cease with named reviews, however. As Scurr comments on the 1999 issue in which McVea and Treglown discussed the *TLS* archive, 'McVea was one of only four women among forty-two contributors to issue No. 5000' (2018).

Inequities in reviewing (both in terms of the reviewer and the identity of the author of the book under review) led to the foundation of VIDA: Women in Literary Arts in 2009. Part of its core activity is an annual count of book reviews in some of the most prestigious of newspapers, journals, and magazines (e.g. the *New York Review of Books* and *New York Times Book Review* in the US). In the UK in 2016, the *TLS* had only 38% of reviews by women, with only 29% of books reviewed by women. The *London Review of Books* proved even more imbalanced, with only 18% of book reviews written by women, and 26% of books reviewed by women (Nash and Squires 2019, p. 140). VIDA opened its count out latterly to become more intersectional, to include counts of gender, race and ethnicity, sexuality and disability. In Australia, the Stella Count has undertaken similar work, with accompanying academic analysis, particularly in the context of declining review space (Harvey and Lamond 2016). The experience of Lesley McDowell, one British reviewer, illustrates more qualitatively some of the issues of gender in reviewing, explaining that she 'carved a niche' career by reviewing books by women:

> In order to make sure I could get enough books to review to pay the bills, I looked for the titles I thought editors would give me, and what wasn't being covered very much [...] surprise, surprise, it was novels by women! Most books reviewers were male, and they tended to choose titles by men.

She then articulates how books by women are more likely to be reviewed by women, and also that 'To be a major reviewer, you have to concentrate on the boys' (McDowell 2012).

Twenty-first-century digital technologies would exponentially increase the amount of space, number of platforms, form of review activities, and, it might therefore be assumed, work towards addressing such inequities. Indeed, Murray has argued that 'Rather than fighting for equal representation within an admittedly prestigious, though undoubtedly shrinking, sector of print culture, feminist attention might be better focused on the potential of the burgeoning *digital* literary sphere' (2018, p. 117). Such a turn, though, risks placing online reviewing within a range of what Driscoll terms feminised, 'middlebrow literary institutions', which are 'placed in a subordinate, inferior position in the literary field' (2014, p. 31). Embracing the opportunities of the digital technologies discussed at the end of the essay should sit alongside a call for equity in traditional, mainstream reviewing practices.

Yet even without the unfurling of opportunities afforded by digital technologies, the landscapes of twenty-first-century reviewing were already more plural than a narrow focus on traditional newspaper reviewing would suggest. A plethora of other printed platforms provide review space for books falling within their respective niches, from pre-publication forums such as the long-established publishing trade journal *The Bookseller*, to specialist and regional magazines such as *Astronomy Now, Horse and Hound, The Ringing World*, and *Cumbria Life*, which focus on reviewing books with subject matter, location, or authors related to their readers' interests. Such reviews vary from lengthy analyses of the books at hand, to simple notices of publication, short round-ups, and one-word or quantitative, starred reviews. Some newspapers 'review the reviews', examining the convergence or disparity of opinion of widely reviewed titles.

Radio and television have given opportunities for the discussion of book titles, from more highbrow cultural discussion programmes – such as BBC Radio 4's *Front Row* and on television (until 2014) BBC 2's *The Review Show* (variously named *Newsnight Review, The Late Review*, and *The Late Show*) – to media book clubs. The TV producer Amanda Ross drew inspiration from the US's extraordinarily successful Oprah's Book Club segment (1996 onwards) on *The Oprah Winfrey Show* to formulate *The Richard & Judy Book Club* (2004 onwards), a mediatised UK book club in which a set of books were chosen each season for discussion, often with the author present. A particular feature of *The Richard & Judy Book Club* was its focus on new books, thus feeding into the immediate marketing and promotion of frontlist titles (Ramone and Cousins 2011; Fuller and Rehberg Sedo 2013). While led by their celebrity presenters, such shows encouraged their audiences to read, review, and discuss themselves, leading to – in an extension of Fuller and Rehberg Sedo's conceptualisation of 'mass reading events' – an idea of 'mass reviewing' that also comes into play with digital technologies.

In addition to pre-publication reviews in trade publications, the practice of publishers, literary agents, and authors seeking pre-publication endorsements – normally from other authors with profile in the particular market sector or genre – might also be seen as a form of review, although one that is short and always positive, and elicited in order to put on the cover of the book before reviews are available, as well as in other marketing materials (press releases, advance information sheets, website copy, in social media). In his study of US endorsements, Maguire writes that, 'In soliciting public endorsements from fellow writers, authors and their publishers wish not only to borrow symbolic capital from recognized authorities but also to situate their work within an affiliative matrix of aesthetically, generically, or thematically similar artists' (2018). Maguire's network analysis of endorsements demonstrates (supposed) literary affiliations and marketplace positioning (and thereby reveals constructions of gender, genre, and race). Within a UK context, one such pre-publication endorsement which could be read through a prism of genre and race is that by Salman Rushdie for

Zadie Smith's debut novel *White Teeth* (2000) (Squires 2007, p. 179). Maguire further comments that while affiliates and friends might also review an author's book post-publication, a key difference is that 'the solicited blurb makes no special claim to impartiality', but that 'readers expect the review of a book not to have any conflicts of interest or relationship with the author', despite friends frequently reviewing each other's titles (2018). As such, the pre-publication endorsement has no intention to take on the role of objective, balanced review, but is there either to sell books, or to confer a form of literary consecration, or both.

In the sphere of academic writing and publishing, the review is also a crucial part of the publishing process, with pre-publication peer review (traditionally anonymous and set up as a gatekeeping, 'gold standard' exercise) arguably having a stronger impact than post-publication reviews in public fora (Butchard et al. 2017). That said, the function of academic book reviews, as argued by a journal reintroducing them to its pages:

> direct readers to research they might not be aware of, strengthening connections between scholarly work on an international and potentially interdisciplinary scale, and a well written review will point out a book's key contributions when scholars often have precious little time to read books.
>
> *Gerrard 2019*

For scholarly monographs, then, both peer review and post-publication reviews are important in terms of the shaping and reception of long-form scholarly ideas, particularly in the arts and humanities disciplines. Scholars, including Fuller and Rehberg Sedo (for their *Reading Beyond the Book* (2013)), also institute informal, or 'DIY' peer review processes among fellow scholars, not in order to make their work more sellable, but to make their scholarship as robust as possible which might, ideally, have the long-term impact of making it circulate further (Butchard et al. 2018). Digital technologies have also enabled innovative, pre-publication forms of peer review, such as Kathleen Fitzpatrick posting an early draft of *Generous Thinking* (2019) online, in order to encourage discussion and feedback of her ideas before the finalisation of the book in its print and e-versions. Such experiments also link to evolving models of peer review including those in open and post-publication review (Butchard et al. 2017).

Alongside its effects in the sphere of academic publishing, digital technologies have affected the landscape of the review, and reviewing practices, in broader and substantive ways. Amazon was established as an internet book retailing operation in 1994, and by 1997 it was already enabling its users to post up comments and reviews of titles (Murray 2018, p. 112). Such reviews were both qualitative (normally brief reviews of the books in question) and quantitative (via a 5-star ranking system) in nature (Ray Murray and Squires 2013, p. 16). Their introduction opened the possibilities for amateur and mass reviewing, leading to the aggregation of reader-reviewer content through quantitative and algorithmic processes. The early days of Amazon's platform for reader-reviewers also led to a boom in evidence for scholars of contemporary reading practices (e.g. Gutjahr 2002; Steiner 2008), as well as much debate around whether they were democratising reviewing (Murray 2018, pp. 111–112). The anonymity or pseudonymity of Amazon's customer reviews could be manipulated for the purposes of sock puppetry (i.e. attacking rival authors' books), writing multiple positive reviews of your own, your friends, or your company's books, and the mass buying of reviews (Ray Murray and Squires, p. 16).

Evolving digital technologies led to further affordances and possibilities for reader-reviews, via sites such as Shelfari and Goodreads (both initially independent, but subsequently bought by Amazon) (Ray Murray and Squires 2013 p. 14). As the twenty-first century progressed, book bloggers became prevalent, and frequently courted by publishers, alongside Booktubers (book reviewers on YouTube), podcasters, and readers using Instagram and its hashtag #Bookstagram, which reached nearly 30 million posts at the beginning of 2019 (even if the latter are more likely to be thought of as visual performances of bookishness than as 'reviews'). Nonetheless, such traces of visual reading and ownership patterns fit alongside a broader 'digital literary sphere' (Murray, 2018).

This sphere, as well as enabling citizen reviewers, also gave much-needed space to more professionalised reviewing on digital platforms such as the *Los Angeles Review of Books* and the *Sydney Review of Books*. Such possibilities led one commentator to ask – and answer positively – 'Could the Internet Save Book Reviews?' (Fay 2012). Whatever position is taken on the quality of these various reviewing platforms (and whether they are economically sustainable places for professional book reviewers to operate), what is clear is that the spaces within which reviewing in the twenty-first century take place are both proliferating and metamorphosing. While many of the same historical issues around the review and the practices of reviewing remain in the current period, as does their complex and conflicted nature, it is also throwing up some new challenges. The role of the review and the reviewer in the circulation and reception of books, in their promotion and their consecration, continues, even if in forms adapting to evolving circumstances and technologies.

References

Allan, S., and Driscoll, B. (2013) Making the list: the value of prizes for women writers in the construction of educational reading lists. In: E. Stinson, ed., *By the book: contemporary publishing in Australia*. Melbourne: Monash University Press, pp. 127–140.

Bayard, P. (2007) *How to talk about books you haven't read*. Translated by: J. Mehlman. London: Granta.

Butchard, D., Rowberry, S., and Squires, C. (2018) DIY peer review and monograph publishing in the arts and humanities. *Convergence* 24(5), pp. 477–493. Available: doi: 10.1177/1354856518780456 [Accessed 29 March 2019].

Butchard, D., Rowberry, S., Squires, C., and Tasker, G. (2017) Peer review in practice. In: S Rayner and R Lyons, eds., *Academic book of the future: BOOC*. London: UCL Press. https://ucldigitalpress.co.uk/BOOC/Article/1/57/

Collini, S. (1998) The critic as journalist: Leavis after *Scrutiny*. In: J. Treglown and B. Bennett, eds., *Grub Street and the ivory tower: literary journalism and literary scholarship from Fielding to the Internet*. Oxford: Clarendon Press, pp. 151–176.

Driscoll, B. (2014) *The new literary middlebrow: tastemakers and reading in the twenty-first century*. Basingstoke: Palgrave Macmillan.

English, J. (2005) *The economy of prestige: prizes, awards, and the circulation of cultural value*. Cambridge: Harvard University Press.

Fay, S. (2012) Could the Internet save book reviews? *The Atlantic*. Available: www.theatlantic.com/entertainment/archive/2012/05/could-the-internet-save-book-reviews/256802/ [Accessed 29 March 2019].

Fitzpatrick, K. (2019) *Generous thinking: a radical approach to saving the university*. Baltimore: Johns Hopkins University Press.

Forster, A. (2009) Book reviewing. In: M. Suarez, S. J. and M. Turner, eds., *The Cambridge history of the book in Britain: volume v 1695–1830*. Cambridge: Cambridge University Press, pp. 631–648.

Fuller, D., and Rehberg Sedo, D. (2013) *Reading beyond the book: the social practices of contemporary literary culture*. New York: Routledge.

Fyfe, A. (2009) The information revolution. In: D. McKitterick, ed., *The Cambridge history of the book in Britain: volume VI 1830–1914*. Cambridge: Cambridge University Press, pp. 567–594.

Gerrard, Y. (2019) *Convergence* book reviews: reflections on the field. *Convergence*. Available: doi: 10.1177/1354856519836014 [Accessed 29 March 2019].

Gutjahr, P. (2002) No longer Left Behind: Amazon.com, reader response, and the changing fortunes of the Christian novel in America. *Book History* 5, pp. 209–236.

Harvey, M., and Lamond, J. (2016) Taking the measure of gender disparity in Australian book reviewing as a field, 1985 and 2013. *Australian Humanities Review*. Available: http://australianhumanitiesreview.org/2016/11/15/taking-the-measure-of-gender-disparity-in-australian-book-reviewing-as-a-field-1985-and-2013/ [Accessed 29 March 2019].

Kijinski, J. (2003) Respectable reading in the late nineties: H.D. Traill's Literature. *Nineteenth-Century Contexts* 25(4), pp. 357–372. Available: doi: 10.1080/0890549032 000167853 [Accessed 29 March 2019].

Law, G. (2010) Reviewing in relation to consumption. In: M. Suarez, S. J. and H. Woudhuysen, eds., *The Oxford companion to the book*. Oxford: Oxford University Press, pp. 1091–1092.

Longley, E. (1998) 'Between the Saxon smile and Yankee yawp': problems and contexts of literary reviewing in Ireland. In: J. Treglown and B. Bennett, eds., *Grub Street and the ivory tower: literary journalism and literary scholarship from Fielding to the Internet*. Oxford: Clarendon Press, pp. 200–223.

Marsden, S. (2018) Writing about writers: mapping the field and moving forward. *Mémoires du livre* 9(2). Available: doi: 10.7202/1046984ar [Accessed 29 March 2019].

McDowell, L. (2012) Woman book reviewer chooses books by women shocker. Available: http://lesleymcdowellwriter.blogspot.com/2012/07/woman-book-reviewer-chooses-books-by.html [Accessed 29 March 2019].

McDowell, L. (2016) ManBooker behaving badly. Available: http://lesleymcdowellwriter.blogspot.com/2016/08/manbooker-behaving-badly.html [Accessed 29 March 2019].

McKitterick, D. (2009) Organising knowledge in print. In: D. McKitterick, ed., *The Cambridge history of the book in Britain: volume vi 1830–1914*. Cambridge: Cambridge University Press, pp. 531–566.

Murray, S. (2018) *The digital literary sphere*. Baltimore: Johns Hopkins University Press.

Nash, A., and Squires, C. (2019) Authorship. In: A. Nash, C. Squires, and I. R. Willison, eds., *Cambridge history of the book in Britain: volume vii the twentieth century and beyond.* Cambridge: Cambridge University Press, pp. 99–145.

Nash, A., Squires, C., and Willison, I. R. (2019) Introduction. In: A. Nash, C. Squires, and I. R. Willison, eds., *Cambridge history of the book in Britain: volume vii the twentieth century and beyond.* Cambridge: Cambridge University Press, pp. 1–38.

Orwell, G. (1946) Confessions of a book reviewer. Available: www.orwellfoundation. com/the-orwell-foundation/orwell/essays-and-other-works/confessions-of-a-book-reviewer/ [Accessed 29 March 2019].

Pool, G., (2007) *Faint praise: the plight of book reviewing in America.* Columbia: University of Missouri Press.

Ramone, J., and Cousins, H. (2011) *The Richard & Judy Book Club reader: popular texts and the practices of reading.* Farnham: Ashgate Publishing.

Ray Murray, P., and Squires, C. (2013) The digital publishing communications circuit. *Book 2.0* 3(1) pp. 3–23.

Sage, L. (1998) Living on writing. In: J. Treglown and B. Bennett, eds., *Grub Street and the ivory tower: literary journalism and literary scholarship from Fielding to the Internet.* Oxford: Clarendon Press, pp. 262–276.

Scurr, R. (2018) Widest sense: celebrating 6,000 issues of the TLS. Available: www.the-tls. co.uk/articles/public/widest-sense-tls-6000/ [Accessed 29 March 2019].

Squires, C. (2007) *Marketing literature: the making of contemporary writing in Britain.* Basingstoke: Palgrave Macmillan.

Steiner, A. (2008) Private criticism in the public sphere: personal writing on literature in readers' reviews on Amazon. *Participations* 5(2). Available: www.participations.org/ Volume%205/Issue%202/5_02_steiner.htm [Accessed 29 March 2019].

Taylor, D. (2016) *The prose factory.* London: Chatto and Windus.

Treglown, J., and Bennett, B., eds., (1998) *Grub Street and the ivory tower: literary journalism and literary scholarship from Fielding to the Internet.* Oxford: Clarendon Press.

7

THE FISH AND THE STREAM

Publishing, genre, and life-writing's crisis of form

Robert Fraser

As a publishing, critical, and pedagogic category, 'life-writing' has attained more and more purchase over the last half-century or so. But the origins of the term are far older. Traces of its application exist as far back as the eighteenth century; its twentieth- and twenty-first-century prominence, however, owes much to a double event: a disturbance, followed by a delay. The disturbance was an aftershock to the work done by Virginia Woolf in the years 1938–1940 towards an authentic life of her deceased friend, the painter and social activist, Roger Fry (1866–1934). The book appeared in 1940, but it caused Woolf no little distress since, as she perceived it, the need to hold herself back in the service of another's talent went against the grain, both of her personality and of her personal gifts. In *Virginia Woolf: An Inner Life* (2005), Julia Briggs evokes the resulting struggle, characterised by Woolf herself as 'appalling grind', 'donkey work…sober drudgery', and by her husband Leonard as 'severe repression' (Briggs 2005, 345). In 1928 Woolf had completed *Orlando: A Biography* with dispatch and delight. A portrait of her friend and lover, the novelist and horticulturalist Vita Sackville-West, that work had however essentially been an exercise in biographical fiction in which Woolf had felt free to let her imagination roam, transporting Orlando/Sackville-West across several centuries, and transforming her as she went from a woman into a man and then back again. But in *Roger Fry* she needed to stick to the facts, and the cold discipline involved proved an agony to her. She found relief in the fitful composition of a memoir entitled 'A Sketch of the Past', taking herself from the nursery to childhood holidays in Cornwall, the death of her mother, and onwards. It was never finished, though it survived in a number of drafts, on all of which Woolf's own biographers were eventually to draw. But only eventually.

Now for the delay. 'A Sketch of the Past' lay dormant, or maybe latent, as a set of manuscript and typescript pages until 1976, when Jeanne Schulkind brought it out as part of a set of previously unpublished autobiographical writings under the collective title *Moments of Being*; there were subsequent editions in 1980 and 2002. As so often with the most innovative works (think of the poetry of Gerard Manley Hopkins, or that of Wilfred Owen), the delay worked in its favour, since with the public airing of this fragmentary sketch came the outing of a previously disregarded passage in which Woolf had discussed the related difficulties attendant on biography, autobiography, and memoir. Against 'moments of being' (equivalent to what Wordsworth had once called 'spots of time'), so she had contended, one needed to pit 'moments of non-being' or 'invisible presences': experiences or influences of whose influence the subject – and by contagion the writer – had been unaware. The passage continued:

Well, if we cannot analyse these invisible presences, we know very little about the subject of the memoir; and again how futile life-writing becomes. I see myself as a fish held in a stream; deflected, held in place, but cannot describe the stream (Woolf 1976, 80).

As is commonly recognised, this was the first occasion on which the hyphenated term 'life-writing' came to be used. It was to be deployed with increasing frequency in the decades following publication, eventually becoming a convenient banner for a cluster of activities, genres, or sub-genres broadly affiliated to the task of narrating a life. The year 2015 saw the publication of *On Life-Writing*, edited by Zachary Leader, a preamble to *The Oxford History of Life-Writing*, the first two volumes of which appeared during 2018, also under Leader's general editorship. For Leader, 'life-writing' is a compendious heading covering 'memoir, autobiography, biography, autobiographical fiction, and biographical fiction, but also letters, writs, wills, written anecdotes, court proceedings…marginalia, nonce writings, lyric poems, scientific and historical writings, and digital forms (including blogs, tweets, and Facebook entries)' (Leader 2015, 1). One might well ask, whatever else is left on the shelves or, for that matter, on the hard disk?

There is, however, another angle from which the question may be viewed. Not merely has 'life-writing' brought together a number of categories of authorship previously regarded as diverse; it has also put pressure of these varieties of literary exercise, encouraging them to merge. From this point of view, generic description is not simply descriptive; it is also prescriptive, proactive, or at the very least suggestive. Autobiography and memoir have ventured to invade biography and *vice versa*, and all of the above have begun to encroach on fiction, and the other way round. The result has been a vigorous process both of convergence and of mutual interrogation. As Woolf had been quick to see, there are difficulties common to all of these forms, and hence a common challenge. To borrow Woolf's own metaphor, if the fish has difficulty in discerning the stream, is the stream necessarily in a better position to observe the fish? And if authors may be compared to anglers placed upon the bank, are they in imminent and perpetual danger of falling in? This essay represents a modest attempt to lend them a helping hand before they sink, and just possibly to dry them out. To which you might well respond that, once writers have tasted the joys of swimming, few are likely to remain on dry land for long. Who, in any case, is much interested in a dry author? Perhaps not even the author him-, her-, or itself.

Prisoners of time

The repercussions of the above process and argument are easy to observe. Life-writing has been through several revolutions since 1976. Essentially, there has been shuffling between genres. The boundary between biography and autobiography used to be rigorously policed; there are now several cross-over points. Both were supposed to be severely factual, though autobiography less so. There is now considerable lee-way in this respect. Some have even argued that both biography and autobiography have become akin to fiction, though what this tends to mean in practice is that an author is expected to stick to the facts, but present them in such a way as to possess imaginative allure. The combined result of these related developments has been a liberation or a distraction, depending on your point of view.

Another way of putting this is that the distinction between author and subject has largely broken down. In 1990 Peter Ackroyd published a 1,000-page biography of *Charles Dickens* in which he himself appears as a character, sometimes in conversation with his long-dead subject, and sometimes in conversation with other authors, or with himself. In the last capacity he is liable to dilate on the art of biography itself, thus:

> Ackroyd (*in interviewer mode*): Do you admire other biographies of Dickens, then?

Ackroyd *auteur* answers that he finds Forster's 1874 life of Dickens prosaic and a little dull. So Ackroyd the interviewer then asks his *alter persona* whether his own book will seem dated in 30 or 40 years' time. It is now almost 30 years since that question was put, and this is how, in 1990, Ackroyd the biographer answered it:

> Ackroyd: (*in interviewee mode*): Every biography is a prisoner of its time, yes, and I am sure that anyone who may happen to open the book in the twenty-first century will recognize at once that it was written in the *fin-de-siècle* of the twentieth century. I have probably made too much of the fact, for example, that Dickens *saw* reality as a reflection of his own fiction.
>
> *Ackroyd 1990, 944*

Ackroyd is himself, of course, a novelist as well as a biographer. What we see in such a passage is the craft of biography straining to release itself from its limitations (or you might say from its job description, again depending on your viewpoint). Ackroyd is very alert to its affinities with the novel in particular, but he is far from peculiar in this respect.

Nor is he unique in addressing his subject directly. In terms of traditional biographical technique, this tendency may appear a *faux pas*. There are, however, precedents for it stretching from Lucian of Samosata's *Dialogues of the Dead*, written in the second century AD, to Lucian's seventeenth- and eighteenth-century imitators. Once re-introduced in the modern period, this particular convention proved transformative, and irresistible. Its ambiguous effects can easily be gleaned by comparing Jenny Uglow's scholarly and restrained biography *Elizabeth Gaskell: A Habit of Stories,* published in the same year as Ackroyd's *Dickens*, with Nell Stevens's imaginative and freewheeling *Mrs Gaskell and Me* released in 2018. Uglow's was a thorough cradle-to-grave account giving full measure to her subject's childhood in Cheshire, her long and fruitful marriage to the Unitarian Revd. William Gaskell, her successive works, and her friendship with the American author Charles Eliot Norton, a fellow Unitarian whom she met whilst holidaying in Rome in February 1855. Stevens's book in stark contrast concentrates almost exclusively on this latter episode which Stevens relates throughout to her own unsuccessful twenty-first-century relationship with a wannabe American author whom she refers to as Max. For Uglow, Gaskell's platonic involvement with Norton, with whom Gaskell continued to correspond for the rest of her life, was joyful and liberating but left her own life essentially intact. For Stevens – confiding *tête-à-tête* with her Victorian predecessor – it has become the traumatic event around which the remainder of Mrs Gaskell's life pivoted. 'It be would be too strong to a say that Elizabeth fell in love with Charles', Uglow sagely remarks. 'He was part of her Italian romance and she fell in love with the whole experience' (Uglow 1990, 418). But for Stevens, who subtitles her lively book 'two women, two love stories, two centuries apart', it is quite necessary that Gaskell's experience should have been every bit as disturbing as her own. At one point Max, with whom she is conducting a medium-distance Skype session, holds up to the screen a reprint of *The Letters of Mrs Gaskell and Charles Eliot Norton 1855–1865*, which he has found on a market stall. 'I didn't realize they would be love letters', he smirkingly observes. 'You didn't tell me they were in love' (Stevens, 2018, p. 58).

If Max is pushing a point, or appropriating one period's and one woman's sensibility to another's, quibbling is surely out of place here, since the Mrs Gaskell of this double fable is not quite the Mrs Gaskell of history, nor is the 'I' of the narrative quite Stevens. As Claire Harman, biographer of Sylvia Townsend Warner, Fanny Burney, and Charlotte Brontë, opined in her *Guardian* review, paraphrasing – and possibly parodying – Stevens's approach, 'Truth is slippery, biography sort of pointless, and autobiography worst of all. Let's just call the whole lot fiction right from the start'.

All the same, to regard this process as an open field day would be a gross over-simplification. Simultaneous with this elision of traditional categories of literary expression, an added sophistication in the world of literary theory has also led to a more refined understanding as to where boundaries do in fact lie, as to what constitutes genuine affinity, and what constitutes difference. Such a heightened understanding can be simply illustrated by reference to that busy field: biographical writing about Marcel Proust. Proust himself had attacked the fallacy of confusing a biographical subject with his real-life counterpart in the person of Charles Sainte-Beuve, an influential critic of his own day who had in his eyes reduced all discussion of contemporary literature to a species of salon gossip (Proust 1971, 211–298). This was not to prevent Proust's own biographers from falling into an equivalent trap. Back in 1959, George D. Painter published a two-volume life of the French writer that was rapidly translated into German, Italian, French, Spanish, and Polish, and taken then to be definitive. Yet Painter had widely connected characters in *A la recherche du temps perdu* with real-life people in Proust's social circle; on occasions there had been, as he portrayed it, an almost one-to-one relation. It took all the scholarship and imagination of Jean-Yves Tadié, the presiding genius of the fourth Pléiade edition of Proust's great novel sequence, to sort out this muddle in his magisterial biography of 1996. No subsequent biographer of Proust has made the same mistake.

Perhaps because of this increase in critical awareness and theoretical understanding, as the twentieth century drew to a close life-writers became markedly more self-critical and self-reflexive. The undeniable fact is that, over the period in question, the more enterprising works in this interconnected nexus of genres, whatever their ostensive subject or subjects, have simultaneously been about themselves as art, the definition of what they generically are: be it biography, autobiography, or memoir, or very often a mix. The object has been to stretch: the author, the reader, and the form.

Multivalent forms

The stretching can take a number of shapes: roughly speaking, the more challenging the subject, the more versatile the shape tends to be. A straightforward subject frequently begets a straightforward life. Fortunately, not that many subjects are that straightforward.

It may be appropriate to demonstrate this argument by looking at two extreme instances: one the life of a sort of non-entity, the other the life of a bird. Some subjects, it may be said, hardly exist at all, except in the minds of their creators. In 1999, on the cusp of the century, Granta Books issued a quaint and excellent book entitled *Rodinsky's Room* which was revolutionary in several respects. The David Rodinsky of the title was an Orthodox Jew of scholarly and reclusive habits, who had disappeared without trace from his room above a Spitalfields synagogue in 1969 and had not been heard of since. In 1980, when the Synagogue was being renovated, his room was unlocked and found just as he had left it: with writing materials on his desk and dictionaries in many exotic tongues on the shelves. Nobody knew what had happened to him, and few could remember who he was. His room, which was later to become a shrine, was a virtual landlocked Marie Celeste, complete with mystery and false leads.

This story could have been a biographer's nightmare – where to begin? – but it produced a versatile and game-changing book. The biographers were two: the psycho-geographer Iain Sinclair, fascinated by a hidden aspect of his beloved and reviled London, and a young writer of Polish-Jewish heritage called Rachel Lichtenstein, deeply involved in recovering her cultural roots. In motivation they were distinct if complementary; in literary style they could hardly have been more distinct. Sinclair, who had begun as a poet, wrote in a dense and baroque style of spikey lyricism; Lichtenstein in simple and direct declarative sentences, as lucid as her search was sincere. Sinclair wrote about Lichtenstein, and she about Sinclair; both of them wrote about Rodinsky, whom neither had ever met. They did not know whether he was alive, or whither he had fled. Eventually Sinclair traced him to a psychiatric hospital in Epsom where he had evidently spent some years. In 2010, when I was preparing my own biography of the poet David Gascoyne, who had been treated in the same hospital around the same time, I went to see Sinclair in Hackney; he told me that the medical records of the hospital concerned had been destroyed. Lichtenstein in the meantime had made her way to Poland on her own, deeply personal quest. In the book that they co-authored, their two accounts run parallel, chapter by chapter in alternating styles until, once the circumstances of Rodinsky's death have been unearthed and his pauper's grave in Waltham Abbey revealed, a *Kaddish* is read over his absent soul.

But what manner of book is this? On one level, it is a highly eccentric biography of Rodinsky, though the deceased is remembered in so many different and conflicting ways by such a variety of living witnesses – some casting him as a genius, others as a fool, yet others as an almost criminal sociopath – that the identity of the departed is as open as the form. On another level, this is a twin memoir, with each of the narrators conveying their own individual testimony. On a third level, it represents a sequential autobiography penned by Lichtenstein, following her from her dawning awareness of her racial identity through her passionate search to the moment she herself feels earthed and lays the broken memory of Rodinsky to rest. Cumulatively, it is all of these things and more. Most especially, it is a book about its own making.

Skip to 2014. In that year Helen Macdonald won the Costa Book of the Year for a beautifully etched memoir – to hedge one's generic bets for a moment – entitled *H is for Hawk*. On one level this was an account of a bereavement, quite a vigorous *sub-genre* in itself. Macdonald was grieving for her father, but her self-prescribed course of convalescence took the unusual form of training a goshawk to fly in captivity. The ostensible subjects of her book thus included herself (*H is for Helen?*); her father, and, of course, the eponymous bird. But that was not all, since in 1951 the writer and one-time English teacher T.H. White, better-known for his Arthurian romances, had published a memoir called *The Goshawk*, describing his own experience of training a goshawk in the grounds of Stowe school. White's had been a very masculine book depicting a battle of wills: man against falcon. Throughout her text, Macdonald animadverts to it, contrasting her own falconer's career with White's. There is thus a second memoir shadowing the first, and the second is treated in such a way as to turn this aspect of the book into a biography of White. At least three genres of life writing are therefore involved in this appealing exercise – biography, autobiography, and memoir – the combined result being a hybridised fourth.

The Biographer's walk

In the late twentieth century, an enhanced critical awareness among biographers of the nature and limitations of their craft had been accompanied by a marked professionalisation of their calling. Until that moment, most biographers had been amateurs; subsequently they tended to regard biography as their job. From the point of view of its sources, its funding, and its distribution, biography had become an industry, and a very organised one at that. For a short time, it was big business, commanding large profits out of which six-figure advances to authors were not infrequently paid. A few biographers became stars. There was even a way of sauntering down Piccadilly in Central London casting furtive sideways glances to reassure oneself that one's latest title was on display in the front window of Hatchards or, failing that, of Waterstones. This biographer's walk occasionally culminated, when the relevant title was present, in attitudes of feigned surprise.

This new breed of biographers were mostly serial offenders. Michael Holroyd adopted his sardonic tone from Lytton Strachey, his two-volume life of whom graced the Hatchards window in 1967 and 1968. He subsequently dispatched Augustus John in two volumes (1974 and 1975), and Bernard Shaw in four (1988, 1989, 1991, and 1992). Lady Antonia Fraser (born 1932), daughter of the biographer Elizabeth Longford, serviced Mary Queen of Scots (1969), Cromwell (1973), Charles II (1979), Boadicaa (1988), the six wives of Henry VIII (1999), Marie Antoinette (2001), and herself (2015). Victoria Glendenning (born 1937) covered Elizabeth Bowen (1977), Edith Sitwell (1981), Vita Sackville-West (1983), Rebecca West (1987), Anthony Trollope (1992), and Jonathan Swift (1998). Claire Tomalin (born 1933) did for Mary Wollstonecraft (1974), Shelley (1980), Katherine Mansfield (1987), Nelly Tiernan (1990), Jane Austen (2000), Samuel Pepys (2002), and Thomas Hardy (2007), and, again, Charles Dickens (2011) and herself (2017).

Many of these biographies aimed to be definitive, and weighed in at more (sometimes far more) than 500 pages. The reason had partly to do with methods of working, drawing extensively on primary sources held usually in university libraries, many of them in the US. Indeed, so anxious were some American institutions for international scholars to use their collections, they very often paid them to do so. The holdings tended to be extensive, and the resulting works became so too. Biographers treating a human subject for the first time felt a strong need to share their precious findings. 'You know', I was told by Ann Thwaite (born 1932: Edmund Gosse 1985, A.A. Milne 1990, Emily Tennyson 1997, and Philip Gosse 2002), 'I always feel a need to put everything in. Do you feel the same way?'

With the millennium, conditions dramatically shifted. The bottom fell out of the biography market and, henceforth, gargantuan advances were in short supply. With the inception of Amazon in 1994 and the patenting of the Kindle in 2009, methods of distribution slowly moved from bookshops to the internet. Henceforth the Biographer's Walk became the Biographer's Click as anxious authors logged into Amazon each morning to see where the rankings of their latest title lay and, in the open reviews, what the wonderstruck of Wimbledon opined.

Though cradle-to-grave lives were still hammered out, fashion now favoured a less literal and inclusive approach. The two primary parameters of life writing have always been time and space. In some of the more adventurous sorties of the form, each of these now expanded to occupy the whole of the canvas. In 2002, the American historian John E. Wills devoted the whole of his *1688: A Global History* to a panorama of that one year that took in China, Mexico, Brazil, the Cape of Good Hope as well as provincial 'Glorious' Revolution in England. This lateral expansion of time was to prove especially rewarding in historical biography, not so much by disturbing chronological sequences – though that occurred as well – as by intensifying them. Thus *A Gambling Man*, Jenny Uglow's 2009 biography of King Charles I, concentrated exclusively on the decade between 1660 and 1670 when the monarchy re-established itself in a nation exhausted by war and Puritanical self-denial. Across those years Charles imposed his personality on Great Britain, reviving and liberating it in ways that have since become proverbial. It was a risk, hence the title of the book, and encompassed set-backs as extreme as the Great Plague of 1665 and the Great Fire of the following year. Theatre was emancipated, and manners were relaxed: Uglow even took to speculating on the length of Charles's penis. But these were also heroic years and, as the fire gripped London, Charles and his brother James, later extirpated and reviled, rose to the challenge and took their part in the saving of the capital by literally rolling up their shirt sleeves. This was as much a biography of a period as a three-dimensional portrait of a man. The canvas was crowded with figures great and small as, for a short time, the life of the monarch became the life blood of the people.

Such temporal distension proved a valuable way of injecting fresh life into frequently visited biographical subjects worn thin by over exposure. Shakespearean biography, for example, had languished in a rut in the later twentieth century until, in the early years of the millennium, the American scholar James Shapiro salvaged it through the brilliant expedient of homing in on particular years in which the development of the age's most original playwright meshed memorably with the general pulse of London, and of public and political events. In an essay contributed to Zachary Leader's 2015 volume *On Life Writing* Shapiro exposed the failings implicit in so much conventional literary biography. First, there had been the tendency to read the life through the work, a double fallacy since 'reading the life through the work leads not only to a distortion of that life, but also, I think inevitably, to a misreading of the work' (Leader, 20). This tendency had been particularly disastrous in the case of Shakespeare's life, about which only a handful of facts are known with any certainty; in the absence of further documentation his biographers had fallen back on supposition, and sometimes on pure make-believe. The result had been a series of cradle-to-grave accounts vitiated by 'circularity' and 'arbitrariness'. Instead, Shapiro championed an alternative approach. Taking a leaf out of the books of Charles Nicholl (2007) and James Bednarz (2012), he excavated finite moments in history, focussing in his words 'on what can be known with greater confidence: the 'form and the pressure' of the time that shaped Shakespeare's writing'. The result was the kind of cross-segment observable in Shapiro's account of the year 1599, when the playwright was 35. 'In 1599', Shapiro writes, 'Elizabethans sent off an army to crush an Irish rebellion, weathered an armada threat from Spain, gambled on a fledgling East India Company, and waited to see who would succeed their ageing and childless Queen'. In the same year Shakespeare 'completed *Henry the Fifth*, wrote *Julius Caesar* and *As You Like It* in quick succession and then drafted *Hamlet*' (Shapiro 2005, xv). Moving from the events to the plays and back again, Shapiro builds up a diorama of a year that left an indelible impression on English culture and society. He followed this success with an in-depth study of 1606, the year that produced the three magnificent tragedies of *King Lear, Macbeth,* and *Antony and Cleopatra*, his study of which is interleaved with vivid accounts of the early years of the reign of James I, the Gunpowder Plot and its aftermath, an outbreak of the plague, and a visit by the King of Denmark. Uncertainty in the kingdom is matched by a sense of anomie in the plays as, in the telling, political crisis turns into artistic crisis before the reader's eyes.

More recent periods have also provided ample scope for this sort of historically microscopic effect. The centenary year of 2017, for example and obvious reasons, saw a flurry in the biographies of leading figures in the Russian Revolution. None of these proved more rewarding than Catherine Merridale's *Lenin on the Train*, which telescoped an incisive account of the history of the revolution into a succinct narration of one particular episode: the free passage from Switzerland to St Petersburg permitted to Lenin and his friends by the German authorities, in the hope that the ensuing insurgency would help to undermine the Allies. The progress of their party across Central Europe is tracked from day to day. The entire journey took little more than ten days but, from Merridale's time-limited excursion, vistas open out before and after, to encompass the whole history of the time.

Diversifying the cast

Until around 1980, writers and politicians had been over-represented as subjects for biography, probably because both groups have tended to leave behind prolix, frequently self-serving accounts of their lives and activities on which the researching biographer could easily draw. Arguably this was, and is, almost too easy. There are, however, other groups temperamentally less inclined to write or speak directly of themselves. Some of the most absorbing biographies published over recent decades, for example, have been of scientists. The more numerically attuned, and the less verbally inclined the scientist, the greater and more rewarding the challenge. Andrew Hodges's revolutionary *Alan Turing: The Enigma* was originally published in 1983, towards the beginning of the decade when a computer became a common, indeed almost an indispensable, household appliance. At the start of that decade, Turing was not a household name; by the end of the century he most definitely was. The 'Enigma' of Hodges's title was the German-made cryptographic machine the operations of which Turing had worked to decode during the Second World War; it was also the personality of a man whose life and apparently suicidal death were themselves mysteries. Hodges's book represented the appropriation by biography of a fresh domain: it was also a kind of manifesto for Turing's hidden and persecuted sexuality.

Writing the lives of scientists thenceforth became a way of re-considering history. Adrian Desmond and James Moore's co-written *Darwin* of 1991 marked an important milestone in this respect, partly because Darwin is a controversial figure to whom scientists and specialists in other disciplines have both laid claim, whether in the secularist polemics of Richard Dawkins; in the critical work of Gillian Beer, who argued that a Darwinian strand runs through the whole of nineteenth-century literature; or in the debunking account of his life by A.N. Wilson (2017), the very first sentence of which proclaims that Darwin was wrong – a claim which the rest of his book sets out to substantiate. Over the decades since 1980, several well-known scientists have received exhaustively researched and insightful biographical treatment. As with Darwin, there has been a tendency to concentrate on individuals whose work has given rise to controversies that have entered the public, non-scientific, domain. This is definitely true of J. Robert Oppenheimer, the subject of Ray Monk's *Inside the Centre* (2012), whose research towards the Atom bomb and possible flirtation with Communism in the era of McCarthy were bound sooner or later to receive biographical attention.

Some of the most striking scientific biographies of the last recent decades, however, have recorded far quieter, more reticent, lives. In 2003 Jenny Uglow's *The Lunar Men: The Men Who Made the Future* brought to life a group of pioneering natural philosophers, engineers, and mechanical men who flourished in and around Birmingham in the early years of the nineteenth century. The result was both to broaden its readers' conception of the scientific revolution, and to contest the metropolitan bias of so much established biographical writing. Graham Farmelo's *The Strangest Man: The Hidden Life of Paul Dirac, Quantum Genius* took as its subject the originator of quantum mechanics, an individual almost notoriously reclusive and non-communicative, who in his concluding pages Farmelo identifies as fairly severely autistic. This is the kind of character of whom biographers had traditionally fought shy, preferring the outward going and demonstrative. Dirac's 'hidden life', however, proved rich and rewarding, his very strategies of emotional avoidance a match for his mental and mathematical sophistication.

All of these works were to a high degree artful, and all of them drew on the tried techniques of literary biography to describe lives not primarily devoted to literature. To that extent at least, they operated in reaction against celebrity arts-orientated biography. The unexamined assumption that only glamorous lives were worth recording was thus usefully challenged, and to great effect. In 2009 in her book *Sisters of Sinai* Janet Soskice concentrated on one unlikely pair, widowed twins from the Western lowlands of Scotland, who in the 1860s taught themselves oriental languages in middle age and then toiled across the desert to uncover the secrets of one of the earliest manuscripts of the Christian gospels in Syriac. These were lives of decent scholarly obscurity; yet the manner of telling rendered them gripping in the extreme, as so many obscure lives tend to be.

Eccentricity was the fulcrum around which several of these English lives swung. The classical scholar and linguist Jane Ellen Harrison (1850–1928) is a person of vacillating reputation, especially in Cambridge ('Oh, not her!' was the instantaneous response of a Trinity colleague when I proposed her work for an anthology of Classical Verse in Translation). Yet she is a role model of a kind, and as such has recently come into her own, especially among feminist scholars. One of the earliest woman students in Cambridge, who missed a First by a whisker, pioneer of Russian studies in England, companion and possibly lover of T.S. Eliot's later friend, the poet Hope Myrlees, and proponent of the ritualistic and comparative method in classical studies and archaeology, she remains indomitable, even if in her time she was largely ignored. In 2000 the classicist Mary Beard attempted to burrow to the heart of her in the slim but penetrating *In Search of Jane Harrison*. The book proved a thought-provoking not-quite success in that, acknowledging the difficulties thrown in its path, partly by the obtuseness of its subject and partly by the deliberate winnowing of the archive, it ended in post-structuralist angst about the necessary inconclusiveness of all knowledge. That Beard spent this amount of time on so admirable and perplexing person of whom few beyond the world of classical learning have heard was itself admirable and instructive. She later chose Harrison as 'My Hero' in *The Guardian*, concluding with the grateful sentence 'She made it possible for me to do what I do'.

Scholars enjoy oddness, Cambridge scholars especially. The classicalist Simon Goldhill highlighted this source of attraction in 2016 in his pointedly entitled *A Very Queer Family Indeed*, an account of another set of talented siblings, children of a forbidding Archbishop of Canterbury: E.F. ('Fred') Benson of the Mapp and Lucia novels, his brother A.C. Benson, prolific literary scholar, Master of Magdalene College, Cambridge, and lyricist of 'Land of Hope and Glory', their priestly brother and Egyptologist, probably Lesbian, sister. The result, as Tom Crewe wrote when reviewing it in *The London Review of Books*, is a 'slippery' book that attracts attention through its insistence on its subjects' oddness. What, Crewe went on to ask, justifies the effort? 'Are they still being written about just to satisfy our national weakness for eccentrics, forbidding Victorian patriarchs and tales of repressed sexuality?'. The misgivings were well aired, yet an answer lay to hand in Goldhill's many digressions about his own Cambridge life, including his depressions and oblique references to his tense subjectivity. Goldhill perfected a superbly indirect way of talking about himself while not talking about himself, which is precisely what the Benson siblings themselves did, even Arthur ('A.C') in a handwritten diary four million words long.

Relative obscurity attracted several biographers; others were drawn to subjects who had conducted their lives almost wholly in the shadows. The resulting works focussed not on the limelight but on the absences, and the need to fill them. There was, for example, a series of carefully documented lives of people who dwelt in the shade cast by others, be they employers or life partners. In 1990 Claire Tomalin's *The Invisible Woman: The Story of Nelly Tiernan and Charles Dickens* reconstructed from a host of fugitive clues the existence of a woman who was Dickens's mistress for many years after the failure of his marriage. It thus provided a very necessary antidote to Ackroyd's *Dickens* published in the same year, and a supplement to Tomalin's own Dickens biography of 2013. Similarly, in 2001 Carole Seymour-Jones's *Painted Shadow: The Life of Vivienne Eliot* recounted the melancholy and disturbed life of the first Mrs T.S. Eliot, a woman without whom the poet would never have written *The Waste Land*, or Robert Crawford been able to produce the rounded and nuanced account of Eliot's early years contained in his superbly etched *Young Eliot: From St Louis to The Waste Land* (2016). In 2007 Alison Light's *Mrs Woolf and the Servants* meticulously documented the professional and personal lives of the unknown people, mostly women, who maintained the successive households occupied in some comfort by one of the twentieth century's most accomplished authors. It thus supplied a vital accompaniment to Hermione Lee's copious and perceptive life of Woolf published in 1996.

Thus biography, in its attempts to evade the seductiveness of the capitalist creed of celebrity, frequently fled to the margins in search of the occluded, the obscure, and the reviled. The more invisible the life, for some biographers, the better. The problem here has been two-fold: either a too-obvious stance of advocacy ('Methinks the biographer doth protest too much'), or alternatively a patent if inevitable inequality between the biographer or narrator, privileged if sympathetic, and his or her subject who could too easily fall to the position of object of biographical charity. Extreme measures were sometimes necessary to avoid the resulting impression of *de haut en bas*. Perhaps the most resourceful, if not uniformly successful, essay of this kind in recent years has been Alexander Master's *Stuart: A Life Backwards*, later filmed, which describes the relationship between a university-educated physicist and author, and Stuart Clive Shorter (1962–2002) a down-and-out rescued from the backstreets of Cambridge.

Masters avoided the trap of condescension by placing Stuart, at least initially, in pole position. He offered him the first draft of his book, which Stuart peremptorily rejects:

> Stuart does not like the manuscript.
> Through the pale Tesco stripes of his supermarket bag I can see the wedge
>   of my papers. Two years of worth of interviews and literary effort.
> 'What's the matter with it?'
> 'It's bollocks boring'.

Masters 2005, 1

We are never shown this scorned manuscript; nor do we ever quite witness the course of Stuart's life in Stuart's own words. Instead, Stuart directs operations at one remove, obliging Masters to tell his life in reverse so that we can observe the wastage of human potential at close quarters: the disorganised present yielding onto the precious and unique might-have-been. In the process, Masters discovers much: about Stuart, about himself, and about the fraught development of this making and this relationship. Arguably the result is a partial failure since, despite his best efforts, the biographer never quite transcends himself – which biographer ever does? The attempt, however, served to raise important questions as to who owns any given life. Stuart's had been one long act of protest: against exclusion, against poverty, essentially against the ways in which he was *seen*. In that sense it had been a protest against the very act of biography itself since, however hard he tries, Masters is one of many *voyeurs*. And so is each reader, joining hands with the biographer in a posture of compassionate contempt. In none of these studies of occluded lives do we ever quite evade the impression of 'some mute inglorious Milton'. Obscurity ultimately proves as precarious a focus as celebrity. Biography is an ever-collapsing bridge.

Enter the crowd

During the early years of the twenty-first century, many of the truisms regarding biography were thus brought into question. There was, for example, the widespread assumption that a biography narrates the life of an individual. Many of the most accomplished biographies of recent years by contrast have concentrated on pairs, or on groups. Several, but by no means all, of these books described couples, or else families. Having resurrected Vivien Eliot, in 2008 Seymour-Jones turned her attention in her double-biography *A Dangerous Liaison* to those darlings of the post-war Left Bank: Simone de Beauvoir and Jean-Paul Sartre. There was no point in her arguing that Beauvoir existed in Sartre's shadow, which did not prevent her trying. Instead, she de-constructed the cult of celebrity by proving beyond doubt that each of these radical stars possessed feet of clay. De Beauvoir had been a serial sexual harasser banned from teaching because of her relationships with several girl pupils; both partners were, during the German occupation of Paris, a lot closer to the Nazi occupiers than either liked to make out. Seymour-Smith's was a more personality-driven and bilious treatment of a period and movement more engagingly covered eight years later in Sarah Bakewell's well-researched and unmissable *The Existentialist Café: Freedom, Being, and Apricot Cocktails* (2016).

Seymour-Jones, who died in 2015, belonged to the incriminatory school of biographical writing, but group biography was more usually given over to celebration. In 1975 Penelope Fitzgerald, a self-effacing and multi-faceted writer who could hardly put a foot wrong, had told the story of her father and her uncles: the extra-ordinary clan of *Knox Brothers* (1975) that included a cryptologist, an editor of *Punch*, and two priests. The disparity between their several occupations only served to emphasise the common spirit of enquiry that drove these remarkable men on. In effect all of Fitzgerald's biographies were of groups of likeminded people, whether of the Pre-Raphaelite Brotherhood in her 1977 book on *Edward Burne-Jones*, or in her *Charlotte Mew and Her Friends* (1984), of life on the fringes of literary London. Once again, it was a hidden – apparently unfulfilled – life that proved so heroic and rewarding.

Superficially, individual and group biography exists at opposite ends of a spectrum; but there are many shades in between. This is especially true of books about families. Since all individuals are the products of families, and all families composed of individuals, things could scarcely be otherwise. One traditional, and sometimes rather tedious, formula had been to begin with a closely observed study of a family across several generations, and slowly to watch the individual subject emerge from out of that background. A more imaginative approach has been to reverse this order of events. Edmund de Waal's *The Hare with Amber Eyes: A Hidden History* of 2010 is arguably the supreme modern exemplar of that second, alternative approach. De Waal, a ceramicist by trade, is a descendant of the Ephrussi, one of the grand Jewish dynasties that dominated central European business in the late nineteenth and earlier twentieth centuries. From his account it is clear that he grew up in relative ignorance of this fact. His father Victor was a high-ranking Anglican clergyman, latterly Dean of Canterbury; although born in Vienna, his paternal grandmother Elizabeth had married a Dutch businessman, settled in Tonbridge Wells after the war, and taken to the Anglican form of the Christian faith.

Beyond the serene, untroubled front lay a convoluted and tragic cultural backdrop which the book unfolds slowly and with meticulous suspense. The open sesame is an exotic family heirloom in the shape of a glass-fronted vitrine containing 264 *netsukes*, tiny ivory figures once suspended from the belts of traditional Japanese kimono gowns, of which the eponymous hare is just one. Edmund had inherited this object from his maternal great-uncle Iggy or Ignace, a Tokyo resident who had, in turn, inherited it from the Viennese branch of the family decimated after the *Anschluss* of March, 1938. That historical event, the violent annexation of Austria by Hitler's Germany, the consequent looting of the family home, the Palais Ephrussi on the Ringstrasse, and the scattering of family members and their treasures, are all vividly described, forming the climactic centrepiece of the work. It is framed by a complex interweaving of personal and collective histories that reach from Central Poland via Odessa in the Ukraine to Vienna and Paris, where Charles Ephrussi, a collector and aesthete and one of the models for Marcel Proust's Charles Swann, acquired those Japanese miniatures and sent them across to Vienna as a wedding present for one of his Austrian cousins.

De Waal's is a tale of obliteration and creation. It is also a fundamental contribution to a growing body of holocaust literature augmented six years later by Philippe Sands's erudite, Ballard Gifford prize-winning *East West Street*, an investigation into the author's Jewish-Ukrainian roots that opens out into a study of the evolution of the legal terms 'crimes against humanity' and 'genocide', and the role that these legal concepts were to play in the Nuremburg trials of 1945, and in the international order of the immediate post-war world.

Daddy I never knew you

The family biography gave rise to a multiple sub-genre: the search for origins taking the form of an agonised attempt by a child to understand its parent. To some extent this style of writing pandered to the sort of appetite as catered for by the television series *Who Do You Think You Are?* But the tendency goes back at least as far as Edmund Gosse's *Father and Son* (1907): it is a variety of life writing that brings together biography and autobiography. It has the additional advantage that it evokes a state-of-affairs experienced by very many of us, from at least one vantage-point, and eventually from both.

Blake Morrison's 1993 memoir *And When Did You Last See Your Father?* was partly written during the months when his dad, a Skipton GP, lay dying of cancer, and revised prior to publication. It is thus to some extent an expression of grief, or rather of proleptic grief, but other emotions enter as well, including rage, love, resentment, puzzlement, and last but not least, jealousy. The son, who moves backwards and forwards between Blackheath and West Yorkshire, enjoys the precarious fame and glamorous metropolitan life; the father the philanthropic calling, the local fan base, and a way with DIY and women. Exasperation is never far from the surface: in the opening essay, the 12-year-old boy has to sit in the back of the family jalopy and watch as his Dad lies and cheats his way into a reserved enclosure at a motor show. During a family holiday in a Swiss ski resort suggestively named Lech, he grinds his teeth in frustration as his middle-aged progenitor gets off with (or is imagined to get off with) the glamorous 19-year-old tour guide called Rachel after whom he himself ineptly lusts. Morris is not ashamed to describe himself lying amid the soap suds in his bath pathetically masturbating. The final, deliberately nurtured, impression is that the much-published son is better at art; the bluff, down-to-earth, father a lot more effective at life, both his own and other peoples'. It is only an impression of course, and from unemphatic clues dropped elsewhere in the text we learn that the son has had his own amorous and practical triumphs. The son is an artefact, and so is the father. All writers of memoir know this to be the case. If one can never entirely trust biography, where the subject is another, can one place any more confidence in memoir, where one of the subjects is the author whose very words one reads?

Inevitably the vista on which a memoirist looks out is a partial one. This fact was brought home to Morrison's readers when in 2002, after his mother's death, he published a complementary memoir entitled *Things My Mother Told Me*. Drawing on his parents' recently discovered love letters and a cache of souvenirs happened on at the bottom of his mother's wardrobe, this is to some extent a contribution to the aforementioned sub-genre of lives-lived-in-the-shadows. But it is a lot more that. In the earlier book, Kim Morrison's cradle Irish Catholicism had been fleetingly hinted at in a half-quotation from Cardinal Newman's hymn 'Lead, Kindly Light' remembered during a rainy camping trip. In his second family memoir Morrison is forced to face the unpalatable fact that his father had been, not only a lecher and a cheat but an atheistical bully who had forced his wife to bury her religion and, with it, many of her childhood associations. Morrison is setting the record straight; but he is also in his own characteristically unobtrusive way, dilating on a clash of cultures and the uneasy process of compromise entailed in many a marriage.

Openness is the key to success in this kind of writing. In 1989 Germaine Greer, having already established herself both as an outstanding Shakespeare scholar and as a leading feminist, produced *Daddy, We Hardly Knew You*, a study of her relationship with her father Reg, a South-African-born newspaper-advertising salesman and, by her account, a rotten and uncaring husband and father. The title implied that she wished the relationship had been warmer, but the book was so tilted by anger and disappointment as to give the impression in some quarters that she was dumping on Reg her entire dislike of the male gender. Or, indeed, the other way round.

Disappointment, however, does not necessarily have this particular fallout. In 2004 the Scottish poet Jackie Kay journeyed to Abuja in Nigeria in search of the birth father who had engendered her in Aberdeen in 1961 on a student nurse, and then promptly abandoned both of them. She was then adopted and brought up by a loving Communist couple and, by the time she tracked down her absconding biological male parent, he had turned into a hypocritically self-righteous evangelical Christian unwilling to acknowledge her lest his fervent co-religionists lose their faith when learning of his 'sin'. Kay's was a far more richly textured book than Greer's, fuelled by genuine curiosity, by horror at her biological father's indifference, and by a glowing gratitude for the manner in which she had been raised in her adoptive home. Like Greer, Kay is disenchanted, but she is inured to the consolations of judgement. One of the funniest scenes in the book occurs when she encounters her ageing and confused biological mother in Milton Keynes and is led a merry dance round the town in search of her mother's church, the location and name of which she has forgotten. Hers is an affectionate, humorous, and passionate study of what it means to have lost a home and to have found one.

Marriage is a subject that encourages tandem biographical treatment. Nigel Nicolson's well-publicised and pruriently televised *Portrait of a Marriage* (1973), which drew on the papers of his parents the novelist Vita Sackville-West and the publisher, Harold Nicolson, blazed a trail in this respect, largely owing to the ambivalent sexuality of both mother and father. Once again, however, it has been the less lime-lit lives that have provoked the quietest and most impressive miracles of art. Vikram Seth's *Two Lives* (2005) is an overlooked masterpiece. At the centre of this unlikely book are two individuals from widely different settings: Seth's uncle Shanti, a one-armed dentist of Bengali descent and his German, Jewish wife Henny. Circumstances threw this devoted pair together in Pre-war Berlin. Shanti, who was obliged twice to qualify, once in Germany and once in England, lost his arm while serving with the allied troops in Italy. He proposed after years of diffidence and delay. Seth draws on their letters, some of which came to light after Henny's death. By no stroke of the imagination were these glamorous lives. Shanti worked from a large, ramshackle detached house in Hendon, latterly with Hetty at his side. There were no children. With an honesty to the facts that reminds one of Naipaul, Seth draws a double portrait that convinces us of the heroism of ordinary lives. The book may have started out as an obligation; it ended as a triumph.

Omniscience and beyond

When Virginia Woolf coined the term 'Life-Writing', it is doubtful if she recognised its full and potential scope. What was implicit in the term from the very beginning, however, was a recognition of its plasticity. It has been adopted as an academic buzz phrase and as a course description, but it is essentially a non-academic banner that invites all of us – livers, writers, and readers – to create and to conflate. The life can be that of a person, as in Ackroyd's *Blake* (1995), of city as in his *London: The Biography* (2000), of a family, a nation, or a world. Sara Maitland's *The Book of Silence* (2008) is at one and the same time a profound memoir and the biography of an attitude: an absence that is also a presence. Yuval Noah Harari's *Sapiens* of 2011 (English translation 2014) is nothing less than a life history of the human race; his *Homo Deus* (2015, English translation 2016) is an account of the race's future.

Beyond that lies scientific speculation: Stephen Hawking's *A Brief History of Time* (1988) was a biography of the universe; David Deutsch's *The Fabric of Reality* (1997) envisages – or, more strictly proposes – a system of parallel multiverses which together encompass all that is, or was, or shall be. In so doing it breaches a divide more entrenched than that between biography, autobiography, and memoir: the academic division between the arts and the sciences. To be honest, this is a Berlin Wall that has been in the process of deconstruction for some time. In 2018 the Italian physicist Carlo Rovelli identified a common strand bringing these once alienated disciplines together. In *The Order of Time* (2018), he interprets the fourth dimension as a Janus head looking both inwards and outwards. If science directs our attention to the elusive realties of space-time, the artistic imagination enables us to explore our own individual sense of temporality through the labyrinths of personal memory, a phenomenon of much interest to the life-writer, but a source of equal fascination to the neurologist. Unsurprisingly, Rovelli has an extended and insightful passage about Proust, whose great novel he describes as a 'detailed meandering among the synapses of Marcel's brain' (Rovelli 2018, 162). Unconsciously too he adopts the image of the steam that represents both the delusion of universal time, invoked from Heraclitus to Newton, and Woolf's private stream of consciousness. If the first has been the classic medium of biography and the second of memoir, modern life-writing has increasingly seen a watershed, and a convergence.

All of which is a long way from Dickens, or else it is a way of peering into his mind, depending on where you are coming from. The philosopher Pascal once famously argued that the individual was greater than the cosmos, since the first cannot contemplate the second, whilst the reverse is never the case. It is the great advantage of recent life-writing that it can observe and contemplate both. Life-writing is an ever-opening eye.

References

Ackroyd, P. (1990), *Dickens*, London: Sinclair-Stevenson.
Ackroyd, P. (1995), *Blake*, London: Sinclair-Stevenson.
Ackroyd, P. (2000), *London: The Biography*, London: Sinclair-Stevenson.
Bakewell, S. (2016), *The Existentialist Café: Freedom, Being and Apricot Cocktails*, London: Chatto and Windus.
Beard, M. (2000), *The Invention of Jane Harrison*, Boston: Harvard University Press.
Briggs, J. (2005), *Virginia Woolf: An Inner Life*, London: Allen Lane.
Crawford, R. (2016), *Young Eliot from St Louis to The Wasteland*, London: Vintage.
Desmond, A. and Moore, J. (1991), *Darwin*, London: Michael Joseph.
Deutsch, D. (1997), *The Fabric of Reality: Towards A Theory of Everything*, London: Penguin.
de Waal, E. (2010), *The Hare With Amber Eyes: A Hidden Inheritance*, London: Vintage.
Farmelo, G. (2009), *The Strangest Man; The Hidden Life of Paul Dirac*, London: Faber.
Fitzgerald, P. (1977), *Edward Burne Jones*, London: Michael Joseph.
Fitzgerald, P. (1975), *The Knox Brothers: Edmund (Evoe) 1881–1971, Dillwyn (1883–1943), Wilfred, 1886–1950, Ronald 1888–1957*, London: Macmillan.
Fitzgerald, P. (1984), *Charlotte Mew and Her Friends*, London: Collins.
Goldhill, S. (2016), *A Very Queer Family Indeed: Sex, Religion and the Bensons in Victorian Britain*, Chicago: University of Chicago Press.
Gosse, E. (1907), *Father and Son*, London: Heinemann, 1907.
Greer, G. (1989), *Daddy We Hardly Knew You*, New York: Fawcett Columbine.
Harari, Y.N. (2014), *Sapiens: A Brief History of Humankind*, London: Vintage.
Harman, C. (2018), ‘*Mrs Gaskell and Me* by Nell Stevens – Desire, Satire and Making Things Up’, *The Guardian*, 28 September, 2018.
Hawking, S. (1988), *A Brief History of Time: From The Big Bang to Black Holes*, London: Bantam Dell.
Hodges, A. (1983), *Alan Turing: The Enigma*, London: Burnett Books/Hutchinson.
Kay, J. (2011), *Red Dust Road*, London: Picador.
Leader, Z. ed. (2015), *On Life-Writing*, Oxford: Oxford University Press.
Light, A. (2007), *Mrs Woolf and The Servants*, London: Penguin.
Macdonald, H. (2014), *H is for Hawk*, London: Vintage.
Maitland, S. (2008), *A Book Of Silence*, London: Granta.
Masters, A. (2005), *Stuart: A Life Backwards*, London: Fourth Estate.
Merridale, C. (2017), *Lenin On The Train*, London: Penguin.
Monk, R. (2012), *Inside The Centre: The Life of J. Robert Oppenheimer*, London: Jonathan Cape.
Morrison, B. (1993), *And When Did You Last See Your Father?*, London: Granta.
Morrison, B. (2002), *Things My Mother Never Told Me*, London: Chatto and Windus.
Nicolson, N. (1973), *Portrait of A Marriage*, London: Weidenfeld and Nicolson.
Painter, G.D. (1959, 1965), *Marcel Proust: A Biography*, 2 vols, London: Chatto and Windus.

Proust, M. (1971), *Contre Sainte-Beuve précédé de Pastiches et Mélanges et suivi de Essais et articles*, Paris: Gallimard.

Rovelli, C. (2018), *The Order of Time*, London: Penguin.

Sands, P. (2016), *East-West Street; On the Origins of Genocide and Crimes against Humanity*, London: Weidenfeld and Nicolson.

Seth, V. (2005), *Two Lives*, New York: Little, Brown.

Seymour-Jones, C. (2001), *Painted Shadow: A Life of Vivienne Eliot*, London: Constable.

Seymour-Jones, C. (2008), *Dangerous Liaison: Simone de Beauvoir and Jean-Paul Sartre*, London: Century.

Shapiro, J. (2005), *1599: A Year in the Life of William Shakespeare*, London: Faber.

Shapiro, J. (2015a), *1606: William Shakespeare and the Year of Lear*, London: Faber.

Shapiro, J. (2015b), 'Unravelling Shakespeare's Life' in *Leader* 2015, 7–24.

Sinclair, I. and Litchenstein, R. (1999), *Rodinsky's Room*, London: Granta.

Soskice, J. (2009), *Sisters of Sinai: How Two Lady Adventurers Found the Hidden Gospels*, London: Vintage.

Stevens, N. (2018), *Mrs Gaskell and Me: Two Women, Two Love Stories, Two Centuries Apart*, London: Picador.

Tadié, J.-Y. (1996), *Marcel Proust: Biographie*, Paris: Gallimard.

Tomalin, C. (1990), *The Invisible Woman: The Story of Nelly Ternan and Charles Dickens*, London: Viking.

Uglow, J. (1990), *Elizabeth Gaskell: A Habit of Stories*, London: Faber.

Uglow, J. (2003), *The Lunar Men: The Friends Who Made The Future, 1730–1810*, London: Faber.

Uglow, J. (2009), *A Gambling Man: Charles II and the Restoration*, London: Faber.

Wills, J.E. (2012), *1688: A Global History*, New York: Norton.

Wilson, A.N. (2017), *Darwin: Victorian Mythmaker*, London: John Murray.

Woolf, V. (1928), *Orlando*, London: The Hogarth Press.

Woolf, V. (1940), *Roger Fry*, London: The Hogarth Press.

Woolf, V. (1976), edited by Shulkind, J. *Moments of Being: Unpublished Autobiographical Writings of Virginia Woolf*, London: University of Sussex Press.

8

CREATIVE WRITING COURSES AND THE PRAGMATICS OF PUBLISHING

R. Lyle Skains

Introduction

Writing for publishing is a specific topic that was rarely covered in my undergraduate and postgraduate programmes in creative writing, though the dominant assumption of the creative writing workshop is that the students' goals are always to become published authors. When it was covered, it was always in terms of the mechanics of submission: crafting the query letter, honing the first three chapters to perfectly hook the reader, and how to find agents and editors who might accept the work. When I began teaching aspects of writing for publishing as a postgraduate teaching assistant, though I had been published several times, I still had very little idea of how the publishing industry worked, much less its history or strategies. The workshop-dominant structure of my undergraduate and MFA in creative writing, like most, failed to prepare me thoroughly for publishing my own writing and for teaching other creative writers how to publish – particularly in today's volatile digital environment. Teaching creative writing has evolved beyond the workshop (for many reasons, including diversity and authority); to best serve our students, it calls for a multi-pronged, mixed-methods approach that prepares students not only in terms of critical thinking and craft, but also in terms of skills and vocation.

Creative writing in higher education is generally acknowledged to have begun in the Iowa Writers Workshop in the 1930s (Bishop, 1990; Fenza, 2000; Brayfield, 2009; Vanderslice, 2010; Bennett, 2014). Its creators, Norman Foerster followed by Paul Engle (Fenza, 2000), created it to provide a community for writers to hone their talent, not to teach writing; their philosophy was that writing could not be taught, merely nurtured (Bishop, 1990; Donnelly, 2010). Stephanie Vanderslice notes it was created for *polished* writers, to toughen them up for facing critics, and largely consisted of men attending university on the U.S. G.I. Bill (2010, pp. 30–32);

its assumptions were that its students were homogenous in their culture, experience, commitment, and ability (Haake, 1994, p. 80). The workshop itself is highly restrictive: the number of students is limited, with 10 noted as an ideal; its focus is on writing, and rarely reading outside the workshop pieces; it institutes a 'gag rule' silencing the author whose work is being discussed; it focusses on flaws in the work according to the group consensus rather than publishing or audience analysis; it focusses on the final product over the process of producing work; it is usually restricted to the 'the three-headed Iowa canon' of minimalist realism, verbose realism, and magical realism (Bennett, 2014, p. n.p.), eschewing all other genres in its servitude to literature (Bizzaro, 2010, p. 38). Its model is one that persists despite changes in the student body, universities, and publishing industry, mostly because its instructors simply teach as they themselves were taught (Amato and Fleisher, 2001); for example, Gill James's presentation of her workshop model differs little from Paul Engle's early twentieth-century construction (2009).

Yet creative writing researchers and instructors have been urging their peers to update their teaching methods for decades. They have condemned the Iowa model as an invitation to 'laziness, calcified thinking and emotional abuse' (Kennedy, 2012, p. 202), an oppressive space that perpetuates patriarchy and bourgeois economics (Koehler, 2015, p. 17) and silences many who may already feel alienated and disempowered (Kearns, 2009, p. 794) in a multicultural and multilingual community (Brayfield, 2009, p. 210). It places ultimate authority in the instructor, reifying a New Critical perspective that privileges 'norms' of literature rather than encouraging writers to experiment (Bizzaro, 1994, p. 238), focussing on polishing writing and pushing it towards this 'common, safe, and neutral ground' (Webb, 1990, p. 332), and actively suppressing minority voices and avant-garde expression (Amato and Fleisher, 2001). Wendy Bishop argues for a 'transactional workshop' led by students and empowering the author's voice to direct their own feedback, situated in the context of their goals and practice (1990). Most creative writing pedagogical discourse echoes this notion and builds upon it, espousing student-led workshops (Bizzaro, 1994; Amato and Fleisher, 2001), encouraging integration of cultural discourse and theory (Garber and Ramjerdi, 1994; Ostrom, 1994; Donnelly, 2009; Haake, 2010; Vanderslice, 2010; Kostelnik, 2014), and development of critical thinking and transferable skills that are more applicable to the modern digital workforce (Cope and Kalantzis, 2009; Clark, 2010; Moxley, 2010; Brandt, 2015; Koehler, 2015).

If creative writing in higher education's goal is to produce published writers, then we must acknowledge the significant changes occurring in the publishing industry; it is no longer sufficient to teach the art of the query letter to twenty-first-century authors. While royalty publishing is certainly not obsolete, nonetheless publishing has become democratised: the digital age has produced a writing-literate culture (Brandt, 2015) that is already participating in mass authorship (Laquintano, 2016). Timothy Laquintano defines publishing both as a professional practice and as 'a literacy practice that develops under conditions in which ordinary people have the ability to publish their writing using digital infrastructures' (ibid., 12), leading to mass authorship. Writers who intend to participate within these practices must be aware of the trends in the industry (which necessitates knowledge of its history and structures) and their options within and without it. Creative writing continues in the traditional form of the book distributed via royalty publishing; it is also erupting in indie publishing through e-books and print-on-demand, fanfiction on sites like Wattpad and Archive of Our Own, and digital-born forms like Twine games and webcomics. Authors are utilising alternative funding models, including crowdsourcing through Kickstarter and Unbound and patronage through Patreon, as well as mixed media forms, including interactive narratives, podcasts, and transmedia texts (Skains, 2019). The digital medium makes publication easy for creative writers; it also introduces new contexts, forms, and considerations such as how to find and grow audiences in such fragmented spaces of attention (Goldhaber, 1997; Bhaskar, 2013).

The result of these various shifts in creative writing and publishing contexts calls for not just updates to the pedagogical model of the Iowa workshop, but for broader inclusion of publishing and writing for publishing in creative writing programmes. The study of publishing in higher education is a much more recent trend than creative writing, emerging only in the 1970s (Geiser, 1997). Publishing as an academic subject has largely remained a distinct study from creative writing, focussed primarily on the business aspects of what has often been called an 'accidental' profession (Greco, 1990, p. 18) – despite the clear overlap of creative and business endeavours. Indeed, many students of creative writing enter the publishing industry as editors (Logan and Prichard, 2016; *What can I do with a creative writing degree?*, 2018). In order to best prepare our writing students for their careers – whether they be published authors, editors, or other vocations drawing on their multiliteracy skills – it is vital to expand their rudimentary understanding of professional writing and publishing, and to dissuade their Romantic notions of creative genius in favour of developing robust process and critical thinking skills.

Towards that end, this essay models two undergraduate modules I have developed combining creative writing and publishing: Professional Publishing and 21st Century Writing & Publishing. The following sections discuss the ways that digital technology and economic and administrative challenges have changed the creative writing student and classroom. This discussion is followed by descriptions of each module, and the pedagogical philosophies behind their structures. A discussion section ensues, parsing this approach with regard to meeting student, instructor, university, and even cultural goals for the creative writer.

Creative writing in today's higher education environment

Digital technologies, like many technologies before, are changing what it means to write and publish. The Romantic notions of the writer as an isolated, creative genius and the publisher as an arbiter of taste and culture cannot hold up in today's environment of microblogging, indie publishing, fanfiction, and risk-averse publishing economies (if they were ever accurate at all). Contemporary publishing can mean posting on a blog, constructing a fictional Twitter persona, formatting an XML file for indie e-book distribution, crafting hypertexts and literary games, launching a Kickstarter campaign – or a combination of all of the above, and then some (Moxley, 2010; Laquintano, 2016; Skains, 2019). For creative writers to succeed in a context where 'writing has widened beyond the page' (Koehler, 2015, p. 26), they must be literate in more than just the three-act structure. A multiliteracies approach (Cazden et al., 1996; Cope and Kalantzis, 2009) is called for, wherein students can gain practical experience, the ability to conceptualise their experiential knowledge and analyse their work and the work of others with regard to relationships of power, and the ability to apply all of this to work in the real world.

This same digital technology has also altered the audiences for creative writing. Despite pessimistic claims that the book is dead and literature along with it, audiences read more now than they ever have before – just in more media than the mere codex. Creative narratives occur in many spaces, including books, e-books, blogs, fanfiction sites, social media, games (Ensslin, 2014), Reddit forums (Alexander, 2016), and even ecommerce reviews (Skains, 2018). The book – or rather, the narrative, as the materiality of the book dissolves in digital spheres – is enabled as a read-write medium (Lessig, 2008; Laquintano, 2016), wherein the boundary between readers and writers is permeable, texts are mutable, and even the most fringe genres can find a home and audience. This fracturing of the twentieth-century communication hierarchy of author->fixed text->reader has fragmented audiences in a many-to-many democratisation of media communication, thinning attention to any one form, genre, or author. Today's writers and publishers compete in an attention economy, as our ability to consume media has been far outpaced by our collective ability to create new texts (Goldhaber, 1997); everyone can create, thanks to digital media, but it's harder than ever to collect more than a modicum of the audience required to convert that attention capital into cultural or financial capital.

In addition to the writing and publishing world they will encounter once they depart our hallowed university halls, the culture and economy *within* our institutions have changed significantly since the formation of creative writing programmes in higher education. Foerster and Engle's dedicated (and distinguishing) community of critique for writers with established talent has evolved into a cash cow market for universities (Hancock, 2008; Simon, 2015), particularly in an age of austerity. The drive to recruit more students paying higher fees, combined with government-driven efforts to widen participation in higher education (Leathwood and O'Connell, 2003), have resulted in creative writing programmes with a diverse set of students in terms of experience, culture, motivation, and career goals. The perception that a university education boosts career prospects and earnings – aside from any loftier goals of creating better citizens – leads to pressure on universities for development of 'transferable skills', that is, vocational training applicable to the wide range of careers that students of English and creative writing matriculate into: design, media, arts, business, marketing, public relations, and sales (Logan and Prichard, 2016; *What can I do with a creative writing degree?*, 2018). The pressure is thus on creative writing instructors not only to hone the creative writing techniques of a non-homogenous, ever larger group of students, but also to 'scaffold students' development of critical thinking, communication, collaboration, problem-solving, and metacognitive skills necessary to thrive in the complex and globalized society of the future— and today' (Howe and Van Wig, 2017, p. 139).

Likewise, this non-homogenous group of creative writing students has a non-homogenous set of goals. Katharine Haake notes that in the beginning, creative writing programmes were designed primarily to enable students to become published writers, and secondarily to become creative writing teachers (1994, p. 79). The students entering our programmes, however, have distinct and complex goals for themselves. Most are seeking assurance that they *can* write, overcoming the still-dominant Romantic myths about creative genius (Bishop, 1990, p. 2), not only to confirm their own capabilities but also to determine if creative writing is the best vocation for their abilities (Webb, 1990, p. 333). Bishop also notes that many enrol in writing programmes 'for the structure and prompting and prodding, for the demands and deadlines and activities that will help them generate new work' (1990, p. 62). Many of my students enter their programme with the anticipated goal of becoming a 'published author', generally defining this as the narrow notion of having a novel published by a royalty publisher. Most of them leave, however, with a much wider knowledge of the possibilities for writing careers, including web writing, indie publishing, media production, screenwriting, playwriting, writing for games, journalism, feature writing, travel writing, and much more. It is insufficient to simply play into their naïve expectations of writerly ideals; as twenty-first-century creative writing instructors, we have an obligation to expose them to as many possibilities for their success as possible.

This can be a daunting task for creative writing instructors, particularly as the Iowa model rarely leaves room for training them as teachers, leading them to simply mimic the way they were taught (Amato and Fleisher, 2001). We have largely been indoctrinated to the strictures of the creative writing workshop – the 'gag rule', focus on flaws, and realism genres – which perpetuate 'patriarchal forces and bourgeois economics that, ultimately, turn the fiction workshop into a politically and culturally oppressive space' (Koehler, 2015, p. 18). To better serve our students and their potential for significant contribution to culture, we as creative writing instructors need to abandon this constrictive model that assumes a certain type of student and privileges a particular approach to literature; in fact, we need to break free from the notion that as creative writing instructors and students that we are in *service* to literature. My goal as an instructor is to arm my students with creative writing skills, yes, but also to instil multiliteracies: to develop their critical thinking skills, to empower them to break free of canonical expectations and socio-cultural power structures, to take the processes and practices they learn on their modules and apply them to their life and career post-university.

The challenge for instructors is to create a classroom/programme environment that permits pursuit of the goals of all parties involved: students, instructors, and universities. Students want to be 'good writers'; because of the dominant cultural and educational models, they expect to become good writers by sitting in workshop circles, ideally with prominent writers telling them how to do it 'correctly'. As instructors, we know that excellent writers are not necessarily excellent teachers, and vice versa; we are beginning to understand that the workshop model has fundamental flaws. So as we try to introduce alternative methods, we face resistance from students, as we are not meeting their inexperienced expectations. The pressures of measures such as the UK's National Student Survey, RateMyProfessor.com, and universities' financial need to please students as customers further complicate the maze of expectations instructors must negotiate. Universities want us to match marketing campaigns and do whatever will make our students/customers give us excellent scores on the litany of surveys and evaluations that pretend to measure teaching quality; it is difficult to push back on both these fronts to meet our own goals of empowering creative writers as purveyors of culture and as citizens of the modern world.

Nonetheless, that is what I have sought to do in developing the various modules I teach, and in particular the writing and publishing modules profiled in this chapter. Publishing is not often taught in parallel with creative writing in the workshop model – when it is, it rarely pushes the creative writer into the digital age, exposing them to the multitude of publishing, distribution, and monetisation platforms that are enabling writers to reach their audiences and make a living. I attempt to fill that gap with the modules I offer, not only building my students' creative and vocational skillsets, but also incorporating pedagogical techniques that improve their multiliteracy skills, better preparing them for the changing demands of the current workforce, for the power imbalances in their social structures, and for navigating issues of self and culture in digital environments.

Teaching writing for publishing: model modules

I have taught various 'writing for publishing' modules over the last decade or so, and my methods have evolved significantly. Early on, I focussed on what I myself had been taught: how to write for a market (commercial rather than literary; as a speculative fiction enthusiast, I greatly resented being forced to write literary fiction as a creative writing student), and how to get agents and editors on board with a particular novel project. I had little awareness of the history of publishing, the work of editors, the trends in the current industry, and what developments were on the horizon. My research interest in digital media and its effects on creative writing, however, led me to widen my focus to include its effects on *publishing* creative writing, and my growing awareness that the publishing industry is in the midst of a paradigm shift of Gutenberg proportions. Thus I continually push my modules to include discussion and evaluation of this shift, to better prepare my students for the writing and publishing atmosphere they will launch themselves into. The two modules profiled here, Professional Publishing and 21st Century Writing & Publishing, immerse students in current publishing trends, arming them with creative and analytical skills to traverse this ever-evolving landscape.

Professional Publishing

I created 'Professional Publishing' to meet the needs of a select few third-year students in our creative writing programme, thus it was a small module of four. The module's aims for the students were simple: to gain professional skills in writing, editing, and publishing creative writing in the current marketplace; to gain experience working in professional groups; and to gain awareness of publishing industry trends. All students on the module were members of the 'Editorial Board'; the instructors (my colleague Eben Muse and I) were the 'Editors-in-Chief'. The Editorial Board was tasked with writing, commissioning, editing, designing, and publishing a collected volume of creative writing by the end of the semester. The requirements for this volume were: (1) it must be published as both a print-on-demand and a reflowable e-book with the major online booksellers, and (2) it must reflect positively on the publishing body (the university).

The assessments were designed in approximation of Linda B. Nilson's 'specifications grading' (2014), in which the module incorporates multiple pass/fail assessments – the more passing marks, the higher the overall module mark.[1] The assessments were part of the editorial and publishing process: (1) a 3,000-word creative piece for the collection, (2) a commissioned short story for the collection, (3) two developmental editorial reviews of submitted stories, (4) two copyedits of submitted stories, (5) layout/design of two of the stories, and (6) peer reviews for each of the weekly editorial board meetings. All assessments, however, were not mandatory; in order to achieve a passing mark (D in our university's A–F scheme), students only had to perform satisfactorily in assessments 1 (creative work), 3 (editorial reviews), and 6 (peer reviews); the more satisfactory assessments a student completed, the higher their overall mark (see Table 8.1). Assessments 4–6 were marked pass/fail; assessments 1–3 were marked according to the decisions of the Editors-in-Chief as to acceptance of each piece for publication: 'Publish as-is' (an A mark), 'Publish, minor editing' (B), 'Reject; editing required' (C), 'Reject; significant editing required' (D), and 'Reject' (F). A token system, with three initial tokens per student, allowed students to trade a token to revise and resubmit a piece for a better decision; students could also trade tokens among one another in return for favours, such as help editing with a difficult piece, or copyediting if that was not a particular student's strength.

TABLE 8.1 Final marking table

Satisfactory assessment	Marking ranges				
	A	B	C	D	E
1. Creative work	•	•	•	•	•
2. Commissioned work	•	•			
3. Editorial reviews (2)	•	•	•	•	
4. Copyedits (2)	•	•	•		
5. Layout design/edits (2)	•	•			
6. Peer reviews	•	•	•	•	•
Average 'excellent' peer review of performance	•				
'Publish as-is' decisions on at least two of:	•				
• Student's own work • Edited works					

Only half the module topics are planned in advance: coverage of practicalities such as promoting a call for works, conducting various levels of edit, marketing strategies, publishing options, technical lessons on design and layout, and copyright issues. The students, based on their self-identified needs, can request remaining scheduled lecture sessions. These included author contracts, budgeting, working in groups, and organising a book launch. The Editorial Board sets their own schedule and deadlines for each assessment based on the final deadline for publishing the collection, and each student performs various group roles in their weekly meetings and throughout the semester: chair, secretary, treasurer, marketing officer, etc. By midway through the semester, the Editors-in-Chief very much served an advisory role, aiding with group conflicts as we would in any workplace, reviewing the submitted work as scheduled, and identifying resources as necessary.

21st Century Writing & Publishing

21st Century Writing & Publishing is an on-going module that I have taught, progressing through various iterations, for around eight years. In its current iteration, it is a joint module for second- and third-year undergraduates, taught every other year. Its aims are focussed on developing understanding of digital publishing and epublishing; developing proficiency in designing narratives for publication; and understanding the effects of digital media on publishing, writing, and reading narrative in current environments, including relevant critical theory. Students on this module write a piece of original fiction in a chosen medium (prose or digital fiction) and submit it for publication or self-publish the work. The module often involves advanced hypermedia techniques, writing in multiple modes of communication, and questions about the economic possibilities for writers in the digital age.

This module, too, incorporates a specifications grading model, in a three-pronged approach. Students complete weekly tasks developing two individual assessments: the creative work for publication, and an argumentative essay based in the practice of writing and publishing their creative work. The third assessment incorporates on-going discourse to the module; its form has changed over the years, from participating in weekly blogs or discussion forums on module topics to, currently, group student-led seminars. The student groups are each assigned a week to lead seminar discussions and exercises based on the relevant critical and creative readings assigned that week. These sessions are peer-reviewed; the mark on this assessment incorporates both performance in leading the seminar discussion for the group, and submitting individual peer reviews for all the other groups. All tasks assigned for this module are marked on a modified pass/fail system: 0 denotes a task that was not submitted; 1 denotes a submitted but failing task; 2 denotes a pass; and 3 denotes an exceptional task, one that surpasses expectations in terms of critical thinking or incorporation of readings. Final marks for each of the three assessments are based on the number of satisfactory marks they receive for tasks related to the assessment: submitting and receiving mostly satisfactory '2' marks falls in the B-range, whereas mostly '3's falls in the A-range. The minimum requirements for each assessment are the final deliverables: the published creative piece, the essay, and participation in leading a seminar. Because of the system, however, a student who *only* delivers the final product can earn a maximum mark in the D-range, regardless of the quality of that product (see sample marking rubric in Tables 8.2 and 8.3). As with Professional Publishing, each student is awarded tokens they can trade for resubmission of a '1' task or submission of a late task.

TABLE 8.2 Task breakdown for creative assessment

MINIMUM REQUIREMENT to PASS

Creative Portfolio
 2000-word work of creative writing, created and published (or submitted for publication) during the semester.

OPTIONAL TASKS for HIGHER MARKS

Creative Exploration Task
 Submit 3 creative exercises in *different media,* with a 200-word discussion on how they influenced the creative choices for your portfolio.

Pitch Peer Assessment Task
 Submit 3 Peer Assessment reviews of fellow students' creative pitches.

Peer Workshop/Beta-Test Task
 Complete and submit feedback for at least 3 peers on their creative portfolio.

Revision Task
 Describe how you used the workshop feedback you received on your creative work to revise the work. Max 200 words.

TABLE 8.3 Creative assessment marking criteria

Mark	Criteria
A	Meets all of the D-level standards, plus *all* 5 elements received *3* marks. A+ Work exceeds professional standards in terms of innovative approaches to creativity and/or publication. A Work achieves basic professional standards. A− Work needs some revision in order to achieve professional standards/recognition.
B	Meets all of the D-level standards, plus: B+ Four tasks submitted, and at least three of five elements received *3* marks B Four tasks submitted at *2* level B− Three tasks submitted at *2* level
C	Meets all of the D-level standards, plus: C+ Two tasks submitted, and at least two of three elements received *3* marks C Two tasks submitted at *2* level C− One task submitted at *2* level
D	Creative work sufficiently demonstrates the achievement of Learning Outcomes (LOs). D+ Work exceeds minimum standards D Work is sufficient to meet minimum standards D− Work is insufficient in some aspects of creative and/or publication execution
E	Portfolio insufficient to demonstrate achievement of LOs. E+ Work approaches achievement of LOs, but has poor clarity of expression or significant deficiencies in its structures E Work is insufficient in 1 LO E− Work is insufficient in 2 LOs
F	Portfolio insufficient to demonstrate achievement of LOs. FI Work was not submitted for publication F2 Work is insufficient in all 3 LOs F3 Work is incomplete F4 Work not submitted

The topics covered on the module progress from a look at the history of royalty publishing and the establishment of copyright law, through digital book publishing to the current variety of genres and methods of publishing. These latter comprise the bulk of the semester: alternative funding methods such as crowdsourcing and patronage; interactive media and literary games; collaborative storytelling through social media and/or webcomics; serial publishing, blogging, and/or podcasting. For each method we examine successful case studies for creative readings. For critical theory readings, the reading list includes publishing history and trends, the effects of disruptive technologies, copyright history and trends, and digital and Internet culture. Some readings are of a more practical nature, such as how to format XML files or record and publish a podcast, and serve as resources for current and future projects. It is a very wide-ranging module, but the effect is that students get a good survey of the digital publishing landscape, and awareness that there is more to writing and publishing than the royalty model.

Pedagogical approaches

My philosophy on teaching is shaped in large part on what I value as a writer, researcher, and teacher: I think writers should be well rounded in terms of knowledge, critical thinkers, and capable of working independently. The creative writing workshop at best helps them develop criticality; at worst it helps them develop biased criticality based on not much more than subjective and emotional opinions. Thus I have largely eschewed the workshop model in my classroom as I have progressed as an instructor (not to mention as enrolment numbers have soared beyond what is feasible for workshops), in favour of what Haake terms a 'hybrid classroom', in which 'the class is more or less evenly split between its reading and its writing expectations, ... the reading all proceeds from a writerly perspective and that the "critical" work we do is always "creative"' (2010, p. 187). The assessments are split between creative and critical; the weekly readings include both creative texts and critical cultural, literary, and publishing theory; and module discourse centres on the interchange between cultural and critical awareness and the writerly goals of contributing thoughtfully and critically to the art and culture of society.

As Kate Kostelnik notes, students are often resistant to this hybridity (2014, p. 439), desiring the much easier path to write, workshop, be told what to fix, and resubmit. Often, this resistance is reflected in these students' module evaluations, particularly for low-attending and/or -participating students; these students in particular generally fail to grasp how this combination of theory and practice aids them in their pursuit to be 'good writers'. Nonetheless, it is my duty as the instructor, as one who 'knows better' and is supported by research (Bizzaro, 1994; Camoin, 1994; Haake, 1994; Ostrom, 1994; Kostelnik, 2014), to persuade them this hybridity benefits them and to push back against university administrators who would urge me to alter my methods to make the students happy,[2] to the detriment of the creative writer who seeks to engage in matters of consequence through their published writing (Goodfellow, 2011, p. 138).

In order to meet both my pedagogical goals and those of my students – who wish not only to write, but to *publish* – I focus my modules on *process* rather than product. To be successful in reaching their goals as published writers, and to meet my goal of creating independently, they must be able to continue their creative work once they have graduated, and no longer have the luxury of a room full of peers and an instructor to provide structure, deadlines, and feedback. For one, the creative writing classroom is often a biased one, led by instructors with subjective preferences and filled with students who have internalised the Iowa model's notions of talent and privileging of literary fiction (Bishop, 1990). The creative writing classroom as an audience is not reflective of *all* audiences; it is more beneficial to the creative writing student to develop the ability to analyse their audience, their genre, their publishing culture, and adapt their writing to fit – and vice versa, to be able to analyse their own work and place it within the appropriate publishing and readerly contexts. By assigning marks according to the process of creating their final assessments, my own bias as an instructor – bias about what genres I like, which students I like, what type of writing or media I like – is mitigated. Likewise, by asking students to publish their work in an appropriate publishing pathway and analyse those choices, they develop a practice of critical thinking that can be used in their future contexts of writing and publishing.

In addition to developing these independent skills, this model empowers them in their writing process, boosting their confidence as writers, thinkers, and workers in general. Bishop advocates for a 'transactional workshop', in which peer-to-peer interaction is preferred over the hierarchy of teacher/expert-led instruction (1990); in the transactional workshop, the writer leads the discussion of their work, rather than passively taking the 'beating' inherent in the workshop model. The transactional workshop is much preferred particularly for writing and publishing modules, as it leaves room for the students to have authority over the knowledge of their genre, medium, and audience; it is impossible for the creative writing instructor to be 'expert' across the wide range of niche audiences and quickly emerging publishing platforms (each year I have to delete the defunct and add the new) available to today's digital author. Re-distributing this authority from the instructor to the student empowers the student to pursue their particular goals, and the class as a whole to expose one another to the astonishingly wide array of publishing possibilities. It also 'de-apprentices' the creative writing classroom, wherein the hierarchy of instructor-as-expert drives the students to appropriate the instructor's way of working, style of writing, and pathway to publication (Bizzaro, 1994, p. 242), leaving the student freer to establish independence and ostensibly greater originality in their writing endeavours.

From my perspective, Professional Publishing and 21st Century Writing & Publishing have been highly successful modules. While the former was a one-off module for only four students, the work they produced was of professional quality; two of the students have gone on to form their own imprint and continue to commission and publish short fiction anthologies. The latter has resulted in an impressive array of published works, including podcasts, Twine games, interactive blogs, Kickstarter novels, indie published e-books, webcomics, and even a few traditionally submitted query letters. Students have used an incredible array of publishing platforms: Amazon Kindle Direct Publishing, social media, Patreon, Wattpad, Kickstarter, podcasting, and Storify. Most of these are genres and platforms in which I have very little practical experience, which indicates the teaching model I have incorporated is 'de-apprenticing' my students from my own practice, and empowering them within their own practice to analyse and pursue pathways that best suit their writing.

Discussion and conclusions

The approach I've taken with my writing and publishing modules is an attempt to meet the varied goals of all parties involved: student, instructor, and university. Students who want to write creatively in any way as part of their careers benefit from experiential knowledge, linking learning, thinking, and doing (Rhodes and Roessner, 2009, p. 305). The publishing industry expects more and more out of its writers, whether they opt for royalty or indie publishing. Thanks to fracturing audiences among media and publishers, royalty publishers are cutting costs in any way they can, which includes favouring 'celebrity' authors who already have significant attention capital, and reducing the number of unknown properties (or even mid-list authors) they take on. It also includes reducing services to the authors they do publish, 'placing increased obligations on authors to become involved in the management and dissemination of work' (Baverstock and Steinitz, 2013, p. 211), and focussing marketing efforts on niche audiences while spreading content across diverse media channels (Thompson, 2012, p. 247). Writers no longer have the luxury, even when working with royalty publishers, of turning in a manuscript and simply allowing the wheels of the industry to churn their work out for them (if they ever really did).

Alternatively, writers now have a multitude of options open to them for publishing their own work – often in combination with royalty publishing. The stigma of self-publishing is fading away in light of the indie published successes of Hugh Howey, Marco Koska (Flood, 2018), and even E.L. James. By exposing students to the variety of options and asking them to evaluate and choose those that best suit their writing and practice, students gain valuable insights into the industry in which they want to work, and experiential knowledge that gives them confidence in their future writing and publishing endeavours (Baverstock and Steinitz, 2013, p. 221). This confidence grows as well from the greater authority they are given in the classroom, as the instructor facilitates knowledge and advises students rather than dictates choices (Rhodes and Roessner, 2009), developing not only their writing and publishing skills but also group coordination, presentation, research, analysis, and problem-solving abilities. This multiliteracies approach is designed to arm them with critical transferable skills that will serve them well regardless of their eventual career outcomes.

Integrating theory and practice in their multiliteracy practices also has significant personal and socio-cultural effects for creative writing students. The history of English literature is strongly embedded in socio-cultural discourse, as Terry Eagleton describes its rise as a binding agent, as it were, for Anglo-American culture in the wake of religious fragmentation, cultural revolutions, and rising literacy (2008). Yet the Iowa workshop model is criticised for its homogeneity, its silencing of disparate voices, and its perpetuation of narrowly defined and increasingly out-dated literary 'norms'; creative writers must be exposed to a wide variety of discourse and voices, both within their own culture and without, in order to contribute in a meaningful way to culture. They must be aware of the conversations they are entering, of the power structures they are participating in as writers, as publishers, and as readers, not only to navigate them for their own sake, but to effect change in their role as cultural reflectors and prognosticators. As Mary Ryan notes:

> The arts are powerful spaces to interrogate how our own personal understandings are mediated by contexts of schooling, curriculum and sometimes by hegemonic views of the world – important considerations in becoming literate in a rapidly changing, globalised world.
>
> *2014, p. 5*

Students cannot gain this literacy without reading and synthesising both theory and creative texts from diverse voices on diverse topics.

Gaining a more nuanced cultural perspective, as well as exposure to the wealth of publishing options, also serves both student and instructor goals: it often leads to innovations in their writing. I find my students are often very concerned with the notion of originality, enough to keep many from progressing in their work. It is difficult to write 'the new' if you are unaware of what has come before, or what options are available for your work. Digital media have opened up a wide array of writerly options: indie publishing, blogging, social media, podcasting, serials, digital fiction, games, collaborative writing, interactive storytelling, multimedia storytelling, transmedia storytelling, and much more. It has expanded the form and structure of narrative, opening new pathways not only for publishing but also for creative story construction. For students who worry that nothing they do is unique, simply trying something new can lead to astonishing creativity, which writers crave; it is no coincidence that the e-book 'revolution' was driven not by business writers, as expected, but by fiction writers (Thompson, 2012, p. 322).

This is not all to say that I have perfected the module models I have presented here. I plan a number of future interventions in these modules to further address balance of authority, multiliteracies, and writer ownership of their texts. Bishop advocates against a lecture-based teaching model, which reinforces student passivity (1990), a significant issue in British-educated students whose secondary school structures indoctrinate them in passivity, hierarchy of authority, and rote memorisation. It is also an issue given the push by British universities to recruit more and more students – not all of them are equally enthusiastic about their studies, an imbalance that many creative writing instructors note leads to rushed or incomplete work and failure to read assigned texts (Donnelly, 2010, pp. 12–13). When teaching writing and publishing theory and history, however, I find it quite easy to fall back into the lecture structure, particularly as I rarely have to prepare anything from scratch anymore. A simple solution I have used in the past is to assign the readings with key discussion questions, and then give the students time at the beginning of a 'lecture' session to discuss these in groups, perhaps even filling in a worksheet with their responses (which keeps them on task). Ideally, I will also assign students a weekly exercise task regarding these readings, so they will have engaged on several levels with the material before turning to me for interpretation and explanation. Once their group discussion winds down, I ask them to share their observations and questions with the entire class for a larger discussion. I always tell the students that if these discussions take the entire 'lecture' session, and I never get to my lecture notes, then great! They've read and synthesised the material via these activities far more than they would by falling asleep to the sound of my voice. It also puts more authority in their hands, as they are responsible for preparing for class ahead of time with the exercises and discussion questions, and for contributing to the discussion.

I am also planning to revise my critical essay assessments. While these are standard academic learning tools, and arguably an effective method for teaching and evaluating key multiliteracies skills such as research, written communication, and critical thinking, they are a very specific task for a very specific career: academia. Students and universities are both placing more vocational expectations on their studies, and only a small percentage of these students will go on to postgraduate work – even smaller to careers in academia. Knoeller argues for 'imaginative response', offering students a wide array of discourse-based options, both creative and critical, for responding to the readings and topics covered on a module (2003). I have often given exercises of this sort, for example, responding to a short story with a creative work of Bakhtinian discourse. Opening their argumentative essays into alternate forms such as feature articles, proposals, fictocriticism, wikis, and other creative responses gives them a more personally meaningful mechanism through which to synthesise and display what they've learned on the module. It also develops relevant multiliteracies for creative writers who do not plan to enter academia, but may eventually write nonfiction work for other purposes, such as websites, business, law, and others.

The goal of creative writing programmes since their inception has been to produce published authors; the goal of students on these programmes has been to hone their skills to that professional level. It is startling, then, that creative writing and publishing have not been integrated more as complementary studies in higher education. Particularly in the current era, when digital media is so vastly transfiguring the landscape of both, it is vital that creative writing students gain understanding of and experience with publishing practices and power structures. Embracing a multiliteracies pedagogy, emphasising student-led activities, integrating theory and practice from diverse voices, and focussing on process rather than product enable a classroom in which creative writers can develop their voice, find their audience, and innovate through new forms and publishing pathways. The skills they gain enhance their abilities not only as creative writers seeking to become published authors but also as workers entering a diverse and globalised economy. By demolishing the creaking century-old structure of the Iowa workshop, we as creative writing instructors can scaffold our students with innovative, flexible, and insightful practices that will benefit our classrooms, their careers, and our culture as a whole.

Notes

1 I maintain a full breakdown of my specifications grading module model, including links to sample module documents, here: http://lyleskains.blogspot.com/2018/09/my-take-on-specifications-grading-or.html. Note that the Professional Publishing module was the first in which I had incorporated this model, and thus its structure has been modified since.

2 It is important to acknowledge that I have a permanent position in a high-performing department, and therefore have a level of job security that is not afforded to many creative writers on zero-hour and other precarious contracts. In these cases, it is vital that instructors have the support of key faculty such as line managers and/or Directors of Teaching & Learning.

References

Alexander, L. (2016) '_9MOTHER9HORSE9EYES9: The Mysterious Tale Terrifying Reddit', *The Guardian*, 5 May. Available at: www.theguardian.com/technology/2016/may/05/9mother9horse9eyes9-the-mysterious-tale-terrifying-reddit (Accessed: 17 June 2016).

Amato, J. and Fleisher, H. K. (2001) 'Reforming Creative Writing Pedagogy: History as Knowledge, Knowledge as Activism', *Electronic Book Review*, 12. Available at: www.altx.com/ebr/riposte/rip2/rip2ped/amato.htm (Accessed: 4 October 2018).

Baverstock, A. and Steinitz, J. (2013) 'Who Are the Self-Publishers?', *Learned Publishing*, 26(3), pp. 211–223. doi: 10.1087/20130310.

Bennett, E. (2014) 'How Iowa Flattened Literature', *The Chronicle of Higher Education*, 10 February. Available at: www.chronicle.com/article/How-Iowa-Flattened-Literature/144531 (Accessed: 4 October 2018).

Bhaskar, M. (2013) *The Content Machine: Towards a Theory of Publishing from the Printing Press to the Digital Network*. London: Anthem Press.

Bishop, W. (1990) *Released into Language: Options for Teaching Creative Writing*. Urbana, IL: National Council of Teachers of English.

Bizzaro, P. (1994) 'Reading the Creative Writing Course: The Teacher's Many Selves', in Bishop, W. and Ostrom, H. A. (eds) *Colors of a Different Horse: Rethinking Creative Writing Theory and Pedagogy*. Urbana, IL: National Council of Teachers of English, pp. 234–247.

Bizzaro, P. (2010) 'Workshop: An Ontological Study', in Donnelly, D. (ed.) *Does the Writing Workshop Still Work?* Bristol: Multilingual Matters, pp. 36–51.

Brandt, D. (2015) *The Rise of Writing: Redefining Mass Literacy*. Cambridge: Cambridge University Press.

Brayfield, C. (2009) 'Babelfish Babylon: Teaching Creative Writing in a Multi-Literate Community', *New Writing*, 6(3), pp. 201–214. doi: 10.1080/14790720903556189.

Camoin, F. (1994) 'The Workshop and Its Discontents', in Bishop, W. and Ostrom, H. A. (eds) *Colors of a Different Horse: Rethinking Creative Writing Theory and Pedagogy*. Urbana, IL: National Council of Teachers of English, pp. 3–7.

Cazden, C. et al. (1996) 'A Pedagogy of Multiliteracies: Designing Social Futures', *Harvard Educational Review; Cambridge*, 66(1), p. 60.

Clark, J. E. (2010) 'The Digital Imperative: Making the Case for a 21st-Century Pedagogy', *Computers and Composition*, 27(1), pp. 27–35.

Cope, B. and Kalantzis, M. (2009) '"Multiliteracies": New Literacies, New Learning', *Pedagogies: An International Journal*, 4(3), pp. 164–195. doi: 10.1080/15544800903076044.

Donnelly, D. (2010) *Does the Writing Workshop Still Work?* Bristol: Multilingual Matters.

Donnelly, D. J. (2009) *Establishing Creative Writing Studies as an Academic Discipline*. PhD. University of South Florida.

Eagleton, T. (2008) *Literary Theory: An Introduction*. Anniversary. Minneapolis: University of Minnesota Press.

Ensslin, A. (2014) *Literary Gaming*. Cambridge, MA: MIT Press.

Fenza, D. W. (2000) 'Creative Writing & Its Discontents', *AWP: The Writer's News*, 1 March. Available at: www.awpwriter.org/magazine_media/writers_news_view/2871/creative_writing_its_discontents (Accessed: 4 October 2018).

Flood, A. (2018) 'French Bookshops Revolt after Prize Selects Novel Self-Published on Amazon', *The Guardian*, 15 September. Available at: www.theguardian.com/books/2018/sep/15/french-bookshops-revolt-after-prize-selects-novel-self-published-on-amazon (Accessed: 16 October 2018).

Garber, E. and Ramjerdi, J. (1994) 'Reflections on the Teaching of Creative Writing: A Correspondence', in Bishop, W. and Ostrom, H. A. (eds) *Colors of a Different Horse: Rethinking Creative Writing Theory and Pedagogy*. Urbana, IL: National Council of Teachers of English, pp. 8–26.

Geiser, E. A. (1997) 'Publishing Education', *Publishing Research Quarterly*, 13(3), pp. 110–117. doi: 10.1007/s12109-997-0003-2.

Goldhaber, M. H. (1997) 'The Attention Economy and the Net', *First Monday*, 2(4–7), p. n.p. Available at: http://firstmonday.org/article/view/519/440 (Accessed: 29 December 2017).

Goodfellow, R. (2011) 'Literacy, Literacies and the Digital in Higher Education', *Teaching in Higher Education*, 16(1), pp. 131–144. doi: 10.1080/13562517.2011.544125.

Greco, A. N. (1990) 'Teaching publishing in the United States', *Book Research Quarterly*, 6(1), pp. 12–19. doi: 10.1007/BF02683729.

Haake, K. (1994) 'Teaching Creative Writing if the Shoe Fits', in Bishop, W. and Ostrom, H. A. (eds) *Colors of a Different Horse: Rethinking Creative Writing Theory and Pedagogy*. Urbana, IL: National Council of Teachers of English, pp. 77–99.

Haake, K. (2010) 'Re-envisioning the Workshop: Hybrid Classrooms, Hybrid Texts', in Donnelly, D. (ed.) *Does the Writing Workshop Still Work?* Bristol: Multilingual Matters, pp. 182–193.

Hancock, P. (2008) 'Novel Thinking', *Times Higher Education (THE)*, 10 July. Available at: www.timeshighereducation.com/features/novel-thinking/402673.article (Accessed: 15 October 2018).

Howe, L. and Van Wig, A. (2017) 'Metacognition via Creative Writing: Dynamic Theories of Learning Support Habits of the Mind in 21st Century Classrooms', *Journal of Poetry Therapy*, 30(3), pp. 139–152. doi: 10.1080/08893675.2017.1328830.

James, G. (2009) 'The Undergraduate Creative Writing Workshop', *Creative Writing: Teaching Theory & Practice*, 1(1), pp. 48–62.

Kearns, R. M. (2009) 'Voice of Authority: Theorizing Creative Writing Pedagogy', *College Composition and Communication*, 60(4), pp. 790–807.

Kennedy, A. L. (2012) 'Does That Make Sense? Approaches to the Creative Writing Workshop', in Morley, D. and Neilsen, P. (eds) *The Cambridge Companion to Creative Writing*. Cambridge: Cambridge University Press, pp. 201–214.

Knoeller, C. (2003) 'Imaginative Response: Teaching Literature through Creative Writing', *The English Journal*, 92(5), pp. 42–48. doi: 10.2307/3650423.

Koehler, A. (2015) 'Screening Subjects: Workshop Pedagogy, Media Ecologies, and (New) Student Subjectivities', in Clark, M. D., Hergenrader, T., and Rein, J. (eds) *Creative Writing in the Digital Age: Theory, Practice, and Pedagogy*. London: Bloomsbury, pp. 17–28.

Kostelnik, K. (2014) 'Innovative Frameworks and Tested Lore for Teaching Creative Writing to Undergraduates in the Twenty-First Century', *Pedagogy*, 14(3), pp. 435–454.

Laquintano, T. (2016) *Mass Authorship and the Rise of Self-Publishing.* Iowa City: University of Iowa Press.

Leathwood, C. and O'Connell, P. (2003) '"It's a Struggle": The Construction of the "New Student" in Higher Education', *Journal of Education Policy*, 18(6), pp. 597–615. doi: 10.1080/0268093032000145863.

Lessig, L. (2008) *Remix: Making Art and Commerce Thrive in the Hybrid Economy.* New York: The Penguin Press.

Logan, E. and Prichard, E. (2016) *What Do Graduates Do?* HEFCU: Graduate Prospects Ltd. Available at: www.hecsu.ac.uk/assets/assets/documents/What_do_graduates_do_2016.pdf.

Moxley, J. (2010) 'Afterword: Disciplinarity and the Future of Creative Writing Studies', in Donnelly, D. (ed.) *Does the Writing Workshop Still Work?* Bristol: Multilingual Matters, pp. 230–238.

Nilson, L. B. (2014) *Specifications Grading: Restoring Rigor, Motivating Students, and Saving Faculty Time.* Reprint Edition. Sterling, Virginia: Stylus Publishing.

Ostrom, H. A. (1994) 'Introduction: Of Radishes and Shadows, Theory and Pedagogy', in Bishop, W. and Ostrom, H. A. (eds) *Colors of a Different Horse: Rethinking Creative Writing Theory and Pedagogy.* Urbana, IL: National Council of Teachers of English, pp. xi–xxiii.

Rhodes, L. and Roessner, A. (2009) 'Teaching Magazine Publishing through Experiential Learning', *Journalism & Mass Communication Educator*, 63(4), pp. 303–316. doi: 10.1177/107769580806300403.

Ryan, M. (2014) 'Reflexivity and Aesthetic Inquiry: Building Dialogues between the Arts and Literacy', *English Teaching*, 13(2), pp. 5–18.

Simon, C. C. (2015) 'Why Writers Love to Hate the M.F.A.', *The New York Times*, 9 April. Available at: www.nytimes.com/2015/04/12/education/edlife/12edl-12mfa.html (Accessed: 15 October 2018).

Skains, R. L. (2018) 'Dissonant Fabulation: Subverting Online Genres to Effect Socio-Cognitive Dissonance', *Textus*, 2018(2), pp. 41–57.

Skains, R. L. (2019) *The Digital Author: Publishing in an Attention Economy.* Cambridge: Cambridge University Press.

Thompson, J. B. (2012) *Merchants of Culture: The Publishing Business in the Twenty-First Century.* 2nd edn. Cambridge: Polity Press.

Vanderslice, S. (2010) 'Once More to the Workshop: A Myth Caught in Time', in Donnelly, D. (ed.) *Does the Writing Workshop Still Work?* Bristol: Multilingual Matters, pp. 30–35.

Webb, C. H. (1990) 'Teaching Creative Writing', *Mississippi Review*, 19(1/2), pp. 331–333.

What Can I Do with a Creative Writing Degree? (2018) *Prospects.ac.uk.* Available at: www.prospects.ac.uk/careers-advice/what-can-i-do-with-my-degree/creative-writing (Accessed: 23 September 2018).

9

THE MODERN LITERARY AGENT

Angus Phillips

The literary agent is prominent in trade book publishing in the UK and the US, whilst the role is rarer in other publishing markets, such as in continental Europe. What started as an intermediary between the author and publisher has developed into a much broader function, acting on behalf of the author, with elements of business, editorial, and marketing. The agent is a key gatekeeper into the mainstream publishing world for authors, especially in the area of fiction. Literary agents champion authors, offer them invaluable support and advice, and may be the single point of continuity throughout their writing career.

There are significant challenges to the established media gatekeepers: authors may find an audience through social media, podcasting, fanfiction, or self-publication in e-book form. Yet there remains the cachet of publishing with an established publishing house, plus the publisher has access to high street retail for the print edition. Agents carry out a valuable function for publishers, acting as a filter for new authors and projects, and undertaking considerable editorial work.

As diversity has become such a live issue in contemporary publishing, questions arise as to how the agent's gatekeeping role is exercised. Possible threats to the role of the agent come not only from self-publishing but also from the continuing consolidation among publishing companies, publishers dealing directly with authors, and the erosion of authors' incomes.

A brief history of the literary agent

The work of the literary agent can be traced in the UK back to the later years of the nineteenth century. The agency A. P. Watt was started by Alexander Pollock Watt in the 1870s, working for both authors and publishers. For authors, working on a commission of 10%, he read their work and helped place it with publishers. His authors included Conan Doyle, Kipling, and Rider Haggard.

For publishers he would help them place serial or other rights; and find suitable authors as required. Mary Ann Gillies views the principal task of the agent from this time as 'to recognize a work that would sell. There was no sense in trying to place material for which there was no market, especially when the agent's earnings depended on a commission from the sale' (Gillies, 2007, page 30).

The role of the agent came under scrutiny, and by the beginning of the twentieth century the Society of Authors recommended that authors should be wary of using agents as they were seen as too allied to the interests of publishers. It was suggested that agents could place more books by keeping the agreed royalty rates paid by publishers at a lower rate; and that they would make more money for themselves overall with this approach (Hepburn, 1968). But this would be at the expense of the earnings of individual authors. George Bernard Shaw regarded the literary agent in an unfavourable light, commenting that 'The literary agency is a ... favourite resort of persons who have not ability enough either for ordinary business pursuits or for literature' (*The Author*, 1 November 1911).

The Society of Authors was also concerned about dubious practices such as charging a fee for reading manuscripts – seen as a business model in its own right for agents. In the *Writers' and Artists' Yearbook* of 1930, there is to be found a cautionary note:

> Owing to complaints of the methods of some literary agents it has been deemed advisable, in the interests of writers, to cut the usual details of the terms upon which business is negotiated. Anyone needing the services of an agent is likely to make a more careful choice if preliminary investigation is a forced necessity.
>
> *page 168*

The practice remained controversial and in post-war New York the successful agent Scott Meredith charged a reading fee. At times the service read over 3,000 scripts annually, and when Arthur Klebanoff took over running the agency in 1993, he introduced a flat fee for a read of $450. The income covered the overhead of the agency (Klebanoff, 2002).

Sterling Lord, who represented authors such as Jack Kerouac and Ken Kesey, talked about the kind of person who was a literary agent in the 1950s in New York:

> [they] were people who were in the business because they liked writing, rather they liked books. It wasn't all about money, and for a long time, the money really wasn't very good. For example, when I started out, many agents weren't interested in the movie business at all, because they thought those guys out there were thugs.
>
> *Albanese, 2013, page 20*

The role of literary agent, however, became more professional and to be seen as commonplace within mainstream trade (or consumer) publishing. In the 1960s and 1970s new opportunities arose to exploit the rights in books: for example by selling film rights. There was also 'the massive expansion of the market created by the rise of the retail chains. ... books were increasingly made available to consumers in ways and on a scale that had simply not been possible before' (Thompson, 2012, page 62). By the mid-1990s Michael Legat viewed agents as both 'an accepted and respected part of the literary scene' (1995, page 13). This was also the era of the super-agent: a prominent example was Andrew Wylie in New York, who was willing to challenge what he saw as a cosy relationship between agents and publishers, and to poach top literary names to bring into his stable of authors.

> Dubbed 'the Jackal' for his aggressive poaching of other people's clients, his distaste for commercial fiction and his disinterest in social media [are] legendary. He is the reigning king of the backlist, profiting mainly off classic titles rather than taking risky bets on new ones. His only criterion is enduring quality, and his client list is eye-popping: Amis, Nabokov, Bellow, Rushdie, Roth.
>
> *Bennett, 2013, page 26*

Wylie began his agency in New York in 1980 and in 1995 Martin Amis dispensed with the services of his agent, Pat Kavanagh, to sign up with Wylie. This opened up a rift between Amis and Kavanagh's husband, Julian Barnes. When asked in 2016 about his relationship with Amis, Barnes said: 'When we meet, we talk ... It's not a problem. He lives in Brooklyn and I live in Tufnell Park' (*Radio Times*, 5 December).

The period before the turn of the century coincided with further growth in retail for books, from supermarkets to book superstores and Amazon, and the book market offered higher incomes for successful authors. The hardback market expanded and publishers were keen to secure the best books and authors through the offer of large advance payments. With publishers willing to put up advance payments to secure a deal, the author would receive substantial cash sums not just the promise of royalties to be earned in the future. Additional opportunities for income streams came from subsidiary rights – from film rights to translations – whilst agents could divide up volume (book) rights by territory and increase the overall pot. For example, they might sell US rights separately to one company in New York, and UK and Commonwealth rights to a publisher in London, whilst selling the rights in several languages.

A long-established network of literary scouts, acting on behalf of international publishers, facilitated the sale of translation rights. They were in regular touch with agents and publishers in New York and London in order to alert their publishing houses as early as possible to exciting new books and authors.

every major trade publisher – from Korea to France and from Italy to Finland – has a scout in America and possibly also one in England, so that even the slightest buzz in New York or London about a new young writer is immediately, and often simultaneously, transferred to dozens of European publishers, whose concurrent interest and heated bidding regularly have a self-fulfilling effect on the announcement that the writer in question has written an 'exciting' book, about which – as the curious expression goes – 'everybody is jumping up and down'.

Asscher, 1993, page 27

The agent takes a prominent role in trade publishing, acting as a gatekeeper for new authors, and pitching books to publishers. This contrasts to the role of the editor, now significantly diminished, especially as the decision to publish a book must align with the opinions of colleagues in sales and marketing. Of publishing in the twenty-first century, Sterling Lord wrote:

[it] has come to resemble less the selling of paintings or other creative work and more that of carpets or refrigerators. Books are no longer bought by publishers on the basis of one editor's commitment. The editor and sometimes even the publisher have to check with other editors, advertising, sales, promotion, or a higher authority, or all of the above. It is 'committee publishing'.

2013, page 291

The *Writers' and Artists' Year Book* from 1930 recorded 30 agents in Britain – all but two were in London. By the 2019 edition (published in 2018), there were 182 listed in the UK and Ireland and in a more diverse range of locations, although the overwhelming majority were still based in London and the South-East (only seven in Scotland and Ireland, and none in Wales). The large agencies in London have a number of agents working for them (Table 9.1).

After the financial crisis of 2008, the book market found growth to be more elusive, compounded by the difficulties of high street retail, the rise and fall of e-books, and a decline in the readership of literary fiction (Phillips, 2017). Editors came under pressure to publish fewer and more commercial books, and author incomes suffered as the market favoured a relatively low number of highly successful titles each year.

TABLE 9.1 Number of literary agencies in Britain – source *Writers' and Artists' Yearbook*

1930	1946	1975	1995	2003	2008	2019
30	39	80	138	161	161	182

The present role of the agent

Storytelling can now take many different forms – from a podcast to a Netflix series – and the agent has become what Jonny Geller from Curtis Brown calls a literary manager. Those forms are

> a huge opportunity for us because now we can have a good storyteller tell a story and I can think well actually this would work better as a ten part series and then the book. It depends on what the author wants.
>
> *Geller, 2019*

In today's world of book publishing the mainstream publishers do not accept unsolicited manuscripts from authors – the so-called slush pile has either moved online (to sites such as Wattpad) or to the offices of agents. To win a publishing contract with a publisher, a first-time novelist must first secure an agent to represent them. Successful agents working with a stable of brand authors will find it difficult to make room for new authors but many agents will still review submissions from new authors. Although the odds are stacked against them (a large agency can receive up to 15,000 submissions a year), there is a continuing appetite for new authors within the industry – there is an ongoing search for fresh talent with an appealing back story and seen as promotable.

Agents will source new authors from the slush pile, through social media, or perhaps from the range of creative writing degrees – around 50 universities in the UK offer a course at master's level. Networking with agents and editors can be one of the key selling-points of a creative writing programme. The agency Curtis Brown launched its own creative writing courses in 2011. Often, however, agents will source new talent through personal recommendation, creating a network into which it is hard to break into without the right connections.

It is in the Code of Conduct of the UK Association of Authors' Agents that no reading fee is charged to authors without prior consent in writing. Separately there are author service companies that will carry out paid work on manuscripts – mostly this is with an eye to the author self-publishing.

The agent acts as a gatekeeper within the industry, and carries out initial filtering for the publisher (Bhaskar, 2013). It is very hard to get in the front door and secure an agent's services but once an author has an agent, their chances of securing a publishing deal are significantly enhanced. The prominent agent Carole Blake (1946–2016) wrote:

> If a writer has an agent, a publisher knows the writer has passed through at least one level of screening, and that another professional in the trade, the agent, believes the author has a future. The agent's reputation says something about the author's abilities, too.
>
> *1999, page 45*

If the agent sees the potential of a book – on receipt of a synopsis and a few chapters in the case of fiction – they may then request the full manuscript. On agreement to represent the author, they will work with the writer to secure a publishing deal. The agent does not receive any financial return before such a deal is signed. They will set out to improve the proposal and sample material from the author, until these are ready to show to selected editors. The agent will maintain good contact with publishers and will know who is likely to be interested. A new book may sell to one publisher or go to auction among a number of interested players. The agent's job is to advise on the best deal and to find the right fit for the author, in terms of the relevant publishing list and the proposed marketing and publicity. Securing a high advance is likely to lead to the publisher allocating a high proportion of their marketing budget to the book.

The division of rights is a source of tension with those publishers that want to purchase world rights. A publisher seeks to secure as many rights as possible whilst the agent wishes to sell them separately or reserve them in case of a deal in the future. A global publisher will argue that they can publish around the world; an agent sees the benefit in signing individual deals by territory and language. A first-time author may be tempted by a good offer for world rights from a big name publisher, perhaps fearing less success elsewhere; a good agent will recognise that advance payments from a number of sources will increase the overall sum that a book will command. There is also a potential benefit from domestic publishers championing the author in their markets. Ebook rights would now be regarded as part of the volume rights for a book, acquired by the publisher with the print rights, and with a standardised royalty rate, but no similar arrangement yet exists for audio rights (a fast-growing part of the market). Yet many publishers would now expect to take audio rights as part of any substantial deal.

Translation rights may be sold by country through sub-agents in other territories or through international work: for example, at the major book fairs, such as Frankfurt and London, or at Bologna (children's). The larger agencies will have departments that concentrate on the sale of translation rights.

Serial rights – extracts sold to a newspaper – will most likely be reserved by the agent. Their value has shrunk in recent years as the sales of newspapers have fallen, but there may be significant publicity value in some deals. Options may be sold for film or TV rights but only a few titles will go into production. The larger agencies will have a separate division that deals with Hollywood and the streaming services such as Netflix and Amazon. Agencies will manage the literary estates of successful authors: for example Roald Dahl (David Higham) and Ian Fleming (Curtis Brown).

At the same time as doing deals agents will be carrying out editorial work – in-house editors have less time to edit as their responsibilities have broadened. Specialist readers for agencies may help with tackling the slush pile, whilst the agents work on improving proposals and helping their authors (especially new ones) develop their next books – from helping shape the structure to line-by-line editing. They will read drafts for the author, who may then get a new set of comments from the editor at the publishing house. Editors seeking authors for a new non-fiction project or publishing list may enlist the help of agents, or decide to approach authors directly.

Much editorial work has in effect been subcontracted from publishers to agents, reducing the overheads of publishing houses. This was highlighted by Eric De Bellaigue:

> In the 1960s and '70s, some agents barely read manuscripts before passing them on to the publisher, safe in the knowledge that the latter's editorial resources were comprehensive. Not today. The agent's role will now cover the pre-selection of publishable texts, work on authors' presentations to publishers, followed by editorial work - sometimes considerable - on the text ahead of submission - all of which also has the practical advantage of cutting down the time to publication.
>
> *2008, page 112*

Books that are ready to go, with little need of editorial work, are more saleable and likely to attract higher advances from publishers keen to fill their forward lists.

Agents will guide the careers of their authors, conscious of market trends: whether psychological thriller (*The Girl on the Train*) or up-lit (*Eleanor Oliphant is Completely Fine*). As Sophie Lambert of C&W comments, 'We have to offer more and more strategic advice to authors, in terms of what their long-term goals are ... writing beautiful, quiet fiction is not going to be a recipe, for the most part, for commercial success' (Lambert, 2019). There are performative aspects to authorship, with an expectation that they are active on social media, be visible in the media, read the audiobook, and participate in literary festivals. In a broader business role, agents today work with authors around their websites, promotional campaigns, and their backlist. They will champion their authors' views to the publishers around book covers. To work with non-fiction authors in particular, some agencies have launched services offering writers for events, talks, and after dinner speaking. If a publisher is not selling enough copies of an author's backlist, the agent may seek to move the books to another publisher or assist in the self-publishing of the titles. The Ed Victor Literary Agency in London set up Bedford Square Books in 2011 to publish POD (print on demand) editions and ebooks of titles that have gone out of print or are unavailable. From the agency Charlie Campbell said:

> We expanded into e-publishing purely as a service to our authors. Of course, there is the possibility of a conflict of interest, but we are doing all we can to avoid such a thing. We would always prefer to be the agent than the publisher, and so, if a suitable offer was made by a publisher, we would accept that and revert to being the agent on the deal.
>
> *Spavlik, 2011, page 9*

The role of the agent is of little significance in other parts of publishing, for example, in academic publishing, since the level of royalties received does not justify the use of an intermediary. However, the expansion of the number of agents has led to some academics being invited to sign up with an agent for their books for a broader general market. Some academics writing for a trade market may still find it useful for their agent to be involved in, say, a college textbook deal.

The reason why there are agents in US and UK publishing is that the returns available to authors are higher than in other markets. Writing in the English language opens up a range of international markets, whilst global exposure encourages sale in translation (the two strongest world markets for the exploitation of copyrights are the US and Germany).

> With the global dominance of the English language, and now translations from English, an unfair advantage has developed, with a momentum of its own, regardless of the quality of the books. This also has implications for authorship, with some authors choosing to write for an international readership, with a consequent shift in content and style.
>
> *Phillips, 2014, page 103*

Indeed some authors choose to write in English and then be translated for the edition in their domestic market. The well-established network of agents and scouts facilitates the sale of subsidiary rights, from film and TV to translation. A book written in a smaller language will have less initial exposure and requires specialist readers to assess its potential for other markets – a sample translation may be required to stimulate rights sales. No such issues exist for books in English.

Sums payable to the author from a publisher will first be paid through their agent – a practice that dates back to the days of A. P. Watt. Originally established by Watt at the level of 10%, the commission is now at a base level of 15%. Just as publishers make their profits from a base of bestsellers, alongside their bets on other titles, agencies will find that their successful authors help to subsidise their work with new authors (yet to bring in income), and their midlist authors – yet to make a breakthrough with their sales. Sometimes they have to make tough decisions, dropping midlist authors in favour of new talent. An author who does not sell may be dropped by both publisher and agent.

With a greater emphasis in the publishing industry on frontlist titles and bestsellers, the income of agencies is derived in a higher proportion from advance payments, and less from royalties once advances have been earned out. A successful agency will aim for a split of 70:30 in favour of new business (Geller, 2019). This makes income uncertain and with advances reduced since the financial crash of 2008, the job of the agent that much harder work.

The rates of profitability at the top publishing groups contrast with diminished incomes for authors: it was estimated that in 2016 the shareholders of the big five publishers received up to three times the amount paid out to authors

(Solomon and Atkinson, 2018). A 2017 Arts Council England (ACE) report into literary fiction concluded that there are only around 1,000 novelists in the UK who can make a career from their sales alone. Taking a hardback book which sells around 3,000 copies:

> For the sake of simplicity, that represents £30,000 of total revenue of which the retailer is likely, on average, to take half – so publisher, agent and author must make do with £15,000 between them. Selling 3,000 to 4,000 books is not unrespectable. However, making a living as a writer at this level of sales is exceptionally difficult, to say the least.
>
> *Arts Council England, 2017, page 16*

Authors will have received an advance against royalties but the report supported the view that advances have been on a downward trajectory. Huge six-figure advances hit the headlines, but they are largely the exception, and the floor for advances may be only a few thousand pounds. For agents an advance in the region of £5,000 to £15,000 will earn them from £750 to £2,250. Simone Murray concludes:

> financial realities have contributed to a marked polarization of authorship into authorial celebrities at one end who may be marketed as virtual brand-names, and the mass of other authors, formerly denoted 'midlist', who struggle to maintain publisher support and must fight among themselves for editorial and marketing attention.
>
> *Phillips and Bhaskar, 2019, page 49*

Saturation in the market, as can be seen from the number of agencies, reflects the presence of smaller agencies, close to lifestyle businesses, with low levels of turnover. Eric de Bellaigue commented on the 'one striking characteristic of the industry, namely the Lilliputian scale of so many literary agencies. This is as true of the United States as it is of the United Kingdom, with numerous instances of one-man or one-woman firms' (2008, page 114). The agents may have worked previously for publishers, perhaps as editors, and are content to work with only a few authors.

Occasionally publishers break away from the established pattern of working through agents, and hold open submissions – aiming to attract new books and authors directly. But mostly editors are happy to work with agents, who feed their publishing programmes. In *Merchants of Culture*, John Thompson writes,

> For the most part it is agents, not editors or publishers, who are expected to discover new talent, to find new writers whom they think are promising and to work with them to turn an idea or draft manuscript into something that an editor or publisher would recognize as an attractive project and potentially successful book.
>
> *2012, page 75*

Professionals in publishing move around frequently and stability for authors is maintained through their agent, whilst their editor may have moved on to another publishing house. When Julian Barnes's editor, Liz Calder, left to co-found the publishing house Bloomsbury, he chose to remain at Jonathan Cape. 'Why would I want to go with her when it is she who has left me?' (Maschler, 2005, page 85) As George Greenfield observed,

> many authors have discovered that, with all the chopping and changing that has taken place and will most likely continue to take place in the ownership and staff of publishing houses, the one fixed point in a fluctuating world is their literary agent.
>
> *1993, page 197*

Editors also become agents, perhaps sick of the round of musical chairs that is often the state of commercial publishing. Editors are measured on their sales and they have to bet on projects, and sometimes bet big in order to impress. Moving on may be their own decision or it is forced upon them.

In turn, authors may decide to move publishing house, to be reunited with their editor, or to seek improved terms or greater attention for their books. Robert Gottlieb, former Editor-in-Chief of Alfred A. Knopf, writes:

> There are many reasons writers switch publishers. Money certainly is one of them: When a writer or his agent wants more than the publisher thinks is prudent to pay, or another publisher has flashed bigger bucks. When a writer and his editor don't really understand (or like) each other. When a writer doesn't feel that his publisher really believes in him. When a writer feels that a change of publisher might change his luck. When a writer is having a mid-career crisis and just needs to make changes in his life, which often involves changing spouses as well as publishers.
>
> *2016, page 176*

Sometimes they will decide to move agencies, for a similar set of motivations. Martin Amis, who accepted an advance of £500,000 for his novel *The Information* (1995), negotiated by his new agent Andrew Wylie, broke with both his agent, Pat Kavanagh, and his publisher, Jonathan Cape. Reflecting on this move many years later, he said:

> The person who wants a quiet life, which is 90% of me, should have taken the Cape offer [of £300,000], and that would have been the end of it. These things stay with you. For years it was the number one thing people asked about, and it was not my finest hour.
>
> *Guardian, 14 July 2013*

An agent has to have a broad mindset in today's environment in which books reach many more platforms than ever before, as observed by Juliet Pickering of Blake Friedmann:

> a book on my list, *SLAY IN YOUR LANE: The Black Girl Bible* (2018), gathered traction across radio, TV, podcasting, corporations, and even reached into fashion outlets. There are traditional spaces for books, and an ever-growing opportunity to take books into non-traditional spaces, which the agent has to start thinking about from the point of taking on the book and the author.
>
> *Clark and Phillips, 2019, page 150*

The agent who is well connected with the world of TV and film can help authors source work in the area of screenwriting. Ultimately the role of the agent is to support their author with encouragement and advice, offer sound business advice, guide them in their writing career, and maintain their morale. Mandy Little of Watson, Little says, 'it's not about a book, it's about a long-term relationship between author and agent; developing talent to the extent that the author is capable of, or perhaps challenging him or her into new directions' (2011, page 23).

Diversity in publishing

A key issue in contemporary publishing is that of diversity and inclusion. How can books represent more fully the nature and composition of society? This issue can be examined along dimensions such as the workforce, authorship, and what is published; and around characteristics from race and gender to class. The author Nikesh Shukla, who edited the crowdfunded book *The Good Immigrant*, writes powerfully about the experience of being a person of colour:

> race is in everything we do. Because the universal experience is white. [A] commenter on a short story I once wrote, was pleasantly surprised to see Indians going through the universal experience. Much as I was surprised that I was excluded from the universal experience, it hammered home the knowledge that the universal experience is white.
>
> *Shukla, 2016, page xi*

On the subject of class, the founder of Bluemoose Books, Kevin Duffy writes:

> There is an increasing disconnect between the lives of those who commission books and the real world of readers up and down the country. ... An author I publish was told by a very eminent writer with whom she was studying that 'literature is always middle class; written about, by and for ...' To write in a different way, about different people, the way Ken Loach makes films, is assumed to be political.
>
> *Guardian, 17 June 2014*

For publishers struggling to achieve growth in mature book markets, can they broaden their horizons whether recruiting staff or new authors? Mathangi Subramanian writes about children's books:

> All over the world, children's literature has a diversity problem. In the US, the Cooperative Children's Book Center reported in 2017 that only 6% of published books for children were penned by black, Latino, or native American authors. Regardless of authorship, only 4% of books for children and teens had LGBTQ+ content. The same year in the UK, only 4% of books for children and teens featured a black, Asian or minority ethnic character. In Australia, a recent study by Victoria University found that books for children and teens almost exclusively star middle class, heterosexual, white families, and most protagonists are male.
>
> Hindustan Times, *3 January 2019*

As literary agencies have a prominent gatekeeping role in mainstream publishing, they too must consider the nature of their workforce and how new talent is discovered. Personal recommendation from existing clients when taking on new authors does not broaden the pool from which they originate – it only reinforces the strength of the existing network drawn from a particular class and background. Julia Kingsford comments on her work as an agent, 'Basically my white, middle class authors were only recommending people from their own social circles, who tended to be white, middle class people who had been to top universities, and worked in the media' (Kingsford, 2019). Drawing on authors from creative writing programmes may have a similar result – these are writers with the time and financial resources to develop their craft. 'Whilst talent is universal, the craft of that talent isn't', says Julia Kingsford.

In 2018 a new UK literary agency, the Good Literary Agency, opened its doors to non-agented writers with a focus on 'discovering, developing and launching the careers of writers of colour, disability, working class, LGBTQ+ and anyone who feels their story is not being told in the mainstream' (thegoodliteraryagency. org). The agency, supported by funding from Arts Council England, was founded by Nikesh Shukla and Julia Kingsford. A key aim of setting up the agency was to work with authors that for financial reasons were not getting serious attention to develop their talent and careers. Julia Kingsford says,

> When we talked to publishers about why there was a lack of diversity in publishing, publishers said that they didn't get sent enough. When we talked to agents what they said was that they sent loads – it just didn't get bought or got bought for such small amounts of money that it wasn't necessarily worth their while to pursue. ... Agenting is a business where you have to follow the money.
>
> *Kingsford, 2019*

Publishers are experimenting with blind recruitment processes – hiding details such as name and education – when making an initial selection of candidates. Should agents do the same when inviting new projects? Trade publishers are discussing opening up offices in other parts of the UK, to get away from a London-centric view – should agencies adopt a similar approach? The difficulties should not be underestimated. Research by Melanie Ramdarshan Bold examined whether literary agents can be successful outside London, looking at the case of Scottish-based agents (there were none in Scotland until 1989). She found that it was more difficult to develop expertise given the smaller pool of opportunities available, and concluded that

> the majority of Scottish literary agents are ill equipped to sell rights and either outsource this task to external agencies or sign over the rights to publishers in exchange for larger advances for their authors. Unfortunately, these publishers do not always exploit the rights efficiently, and so lucrative rights are often left unexploited.
>
> *Ramdarshan Bold, 2013, page 16*

A lack of diversity in the UK and US publishing markets is also reflected in the lack of translated works. Chad Post of the Three Percent blog says:

> The big corporate presses are not doing very many of these books. They do the big books that seem like they are built to make a lot of money or have a name—Haruki Murakami, Stieg Larsson, the books that are set to have a large sales base for whatever reason.
>
> *Edgerly, 2016*

Smaller presses may publish high literary titles in translation; and surprisingly it is Amazon with their AmazonCrossing programme that fills the gap in the middle – for example, those genre titles such as mystery or thrillers that do well in their domestic markets. There are definitely some agents interested in the area of translations but if they have to follow the money, often their inclination will be to concentrate on authors writing in English.

The future of the literary agent

Agents remain a fundamental part of the ecosystem of trade publishing, and are valued by both authors and publishers. They continue to spot new talent in their gatekeeping role, and nurture the careers of authors whilst protecting their interests. Can we see any threats to the position of the literary agent? The continuing consolidation of publishers can only depress competition for agented books. The larger publishing groups still allow competition between their imprints when other publishers are in the hunt for a book. This favours authors but how long will this be allowed to continue? Also the aim of securing world rights, if achieved by publishers, will diminish the opportunities for agents to sell works themselves into different territories. In addition, publishers may increase their direct approaches to authors – this is already the case for some commissioned non-fiction titles. Celebrities may use the services of their lawyers to negotiate contracts as books are seen as just one part of the exploitation of their brand.

The impact of self-publishing continues to be felt in the publishing industry. The democratisation of authorship means that there is a ready route to publication which bypasses the mainstream publishers (Phillips, 2014). There are not accurate figures on the sales of self-published books but a large number of titles are published through this route. The aim of the self-published author may be to attract their own audience, and take a higher share of the book's revenue. Some also see the possibility of attracting the interest of a commercial publisher – the large publishing houses keep an eye on successes through storytelling sites such as Wattpad, crowdfunded options such as Unbound or Kickstarter, or e-book publication through Amazon. Such filtering bypasses that done by agents, but those signing up with a mainstream publisher may still feel they need an agent's help when negotiating terms.

Wattpad has moved from simply being a platform to the creation of a whole model around the exploitation of stories through different media. The author Anna Todd posted her story *After* on the platform in 2013, and it went on to be read over 1.5 billion times. The book was sold to Simon & Schuster, and Wattpad received the equivalent of an agent's commission, taking 15% of Todd's earnings. For the Hollywood movie, Wattpad acted in the role of producer (Cuccinello, 2018). Could the filtering role of agents be carried out by AI? – Wattpad thinks so and in 2019 the company announced the opening of its own publishing division and the proposed use of algorithms to aid the process of selecting titles: 'Whereas traditional publishing is based on individual editors' tastes, Wattpad's technology will scan and analyze the hundreds of millions of stories on the app to find themes or elements that might determine a story's commercial success' (*New York Times*, 24 January 2019).

The erosion of authors' earnings has impacted on the work of agents: if more work is required to generate the same level of income, something has to give – from work on the slush pile to the level of editorial input given to new writers. The larger agencies have developed an infrastructure of lawyers, accountants, or PR experts, and these overheads have to be covered from the share of author incomes. Those agents may be forced to restrict themselves to working with the known quantities of successful brand authors. Authors, in turn, may direct their efforts towards projects in the world of audio, TV, or film, away from books. Some agencies, already working across media, are well placed to deal with such a shift, but smaller literary agencies will undoubtedly struggle.

References

Albanese, A. (2013), 'The Agent', *Publishers Weekly*, 18 February.

Arts Council England (2017), *Literature in the 21st Century: Understanding Models of Support for Literary Fiction*. www.artscouncil.org.uk/publication/literature-21st-century-understanding-models-support-literary-fiction [Accessed 15th November 2019].

Asscher, M. (1993), 'The Challenge of Being Small and Unknown', *Publishing Research Quarterly*, Summer.

Bennett, L. (2013), 'The Dastardly Defender of Letters', *New Republic*, 21 October.

Bhaskar, M. (2013), *The Content Machine: Towards a Theory of Publishing from the Printing Press to the Digital Network*, Anthem Press.

Blake, C. (1999), *From Pitch to Publication*, Macmillan.

Clark, G. and Phillips, A. (2019), *Inside Book Publishing*, 6th edition, Routledge.

Cuccinello, H. (2018), '$400M Fiction Giant Wattpad Wants To Be Your Literary Agent', *Forbes*, 24 September.

De Bellaigue, E. (2008), '"Trust Me. I'm an Agent." The Ever-Changing Balance between Author, Agent and Publisher', *Logos*, 19:3, 109–119.

Edgerly, L. (2016), 'Found in Translation: How Amazon Is Filling a Gap in World Literature', https://teleread.org/, posted 27 August.

Geller, J. (2019), Joint CEO of Curtis Brown, interviewed by the author, 14 January.

Gillies, M. A. (2007), *The Professional Literary Agent in Britain, 1880–1920*, University of Toronto Press.

Gottlieb, R. (2016), *Avid Reader: A life*, Farrar, Straus and Giroux.

Greenfield, G. (1993), 'Literary Agents: Where They Come from and Where They Are Going – A Transatlantic Study', *Logos*, 4:4, 189–197.

Hepburn, J. (1968), *The Author's Empty Purse and the Rise of the Literary Agent*, Oxford University Press.

Kingsford, J. (2019), Co-founder of The Good Literary Agency and Kingsford Campbell, interviewed by the author, 16 January.

Klebanoff, A. (2002), *The Agent: Personalities, Politics and Publishing*, Texere.

Lambert, S. (2019, Director at C&W (Part of Curtis Brown), interviewed by the author, 19 February.

Legat, M. (1995), *An Author's Guide to Literary Agents*, Robert Hale.

Little, A. (2011), 'Agenting Now', *Logos*, 22:2, 22–27.

Lord, S. (2013), *Lord of Publishing: A Memoir*, Open Road.

Maschler, T. (2005), *Publisher*, Picador.

Phillips, A. (2014), *Turning the Page*, Routledge.

Phillips, A. (2017), 'Have We Passed Peak Book? The Uncoupling of Book Sales from Economic Growth', *Publishing Research Quarterly*, 33:3, 310–327.

Phillips, A. and Bhaskar, M, eds. (2019), *The Oxford Handbook of Publishing*, Oxford University Press.

Ramdarshan Bold, M. (2013), 'Can Literary Agents Be Based Outside London and Still Be Successful?', *Logos*, 24:1, 7–18.

Shukla, N. (2016), *The Good Immigrant*, Unbound.

Solomon, N. and Atkinson, O. (2018), 'Open Letter on Author Earnings', *The Bookseller*, 29 June.

Spavlik, J. (2011), 'Fitting Literary Agents into the Digital Publishing Equation', *EContent*, September.

Thompson, J. (2012), *Merchants of Culture: The Publishing Business in the 21st Century*, 2nd edition, Polity Press.

The Writers' and Artists' Yearbook (1930), A. & C. Black.

10

THE REAL NEW PUBLISHING

How interconnected 'outsiders' are setting the trends

Caroline Harris

The real new publishing: how interconnected 'outsiders' are setting the trends

When pioneering blockchain author Sukhi Jutla wrote her round-up of takeaways from the 2018 FutureBook Live conference, one of the key insights she highlighted was that 'change comes from outsiders'. The phrase had been used by Emmanuel Nataf, co-founder of Reedsy, a platform that connects authors with publishing and editorial professionals. Nataf was talking about the industry's aversion to technology, but this principle holds more widely. Some of the most exciting, innovative publishing is currently being developed outside the traditional publishing ecosystem. A new generation of publishers are rewriting the rules. Frequently arriving at books from other areas of media, culture, internet business, or the third sector, they are taking advantage of new technologies and digital means to produce, market, and retail their works. Many are creating highly desirable products; often – though not always, as the success of personalised children's book publisher Wonderbly demonstrates – for niche audiences and sometimes in deliberately limited editions.

For these emerging post-digital publishers, there is no 'print versus digital'; no either/or – the two are companions and interconnected. The new entrants publish and share ideas, stories, and images across multiple platforms, from beautifully designed hardback print books, to personalised titles, e-books, magazines, video, web, merchandise, podcasts, events, and social media. In this setting, a book becomes one option among many, chosen when it is the most appropriate form: whether to display images and text in a tactile object, or because a book can so effectively mark a pause, a milestone reached. Sometimes, because a book can help these publishers reach different audiences and amplify different voices. You don't have to be a book publisher to make a book, so what are the motivations for doing so? What are the business models, creative decisions, and technical developments driving these new approaches to book publishing?

This essay investigates the new generation of emerging publishers, focussing on the 'outsiders'. Through a selection of case studies, it identifies and examines four trends in the new publishing ecosystem. These are magazine publishers that also create books; spoken word and live events generating book enterprises, in a reversal of the book festival model; social enterprise and charitable publishing; and tech-enabled businesses. The organisations experimenting with publishing in this way range from the financially self-supporting and successful to micropublishers (generally defined as one- or two-person operations) reliant on funding from the Arts Council or donations.

The primary research underpinning this essay comes from a study of more than 50 organisations and includes material from responses to an online survey and semi-structured interviews. It draws on the growing body of established expertise in the indie magazines sector, which has generated a network of specialist shops (both bricks-and-mortar and online), blogs, and events. Books such as Jeremy Leslie's *The Modern Magazine* (2013) and Ruth Jamieson's *Print Is Dead, Long Live Print* (2015) have begun to analyse the scope, history, and drivers of this sector. However, the existing literature on indie magazines does not specifically focus on book publishing, while for the other trends, this is the first systematic consideration of these publishing phenomena.

The niche ecosystems considered here were initially investigated through a literature search of articles in industry periodicals such as *The Bookseller* and respected blogs such as Stack Magazines, by researching networks of links – often regionally based, such as the Bristol and south west of England hub – and through online searches. To ascertain whether these trends extended beyond the UK, international examples have also been included. After the initial scoping phase, an email survey was sent to a selection of the identified organisations, to provide example case studies. Recipients were given the option of an interview or email questions in place of or in addition to the survey – which was designed to provide qualitative rather than quantitative details. Alongside information about their role, the survey asked respondents about areas such as previous publishing experience (their own and within their organisation), how their books were created and distributed (for example, in-house, or with freelance help, or with a book publisher), and to rate the usefulness of a variety of technologies (from Adobe Creative Cloud and short-run offset printing to e-books, social media, and podcasting). Participants were asked to indicate what had prompted the decision to publish, benefits of the books to their organisation, and if they had plans for future publications. The survey employed a range of multiple-choice questions, to provide comparisons. These, however, allowed multiple answers, in order to capture a more nuanced picture of the variety of business models and experiences. There were also comment spaces for respondents to indicate where their particular organisation and book publishing experience differed from the pre-set answers, or if they had any other comments. These acted as a checking mechanism and also to gather further detail.

Print versus digital: the same old story?

The context for the innovative publishing models discussed here is the landscape of post-digital publishing and self-publishing. Much research and theorising on digital disruption in book publishing has concentrated on e-books and digital reading (for example, Gomez, 2008; Striphas, 2011), with the 'threats' to books debated since before the turn of the millennium. The focus of this research so far has largely been on book publishing as an industry rather than on book publishing as an activity or process. In the traditional book publishing industry, the book is regarded as the core product, supported by associated marketing and promotional activities and, more recently, different formats, whether e-book, audiobook, or video. However, this is not the only way to view the production and place of books. Indeed, Michael Bhaskar, in his 2013 theoretical exploration, *The Content Machine*, contends that publishing is in fact about the selection, manipulation, and distribution of content. He writes how publishers, by defining themselves (incorrectly, he says) as 'makers of books', have 'straightjacketed themselves' (p.4).

Since the mid-1990s we have become used to witnessing the push-pull of the digital-versus-print story as e-books were hyped, then failed to overtake print as predicted; experienced rapid growth in sales after the release of the Amazon Kindle in 2007; and more recently appeared to plateau and drop in popularity. Often unreflectively, each reported rise in print book sales versus each fall in those of e-books was still, at the start of 2019, being narrated as a small 'success'. In his end-of-2018 round-up, Tim Godfray, executive chair of the UK's Booksellers Association, characterised the recent movements as a tide that is 'continuing to turn in favour of printed books and bookshops' (Mansfield, 2019). That year was also the fourth of rising print book sales in the UK, up 2.14% by value in 2018 from the 2017 figure (O'Brien, 2019). However, there are difficulties both with the 'rise' of independent bookshops (which came after massive decline) and with the headline e-book sales reported by Nielsen Bookscan in the UK and the Association of American Publishers and International Digital Publishing Forum in the US. The reported sales figures do not sufficiently take account of non-traditionally published books and those without an ISBN, often from small independents. They also do not consider the titles consumed by readers who have transitioned to subscription services such as Amazon's Kindle Unlimited, which in 2017 was estimated to represent about 14% of the company's e-book reads and is dominated by self-published authors (Friedman, 2017).

The difficulty in quantifying e-book sales exemplifies some of the issues for the traditional publishing industry. It has needed to bolt on newer platforms, data-gathering and outside expertise from rival media sectors (The Bookseller News Team, 2017) to its pre-digital foundations. Amazon, in contrast, is built from the algorithm up. Data collection and exploitation are integral to the whole way the online retailer operates. From this starting position, it has been able to then compete in the more established book industry arena, becoming a publisher and bricks-and-mortar chain. Similarly, for the new entrants in this study, digital is their native environment; it is the air they breathe.

While the relationship between print and digital forms has all too often been portrayed as adversarial, couched in the language of apocalypse and prophecy (Grafton, 2009), or extinction and replacement, the reality is much messier than the rhetoric. The ways in which digital and print forms relate are complex, sometimes complementary. Striphas, for example, points to 'persistent unevenness, or dynamism' in contemporary book culture (2009, p. ix), and this dynamism and unevenness also apply to the newer digital forms.

Author, entrepreneur, publisher, and futurecaster Seth Godin asserts that mobile is the 'real disruption', not the e-book (Flatt, 2018). Godin is among those who think that the publishing industry is 'in dramatic decline', with publishers constantly making the wrong decisions. 'The smartphone changed everything', he stated in his pre-FutureBook Live discussion with organiser Molly Flatt. He points out that the average person now spends nine hours a day reading, compared with 20 minutes a day when he started in publishing: a 27-fold increase. The difference is that this reading is mainly on mobile phones and computer screens. Godin contrasts the connection of smartphone-reading with the *dis*connection of book-reading and argues that 'people are fully hooked on connection'. However, this perceived disadvantage has also been at the core of the so-called 'print renaissance', in both the independent magazine sector and books. Attitudes to digital reading and social media content are complicated, contradictory, and not always positive. Millennials and Generation Z value print books for the 'safe', relaxed, non-digital space they offer (Filby, 2017), with 79% of a sample of US 18–34-year-olds in a 2015 study having read a print book in the previous year – nearly twice as many as had read an e-book (Cox, 2015).

Self-publishing: challenging the gatekeepers

The new generation of publishers have also been facilitated by the maturing of self-publishing and its challenge to established publishing models. In 2017, the total number of self-published titles exceeded one million, according to official US ISBN and data-collection agency Bowker (2018); this was a 28% increase from the 2016 total, which itself had seen an 8% rise from the year before. Interestingly, the number of self-published print books stood at 879,587 titles: an increase of 38% in the year. However, Bowker attributed this largely to the 50% increase at Amazon's CreateSpace platform and agent and commentator Jane Friedman and others have pointed out that Amazon has pushed towards print as it sees that it can charge more for paper copies (2017). So this may be a result of commercial strategy as much as author and consumer preference.

While some champion self-publishing as democratising and revolutionary, others regard it as reactionary and individualistic (Skinner, 2014). Either way, it has focussed attention keenly on the gatekeeper function of publishers. Steve Watson, founder of the independent magazine subscription service Stack

Magazines and a leading commentator on that industry, said in his interview for this research that:

> There is this growing independence ... the barriers are coming down between the people making things and the people consuming things. It wasn't very long ago that you needed a book publisher because they had the distribution lists ... there was a gatekeeper you had to go through. These days that's not as true as it was.

Bhaskar, writing in 2011, had also noted that when 'everyone can communicate with everyone' the gatekeeper function of media companies breaks down. However, he characterises this development as bringing 'super-abundance' and '[o]verwhelming complexity'. His language, of 'fragmentary content production ... barely held together by the forces of centralisation', conveys the anxiety of established book publishers in the face of this loss of control (p.58). Alison Baverstock and Jackie Steinitz's research conclusions are more positive, challenging the prejudice that quality is compromised with self-publication and instead pointing to high levels of motivation and preparation for the process among authors, and sharing of knowledge (2013).

Self-publishing is also generating new co-creation and business models. Author collectives include Triskele Press, Five Directions Press, and Year Zero Writers – the latter of which eschews the title of 'publishing company', instead focussing on the relationship between writers and readers (Year Zero Writers, n.d.). Gill Harry and Brenda Bannister are two of the coordinating team for Silver Crow Books, the co-publishing imprint of Frome Writers Collective, and answered the survey for this research. With over a hundred members, one of the group's aims is to support those who wish to self-publish. Working towards this, the Silver Crow Books imprint collaborates with preferred partners, such as Silverwood Books, Matador/Troubador, and the Self-Publishing Partnership in Bath. Its goal, Harry and Bannister explained in their survey response, is

> to make our services to members accessible, professional and low-cost. If our selected authors do not have the confidence or all the required to become a publisher themselves, we help them to prepare their manuscripts for publication and guide them through the publishing process. We also offer joint promotion and marketing opportunities.

The relationship between authors and readership continues to be transformed. Jutla is the first blockchain-published author (in April 2018), her book *Escape the Cubicle* being published via the UK's Publica (Albanese, 2018). On the evidence of 2018, blockchain was on its way down the Gartner Hype Cycle, which charts the expectations over time for emerging technologies, from the 'Peak of Inflated Expectations' to the 'Trough of Disillusionment' (Panetta, 2018). However, it has possibilities for supporting direct relationships between author and readership.

Publica uses a crowdfunding-style system where authors pre-sell their books via Initial Coin Offerings, or ICOs (Publica, 2019). Other tech-driven possibilities for self-publishing include Reedsy's Discovery platform, launched in 2019, which calls itself 'Goodreads for indie authors' (Reedsy, 2019).

Definitions and study: problems and potential

It is into this new digital-print ecosystem that the emerging publishers surveyed here have been born. They are certainly publishers, as defined by Bhaskar, who theorises that publishing is at its core about content and the 'framing and models, filtering and amplification' of that content. Like other publishers, they make content public and amplify it, scaling it up from one instance to multiple copies (2013, p. 6). However, they are often non-traditional, or non-mainstream, in their approaches when compared with the more established book publishing industry.

Non-traditional is, by general definition, not the norm; not the way things have been done before. It is the 'other', encompassing the new, the as-yet unrecognised, the small-scale, the eccentric, the edgelands. In publishing, the term has been used as a catch-all for self-publishing, on-demand publication of works that are out of copyright, and micro or niche publishing. However, figures from Bowker revealed that even in 2010, non-traditional publishing of this type accounted for eight times the output of traditional publishing (Bradley *et al.*, 2011) – making it, in terms of scale, more the norm than so-called 'traditional' publication. The category of 'non-traditional' is defined by Bradley *et al.* through the author relationship: mainstream publishers pay authors for their work through royalties; non-traditional publishers secure material through other methods. By this definition, the emerging and niche publishers who are the subject of this essay combine both mainstream and non-traditional means. Some self-publish, some produce books for brand clients, some partner with authors, some follow a more mainstream publishing model.

In their combining of multiple platforms and publishing formats these emerging publishers might be called hybrid – except that this term has already been applied to companies that offer authors both the traditional publishing model and various forms of co-publishing where the author pays for some or all of the services (Friedman, 2016). In their seamless distribution of content across multiple platforms, they could be termed omnichannel publishers, a phrase used in marketing and business studies to denote companies and strategies that combine online and offline operations (Wiener, Hoßbach and Saunders, 2018). However, definitions vary. 'Omnichannel publishing' is used by some marketing commentators to denote a seamless integration of channels that is more complete and mature than 'multichannel'. At the same time, it is used more narrowly to describe the pairing of consumer data with targeted content, using analytics to tailor digital communication strategies across channels (New Target, 2016).

While certain features unify the new-generation publishers studied here, they are also characterised by their diversity. They have different aims and operate in different sectors and niches. The criteria for inclusion in this study were that they were perceived to be involved in or have derived from activities other than publishing, or have been facilitated by digital disruptions and developments. The analysis focusses on attempting to identify emerging trends and clusters of similarities. In so doing, naming these trends becomes a tool for focussing on and teasing out what is happening at this point in the dynamic interplay that is contemporary publishing.

Many of the organisations are 'outsiders'. However, as examples such as crowdfunding publisher Unbound, digital-first press Canelo, Miranda West of event-led independent Do Book Company, and Crystal Mahey-Morgan's cross-platform storytelling brand Own It! show, experienced publishing professionals too are either setting up their own enterprises or running their more innovative ventures as side projects. For some, there is a dissatisfaction with the models being offered by traditional publishing. For others, an inkling that there are more innovative, inclusive ways of making books and connecting with potential readers. Benoit Knox, who started BK Publishing from scratch while in the second year of a publishing degree, explained:

> I could see that the traditional publishing industry was unable to cater for the needs of the wider South African market. It had and still has a narrow view of who its readers are and is content with its limited distribution options. To me as a young person this was not the type of industry I wanted to work in.

Echoing this from the UK, John Mitchinson, who as co-founder of Unbound had both publishing and TV experience, compares traditional publishing to 'agri-business', where publishers, in his view, are only looking for the highest yield 'crops'. 'That means that there is a massive amount of interesting and good stuff that just isn't being published. Because it is not easy for a publisher to see the return, real innovation in publishing is compromised', he says (Hussain, n.d.).

This study aims to look instead at the innovation. There is crossover between the groupings in the taxonomy that follows, and the trends sketched here are of course not the only way of categorising these new ecosystems. There are also continuities and overlaps with long-established models and traditional publishing practices among the case studies. In a rapidly changing media sphere, culture, and industry, where developments from Apple's podcast app to HP Indigo digital printing are rapidly absorbed and exploited, this essay can only ever provide a snapshot. It is an attempt to navigate, chart, and question the emerging forms of book producers as we traverse into the third decade of the twenty-first century.

Transferrable skills and aesthetic values: magazines as book producers

It is 20 years since the likes of *The Idler* and *Frieze* art magazine (born of the Frieze art fair) were launched, and nearly 15 since the beginnings of the latest wave of independent magazines (*Little White Lies*, for example, started in 2005). *Print! Tearing it Up*, an exhibition at Somerset House, London in summer 2018, began its homage with the 1914 Vorticist journal *Blast*. This long history, and the current boom, means there is a wealth of templates, and of experience, about how to make a magazine outside the mainstream.

Traditionally, magazine and trade book publishing have operated in separate spheres, with different content forms (collected articles submitted by a multiplicity of authors versus a single-author volume), design styles, business models, and author relationships. However, several factors have in the past decade and more brought areas of convergence between the two industries. These include the maturing independent magazine sector's focus on high-quality print; the disruption of digital and its challenge to the traditional magazine business model; and the maturing of the blogger generation.

In the early twenty-first century, the standardisation and commercially driven formats and content in mainstream magazine publishing prompted a number of independently minded titles to experiment. In their efforts to differentiate themselves, a number of titles explored designs more reminiscent of books, such as the quiet, highly formatted covers of business and design title *Monocle* – innovative when it launched in 2007 – or the single-column typography and broad margins of lifestyle magazine *Kinfolk*, launched in 2011. High production values became a point of distinction. *The Idler* brought out editions in fabric hard cover, a trope also employed by fashion title *PETRIe*, which aims to mix beautiful imagery with serious journalism (Wang, 2017). Travel and lifestyle magazine *Cereal* – one of the most successful of the new wave – perfected a much-copied minimalist style of layout and photography, with weighty, collectable, high-pagination issues produced at first quarterly and then biannually. As editor Rosa Park explained to MagCulture, 'we are of a generation where the way things look is important, and having a brand identity that filters through all of your images and design was very important to us' (2017). *The Hieronymus Journal*, launched in 2018 by the eponymous Swiss stationer, has a foil-embossed cover and open thread stitched spine. With issue one advertised at CHF220 and in a limited edition of 500 hand-numbered copies, this occasional journal takes periodical publishing into the territory of artist's bookwork.

The second factor driving the convergence of books and magazines is the disruption wrought by digital. This has affected both traditional magazine business models, where it has drastically reduced advertising revenues, and delivery platforms, by increasing the number of potential channels for appealing to readers. 'Where once there was a single business model (sell ads and sell copies) now there are multiple ways of making money and distributing magazines', writes graphic designer and industry commentator Jeremy Leslie in *The Modern Magazine* (2013, p.9). *Cereal* carefully curates its commercial relationships, making strategic brand alliances with the likes of British perfume house Penhaligon's or Levi's Made and Crafted. It also generates income by acting as a media agency. Similarly, TCO, publisher of film magazine *Little White Lies* and youth culture title *Huck* delivers targeted editorial across platforms from film to social media to print with brands including The North Face, Nike, and WeTransfer.

The blogging generation, who have grown up with an online voice, have been the drivers of much of the indie magazine expansion. Journalist Lizzie Garrett Mettler argues that the image-led aesthetic and abundant white space in the titles she studied are influenced by platforms such as Pinterest and Tumblr: 'these magazines haven't so much rejected the Internet as brought it off our screens and onto paper' (2014). Leslie notes how producing a printed magazine alongside a website brought a counterpoint to the 'disposability' of blogging for design commentary site *It's Nice That*; advertisers and clients took them more seriously (pp. 214–5).

It is no surprise that alongside book-like magazines these magazine brands are now initiating their own books. Watson pointed out that magazine publishers

> feel like they understand how to bind paper on one side and sell it to people … Anyone who's a magazine publisher will have all of the expertise to lay out a page that could be used for a book, or a page for a magazine.

Some of these magazine publishers produce books themselves, born from their own content and niche subject matter; some work with established book publishers; others create books for clients.

For these magazine producers, facing the financial challenges of the current media market, books can act as an additional income stream, or be another channel to offer clients. Clive Wilson, consultant head of books for TCO and co-founder of book creation business Harris + Wilson, explains that they are 'one element of the TCO offering to brands – alongside other premium content including film, digital and events'. Wilson says that 'white-label, non-trade publications … provid[e] a brand with a premium quality marketing asset'. Examples include the 'thought leadership' publications that the agency produced for Google, entitled *Think Quarterly*, and a book for Microsoft after its acquisition of Nokia in 2014. TCO also produces trade titles with established book publishers as partners, which additionally play a marketing role by amplifying their magazine brands. As of November 2018, 12 *Huck* and *Little White Lies* books were in print, with another six titles due in 2019. These are funded through flat fees and advances from publishers (Laurence King Publishing, US publisher Abrams, and HarperCollins imprint William Collins for the existing titles). The *Huck* book *Paddle Against the Flow* was placed with Chronicle Books in part because TCO was aiming to build a US audience. 'Editorial, design and marketing expertise translates very well from a magazine environment to a book publishing one', says Wilson. There is a 'genuine commitment to the physical, tactile qualities and potential of the printed page'.

Some independent magazines use the book form to collate past issues or compile yearbooks: travel title *Lodestars Anthology*, for example, or German typography blog-turned-magazine publisher *Slanted* with its *Yearbook of Type*. For others, the books speak to the interests of their niche audiences. *Apartamento*, established in 2007 in Barcelona and describing itself as 'an everyday life interiors magazine', has built a list of photo-led, cookery, and even adult colouring books with its own imprint (Apartamento Magazine, 2019). The *Cereal* website offers coffee-table volumes of curated images and words – such as *These Islands: A Portrait of the British Isles* – and city guides in digital and print forms. Editor Rosa Park is the author of an illustrated children's title, *A Balloon Away*, also published through *Cereal*. With events, its agency, and even a gallery project, *Cereal* exemplifies the multi-layered, omnichannel presence of many in this new generation.

London and North America-based *Pom Pom Quarterly*, a journal focussing on knitting, crochet, and craft, was set up in 2012 and conceived as 'a collection of patterns complemented by thoughtful writing and useful tutorials' (2018). By the beginning of 2019, the Pom Pom Press page listed six standalone titles and a six-volume series, *Interpretations*. Readers can purchase digital, print, or gift set editions. In answer to questions for this research, co-founder and editor Meghan Fernandes described its core business areas as magazine or journal publisher, events or festivals, podcast or other audio producer, and niche interest publisher. Fernandes is the only one of the Pom Pom team with previous publishing experience: working 'as an assistant in the picture research department of a lifestyle book publisher part-time as a student. I then helped produce exhibition catalogs [sic] at a small gallery'. They create the books themselves in-house, developing their approach and production schedules with each title, but employing a freelance graphic designer. According to Fernandes, the decision to become book publishers came because they 'saw a gap for more boutique-style books in the craft industry'. The books add value for their audience and Pom Pom plans to continue publishing three to five books a year. Interestingly, Fernandes described Amazon as 'Not at all useful' compared to the importance of social media for this niche craft audience: the high-volume, low-discoverability market hall, where it can be difficult to convey points of distinctiveness, does not always lend itself well to these niche non-fiction publishers.

The story is slightly different for literary periodicals. For these publishers, books – or the aspiration to produce books – are often part of the original plan, and editors are more likely to have a background in book publishing. *Slightly Foxed* was set up by Girl Pirkis and Hazel Wood, formerly of John Murray, in 2004 and began producing Slightly Foxed Editions in 2008 (Slightly Foxed, 2019). These clothbound limited runs of forgotten works are printed by Smith Settle, the same craft printers who have produced the journal since its beginnings. The magazine itself, said Watson in interview, is 'a bookish object, and [Pirkis and Wood] realised they could take these great works … and know this is the sort of stuff that their readers love … It's such a lovely little ecosystem they've got going'. More recently, Laura Jones and Heather McDaid launched 404 Ink first with a literary magazine in autumn 2016, followed by the Kickstarter-funded and widely reported *Angry Women* as their first book publication in March 2017. Both are publishing freelancers, with experience in books and journalism.

This model of mixed journal and literary products is also to be found in poetry. Corbel Stone Press, run by Autumn Richardson and Richard Skelton, has an innovative multimedia list spanning artworks and special editions, journal *Reliquiae*, original books, and paperback editions of out-of-print titles by the founders and others; it also publishes music in cassette, DVD, USB drive, and digital download forms (Corbel Stone Press, n.d.).

Spoken word first: podcasting and events

In recent years there has also been convergence, or perhaps more of a readjustment, between the written and spoken word. Audiobook sales are 'booming', according to a *Bookseller* article based on 2017 figures from Nielsen, having risen 15% by value compared with 2016 in the UK and doubling in the five years from 2012 (Wood, 2018). Podcasts are reaching six million people a week in the UK (Ofcom, 2018), with podcast publishers reporting close to 150 million downloads globally a month (Statista, 2019). Magazines such as *Little White Lies* produce podcast editions, while Stack Magazines has a long-running 'behind the scenes' podcast series. There are also podcast-to-book ventures, such as the Lunar Poetry Podcasts anthology, *Why Poetry?*, and more interwoven co-productions, such as the podcast-plus-pocketbook output of Radiobook Rwanda, a collaboration between Bristol-based No Bindings, Huza Press in Rwanda, and Kwani Trust in Kenya to 'showcase Rwandan and East African creative voices' (Radiobook Rwanda, n.d.).

David Turner, founder of Lunar and co-creator, with Lizzy Turner, of *Why Poetry?*, explained in interview: 'I've always seen the podcast as like a zine or magazine'. Lunar is a series of conversations with poets about the process and theory of writing. He now also publishes the transcripts; thanks to funding from Arts Council England they are available freely through Lunar's website. 'I think a lot of people who are attracted to podcasts want to reject traditional publishing', he said. '[That] was never my choice. I just wanted to have more space'. *Why Poetry?* was published by Verve Poetry Press in 2018 and came about through an invitation from Stuart Bartholomew, co-founder of the press, which itself developed from the Birmingham-based Verve Poetry Festival: 'What I'm trying to achieve with the podcast is what they're trying to achieve with the festival, which is an open view of what poetry is, and not having a division between spoken word and written poetry.' The Turners jumped at the opportunity for someone else to do the distribution, although they were the editors and typesetters for the book. It showcases the work of 30 poets featured in the podcast, woven through with the story of the podcasts, told in a series of interviews.

The Do Book Company sprang from spoken-word events of a different kind. The Do Lectures were set up by David and Clare Hieatt, co-founders of ethical clothing companies Howies and Hiut Denim, and run each year on their farm in Cardigan, Wales. The idea is a simple one: that people who do things can inspire the rest of us to go and do amazing things too. The talks are filmed and made freely available via the website and Do has become a worldwide 'encouragement network'. Impressed by the Do ethos and prompted by a 'desire to run my own independent publishing company', Miranda West, who answered survey questions for this study, set up The Do Book Company as a separate but associated enterprise. Operating from a small office in Shoreditch, London, the company sends a royalty of 5% from the proceeds of each sale back to the Do Lectures. The books are written by speakers from the lectures: 'Our aim is to recreate that same positive change in book form – whether that's the mastery of a new skill or craft, a simple mindshift, or a shot of inspiration to help you get started' (The Do Book Company, 2019). Similarly, the School of Life creative and life-hacking workshops, based in London, have led to its business in linked books and stationery. Unlike many of the new entrants studied in this research, West has more than two decades of established expertise, having been publisher for André Deutsch and editorial director for Ebury Press before moving to Vermilion. 'I would not have started a publishing business without having industry experience,' West commented in her survey answers.

These publishing operations extend the brand and audience reach for the original ventures and add a tangible element for the existing audiences. Events can become both the instigator of a book or publishing operation and the point of sale. However, books can work in another way for events: to capture and explain. 'We needed to find a new way to record an event or programme that is disparate/transient, that can't be captured through photography or video alone,' wrote Rosie Allen, one half of the partnership behind contemporary arts project organisation Field Notes, in her survey responses. A community interest company (CIC), Field Notes produced *The Wanderers* with a young artist publishing collective, using riso printing and traditional binding. Their work is funded on a project-by-project basis, with finance for the first ISBN-registered publication from Arts Council England and Cornwall arts funder FEAST. 'The reception of the book has been perhaps the most surprising thing', said Allen, 'the degree to which it has allowed us to explain the project as a whole has greatly extended the legacy of the project and is helping us to build useful connections for a new programme and publication'.

Books with purpose: social enterprise and charity publishing

Reaching different audiences; amplifying different voices: these aims draw together organisations that are trying to initiate change through their books and publishing projects. They are concerned with social value, not just aesthetic, informational, or financial value. This study identified two main forms of social value publishing: charities that have begun to produce books or have set up a publishing business, and book-related ventures that have formed themselves as a social enterprise or have a social imprint. Although definitions of social enterprise vary, a broad categorisation is that these organisations sit between traditional charities and profit-driven business. They have commercial elements, but aim to create positive social change, reinvesting profits to 'tackle social problems, improve people's life chances, provide training and employment opportunities for those furthest from the market, support communities and help the environment' (Social Enterprise UK, 2016).

Benoit Knox is director/publisher of BK Publishing, a magazine and book producer based in Pretoria. Much of its output is for clients – from small to international publishers and from children's titles and personalised books to poetry and local interest – but BK Publishing also has its own social imprint, Meetse a Bophelo: 'The Water of Life'. This currently publishes two to three titles a year – and Knox hopes it will be more in future. 'Social value extends far beyond the cultural value of books', he wrote in his survey answers. 'Our books and magazines and distribution models are designed to create a book-reading and book-buying culture in the disadvantaged communities in South Africa'. He wants to appeal to a diverse audience, and BK Publishing has been experimenting with reaching people who would not usually buy books, by hand-selling and distributing through alternative outlets such as 'pop-up bookshops on our street corner' and 'spaza-shops' (informal traders of groceries and sweets).

In the US, Anne Trubek is the owner and publisher at Belt Publishing, 'a platform for new and influential voices from the Rust Belt and Midwest' (*Belt Magazine*, 2018). Trubek wrote that she was prompted to produce books by a '[d]esire to tell stories that were not being otherwise told'. She also founded *Belt Magazine*, a journalism website focussing on the politics and culture of the region, and now a separate non-profit organisation supported by readers, donations, and grants.

The aim of facilitating diversity, inclusivity, and access to the industry has encouraged a number of organisations to provide mentoring and support. Verve Poetry Press, for example, has plans to assist the development of emerging poets through workshops, writing opportunities, and the support of the press's published poets (2019). The Good Literary Agency was set up by author Nikesh Shukla and his agent Julia Kingsford to focus on 'discovering, developing and launching the careers of writers of colour, disability, working class, LGBTQ+ and anyone who feels their story is not being told in the mainstream' (2019). While there are no plans to become a book publisher, Shukla also edits *The Good Journal*, a quarterly journal showcasing British writers of colour. Its status as a social enterprise is important, said Kingsford in her interview responses, 'because there is a clear social purpose to the agency'. The structure is also necessary, as the venture is partially funded by Arts Council England. Currently working with more than 40 authors, it has received an 'incredibly positive' response from publishers, with many providing low-level funding.

Trigger exemplifies a model of charity-related publishing driven by the aim of widening audience and access. Adam Shaw, chair and founder of The Shaw Mind Foundation, had struggled for over 30 years with debilitating OCD. On recovering with the help of psychologist Dr Lauren Callaghan, he wanted to support people who might not have access to the private therapy he had benefited from. 'His Pulling the Trigger books series aims to provide evidence-based recovery tools written by clinical psychologists and psychiatrists', explained editor

Stephanie Cox, answering on behalf of Trigger. Callaghan is a founder of the press, which means that 'every book we produce has a professional stamp of approval, which is vital when putting out such important books'. The press began with a seasoned copywriter and editor, and graduates as publishing coordinators. It has now grown to include a range of imprints and brought in directors from Palgrave MacMillan and Quarto group alongside highly experienced sales and publicity managers. There are plans to move into children's publishing and to become more of a 'mental health and wellbeing publisher'. Proceeds from the books, aside from author royalties, fund The Shaw Mind Foundation's mental health projects. 'Information about the charity is shared inside our books and we cross-promote our services at events and other ventures', explained Cox.

The Ellen MacArthur Foundation also finds that books help them reach different audiences, as editorial lead Ian Banks stated in his survey answers.

> Our standard format of publication has been the research report, but a book offers access to a different readership (e.g. academics), allows for outside authorship and contributions, and is a place where we can explore concepts and ideas related to but outside the remit of our reports,

he explained. The Foundation is a charity that aims to accelerate the transition to a circular economy and promote positive economic change globally. It does this by engaging with decision-makers from government, business, design, and academia. It offers in-depth reports, workshops and learning activities, and web-based resources. By the end of 2018 it had released three books under its own imprint. However, being a new entrant to publishing, especially one (unlike magazine businesses) not used to trading, expectations of distribution figures 'sometimes exceeded what might be normally expected for that type of book', wrote Banks. A subsequent book collaboration was undertaken with a mainstream publisher to strengthen distribution, marketing, and revenue collection – as well as to bring in outside help for design and graphics, as for previous books – due to lack of capacity as well as gaps in expertise. For the Foundation, their books also provide evidence of dissemination and impact for funders and stakeholders.

What these organisations share is that their publishing-related operations are concerned with making a difference. They also aim to create a virtuous circle, where the different areas of the organisation support and amplify each other. This circularity and mutual support, which contrasts with a linear, 'broadcast', get-it-out-there-and-promote-it model, is a feature of this interconnected publishing.

Digital enabling: platforms and relationships

In the current world of post-digital reading, distribution, and marketing, new platforms and technological developments have enabled connection between readers, authors, and books in a variety of ways. Social media platforms were highly valued by the survey and interview respondents in this research but, beyond that, each pinpointed their own bespoke combination of tech-related enablers, whether digital printing, or e-books, or Amazon, or lower-cost equipment and software. The availability of industry-standard graphic design programme InDesign on subscription service Adobe Creative Cloud has had a particular impact in lowering the financial barriers of production, especially for micropublishers. Instead of a substantial up-front software investment, new entrants can pay month by month, with free trials and reductions for students and in promotions.

Other publishers established over the past decade have been tech start-ups as well as publishing companies. John Mitchinson, who co-founded Unbound in 2011, noticed how, while many small, independent presses had sprung up in the gaps left by the big publishers, 'no one seemed to be doing anything in the technology space. Nobody seemed to be challenging the relationship between readers and writers' (Hussain, n.d.). Unbound has taken the crowdfunding model and applied it to book publishing, with its own dedicated platform in the foreground, backed up by traditional editorial services and, since 2018, in-house sales and distribution (Onwuemezi, 2018). It has published more than 150 books, with Shukla's prize-winning *The Good Immigrant* a particular success, having sold more than 70,000 copies (Myers, 2018; *Courier*, 2018). David Hieatt's book *Do Purpose*, part of the Do Book Company series, was funded via the Unbound platform. The publisher has combined technological with editorial, business, and marketing innovation, pursuing a policy of publishing underrepresented writers, giving authors 50% of profits from their title and importing the reader-author relationships fostered by social media and Kickstarter-style crowdfunding into the publishing model itself. In the style of the newly interconnected publishing, it has also launched an online journal, *Boundless*, with content ranging from essays to reviews, a podcast and unpublished fiction, edited by established journalist and critic Arifa Akbar. Alongside providing literary value, Mitchinson has said *Boundless* is 'a way of enlarging our data set, with relatively minimal investment' (*Courier*, 2018).

While some publishers, such as digital-first Canelo and Hera, have moved away from print, for Wonderbly the book experience is crucial, even though it is enabled by a host of back-end technological developments. The personalised book company was originally called Lost My Name, in reference to its first product, *The Little Boy/Girl Who Lost His/Her Name*, which by 2017 had sold 2.7 million copies and, according to the company's website, was the bestselling picture book of 2018 in the UK (Wonderbly, n.d.). Chief product officer Nick Marsh said in his interview for this research that the company had been on a 'big journey' through a rapid growth phase to its current position as a 'slightly more mature medium-sized business'. Wonderbly sees itself as 'really just a children's publisher, it's just that our USP is personalisation'. Marsh stated:

> We don't have this as our customer-facing value proposition, but personalised books are personalised in order to make the stories inside them and the messages children take from them more impactful and more memorable and more valuable to them.

Wonderbly is a 'microcosm' of the publishing industry, he continued: a publisher, an ecommerce retailer, manufacturer, and marketer all in one. Marsh's own background is in graphic design, while the four founders – Asi Sharabi, Tal Oron, David Cadji-Newby, and Pedro Serapicos – had some writing and design experience, but none in publishing; the group's core expertise lay primarily in digital marketing, internet business, and start-ups. They took the format of the personalised book and made it into a high-quality product, with fine attention to the detail of story, scripting, and illustration.

The digital driver in the company's growth was 'the opening up of Facebook as a digital marketing platform'. This, Marsh revealed, took the *Lost My Name* books from a niche product to a mass-appeal product. He also pointed to developments such as the browser technology that renders the personalised book previews on the website and high-resolution PDFs that are sent to print: 'our website is basically a website that allows you to print off another website', he explained. Then there are the standards around image and rendering technologies and graphics processing, and the 'high-quality, high-volume digital print' allowed by the slightly older technology of HP Indigo digital offset presses.

Turner of Lunar Poetry Podcasts noted the rise of easily accessible platforms on which to publish audio, together with cheaper equipment aimed at beginner podcasters. He uses Soundcloud, because 'when you share the link through social media it automatically embeds with a player that is compatible with just about every device'. He wanted engaging with the podcast to be as easy as picking up a magazine. This compatibility, and accessibility of the means of making, is important to Turner, who says of the current upsurge in indie production:

> I liken it very much to … the 70s [when] there were photocopiers popping up in public buildings and offices and then zine culture really exploded because suddenly you could just run off a hundred copies – behind your boss's back.

Why a book?

The new generation of publishers in this study all had their own particular reasons for publishing books – from being invited, to financial, to championing diversity, to audience-building, to documenting, to the desire to run their own press. For all of them, however, books offer a special and particular value. In *The Revenge of Analog*, David Sax argues that the ubiquity and efficiency of digital has re-valued analogue technologies, including paper and physical books. Initially, digital makes the analogue versions 'worthless', but when digital becomes the default, the 'honeymoon' with the next new tech product ends: each technology can then be judged on its true merits (2016, p. xvi). In Sax's view, the older analogue tool is then either recognised as working better or coveted for its inefficiency. This to an extent holds true in publishing, in particular for the indie magazine sector and with limited editions, but in the interconnected publishing researched here, it is more the case that digital and print are woven together. Each technology has its particular role and strengths. There is a continuum: from ephemerality and disembodiedness towards longevity and 'weight' – from social media to website to print magazine – with a book sitting, logically, as the farthest point.

The bound-ness of books has been contrasted in negative terms to the supposed freedom of digital forms. However, in an era of in-finite information and scrolling without end, the finiteness of a book becomes a point of difference: a benefit. The artisan aspect of print has also been re-valued, with letterpress printing a growth area that has spawned its own magazines, including Alberta-based *Uppercase* (which also produces books) and *Pressing Matters* from Bristol. Turner referred to a conversation with Michael Curran, who started Tangerine Press around the time that the Amazon Kindle came out:

> People said: 'You're crazy, people don't want books any more.' And …
> because he does really nicely handbound books, and everything's really
> considered and everything's really beautiful, he said that he only saw a rise in
> sales because people don't want one thing or the other, they want choice …
> They're very different experiences: holding a book and reading words.

Among his examples, Sax analysed the success of Moleskine and discussed how the company positioned its notebooks as 'the ideal companion to smartphones' (2016, p.31). Perhaps this is a way to view the print books being produced by these new publishers: as companions. This terminology at least questions the adversarial tenor of debate around how the disruptive potential of digital will play out, and the language of challenge and defence. As *Cereal* editor Park has stated, 'I don't think that digital is on a different par to print, it's equally important. But it's difficult to compare because they are so different. They're dependent on each other' (MagCulture, 2017).

Many of the emerging publishers studied here are niche and have built a close relationship with their audiences and online communities through digital means. However, niche does not necessarily mean small, especially as publishing enterprises expand their omnichannel presence. By 2019 *Monocle* had become a global lifestyle and publishing brand, spanning designer goods to radio and film, and from annual Quality of Life conferences to cafés in London, Tokyo, and Zurich. It has a book list published with German house Gestalten (Monocle, 2019).

As shown by the examples of Google and Microsoft, leading global brands are themselves looking towards print and books, sometimes as vehicles for internal communications. Brands have for several decades produced books as part of their marketing and brand development. The Soho House group of clubs and hotels, which for a time had their own publication programme including magazines, has produced two books with Preface Publishing; Harris + Wilson created a series for Octopus Publishing Group with organic children's food brand Ella's Kitchen. In a more unusual move, fashion retailer COS itself published *Creating with Shapes* by fashion designer and long-time collaborator Usha Doshi.

Books bear great cultural and informational significance. They have for centuries played a central role in 'how people have given material form to knowledge and stories', as Leslie Howsam writes in the introduction to *The Cambridge Companion to the History of the Book* (2015, p.1). In 2019, Sharmaine Lovegrove, publisher at Dialogue Books, called on the publishing industry to be 'bolder and braver' and 'appeal to the full range of potential readers'. Her rallying cry was predicated on a view that books are the 'foundation of culture' or that they should be (Lovegrove, 2019). Books are still seen as special: a category apart. However, they are no longer the primary information channel. In his 2011 deconstructionist analysis of the book, Striphas was suspicious of the hegemony of print: 'So much of the work of the world in the age of the [printed] book has been the exercise of dominion and domination over not only the forces of nature but other men and women, cultures and societies', he wrote (p. xii). Ironically, with the new hegemony of digital big business, print offers possibilities as a vessel for alternative viewpoints and as a vibrant space for experimentation.

Digital culture commentator Craig Mod wrote in *Wired* how the 'Future Book' is not what we thought it would be. Rather than 'interactive, moving, alive … lush with whirling doodads, responsive, hands-on', it is exemplified by an independently produced special edition to mark the 40th anniversary of the Voyager spacecraft; a multiplatform, crowdfunded publication that was 'complex and beautiful, with foil stamping and thick pages, full-color, in multiple volumes, made into a box set … for a weirdly niche audience, funded by geeks like me who are turned on by the romance of space' (2018). Mod calls the whole of the digital communication and production infrastructure that led to the final products the 'book' – a classification that could be questioned. His highlighting of the changing 'latticework' that goes into creating books, however, chimes with the findings of this study.

The 'outsider', emerging publishers discussed here use the whole of the digital-print continuum, in a way that is interconnected and that listens and responds to their audiences. They may not be *the* future of book publishing, but they are certainly indicative of how publishing is being transformed and remade in post-digital times.

References

Albanese, A. (2018) 'London Book Fair 2018: meet the world's first #1 bestselling "blockchain" author', *Publishers Weekly*, 11 April 2018. Available at: www.publishersweekly.com/pw/by-topic/international/london-book-fair/article/76592-london-book-fair-2018-meet-the-world-s-first-1-bestselling-blockchain-author.html (Accessed: 14 May 2019).

Apartamento (n.d.) *Home*. Available at: www.apartamentomagazine.com/ (Accessed: 15 May 2019).

Baverstock, A. and Steinitz, J. (2013) 'Who are the self-publishers?', *Learned Publishing*, 26(3), pp. 211–223.

Belt Magazine (2018) *Belt Publishing*. Available at: https://beltmag.com/belt_publishing/ (Accessed: 27 July 2018).

Bhaskar, M. (2013) *The content machine: towards a theory of publishing from the print press to the digital network*. London and New York: Anthem Press.

Bookseller News Team, The (2017) 'Firms look outside trade for senior appointments', *The Bookseller*, 18 August 2017, pp. 6–7.

Bowker (2018) 'New record: more than 1 million books self-published in 2017', *Bowker*, 10 October 2018. www.bowker.com/news/2018/New-Record-More-than-1-Million-Books-Self-Published-in-2017.html (Accessed: 11 March 2019).

Bradley, J., Fulton, B., Helm, M. and Pittner, K.A. (2011) 'Non-traditional book publishing', *First Monday*, 16(8), 1 August 2011. Available at: https://journals.uic.edu/ojs/index.php/fm/article/view/3353/3030 (Accessed: 11 January 2019).

Corbel Stone Press (n.d.) *Home*. Available at: www.corbelstonepress.com (Accessed: 15 May 2019).

Courier (2018) 'The pig-farming book publisher', *Courier*, 7 February 2018. Available at: https://couriermedia.co/2018/02/07/pig-farming-publisher-john-mitchinson-unbound/ (Accessed: 9 March 2019).

Cox, E.L. (2015) *Designing books for tomorrow's readers: how millennials consume content: White Paper from Publishing Perspectives and Publishing Technology*. Available at: www.ingenta.com/wp-content/uploads/2014/10/White-Paper-How-Millennials-Consume-Content.pdf (Accessed: 15 May 2019).

Do Book Company, The (2019) *About us*. Available at: https://thedobook.co/pages/about-us (Accessed: 1 March 2019).

Filby, E. (2017) 'What publishers need to understand about Generation Z', *The Bookseller*, 22 November 2017. Available at: www.thebookseller.com/futurebook/what-publishers-need-know-about-generation-z-676631 (Accessed: 15 May 2019).

Flatt, M. (2018) 'Seth Godin's mini-guide to publishing, selling and marketing books now', *The Bookseller*, 12 November 2018. Available at: www.thebookseller.com/futurebook/seth-godins-mini-guide-bookselling-and-marketing-now-890756 (Accessed: 12 November 2018).

Friedman, J. (2016) 'What is a hybrid publisher?', *Jane Friedman*, 7 December 2016. Available at: www.janefriedman.com/what-is-a-hybrid-publisher/ (Accessed: 10 March 2019).

———. (2017) 'The myth about print coming back (updated)', *Jane Friedman*, 26 March 2017. Available at: www.janefriedman.com/myth-print/ (Accessed: 25 March 2019).

Garrett Mettler, L. (2014) 'The great indie magazine explosion: a survey', *Vogue*, 26 September 2014. Available at: www.vogue.com/article/indie-magazine-independent-bookstore-explosion (Accessed: 23 February 2019).Gomez, J. (2008) *Print is dead: books in our digital age*. London: Macmillan.

Good Literary Agency, The (2019) *Home*. Available at: https://thegoodliteraryagency.org/ (Accessed: 28 February 2019).

Grafton, A. (2009) 'Codex in crisis: the book dematerializes', in Levy, M. and Mole, T. (eds.) (2015) *The Broadview reader in book history*. London: Broadview Press Ltd, pp. 555–573.

Howsam, L. (2015) *The Cambridge companion to the history of the book*. Cambridge: Cambridge University Press.

Hussain, H.M. (n.d.) 'Interview: John Mitchinson, co-founder of Unbound', *Dundee University Review of the Arts*. Available at: https://dura-dundee.org.uk/2018/04/11/interview-john-mitchinson-co-founder-of-unbound/ (Accessed: 3 March 2019).

Jamieson, R. (2015) *Print is dead, long live print: the world's best independent magazines*. Munich: Prestel.

Jutla, S. (2018) '#FutureBook18 Conference – a summary', *LinkedIn*. Available at: www. linkedin.com/pulse/futurebook18-conference-summary-sukhi-jutla/?published=t (Accessed: 6 December 2018).

Leslie, J. (2013) *The modern magazine: visual journalism in the digital era*. London: Laurence King Publishing Ltd.

Lovegrove, S. (2019) 'We need to put books back at the heart of British culture', *The Bookseller*, 9 January 2019. Available at: www.thebookseller.com/futurebook/we-need-put-books-back-heart-british-culture-926496 (Accessed: 24 January 2019).

MagCulture (2017) 'Independence: Rosa Park', *MagCulture*, 7 August 2017. Available at: https://magculture.com/rosa-park-cereal/ (Accessed: 25 February 2019).

Mansfield, K. (2019) 'BA exec chairman hails booksellers bucking high street trend', *The Bookseller*, 2 January 2019. Available at: www.thebookseller.com/news/ba-chief-exec-hails-booksellers-bucking-high-street-trend-922061 (Accessed: 5 January 2019).

Mod, C. (2018) 'The "Future Book" is here, but it's not what we expected', *Wired*, 20 December 2018. Available at: www.wired.com/story/future-book-is-here-but-not-what-we-expected/ (Accessed: 15 May 2019).

Monocle (2019) *About Monocle*. Available at: https://monocle.com/about/ (Accessed: 24 February 2019).

Myers, N. (2018) 'Small independent presses: interview with John Mitchinson', *Book Machine*, 25 May 2018. Available at: https://bookmachine.org/2018/05/25/small-independent-presses-interview-with-john-mitchinson/ (Accessed: 9 March 2019).

New Target (2016) 'Transitioning from multi-channel publishing to an omni-channel digital web strategy', *New Target*, 4 May 2016. Available at: www.newtarget.com/about/web-insights-blog/transitioning-multi-channel-publishing-omni-channel-digital-web-strategy (Accessed: 10 March 2019).

O'Brien, K. (2019) 'Print market posts fourth consecutive year of value growth', *The Bookseller*, 2 January 2019. Available at: www.thebookseller.com/news/print-market-posts-growth-fourth-consecutive-year-922081 (Accessed: 6 January 2019).

Ofcom (2018) *Podcast listening booms in the UK*. Available at: www.ofcom.org.uk/about-ofcom/latest/media/media-releases/2018/uk-podcast-listening-booms (Accessed: 5 April 2019).

Onwuemezi, N. (2018) 'Unbound brings sales and distribution in-house', *The Bookseller*, 28 February 2018. Available at: www.thebookseller.com/news/unbound-brings-sales-and-distribution-house-742811 (Accessed: 7 September 2018).

Panetta, K. (2018) '5 trends emerge in the Gartner Hype Cycle for emerging technologies, 2018', *Gartner*, 16 August 2018. www.gartner.com/smarterwithgartner/5-trends-emerge-in-gartner-hype-cycle-for-emerging-technologies-2018/ (Accessed: 31 March 2019).

Pom Pom Quarterly (n.d.) *Story*. Available at: www.pompommag.com/story/ (Accessed: 27 July 2018).

Publica (2019) *Introducing the book ICO*. Available at: https://publica.com/ (Accessed: 15 May 2019).

Radiobook Rwanda (n.d.) *About*. Available at: www.radiobookrwanda.com/about (Accessed: 15 May 2019).

Reedsy (2019) 'Big announcement! We've launched a new book marketing tool', *Reedsy*, 4 March 2019. Available at: https://blog.reedsy.com/announcing-reedsy-discovery/ (Accessed: 15 May 2019).

Sax, D. (2016) *The revenge of analog*. New York: PublicAffairs.

Skinner, A. (2014) 'Self-publishing is not revolutionary, it's reactionary', *The Guardian*, 29 May 2014. Available at: www.theguardian.com/books/booksblog/2014/may/29/self-publishing-revolutionary-reactionary-authorpreneurialism (Accessed: 10 March 2019).

Slanted (2019) *Profile*. Available at: www.slanted.de/en/publisher/profile-contact/ (Accessed: 24 February 2019).

Slightly Foxed (2019) *Slightly Foxed: a potted history*. Available at: https://foxedquarterly. com/a-history/ (Accessed: 26 November 2018).

Statista (2019) *Leading podcast publishers worldwide in March 2019, by unique streams and downloads (in millions)*. Available at: www.statista.com/statistics/613724/global-podcast-streams-downloads/ (Accessed: 5 April 2019).

Striphas, T.G. (2011) *The late age of print: everyday book culture from consumerism to control.* 2nd edn. New York; Chichester: Columbia University Press, 2011

Verve Poetry Press (2019) *About*. Available at: https://vervepoetrypress.com/about/ (Accessed: 2 March 2019).

Wang, G. (2017) 'Fashion magazine PETRIe is not afraid to challenge its readers', *Stack Magazines*, November 2017. Available at: www.stackmagazines.com/current-affairs/ petrie-magazine-interview-zadrian-smith/ (Accessed: 9 August 2018).

Wiener, M., Hoßbach, N. and Saunders C. (2018) 'Omnichannel businesses in the publishing and retail industries: synergies and tensions between coexisting online and offline business models', *Decision Support Systems,* 109(2018), pp. 15–26. Available at: https://reader.elsevier.com/reader/sd/pii/S0167923618300186? token=F979B78E4F241BACFEB902E243EBAA463D4095C949DD2707D 9906669A0D4F2CD2438587D90FAB63CE582E0C27D2C46F3 (Accessed: 10 March 2019).

Wonderbly (n.d.) *The Little Boy or Girl Who Lost Their Name*. Available at: www.wonderbly. com/uk/personalized-products/lost-my-name-book (Accessed: 9 March 2019).

Wood, H. (2018) '"Booming" audiobook sales double in five years', *The Bookseller,* 9 April 2018. Available at: www.thebookseller.com/news/audio-sales-double-five-years-764431 (Accessed: 5 April 2019).

Year Zero Writers (n.d.) *About Year Zero Writers*. Available at: https://yearzerowriters. wordpress.com/about-year-zero-writers/ (Accessed: 31 March 2019).

11

PARALLELS BETWEEN FICTION AND FOOD WRITING

Amy Burns

This essay reflects two aspects of my life. Professionally I am an academic concerned mainly with the business of food preparation and marketing, while at the same time I am heavily drawn to the broader culture of food, books, and the media. I enjoy fiction as much as I do guides to cooking, and it has become evident to me that these two genres of writing have developed striking similarities over the past few decades.

I will begin with details of a survey in which participants were asked the same questions in relation to their perceptions of both cookbooks and fiction; and in this regard my professional persona and style will predominate. It will, of necessity, sound like a brief scientific paper. Thereafter, the remainder of the essay will address the parallels between the two genres and give particular attention to the questions in the survey. In the process I hope to cast off the cloak of dry academia and do my best to make serious points in a more accessible – and I hope at times appropriately witty – manner.

In order to identify stages and factors that may influence consumers when purchasing a novel or cookbook and to measure general purchasing behaviour in relation to novels and cookbooks, an online survey was designed and distributed using social media sites (Facebook, Twitter, and LinkedIn) and personal email contacts. A total of 520 participants completed the survey of which 49% were male and 51% female. The age of participants ranged from 18 to over 60 and their purchasing habits varied from one to five books per year to over 20. See Table 11.1 for further demographic information on the sample.

TABLE 11.1 Demographics and purchasing habits of survey participants

Variable	Percentage
Age	
18–24	10
25–30	15
31–45	40
46–60	22
60+	13
Highest education level	
School	41
University degree	47
MSc	6
PhD	6
Number of books purchased per year	
1–5	32
6–10	43
11–15	24
16–20	0.5
20+	0.5
Source of information on new books	
Newspaper reviews	38
Recommendation from family/friends	30
Online/media promotion	23
Book shop browsing	9

Dewey's five stages of the buyer decision process were first introduced in the early twentieth century (Dewey, 1910). Since then studies have expanded on his initial findings but their essential validity remains – and will be the lens through which I consider my responses. Dewey's five stages are:

1. Problem/Need Recognition – recognising what the problem or need is and identifying the product or type of product which is required.
2. Information Search – the consumer researches the product which would satisfy their recognised need(s).
3. Evaluation of Alternatives – the consumer evaluates the searched alternatives. Generally, the information search reveals multiple products for the consumer to evaluate and understand which product would be appropriate.
4. Purchase Decision – after the consumer has evaluated all the options and is intending on purchasing the product they may still not purchase as the product has poorly judged by reviewers or due to unforeseen circumstances: for example it is too expensive.
5. Post Purchase Behaviour – after purchasing the product the consumer may experience post purchase dissonance feeling that buying another product would have been better. There is a need to address post purchase dissonance as not to do so decreases the chance of frequent repurchase.

These five stages are a useful framework to evaluate customers' buying decision process of any product. While many consumers pass through these stages in a fixed, linear sequence, some stages such as evaluation of alternatives may occur throughout the process. Furthermore, the time and effort given to each stage will depend on the type of consumer and the product they are purchasing.

In the case of purchasing a book, more specifically a novel or cookbook, the five stages are clearly relevant. However, there may be even more specific factors within the various stages that influence a consumer to purchase a novel or cookbook. My theory was that there are four key influencing factors that influence consumers: namely entertainment; education/self-improvement; celebrity status of the author; and finally style of writing/story-telling. To put this to the test a series of seven-point Likert scale style questions were included in the online survey. The questions asked participants how important the three factors were to them when purchasing a novel or cookbook and responses ranged from 1 = extremely unimportant to 9 = extremely important. The mean scores (x) for each factor for novels and cookbooks can be seen in Table 11.2.

As expected the entertainment factor of a book scored significantly higher (x = 5.9) when making a decision to purchase a novel and significantly lower (P < 0.01) (x = 2.3) when purchasing a cookbook (P < 0.01). Inversely the importance of education/self-improvement scored significantly lower (P < 0.01) when purchasing a novel (x = 3.4) and significantly higher (P < 0.01) when purchasing a cookbook (x = 6.9). However, the celebrity status of an author scored highly when purchasing a novel (x = 6.1) or cookbook (x = 6.8). While the novel outscored cookbooks in terms of style and narrative/story-telling an unexpected proportion of participants gave attention to these factors, which we routinely associate almost exclusively with literature (x = 6.0 vs x = 5.5).

TABLE 11.2 Quantitative survey results

	N	Minimum	Maximum	Mean	Std. deviation
Novel entertainment factor	520	4.0	7.0	5.9	0.95
Novel education/self improvement factor	520	2.0	5.0	3.4	0.68
Novel celebrity status	520	3.0	7.0	6.1	0.70
Novel style of writing/story telling	520	4.0	8.0	6.0	1.6
Cookbook entertainment factor	520	1.0	4.0	2.3	0.85
Cookbook education/self-improvement factor	520	5.0	7.0	6.9	0.24
Cookbook celebrity status	520	6.0	7.0	6.8	0.43
Cookbook style of writing/story telling	520	3.0	8.0	5.5	1.60

In what follows I will extrapolate this purely statistical survey into an essay which explores in detail the parallels between contemporary fiction and cookbooks. I will give emphasis to the issues which feature most prominently in the survey – notably entertainment versus self-improvement/education, the celebrity status of the author, and the more complex notion of style/story-telling – and speculate upon what lies behind the responses of participants.

There are a number of semiotic studies that examine food and literature as part of the same complex network of cultural sign-systems, but at a far more basic level literary writers seem largely unconcerned with food. Most aspects of bacchanalia, depravity, or horror find welcoming homes in verse or fiction: sex, drink, drugs, and death are notable favourites. It seems odd, therefore, that there are very few passages of any length in fiction (and virtually none in poetry) dedicated to eating, and hardly any to cooking. Unless you are dying of starvation Virginia Woolf's account in *In the Lighthouse* of *Boeuf en Daube* will be disappointing. It is a prompt for our sense of the emotions that swirl around the table but there is no sense of whether the dish poor old Mrs Ramsey spent days preparing pleasured the diners in any way. Proust's young narrator is distracted from the ethereal beauty of the ranks of peas and asparagus by his imagining of the violence visited on the star of the show, specifically the dead chicken, before the meal takes place. Once more, food is used as a symbolic transference mechanism, a way of focussing our attention to ensure we concentrate on something else. The mechanics and the sheer pleasure of eating and drinking seem unsuitably vulgar topics for literary art. Even Martin Amis, a writer enchanted by the sleazy protocols of modern existence, seems a little prudish. His most grotesque creation is John Self (*Money*, 1980), a drug taking alcoholic, who smokes a record number of cigarettes and purchases sexual encounters almost as regularly. He is also addicted to junk food – burgers and chips, we think – but Amis spares us the minutiae of his artery-clogging takeaway consumption while providing us with unsparing details on his other excesses. Obviously Big Macs are not as exciting as cocaine or blow-jobs after lunch.

Regarding the ways in which contemporary writers have represented such activities as cooking and eating the present-day differs little from the past: there is little to detect or say. More interesting is the rise of the cookbook – and along with it the celebrity author, often with regular TV series of their own – as a cultural phenomenon in its own right. It might not have self-consciously attempted to replicate elements of contemporary fiction but there are some extraordinary parallels.

The cookbook dates back to fragments of recipes attributed to the Roman gourmet Marcus Gavius Apicius, sometime in the first century AD, which first went into print in Europe in 1483. Several centuries earlier the Chinese Tang Dynasty had made records (now almost entirely destroyed) of cooking methods, and throughout the European Renaissance and the eighteenth century there was a regular output of books on the preparation of food aimed at those employed by the aristocracy to run the kitchens of houses from manors to palaces.

The shift of emphasis towards 'ordinary' people as potential purchasers of cookbooks came in the mid-nineteenth century. Suburbs were expanding and the women of the house, perhaps assisted by a maid, would be in charge of the kitchen. Eliza Acton was the first to spot this gap in the market and published her *Modern Cookery for Private Families* in 1845, Isabella Beeton's *Mrs Beeton's Book of Household Management* (1857–1861; reprinted by Benediction Press, 2010) is now far more famous but Acton had set the basic standard for what-goes-with-what, cook-for-how-long, serve-with formulae. Acton and Beeton had created a template. Essentially, their books were food-grammars. The basics of noun-verb-adjective formulae were replaced by rules on what vegetables would go with, say, cod or pork chops (and by implication which would be unsuitable) and how the two parts of the formula should be caused to react with each other.

In the UK and Europe little changed over the following eighty years, and the food rationing regulations in the UK during the Second World War placed restrictions on the imaginative range everyone from the metropolitan chef to the housewife. After the war Fanny Cradock (1909–1994), and her baleful husband Johnny, transformed things by appearing on BBC television in the late 1950s and early 1960s while at the same time publishing cookbooks. The Cradocks were more adventurous than their predecessors in terms of their attempts to internationalise the standard British cooking habits. She played particularly upon the exotic nature of dishes that, she alleged, originated in France and Italy, and is credited with introducing the British domestic cook to the pizza and the prawn cocktail, though her claim that the latter was a favourite of Mediterranean fishermen is open to doubt. They succeeded not because they tapped into a previously unsourced appetite for gastronomic otherness in 1950s Britain. In truth most ordinary cooks and diners were fully satisfied by the standard retinue of boiled vegetables, roast meat, fry ups, and fish and chips. The factor that projected the prawn cocktail into the menus of all ambitious eateries, dinners, and dances and onto the tables of newly married hosts was rather that of the Cradock's other-worldly personae. Fanny was at heart an actress, of the type played by Gloria Swanson in *Sunset Boulevard*: over-demonstrative, egotistical, and convinced that her histrionic persona would override usual notions of the real world. She would appear in the studio kitchen in ball gowns, heavily made-up and her preparation of each dish would be as much a performance as a demonstration of the practice of gastronomy. Johnny was her straight-man, subdued, and frequently admonished as the insignificant secondary. For the more prudish she might have come across as a showily oversexualised middle-aged woman but at the same time this was vital to her appeal: her sheer explosiveness would have been attractive to viewers, especially women, in working-class households with their new black and white televisions. She ruled by personality and she set the precedent for a cultural phenomenon.

In contrast to the Cradocks the middle classes of post-war Britain were receiving instruction from a self-appointed guru of continental gastronomic sophistication. In the 1930s Elizabeth David (1913–1992) had studied art in Paris, attended courses at the Sorbonne, and, bored with her studies, spent much of her time in the kitchen of the Parisian family with which she lodged. Inspired, she travelled through the French countryside picking up on the inventive synergies between regional habits and available produce. The result was her first book, *A Book of Mediterranean Food* (1950) which was an overnight success, due mainly to reviews in the quality broadsheets. Unlike the Cradocks, David limited herself almost exclusively to writing and rarely appeared on television, which carried a whiff of cultural elitism often echoed in the reviews of her books. Aside from enjoying the menus reviewers seemed to regard her as a vanguard for internationalism, the avoidance of humdrum Britain in favour of the wistful romanticism of being abroad. *French Country Cooking* (1951), *Italian Food* (1954), and *French Provincial Cooking* (1960) were much as travel guides for those inclined to favour travelling on the continent – that is the reasonably well-educated and well-off – as food books. While Fanny Cradock exemplified the popular culture of food writing and its new relationship with the media Elizabeth David was the high cultural *litterateur*. As we shall see this bipolar division between the two women became less evident later, with the stars of gastronomic discourse dividing their personae between high art and the fundamentals of food preparation.

Less than a decade later Delia Smith and Keith Floyd followed Fanny's example by making themselves as important as their ingredients and methods of preparation. Delia was the equivalent of Wendy Craig in the sitcom of the same period, *Butterflies* (1978–1983): resigned with her stable, middle-class existence but exhibiting signs of eccentricity, even rebellion. Keith was a witty, exuberant version of Basil Fawlty; you, the viewer, are his guest and you are never quite sure how he might behave or what the raconteur might come up with after his next swig of wine. Floyd became the Fanny Cradock televised food programmes.

Since then, many others have redesigned the chef-persona with relative degrees of success. Jamie Oliver is the Jack-the-lad Essex boy, almost admitting to philistinism but cancelling this suspicion with his espousal of gastronomic multiculturalism. Nigella Lawson could have walked out of a novel and into its film adaptation, probably directed by Richard Curtis. She is self-consciously good-looking, part of the educated London upper middle classes, and she seems happy to admit viewers to her up-market West-End home where she prepares dishes for her cultivated guests. Sometimes we get a glimpse of diners enjoying her preparations, but from a distance and briefly. It's rather like being admitted momentarily to a fictional world that will live on only in our fantasies and by now the parallels with the novel should be evident.

Hugh Fearnley-Whittingstall in his television programmes and books has created a narrative where the boundaries between impression, performance, and authenticity become very blurred. He admits to a privileged past – Eton and Oxford – but insists that his Devon cottage and the television programme spawned by the latter involve no fabrications or exaggerations. Several questions arise. Did he buy River Cottage as a going concern and was later approached by Channel Four or was the Cottage paid for by Channel Four as the set for their star performer? Does it matter? Yes it does because if we are a fan of his programmes and books we would not ask. Such enquiries demystify his performance as the main character in a narrative that involves an idyll he joyously brutalises by filming his beloved livestock being loaded for the abattoir, and a cast of locals who regularly help him out and are rewarded with invitations to feasts in his kitchen and garden. If a piece of fiction beguiles us sufficiently to create a suspension of disbelief, we do not ponder the absolute verity of the details offered by the narrator. This would be the equivalent of engaging fictional characters in a conversation with a view to checking on aspects of their personality or background that seem slightly suspect. Certainly, novelists make use of the raw material of the known world to embed their stories in a setting that is convincing and familiar, yet at the same time they distort this material to their own ends. In this respect the parallels between the celebrity chef, in print and on TV, and the work of fiction are intriguing and extraordinary. We are fully aware that the likes of Jamie Oliver, Nigella Lawson, and Hugh Fearnley-Whittingstall exist as actual individuals beyond their appearances on screen and their manifestations as authors of texts but in the latter our sense of them as real is activated by a complex fabric of transformative discourses and socio-cultural framings.

A sceptic might point out that an obvious difference between the two genres is that food books and programmes are dedicated to the pragmatic, instructive transference of information on the nature of food and its preparation. Novels, generally speaking, are not guide books, even if one includes those works of fiction designed to inculcate some political or moral ideal. As Table 11.2 indicates participants regarded cookbooks as almost twice as important as fiction in terms of information/instruction, and it is also notable that the proportionate relationship between the two genres in terms of entertainment was very similar. This distinction begins to fade when we look at how celebrity chefs have gradually turned food into a conceit for less specific affects and impressions. Floyd pioneered this with his tours of various parts of Britain, Ireland, Asia, and the US; he had a particular affection for France. His evocations of a region, with its cultural habits, its landscape and architecture became framing devices for his performances, glass in hand, in a kitchen borrowed from an agreeable local, in a square, or on a piece of windswept moorland. The food was interesting enough, but no more so than a novelist's description of the cut of a man's blazer as part of a much broader spectrum of representational nuances. Rick Stein took up where Floyd left off, his television programmes and books becoming travel narratives in all but name. The classic Stein work is *Rick Stein's French Odyssey* (TV programme and printed text) in which we accompany him on a giant barge along the canal de midi from Bordeaux to the Mediterranean. As with Floyd the food itself becomes part of the narrative thread, always linked to the habits and local produce of the areas framed by Stein's presence and eloquence.

In many ways food television programmes and books closely resemble the sub-genre of popular fiction involving crime, the thriller, and romance. In the best of the latter a balance is found between escapism – including ghoulish fetishism regarding topics we would prefer to avoid in real life or which we can only fantasise on – and aspects of the 'literary' novel, where we are obliged to confront, via the characters, ethical and existential dilemmas. In this regard, John le Carré is probably the most accomplished recent practitioner. Similarly, celebrity chefs, as performers and authors, furnish their stories with seemingly sincere questions regarding the environment, the ethics of farming and animal management (Fearnley-Whittingstall, particularly), and the current obsession with health, fast food, and obesity (Oliver outranks the others in this regard).

There is a fascinating similarity between contemporary food writing and media presentations and a genre of contemporary fiction which is too fluid to merit a title, as yet, but which involves notable unifying features: 'Chick List' exemplified, some would argue invented, by the Bridget Jones novels of Helen Fielding. *The New York Times* offered a blunt explanation for the success of the first book in the series, *Bridget Jones' Diary* (1996). 'It captures neatly the way modern women teeter between "I am a woman" independence and a pathetic girlie desire to be all things to all men' (Gleick, *New York Times*, 31 May, 1998).

We learn of Bridget's thoughts and activities predominantly via her diary entries but Fielding sets up a tension with each of these between her public and private persona. The former involve what the *Times* refers to as her '"I am a woman" independence', benefitting as she does from the recent legacy of the feminist movement of the seventies and eighties. The latter brings us closer to another aspect of Bridget: continually nervous about her weight and appearance, convinced that her 'career' in the media will lead nowhere and concerned ultimately with finding a reliable, sexy, long-term partner, preferably with a healthy bank balance.

In this regard the novel might be treated as a celebration of narcissism, self-delusion, and hypocrisy but there is something about the ever-dissembling Bridget that is rather enchanting. We take pleasure in her persistent shifts between sincerity and performance, and for some readers she offers a hint of salvation by contingency. The profundities of a new courageous mindset – in her case the 'independent woman' – can be played off against the conservative securities of her mother's generation. There are, of course, echoes of Jane Austen's heroines here but within the context of contemporary reading we might also liken her to the celebrity chef. The latter is naturalistic – he or she exists as an authentic individual – but on screen or on the page they also seem to allow the uncertainties of chance and improvisation to undermine uncertainty. The pressing routines of Bridget's world – principally the pursuit of a good job, the maintenance of a fulfilling self-image, and the search for a love life – are always part of a precarious relationship between ambition and reality. We watch with fascination as she does her best to create an ideal from chaos. Similarly, chefs perform tricks by selecting ingredients, preparing them, matching them, and bringing them to a beautifully successful conclusion while all the time maintaining the illusion that they are undertaking an experiment in the unforeseen, that at any point something might go catastrophically wrong. In this respect the relationship between the style of food writing, its status as a narrative, and the same factors in fiction becomes intriguing. And we should here bear in mind the surprising findings of the survey, where participants responded in a significant number to the ways in which cookbooks create a narrative effect.

Bridget's diary is very much like a series of chance-laden recipes. Each entry opens with her weight and a record of alcohol, food, and cigarettes recently consumed. Thereafter Bridget the author is fed into a narrative of possibilities and potential encounters – with friends, boy-friends, colleagues, and family – and we wonder with a growing sense of sanguine weariness what will happen to her at the close of the next episode. Continually, charmingly, she digresses, recalling incidents from her past, speculating on her future, alluding to books she's read or films she's seen, often in a way that seems authentically improvised. The closest parallel will be found not in fiction but in the mature writings of Delia Smith. At one point in *Delia's Happy Christmas* (BBC Books, London, 2008) she interrupts her account of how to prepare a seasonal dish.

> Christmas is a thoroughly good thing – something Charles Dickens instinctively understood when he wrote his famous *Christmas Carol*. The main character, Ebenezer Scrooge was a cynic...The story of his conversion, and how he became an ardent lover of Christmas is a perceptive and powerful observation on human life. Dickens understood the innate need we have to step aside from the daily grind and take time out from feasting and having fun.
>
> *p 10*

For someone who has bought the book for the sole purpose of instructing themselves on Christmas recipes this passage would be of questionable relevance. But as Smith is fully aware, her readers are drawn to her writing for very different reasons, having since the end of the 1990s become familiar with her as more than an instructor. Cooking is one of many tropes that constitute the personality of Delia Smith, a pseudo-literary presence whose idiomatic habits and, slightly introverted, Englishness convert easily from her on-screen manifestation to her prose.

Elizabeth Jane Howard, Margret Drabble, and Joanna Trollope differ commendably in the particulars of their craft but for all three middle-class England – predominantly the gentrified areas of London, the Cotswolds, and the South West – provide the setting for Bridget Jones in her maturity. Bridget's list of concerns takes on a less farcical edge. For Howard's, Drabble's and Trollope's characters, marriage breakdown, mental or terminal illness, serial adultery, sibling rivalry, and the distressing effects of age are all borne with a compensatory degree of refinement and endurance. But there are nonetheless similarities between the coquettish youngster and her comfortably off middle-aged counterparts. Characteristically Trollope opens each chapter with a reflective passage, enabling her character or narrator to set the scene – usually involving a calmness that belies the turmoil to follow – and allow something a sense of mood, an essence of personality to inform the actual events of the longer narrative. The principal character, usually in alliance with the narrator if in the third person, absorbs, often ameliorates the routine of crises and challenges which make up the constituent parts of the story.

> The house Beth shared with Clare had been bought just before Tower Hamlets became a modish destination for young entrepreneurs of the new technology. When they were first together – a junior academic and a trainee lawyer dissatisfied with the law – they had a flat in the old market in Spitalfields, a series of small dingy rooms whose only advantage was the view from the sitting room window of Christ Church, Spitalfields, in all its Hawksmoor – although as yet unrestored – glory. The bedroom windows looked down into the shabby ordinariness of Brushfield Street, and the smell of perpetually cooking curry permeated the whole area like fog.
>
> *City of Friends, Pan Macmillan, London, 2017, p 52*

Beth and Clare are not the narrators but they might as well be. Their third person proxy mirrors their confidence and self-possession. All three are able to absorb the nuances of place and region in their weighted, suitably erudite manner. They embody a stability which will stand them in good stead for encounters with the actual events of the novel – redundancy, failed relationships, ageing parents, etc. The problems that confront Beth, Clare, Melissa, Gaby, and Stacey reflect the unwelcome but inevitable challenges of their readers' lives, and while Trollope does not play them down she subtly offers the novel as a palliative substitute for the real world. Her figures have sufficient strength to absorb and disperse pain. We recognise aspects of our lives in theirs but at the same time we take comfort in their resilience. As fictional presences they almost become counsellors.

The following is Nigel Slater's entry for January 1st in *The Kitchen Diaries* (2006):

> There is a single rose in the garden, a faded bundle of cream and magenta petals struggling against grey boards. A handful of snowdrops peeps out from the ivy that has taken hold among the fruit trees... January the 1st is the day I prune back the tangle of dried sticks in the kitchen garden, chuck anything over its sell by date from the cupboards, flick through the seed catalogues and make lists of what I want to grow and eat in the year to come. I have always loved the first day of the year, a day ringing with promise.
>
> *p 4*

In a novel this could be a cautionary, evasive preamble to something more profound, an issue he would rather postpone by focussing on the place that diverts him from the immediacies of the world beyond his beloved garden. Like Trollope's Beth and Clare he might be enfolding the narrative in his calming mindset; a way of dealing with it. What follows, however, is not his encounter with divorce or redundancy, but the challenge of the next recipe. Cookbooks have indeed become 'literary' at least in terms of their formal and stylistic borrowings from devices routinely employed by fiction writers.

Nigella Lawson, in *Nigella's Christmas*:

> I can't deny that I am, simply put, a heathen. Although I have not been able to stop myself from writing about the joys – and the stresses, I don't dispute – of cooking for Christmas, I felt a certain reserve at interjecting myself a little too presumptuously into other people's feast and faith. But the truth is the Christmas we celebrate in our kitchen is not the Christmas that is celebrated in church. Yes of course they coincide, and for many the latter corroborates and gives meaning to the former, but the Christmas feasting, the Christmas lights, the carousing and gift giving, these come from much further back than the birth of Christianity.
>
> *2008, p VI*

We know that Ms Lawson is ideologically secular, while retaining a nostalgic respect for her Jewish background. But we are aware of this because of her presence as a media celebrity, the regular subject of news reports on her personal life, along with interviews and high-quality magazine profiles. She is a wonderful example of intertextuality, demolishing the boundaries between her discourse/media persona and her actual presence. What, one might ask, is the difference between this and the now cliched device of having the author walk into his/her novel and elide the distinction between the world they have created and the one they inhabit? In her books Nigella reinvents herself, becomes a performance artist, while never quite leaving behind the 'real' Nigella of tabloid features and magazine interviews.

Nigella's profile, actual and created, is highly sexualised. On television her gestures and use of food items as objects, some apparently prophylactic, verge upon a kind of pornographic self-caricature and while this is less evident in her books she is able to superimpose on her recipes something that we would more often associate with *Fifty Shades of Grey*.

> I am in the middle of a love affair with salted caramel. It's heady, it's passionate, it may – like the stalker's obsessive focus – not be entirely healthy, but I take the view that few in this world have the luxury to be blasé about pleasure. There's simply not enough of it about for us to gainsay what gifts are offered up for our enjoyment. True for many, self denial has its own exquisite agony, but I am not among their number (Lawson), 'My Love Affair With Salted Caramel'.
>
> *Stylist Magazine, December, 2011*

Nigella Lawson's counterpart at the other end of the gender-spectrum is Jamie Oliver. In his later books, often based on tours of various regions, we encounter a blokish dramatic monologue. He is certainly not sexist or implicitly misogynistic in his manner – he does not wish to alienate half of his readership – but at the same time he is comfortable with an idiom that bespeaks working-class Essex-based maleness. *In Jamie's Italy* (Michael Joseph, London, 2005):

> The truth is, when I'm in Italy I feel Italian – even with my very basic grasp of the language I manage to get by, and you know why? Because, like all Italians I love my family for better or for worse and because food has been something I've grown up around. If you are at the market and you ask the fruit man if you can taste one of his beautiful grapes, he will immediately recognise you as someone who cares and will give you respect. When I found myself at a vegetable stall in a small village in Tuscany, being served by a dishevelled old bloke, I told him I was going to be cooking for some grape-pickers and he questioned me straight away, saying it was too early to be picking grapes because 'The sangiovese is not ready yet...'
>
> *p X*

The unreflecting familiarity of the prose brings to mind a loquacious – rather frank, but equally distracted – young man who joins you in a bar and, without properly introducing himself, becomes the voice in your head. The fact that he is apparently preoccupied with local food is marginal. More interesting is his presence, a figure seemingly addicted to chains of loose syntax for their own sake. The unstoppably chatty first person narrator is a commonplace of modern fiction and Jamie's closest counterpart will be found in the sub-genre which emerged in the 1990s: 'lad lit'. The narrator of Nick Hornby's *Fever Pitch* (1992) treats us to a memoir-monologue in which he combines self-evident wit and intelligence with a coat-trailing preoccupation with sub-culture, specifically football. That the narrator is Hornby himself points up the ways in which the boundary between first person fiction and non-fiction can be blurred. The parallels with Oliver are striking and it is intriguing that in Hornby's second book, *High Fidelity* (1995), he hands over the narrative to his fictional proxy, Rob Fleming. In stylistic terms the texts are virtually identical. Rob is obsessed not with football but with contemporary popular music, but once more the ostensible topic of his monologue is less significant in its own right then as a sounding board for nuances of his background, character, and temperament. For Hornby, football and music, and for Oliver, food. There are gradations, shifts in emphasis between the narrator and topic but in each instance the notion of a three-dimensional presence – by parts charming, idiosyncratic, solipsistic, and casually entertaining – absorbs the notion of non-fictional subject matter.

Will in Hornby's *About a Boy* (1998) relinquishes any pretence to an interest in a particular activity; he is a more honest version of Fleming and Rob, concerned primarily with himself. Hornby should be commended in creating a character so self-absorbed who is also wickedly captivating. We know we ought to dislike him but we can't help enjoying his company. Tim Lott's estate agent anti-hero in *White City Blue* (1999); Simon Armitage's Felix Fenton, a social worker with a taste for beer and barbecues (*The White Stuff*, 2004); and Ben Elton's Sam, the BBC middle-ranker and frustrated writer (*Inconceivable*, 1999), follow a similar template. They are troubled by relationships with women, in Sam's case his partner's tragic-comic desperation for a child, but such factors merely provide settings for excesses in self-portraiture.

Along with Oliver, their other associates in food writing include James Martin. Martin, like Floyd and Oliver, has succeeded in creating a hybrid from the travel narrative and the recipe book, and much as one might be distracted by his versions of French and US dishes our attention is drawn primarily to the demonstrative Yorkshire man who manages to incorporate elements of his dialect into his account of regional eccentricities. But for the most fascinating example of intergeneric interface compare Hornby's mutations of non-fiction into novels with Jay Rayner's *The Man Who Ate the World: In Search of the Perfect Dinner* (2008). Like Hornby in *Fever Pitch* Rayner digresses restlessly, taking us back to his childhood, picking out anecdotes from his youth, his travels, his earlier career, and interspersing the main narrative with minor memoir-short stories, all of which hang upon a love-hate relationship with, respectively, football and food. Both books were bestsellers and generously reviewed in the mainstream press, but their popularity and acclaim had little if anything to do with their readers' dedication to the beautiful game, eating or cooking. Many reviewers pointed out that they were anything but proselytising books; they did not convert the disinterested reader to a love for food or sport. Rather, their subjects became an element of their narrators' addictively quirky disposition and their adeptness as story-tellers. Heston Blumenthal pioneered what he called 'multi-sensory' cuisine which deliberately challenged the consumer's expectations of what should and should not belong in the same recipe. His repertoire of shocks was extraordinarily diverse but experiments with snail porridge and bacon and egg ice cream in particular hit the headlines. Parallels with the poetic function are self-evident in that in both instances there is a clash between what we are accustomed to and what we receive. But there is something more intriguing than similarities between the 'text' of the dish and the literary work. Blumenthal is by the nature of his enterprise an extrovert and in this respect he is no better and no worse than his competitors in the field of celebrity-chefism. Each wish to impose upon their dishes a sense of their own distracted idiosyncrasy, and in this respect Blumenthal's closest literary counterpart is probably Will Self. In one of his first novels, *My Idea of Fun* (1993) Self combines naturalistic detail with the grotesque and the horribly ludicrous – in one instance abortion via a vacuum cleaner – and he has maintained his signature mode since then, as has Blumenthal. Food and language are necessities; without either we would cease to exist. At present the culture of food and literature seem to have little concern for either, but treat them rather as vehicles for self-promotion.

On 6th October 2018 the Literary Review section of *The Guardian*, opened with articles by the columnist Bee Wilson and novelist Jeanette Winterson on the contemporary phenomenon of food writing. The main subject was Nigella Lawson but throughout both pieces Wilson and Winterson make tentative attempts to build bridges between fiction and books on food. Wilson, for example, praises Lawson's *How to Eat* for its exclusion of photographs; it was 'non-visual and writerly', using words in the manner of the best prose fiction to create images in our mind and, implied Wilson, a collateral effect on our palate. Winterson goes further: 'Recipes are like plot summaries of Shakespeare's plays; we know what's supposed to happen but the real pleasure is in the writing'. The parallel is compelling and not entirely unfamiliar. One of the routine methods of defining literature per se is to look at the difference between a literary text and the text or statement whose primary purpose is the transparent conveyance of a message – essentially all forms of linguistic exchange that do not involve deliberate or negligent distortions of fact. Literature, for seemingly arbitrary reasons, distorts the message by foregrounding the medium, and according to Winterson so does the best food writing. Winterson's point is seductive but not by virtue of its intrinsic validity. We live in an era which all but forbids aesthetic hierarchies. Within academia high art and notions of a canon of great texts are functional necessities but the values that underpin them are treated with contempt, and most of the present-day intelligentsia have been in various ways influenced by the changes in Arts/Humanities of the past four decades. So while Wilson and Winterson toy with similarities between food writing and literature they studiously avoid the question of whether the former has any qualities as art. They have opted for, without acknowledging, the get-out clause of present-day egalitarian anti-aesthetics: promote the culturally low-brow as 'literary' while ignoring its implicit claim to artistic value. In truth Lawson and the other major presences of the food-writing sub-genre are competent stylists. Winterson states that 'It doesn't matter if you actually cook the food…When I read Nigella I'm there for the story' and she compares each recipe with a short story, a delicious escape from actuality that can be admired equally for its mannered artfulness. It is quite astonishing that one of the most celebrated novelists of the past two decades can treat a food writer as her equal, and one has to ask the question of why she does so.

There are no records as to the number of food authors who rely on 'ghost writers' for their books, and despite having contacted six major publishers for information on this all of my enquiries have been rejected.

In an article for *The Financial Times* ('Cooking the Books',15 July 2006) R Ehrlich affirms that authors who are best known for something completely different from writing should not be regarded as the sole-authors of books about their activities: 'If tennis players aren't assumed to be good writers, why should we expect this skill of cooks?' Do Nigella or Jamie write their own prose? Who knows? But what is clear – despite Wilson's promotion of Nigella as a pseudo-fiction writer – is that it is her image beyond the text, rather than her contribution to it, that ensures sales. Ehrlich continues: 'The problem is that in our celebrity-obsessed age readers of cookbooks don't just want recipes that work. They also buy into a dubious notion of personality. They're not just looking for minestrone, they're looking for X's minestrone'. As already stated, a number of celebrity chefs have become associated with a signature prose style that corresponds with their assembly of images established via other media. Jamie Oliver's Twitter presence of 2009 was, he stated, a way 'to create a way to create a more personal relationship between us all' and throughout that year he accompanied virtually all of his messages, irrespective of their ostensible topics, with an insistence that for all his followers he was 'real'. For example: 'of course it's the real me on this and the real me is so excited that that so many have pledged to support British bacon' (9.24 am, 29 January 2009). There was no reason for any of his growing army of followers to suspect that they were in touch with some kind of Jamie-proxy and one has to wonder why he is apparently so astonished by his own actuality. Could it be that the stream-of-consciousness style of his Twitter account, with the conventions of syntax often exchanged for unpunctuated Essex-idiom, are a little closer to the 'real' Jamie of the television appearances and interviews than the one that disappears behind the more crafted, grammatically measured prose of his books? All of this raises a question about the apparent parallels between food writing and fiction, considered above, especially those where the food writer takes time to digress from the mundane details of the recipe and reflect on some regional or cultural aspect of food, eating, and their nuances. What if the figure responsible for these excursions into food-as-literary-art is not the one whose name appears on the cover, but a 'ghost' with well-tuned writerly skills that have nothing to do with the preparation or appreciation of food? Roland Barthes was responsible for a thesis that caused us to wonder if the image of the figure behind the words in a text is real or the product of various competing interpretive and cultural forces; he declared, with tongue somewhat in cheek, 'The Death of the Author'.

The validity of Barthes's ideas regarding literary works has been questioned by more conservative thinkers but it seems to have a particular, literal relevance for food-writing. In epistemological terms it is easy enough to undermine Barthes's thesis. Archived documents, often cited by biographers and other scholars, provide verifiable evidence of manuscripts prepared by the likes of Dickens or Evelyn Waugh, alongside correspondence between editors and documents pertaining to payments and dates of publication of novels. We can prove that major authors exist and that they are the sole-authors of their works. No such evidence will be available regarding food authors, now or in material sent to university archives. Why? Because ghost writers and copy-editor authors are contracted on terms that involve them being unable to prove that they stood in for the ostensible author. It is, I would argue, reasonable to conclude that if food writing is a literary sub-genre it is unique, essentially a celebrity form whereby the division of labour regarding the creation of the book involves both the corporate manufacturing of an image for the alleged 'author' and the deliberate obscuring of the process of authorship and its various participants.

Common sense tells us that a food book submitted to a publisher or agent by a person without a reputation in the expanding sub-culture of consumption, food preparation, eating, and cooking would be rejected without consideration. Food authors must be major presences in food culture before they can write about it, or have someone else do so on their behalf. And at this point we can see how food books both diverge from fiction and reflect the worst elements of it. Michael Ruhlman, a high profile US food writer and media figure, produced an online article (3 April 2009) called 'On Food Writing' in which he addresses the question asked of him by numerous members of the public: how do I become a food writer? He comes up with the standard retinue of responses made available in *The Writer's and Artist's Yearbook* and various 'how to…' guides for aspiring writers: perfect a prose style of your own; diverge from precedent; create original menus; digress on matters such as region, places you've enjoyed specific dishes, private memories, etc.; prepare a proposal that will convince an agent or open-submission publisher that your project will chart new territory and find a profitable niche market. It all sounds like a commendable exercise in common sense, the model for selling a new piece of fiction adapted to food books, but it exists only as a fantastic hypothesis (see also, *Get Started in Food Writing*, by Kerstin Rodgers, Teach Yourself Books, 2015). Finding a reputable publisher for anything is extraordinarily difficult but as figures such as J K Rowling have shown faith in the quality of your material and a belief that a commissioning editor will share your opinion sometimes pays off. Sometimes the product wins out irrespective of the obscurity of the producer, so why should we doubt Ruhlman's guidance on food writing? For the simple reason that no food writer has ever risen to prominence by taking the route he recommends. Ruhlman's exercise in aspirational delusion is but a spin-off from a work that tells us much more, albeit involuntarily, about the nebulous, almost metaphysical, status of the food author, Dianne Jacob's *Will Write for Food* (De Capo Books, first pub, 2005; updated 2015). The book has been very well reviewed, and paperback sales had reached six figures at the last count. It is admirably detailed and comprehensive in terms of the pragmatics of proposing and selling a food book, which include the difficulties of finding an Agent and a somewhat dispiriting list of reasons why a publisher might not want to publish your book ('They don't like your writing…etc'); and like Ruhlman Jacob appears to be offering the ambitious cookbook author an impartial and instructive account of what to do to get into print. But look closer and it is evident that something almost sinister is happening. In a passage called 'When You Don't Need Agent' Jacob bypasses the fact – not previously addressed – that all major publishers who publish profitable food books will not respond to proposals unsupported by an Agent and instead guides the reader into a field of opportunities, such as those offered by 'Academic presses…', 'Small publishers…', and 'Reference publishers…', naming some of the major players in these areas of the industry but omitting to mention that none of them has published anything resembling the kind of book about food that ordinary people would buy. Jacob's book is an astonishing blend of evasion and fantasy, so much that it rivals the appeal of popular fiction in both respects. With regard to fantasy her guide to 'The Contract' is exceptional. Without conceding that being offered a contract by a major trade publisher is all but impossible for authors without a pre-established cultural or media presence Jacob glides into an explanation of 'The advance' which, she advises, is unlikely to go beyond '$5,000 to $25,000' for 'first time authors'. At this point those in the business of publishing will realise that Jacob either exists in or has created a parallel universe. Sadly, the gullible reader who has bought her book might be lured into it too. I stress this element of the fantasy of becoming a food writer because it points up another overlap between cookbooks and fiction. Vanity publishing and, with the assistance of AI, self-publishing are sustained by a widespread desire among the general population to belong to an elite, to see their name on the spine of a volume that resembles the esteemed products found on the shelves of Waterstones. It seems likely that the desire to become a novelist surpasses all other writing ambitions, but it seems that the celebrity status of food writers is causing the cookbook to catch up.

References

Acton, E., 2011. *Modern cookery for private families.* London: Quadrille Publishing.

Alsop, J., 2007. Bridget Jones meets Mr. Darcy: Challenges of contemporary fiction. *The Journal of Academic Librarianship, 33*(5), pp.581–585.

Amis, M., 2011. *Money.* London: Random House.

Armitage, S., 2005. *The white stuff.* London: Penguin.

Barnes, C., 2017. Mediating good food and moments of possibility with Jamie Oliver: Problematising celebrity chefs as talking labels. *Geoforum, 84,* pp.169–178.

Barthes, R., 2001. The death of the author. *Contributions in Philosophy, 83,* pp.3–8.

Bell, D. and Hollows, J., 2011. From river cottage to chicken run: Hugh Fearnley-Whittingstall and the class politics of ethical consumption. *Celebrity Studies, 2*(2), pp.178–191.

Beeton, M., 2010 *The book of household management.* Oxford: Benediction Press.

Bildtgård, T., 2009. Mental foodscapes. *Food, Culture & Society, 12*(4), pp.498–523.

Bilton, S., 2011. The influence of cookbooks on domestic cooks, 1990–2010. *Petits Propos Culinaires,* (94), p.30.

Bonner, F., 2005. Whose lifestyle is it anyway. In *Ordinary lifestyles: Popular media, consumption and taste,* David Bell and Joanne Hollows (eds), (pp.35–46). Maidenhead: The Open University Press.

Blumenthal, H., 2008. *The big fat duck cookbook.* London: Bloomsbury.

Bruner, G.C. and Pomazal, R.J., 1988. Problem recognition: The crucial first stage of the consumer decision process. *Journal of Services Marketing, 2*(3), pp.43–53.

Caraher, M., Lange, T. and Dixon, P., 2000. The influence of TV and celebrity chefs on public attitudes and behavior among the English public. *Journal for the Study of Food and Society, 4*(1), pp.27–46.

Culver, C., 2012. A pinch of salt and a dash of plot: The power of narrative in contemporary cookbooks. *Journal of the Australasian Universities Language and Literature Association, 2012*(118), pp.33–50.

Cradock, F., 1974. *Common market cookery-Italy.* London: BBC.

Cradock, F., 1973. *Common market cookery-France.* London: British Broadcasting Corporation.

David, E., 1980. *Elizabeth David classics: Mediterranean food, French country cooking, summer cooking.* London: Jill Norman Limited.

David, E., 1999. *Italian food*. London: Penguin.

David, E., 1999. *French provincial cooking*. New York: Penguin.

David, E., 2013. *French country cooking*. New York: Penguin UK.

Darley, W.K., Blankson, C. and Luethge, D.J., 2010. Toward an integrated framework for online consumer behavior and decision making process: A review. *Psychology & Marketing*, 27(2), pp.94–116.

David, E., 2002. *A book of Mediterranean food*. New York: New York Review of Books.

Dewey, J., 1991. How we think (1910). *Ders: The Middle Works*, 6, pp.177–356.

Dunn, D., 2010. 16 Transforming taste(s) into sights: Gazing and grazing with television's culinary tourists. *Tourism and Visual Culture: Theories and Concepts*, 1, p.191.

Ehrlich, R., 2006. Cooking the books. *Financial Times*, 15 July 2008.

Ellis, C., 2011. *Fabulous Fanny Cradock: TV's outrageous queen of cuisine*. Stroud, Gloucestershire: The History Press.

Elton, B., 2012. *Inconceivable*. New York: Random House.

Fearnley-Whittingstall, H., 2011. *Hugh Fearlessly eats it all: Dispatches from the gastronomic front line*. London: A&C Black.

Fielding, H., 2016. *Bridget Jones's diary*. Oxford: Macmillan.

Gallegos, D., 2005. Cookbooks as manuals of taste. *Ordinary lifestyles: Popular media, consumption and taste*, David Bell and Joanne Hollows (eds), (pp.99–110). Maidenhead: The Open University Press.

Gleick, E., 1998. A.V fine mess. *New York Times*, 31 May 1998.

Grainger, S., 2007. The myth of Apicius. *Gastronomica*, 7(2), pp.71–77.

Hollows, J. and Jones, S., 2010. Please don't try this at home: Heston Blumenthal, cookery TV and the culinary field. *Food, Culture & Society*, 13(4), pp.521–537.

Hornby, N., 2005. *Fever pitch*. London: Penguin UK.

Hornby, N., 2005. *High fidelity*. London: London: Penguin UK.

Inglis, D. and Almila, A.M., 2019. Creating and routinizing style and immediacy: Keith Floyd and the South-West English roots of new cookery mediatizations. In *Globalized eating cultures*, Jörg Dürrschmidt and York Kautt (eds), (pp.221–244). Cham: Palgrave Macmillan.

Jacob, D., 2005. *Will write for food: The complete guide to writing cookbooks, restaurant reviews, articles, memoir, fiction, and more*. Boston: Da Capo Press.

Lawson, N., 2008. *Nigella Christmas*. London: Chatto & Windus.

Lawson, N 2011. *My love affair with salted carmel, stylist*. https://www.stylist.co.uk/life/my-love-affair-with-salted-caramel/49185

Lott, T., 2000. *White city blue*. London: Penguin UK.

Martin, J. 2008 *The collection*. London: Mitchell Beazley.

McLean, A., 2004. Tasting language: The aesthetic pleasures of Elizabeth David. *Food, Culture & Society*, 7(1), pp.37–45.

McLean, A., 2012. *Aesthetic pleasure in twentieth-century women's food writing: The innovative appetites of MFK Fisher, Alice B. Toklas, and Elizabeth David*. New York: Routledge.

Oliver, J. and Terry, C., 2005. *Jamie's Italy*. London: Michael Joseph.

Piper, N., 2013. Audiencing Jamie Oliver: Embarrassment, voyeurism and reflexive positioning. *Geoforum*, 45, pp.346–355.

Piper, N., 2015. Jamie Oliver and cultural intermediation. *Food, Culture & Society*, 18(2), pp.245–264.

Rayner, J., 2008. *The man who ate the world: In search of the perfect dinner*. London: Macmillan.

Rodgers, S., 2015. *Get started in food writing: The complete guide to writing about food, cooking, recipes and gastronomy*. London: John Murray Press.

Self, W., 1993. *My idea of fun: A cautionary tale*. London: Bloomsbury.

Scholes, L., 2011. A slave to the stove? The TV celebrity chef abandons the kitchen: Lifestyle TV, domesticity and gender. *Critical Quarterly, 53*(3), pp.44–59.

Smith, D., 2008. *Delia's happy Christmas.* London: BBC Books.

Slater, N., 2005. *Nigel Slater: The kitchen diaries.* New York: Viking Studio.

Stein, R., 2013. *Rick Stein's French odyssey.* London: Random House.

Trollope, J., 2017. City of friends. Mantle; Air Iri OME edition.

Versteegen, H., 2010. Armchair epicures: The proliferation of food programmes on British TV. In *The pleasures and horrors of eating: The cultural history of eating in Anglophone literature,* Marion Gymnich, Norbert Lennartz (eds), (pp.447–464). Bonn: Bonn University Press.

Woolf, V., 1992. To the lighthouse. In *Collected novels of Virginia Woolf,* Stella McNichol (ed), (pp.177–334). London: Palgrave Macmillan.

Wilson, B. and Winterson, J., 2018. Bool review. *The Guardian.* 6 October 2018.

12

THE HISTORY AND INFLUENCE OF TRAVEL WRITING

Peter Bolan

Introduction

The desire to travel, to seek out and explore new places, to fuel one's curiosity and experience that which is different is quite simply part of the human psyche. The influences on such desires can be many and varied, especially in today's fast-paced and media-dominated world. One early inspirational influence on travel has been that of the written word. The range is very wide, but whether travel-specific writing with the intention of informing and inspiring others to make similar journeys (e.g. guidebooks), or the influence of novels, poetry, and other written art forms featuring travel and associated choices, there can be no doubting the profound impact this medium has had.

Indeed there can be strong synergies between tourism and the literary world which has given rise to specific forms of niche tourism such as 'literary tourism'. An aspect this essay addresses before examining in more depth the history of travel writing and its influence through the ages from ancient Greece, through the time of the Grand Tour to the advent of the travel blogger and digital influencer of today's modern world. In the travel planning process for the traveller there are many questions to be answered.

What does the tourist expect to experience during their trip? How do they assess the travel experience amid the various other areas of their life? What are their expectations regarding the encounter with host communities, in terms of how they perceive themselves, their home country and their place as tourists? And what historical, cultural, economic, social, and geopolitical processes have constructed these expectations and perceptions at any given time and place? (Mazor-Tregerman, 2015). The answer to many such questions lies in travel writing. The written accounts of other travellers and their experiences, whether in diary form, that of a novel, a poem, or a dedicated guidebook has a profound effect in a myriad of ways. The essence of this essay is to address this.

Literary tourism

Literary tourism is associated with both places celebrated for depictions and any connections with literary figures. People can be drawn towards a location that authors have written about or a location that the author themselves may have been linked with. Travelling to such a location allows the visitor to connect with places closely associated with particular stories, experiences and admired individuals, and a chance to experience the site in person. Herbert observes, 'Literacy places are the fusion of the real worlds in which the writers lived with the worlds portrayed in the novels' (Busby & Klug, 2001, p.319). People interested in literary tourism tend to visit houses where writers lived and worked and also to the landscapes that may have provided the settings for a novel. According to Herbert (2001, 312), 'There is a fascination about places associated with writers that has often prompted readers to become pilgrims'. Such pilgrims, as Herbert refers to them, are very much tourists travelling to other places in search of experiences connected to the authors and their literary work.

In the modern era such connections between travel and the written word have become increasingly recognised. *Visit England* declared 2017 to be Year of Literary Heroes, reporting that one in four Britons visited an English literary location in 2016 (VisitEngland, 2017). A growing demand for books and e-books across countries such as the US, China, and the UK (which are also key tourist generating regions) combined with rising popularity of book groups and digital online literary discussion groups has fuelled these important connections and their influence further still. According to MacLeod et al. (2018, 388), this '... reflects the enduring appeal of the written word and underpins the ongoing desire to travel to expand this interest'.

Johnson (2004, 93) notes that, '...the intertextual arena in which travel writing literally takes place is not confined solely to other travellers' texts but also includes a host of other forms of representation – the visual image, the novel and the spoken word'. What Johnson (2004) is conveying in her work on Dublin's literary landscape is that what we glean travel information and knowledge from is not only travel-specific writing but also visual stimulation from sources such as film and television, literary works such as novels, and the spoken word of others. Literary tourism and the more modern film tourism are therefore similar in many ways. There is a merging of the real and the imaginary, which gives literary places a special meaning to motivate tourists to visit certain sites or locations.

There is according to Johnson (2004, 91) a need to 'develop a better understanding of...how a novel is read as fiction, social document or indeed tourist guide' and as the author further advocates it is a question seldom investigated by researchers partly due to the difficulty in conducting and interpreting audience response to such novels and other works of literature. Recognition nonetheless continues to grow with regard to the influence of literary works on the traveller. UNESCO now includes literature as part its cultural landscape designation (Ruiz Scarfuto, 2013) using such means to officially recognise certain places from Edinburgh to Prague, Dublin to Krakow, Barcelona to Seattle as so-called 'Cities of Literature', a label that provides a certain literary standing in the public consciousness and one which also therefore serves as a marketing opportunity to attract the literary tourist.

Whilst some tourists will avail of the many specialist literary tour operators that now exist and take tailored packages to authors' homes, graves, festivals, museums, and visitor centres, for others it may be more of a personal journey. These travellers will achieve their experience and derive their satisfaction from '… seeking out likely locations and inscribing their own narratives on the landscape without the intervention of any external agency' (MacLeod et al. 2018, 390). Whichever form it may be, to truly examine the influence of literature on travel, it is necessary to go further back into history. As such this essay now explores the history of travel writing and its resulting impact on tourism and the traveller.

Early travel writing and its influence

In tracing the historical influence of the written word on travel, one can arguably begin in Europe in the days of the Greek Empire. Written around 8 BC, works such as Homer's *Odyssey*, which recounts the journey of Odysseus home after the fall of the city of Troy, can be seen as a very early form of written travel account that had an influencing factor in inspiring others to take such journeys. Later, in the time between ancient and classical Greece, the Greek traveller and geographer Pausanis (AD 110) is noted for having explored much of the Greek empire at the time, producing detailed accounts on aspects such as art, history, and architecture of the places he visited. His accounts are said to have later influenced a great many travellers to follow in his footsteps.

Travel being recorded in literature also became particularly prevalent in China around the 1300s. Many accounts from that period in Asia took a cultural and topographical approach, incorporating a blend of narrative, essay, and diary elements in how travel was recounted to the reader. However, travel literature dating from the Song Dynasty (AD 960–1279) arguably fuelled such later travel writing in the fourteenth century. Authors such as Fan Chengda and Xu Xiake and poets such as Su Shi have been noted for the geographical and topographical information their works contain. Japan also holds important examples from such a period. The *Sjorai Moluroku* (AD 804) (Buddhist texts brought back to Japan from China) by author Kukai is said to have been a strong influence upon many travellers of the time. Another prominent example is the *Tosa Nikki* (*Tosa Diary*) by Ki no Tsurayuki (early tenth century), a poetic work which details a 55-day journey returning from the Tosa province to Kyoto (Japan's original capital city). This literary work is not only notable as an early example influencing travel in Japan but can also be seen as particularly revolutionary as it featured a female narrator.

Coinciding with some of this period, Western-based explorers such as Marco Polo also provide detailed accounts of travel in Asia. *Il Milione* (The Million, 1298) charts the story of a Venetian traveller from Europe to China and the Mongol empire of the time. Polo is often credited with being one of the first great travel writers. His own 24-year journey through the Persian Gulf and much of Asia, his travels along the Silk Road, and his time in the court of Kublai Khan (grandson of Genghis Khan) had a profound influence on his writing and, in turn, the desire of others to see and experience such sights. Whilst some doubt the legitimacy or accuracy of Polo and his written accounts, there can be no doubt on the influence of his literary work on later travels along the Silk Road in particular.

While such notable examples provide early evidence of literary works fuelling the desire to travel, it was arguably the eighteenth and nineteenth centuries that saw travel writing, at least in terms of its impact and influence, truly come alive. Diaries from noted explorers such as Captain James Cook, Alfred Russel Wallace, and even Robert Falcon Scott (in the early twentieth century) became bestsellers. Furthermore poems, novels, and plays taking place in a variety of exotic locations from writers such as Charles Baudelaire, Walter Scott, and Lord Byron came to prominence in terms of their influence on those with the means and ability to travel. A newly mobile public, whilst still a minority in general terms, was growing and travel-related literature and its influence grew with it. By 1825, a pocket travel version of Walter Scott's *The Lady of the Lake* had been produced specifically for tourists, whilst part of Ayrshire in Scotland had already been dubbed *Burns Country* by this early part of the nineteenth century.

During such times in the eighteenth century much travel writing was often referred to under *The Book of Travels*. In this form such literary works were mostly maritime journals, but such maritime accounts and stories captured the public imagination and were hugely popular. James Cook's diaries (1784) could be compared to the status of a modern-day bestseller such was the insatiable appetite for them. Eighteenth-century novels such as *Gulliver's Travels* by Jonathan Swift and nineteenth-century works such as *Around the World in 80 Days* by Jules Verne fuelled people's imaginations and their desire for travel to far off exotic lands yet further. It truly was a golden age for literature in relation to travel, inspired and added to by factual exploration and discovery as well as imagination and artistic licence.

The grand tour

The predominantly eighteenth- and early nineteenth-century custom of travelling around key cities of cultural and historical significance in Europe, known as the 'Grand Tour', drew upon the influence of literary works, as well as paintings, music, and other renowned works of art. Whilst largely the preserve of the wealthy elite, this is often seen as a pivotal time in the development of tourism as we know it today. The tour circuit followed by such tourists took place predominantly in France, Italy, Germany, Switzerland, and the Low Countries. The tour was undertaken principally, but not exclusively by the British, until it was later also undertaken (in the nineteenth century) by wealthy Americans who adopted a similar itinerary.

Whilst over time the social class of the tourist on such a grand tour changed and developed, the distinct tour itinerary that was followed stayed largely the same. This would usually comprise a visit to the city of Paris and the court at Versailles, then on to view the classical antiquities of the lower Rhone valley, followed by a tour of the cities of northern Italy, in particular Turin, Milan, and Venice. Florence, Rome, and Naples usually formed the climax to the tour and the return to Britain was generally made through Germany, down the Rhine, and across the Low Countries (Towner, 1985).

The tour itself was influenced in part by previous literary works and accounts of travel experiences. Certain young men of the time were exposed to Greek and Roman history, language, and literature throughout school and university, and when they eventually went abroad, usually chaperoned by a paid tutor, known as a 'cicerone', this classical education was brought to life through the experiences and sights of the Grand Tour. Gradually with increasing wealth and political stability more people began to travel more widely. Whilst a typical Grand Tourist was likely to be a young British man from a wealthy background completing his education, such trips (especially in the later days of such a Grand Tour) also began to be undertaken by artists, designers, authors, collectors, traders in art works, and large numbers of the educated public, including many women.

Francis Bacon's work *Of Travel* (1625) was seen as inspirational for many Grand Tourists of the time and became something of a pocket guidebook. Indeed, to its credit, it can still be seen as such today for the modern traveller. It is often thought that Mary Shelley conceived of *Frankenstein* (published originally as *The Modern Prometheus*) to win a bet while travelling through Europe on a Grand Tour of sorts with Percy Shelley and Lord Byron. Mark Twain was perhaps one of the last to embark on such a Grand Tour. His trip to Europe in 1867 is chronicled in his work *The Innocents Abroad*. The book, which recounts an American's perspective on Europe, sold widely and its influence on subsequent travels was equally far reaching.

The influence of Baedeker

Specific travel guidebooks may be something we take for granted today (many now also in online digital form through various mobile apps), but back in the early 1800s it was arguably Karl Baedeker who hugely developed this concept and captured the attention of the travel world and the tourist of the time. Designed by Baedeker, his guides were created to be carried in one's pocket, produced in a small robust and easy to carry format. Karl and several subsequent generations of Baedekers created an enormous achievement for the time, a tri-lingual set of pocket travel guides spanning 180 years, covering some 40 countries across most of the world's continents.

Karl Baedeker, himself was descended from a family of booksellers and publishers. Inspired by the launch in 1827 of the first passenger steamboat service between Coblence and Mayence on the Rhine, he published the first of his guidebooks in 1832. As such, Baedeker's famous guides (with their distinctive red covers) were born. The first English translation appeared in 1861, with translated versions of guides to Switzerland published in 1863 and Paris in 1865. Baedeker used a star system to rate tourist sites with an asterisk (an innovative approach at the time), and he meticulously collected data, including state-of-the-art maps to provide his guidebooks with everything he felt the traveller needed to know.

The sudden death of Karl in 1859 did not end the influence of his work. Carried on initially by his sons and later by other descendants, the famous red covered guidebooks continued to provide a wealth of knowledge, information, and inspiration for travellers all around the world. Baedeker's guides also gained notoriety in other literary forms such as E.M. Forster's *A Room with a View*, where the Northern Italy Baedeker Guide was used prominently (both in the novel and in the subsequent film). Again, the influence of such travel guides (themselves an important form of literature) cutting across other forms of literature clear for all to see and cementing their huge importance. Whilst Baedeker's pocket guidebooks have evolved and undergone key changes across the years they still centre on the qualities that first drove Karl Baedeker himself: accuracy, reliability, lucidity, portability, and above all facilitating the traveller with an independence to travel armed with knowledge and advice.

Bradshaw's railway guides

A pivotal impact in travel writing occurred in the nineteenth century for the railway mode of transport, thanks in no small part to George Bradshaw. Already having published a series of maps detailing travel routes by canal through northern England (predominantly Yorkshire and Lancashire) in the earlier part of the century, Bradshaw turned his attention to rail travel, publishing in 1839 the first of his tomes entitled *Bradshaw's Railway Time Tables and Assistant to Railway Travelling*. Later to be renamed simply *Bradshaw's Railway Companion*, this publication became synonymous with such a form of travel throughout Britain at the time. Bradshaw later extended such work to Ireland and mainland Europe. It was 1847 that saw Bradshaw's *Continental Railway Guide* published, which extended the narrative, recommendations, and advice for the traveller throughout much of continental Europe. Bradshaw's written work in the field became widely known and consulted.

Indeed, this was so much the case that Bradshaw's guides are referenced in a key number of literary works by many renowned writers of the time and since. In *Around the World in 80 Days*, the character Phileas Fogg carries a *Bradshaw*. Conan Doyle makes mention of Bradshaw's guides in the Sherlock Holmes stories *The Valley of Fear* and *The Adventure of the Copper Beeches*. Count Dracula himself uses a Bradshaw's guide when planning his voyage to England in Bram Stoker's *Dracula*. Mentions also can be found in Daphne du Maurier's *Rebecca* and Agatha Christie's *Death in the Clouds*. Clear evidence of how invaluable and intrinsic Bradshaw's work was in terms of rail travel to be referenced in such renowned literary works.

In the twenty-first century, Bradshaw's literary work in relation to travel has received an enormous revival, indeed renaissance, thanks to another medium, that of television. Michael Portillo's Great Railway Journeys television show (premiering on the BBC in 2010) traces routes around UK, later moving to Ireland and the rest of Europe, focussing on the presenter's use of a Bradshaw's Guide from the 1840s. Recounting passages from Bradshaw, with vivid and colourful descriptions of places together with traveller advice, the television show has not only been hugely successful in its own right but also served to introduce Bradshaw's influential travel writing to a new twenty-first-century audience.

Modern travel writing

The modern tourist guidebook has evolved from the days of Baedeker and Bradshaw but still owes its place to prolific nineteenth-century writers. Zillinger (2006) contends that the guidebook presents the reader (and would-be tourist) with vital information about a particular attraction site. According to MacCannell (1999) an attraction is an empirical relationship between a sight, a tourist, and a marker. In this context, the guidebooks therefore serve as markers. In fact it can be seen in many cases that the tourists' first contact with a sight is not the sight itself, but a representation thereof.

Such modern guidebooks now come from a plethora of specialist publishing companies that focus on the travel domain, e.g. Lonely Planet, Rough Guides, Fodor's, Dorling Kindersley (DK) and Frommer's. Such guidebooks provide travellers with a blend of spatial and social information and in doing so both identify and popularise places as tourist attractions. According to Zillinger (2006, 230) they therefore

...determine the tourists' starting-points as well as provide vector points in advising and guiding them. Hereby the tourists are given propositional presentations of what the place is like and which attractions are worth seeing and experiencing, thus separating desirable from undesirable experiences.

The inherent intangibility of the tourism product requires that travel information regarding diverse tourism components such as transport, food, accommodation, weather, attractions, etc., be conveyed to the tourist. Providing this kind of information allows the traveller to then make destination choices with low perceived risk (Mazor-Tregerman, 2015). One could say that is the ultimate aim of any guidebook. Authors such as Wong and Liu (2011) advocate that guidebooks, with their varied and broad ranging wealth of information, have become both tourism 'gate openers' and risk mitigators for the traveller.

However, the modern tourist guidebook, whilst prevalent in its scope and influence, is not the only form of inspiration for the tourist. Travel writing today, still goes beyond the specific and dedicated industry-centred guidebooks produced by publishers such as Lonely Planet. Travel writing in the form of first person travel accounts, diaries, and humorous anecdotes has a strong influence on the tourist. The work of authors such as Paul Theroux and Bill Bryson stand out as highly prevalent examples of such a form of travel writing.

Bill Bryson's caustically written *The Lost Continent* (1989) set the tone for what was to become a series of bestselling travel-focussed books that have captured the attention of the reading public and fuelled people's own travel desires throughout the 1990s and since. Bryson felt he was writing something of a memoir with *The Lost Continent* (which centred on the US and his Midwestern upbringing in Des Moines, Iowa) and was not specifically aiming to be seen as a travel writer. Nonetheless his recounting of road trips around small-town America interspersed with memories of his childhood and family in Iowa set Bryson on a path to become one of the modern era's most prolific travel writers.

Bryson's attention moved to Europe with the acclaimed *Neither Here Nor There* journeying in his trademark sarcastic and humorous style from Hammerfest in Norway to Istanbul in Turkey, and through it all braving homicidal motorists in Paris, getting robbed by gypsies in Florence and ardently disputing his hotel bill in Copenhagen. It was arguably his later work *Notes from a Small Island* that made his name in the UK however (somewhere Bryson had made his home from 1977 to 1995). Other works including *A Walk in the Woods* and *Notes from a Big Country* (compiled from a series of newspaper columns and published in the US as *I'm a Stranger here myself*) have helped Bryson become a highly recognised travel writer of influence and one whose work conveys such travels in a uniquely different style and tone from the more traditional travel writers and official guidebooks.

When it comes to modern travel writing it is impossible not to mention the work of Paul Theroux. Whilst also known for novels such as *Waldo, Jungle Lovers*, and *The Mosquito Coast*, it is very much as a travel writer that Theroux has become widely known and respected. His account of travelling by train from Britain to Japan and back (shortly after moving to live in London in the early 1970s) entitled *The Great Railway Bazaar*, was his first huge success as a travel writer and is now seen as something of a classic. Others followed, such as *The Old Patagonian Express* (detailing travelling by train from Boston to Argentina), *Riding the Iron Rooster* (an account of travelling by train through China), *Dark Star Safari* (on his travels from Cairo to Cape Town), and more recently *Deep South* (recounting a number of road trips throughout the southern states of the US). Such is the renown for Theroux's work in the travel genre that it has led to some referring to him as the godfather of contemporary travel writing.

In differing ways the work of Theroux and Bryson illustrate the sheer power and influence of the travel writer on today's tourist. When combined with tailored industry-specific guidebooks the impact of travel writing is enormous and far reaching in its scope. However, such traditional writing in printed form has been added to and in some cases superseded with the advent of the digital world, where everyone with a laptop, tablet, or smartphone can now become their own travel writer and influence the world of the tourist around them.

The impact of digital

The internet has offered ongoing options for change in how information can be delivered. Web 2.0 applications such as blogs, message boards, public access video sites, virtual community games, and social networking platforms such as Facebook, Instagram, and Twitter have altered what the internet is used for and have captured the public imagination. Online platforms (Web 2.0 applications) such as blogs (e.g. travelblog.org), message boards (e.g. TripAdvisor), and public access video sites (e.g. YouTube) have become common place.

Tourists now use these 'informal online environments' to publish details of their holidays, their experiences, and their views (good or bad), both textually and visually (in the form of photographs or digital video clips). This provides a new and sometimes very rich source of information for other travellers and in some ways helps to make more tangible something which is inherently intangible – the holiday experience. The advent of travel blogs in particular has allowed almost anyone to become a travel writer and as such a digital influencer in this realm. Their widespread growth and popularity has even led to some authors (such as Cohen & Krishnamurthy, 2006; Hookway, 2008; Schmallegger & Carson, 2008) referring to the *'blogosphere'* or *'blogistan'* to describe the vast online world that blogs and bloggers inhabit.

Tourism has always been among the most popular of content areas on the internet and blogs are no exception to this. Tourists like to share their thoughts and experiences and appear to trust the views of other tourists more than the views or comments of organisations in the tourism industry. Undoubtedly this has helped the growth and popularity of tourism blogs. 'One of the major reasons for this phenomenon is certainly the higher perceived credibility of consumer opinions as compared to traditional tourist information sources' (Schmallegger & Carson, 2008, 102).

Whilst the publishers of specific travel guides, such as Lonely Planet and Rough Guides, now provide truncated mobile-enabled digital versions for the tourist to engage with on their laptop or smartphone, it is the rise of the independent online travel blogger that has evolved the world of travel writing and its reach in the greatest sense. From micro-influencers (social media personalities with between 10,000 and 100,000 followers) to full-blown influencers with many hundreds of thousands of followers these digital writers command huge reach and enormous earning potential (some earning millions per year in endorsements).

Blogs have become for many tourists the media of choice offering characteristics such as freshness, immediacy, interactivity, and personality, which continues to grow as the vast majority of people are now using the internet as their key source to explore, learn, plan, and book their travel (Bolan, 2015). People like to read about the escapades of others. It has been happening since the days of Pausanis and Ancient Greece. The internet through the world wide web has simply enabled everyone to become a Pausanis or a Marco Polo and recount their travel tales to those interested enough to read them.

The sheer proliferation however has caused many to question the level of quality and in some cases the authenticity of the written material provided. In reference to the sheer number of travel bloggers, online influencers, and numerous hastily written commentaries on internet travel review platforms, Bill Bryson has recently stated he feels Britain's heritage is at risk due to 'ill-educated internet critics'. So, whilst the availability and diversity of travel writing are greater than ever, does one need to take some of this with a pinch of salt and not necessarily accept at face value everything such written work conveys? Undoubtedly yes, but then is not all such writing subjective? And has it not always been so? Is not Bryson's own work his subjective view of reality in the places he has travelled? It lies with the reader to make a personal choice with all such written material.

Prior to the advent of the digital influencer, Pratt (1992) observed that travel writers 'produced' the world, where colonising European travel writers constructed domesticated and imperialised views of foreign places and people for their home audience. Tavares and Brosseau (2006, 300) later provide a similar stance stating that representations of other far off places and lands were often embedded in the language, culture and traditions of the 'representer' and thus '... implicated with a great many things other than the *truth* or *reality*'. Whilst a criticism may be levelled fairly at some of today's travel bloggers it is not that different from that which could have applied to some of the earlier travel writers from centuries past.

Dangers with travel writing encouraging tourism

Regardless of accuracy of information and advice (as highlighted earlier) modern travel writers can often be accused of encouraging aspects of mass tourism to destinations and places that are not ready for it, cannot cope with it, and in some cases do not actually want it. Particularly if such writing is about places that are off the beaten track, then a resultant and sudden influx of tourists can actually damage such places and ruin them both aesthetically and for any future generations to enjoy. As Wilde eloquently put, killing the thing we love.

Kohnstamm (2008, 102) acknowledges such consequences in his own travel writing stating ...

> Lonely Planet's seal of approval means that the little fishing village gets a booster shot of global publicity, whether the town wanted it, needed it, could handle it; or not ... while the guidebooks come first, hand in hand with the backpacker front line, the newspaper and magazines are not far behind in the feeding frenzy.

This raises the question therefore, do travel writers have an ethical responsibility to the places they write about? McWha et al. (2017) refer to this as *Lonely Planet Syndrome*. Indeed, Annesley (2004) views such a situation as a true paradox where travel writers identify alternative routes and places still largely free from mass tourism, but these destinations (through the influence of the travel writer) then become inundated with tourists (which is not always a good thing for both local and tourist).

To write about a place is to make it known, to make it visible (regardless of how authentic or not that may be). It can be reasonably argued therefore that travel writers do have some level of responsibility to the places and the people that they write about. Readers, as has been shown through this essay, will be influenced and inspired to seek out such places for themselves resulting in some form of inevitable impact upon the places visited. The impact of which, at least in some part, can be attributed to the travel writer.

Concluding thoughts

People will continue to travel, to seek out new places and new experiences in ever increasing numbers. Some 1.4 billion took an international trip in 2018 (UNWTO, 2019). The written word has and will continue to have strong influence on such travels in terms of choice and experience. 'The diversity of travel writing is immense, ranging from objectively factual guidebooks to much more whimsical short stories or imaginative novels' (MacLeod et al. 2018, 388). From writers of ancient Greece, through the time of the Grand Tour to the advent of the travel blogger and digital influencer of today's modern world, the tourist has been seeking out the places and peoples depicted.

This will undoubtedly continue to be the case. What influences the traveller will vary as the medium through which the tourist receives their written travel information changes and evolves, but then 'Tourism is essentially a fashion industry, and like most fashions, relies on rapidly changing trends' (McWha et al. 2017, 1402). Tourism itself does not sit still and therefore neither should the travel writer. Travel after all is what it is all about.

References

Annesley, J. (2004) Pure shores: Travel, consumption, and Alex Garland's the beach. *Modern Fiction Studies*, 50(3), pp. 551–569.

Bacon, F. (1625) *Of Travel*. 2nd ed. Oxford: Oxford University Press.

Bolan, P. (2015) A perspective on the near future: mobilizing events and social media. In: Yeoman, I., Reobertson, R., McMahon-Beattie, U., Smith, K. A., and Backer, E., eds., *The Future of Events and Festivals*. London: Routledge.

Bryson, B. (1989) *The Lost Continent: Travels in Small Town America*. Devon: Black Swan.

Bryson, B. (1997) *A Walk in the Woods*. Devon: Black Swan.

Bryson, B. (1998) *Neither Here Nor There: Travels in Europe*. Devon: Black Swan.

Bryson, B. (1999) *Notes from a Big Country*. Devon: Black Swan.

Busby, G., & Klug, J. (2001) Movie-induced tourism: The challenge of measurement and other issues. *Journal of Vacation Marketing*, 7(4), pp. 316–332.

Cohen, E., & Krishnamurthy, B. (2006) A short walk in the Blogistan. *Computer Networks*, 50(2), 615–630.

Cook, J. (1784) *Selected Diaries.* Volume I, Sydney: National Library of Australia.

Herbert, D. (2001) Literary places, tourism and the heritage experience. *Annals of Tourism Research*, 28(2), pp. 312–333.

Hookway, N. (2008) Entering the Blogosphere: Some strategies for using blogs in social research. *Qualitative Research*, 8(1), pp. 91–113.

Johnson, N. C. (2004) Fictional journeys: Paper landscapes, tourist trails and Dublin's literary texts. *Social & Cultural Geography*, 5(1) pp. 91–107.

Kohnstamm, T. (2008) *Do Travel Writers Go to Hell? A Swashbuckling Tale of High Adventure, Questionable Ethics and Professional Hedonism.* New York: Broadway.

MacCannell, D. (1999) *The Tourist. A New Theory of the Leisure Class.* London: University of California Press.

MacLeod, N., Shelley, J., & Morrison. A. M. (2018) The touring reader: Understanding the bibliophile's experience of literary tourism. *Tourism Management*, 67, 388–398.

Mazor-Tregerman, M. (2015) Travel guidebooks and the construction of tourist identity. *Journal of Tourism and Cultural Change*, 15(1), pp. 80–98.

McWha, M., Frost, W., & Laing, J. (2017) Sustainable travel writing? Exploring the ethical dilemmas of twenty-first century travel writers. *Journal of Sustainable Tourism*, 25(10), pp. 1401–1417.

Pratt, M. (1992) *Imperial eyes: Travel writing and transculturation.* New York: Routledge.

Schmallegger, D., & Carson, D. (2008) Blogs in tourism: Changing approaches to information exchange. *Journal of Vacation Marketing*, 14(2), pp. 99–110.

Ruiz Scarfuto, R. (2013) Literary routes: Contributions to natural/cultural heritage tourism – how landscape transforms literature and tourism. *Journal of Tourism, Culture and Territorial Development*, 10(1), pp. 37–52.

Tavares, D., & Brosseau, M. (2006) The representation of Mongolia in contemporary travel writing: Imaginative geographies of a travellers' frontier. *Social and Cultural Geography*, 7(2), pp. 299–317.

Towner, J. (1985) The grand tour: A key phase in the history of tourism. *Annals of Tourism Research*, 12(3), pp. 297–333.

UNWTO (2019) *International Tourism Highlights.* 2019 ed. Madrid: UNWTO Publications.

VisitEngland (2017) Discover the land of literary heroes, accessed at: https://visitengland.com/discover-land-literary-heroes

Wong, C. K. S., & Liu, F. C. G. (2011) A study of pre-trip use of travel guidebooks by leisure travelers. *Tourism Management*, 32(3), pp. 616–628.

Zillinger, M. (2006) The importance of guidebooks for the choice of tourist sites: A study of German tourists in Sweden. *Scandinavian Journal of Hospitality and Tourism*, 6(3), pp. 229–247.

13

UNDERSTANDING OUR PLACE

Publishing's role in the reading ecosystem under neoliberal economics

Jasmin Kirkbride

Introduction

In December 2018, I was asked to give a lecture as part of the Kingston University Masterclass series, examining key challenges publishing might face in its future. The topic brought together several thoughts I was having about what the reading ecosystem looks like, where its fault lines are, and what role publishing plays in it.

In this essay, the ideas from that lecture have been put into writing. It will examine the way that ecosystem works, and how it keeps books and reading alive. It will also explore a couple of ways in which this ecosystem is starting to break down, and what that means for the longevity of books. Because of its original audience, there are moments where the essay is aimed towards new publishers, but hopefully these moments will contain some value for old-hands of the industry as well.

Of course, this is a huge topic, so I will narrow it down by focussing mainly on traditional publishing and its authors. We will also be looking at the ecosystem through the lens of neoliberalism – the current economic soil which we all have to till, as it were.

The reading ecosystem

I have worked with books since 2013, when I first graduated from university. During these five-or-so years, I have primarily been an editor and book-trade journalist, both freelance and in-house, with notable roles as a reporter at *BookBrunch* and publishing director at Endeavour Media. I have also worked with social media, digital and marketing, for clients including Hay Festival.

Currently, I am developing my career by undertaking a PhD in Creative and Critical Writing at the University of East Anglia (UEA).

These experiences have given me a broad overview of the industry, and as a result I have developed a theory of the 'reading ecosystem'. The reading ecosystem is a network of book production and consumption, of which publishing is a part, and is a helpful tool to look at how the culture of reading is maintained.

To explain the idea, let's start with the very basics: tracking the journey of a book through its life, from beginning to end. In essence, the journey looks like this: first, a book is written by the author; then it goes through the publishing and bookselling process; finally, it is received and read (Figure 13.1).

As an identifier of the publishing process, this analysis works quite well because it is purely focussed on the product – books! However, in practice it is quite an old-school way of looking at the ecosystem of reading, precisely because it is from that publisher- and product-centric perspective.

In fact, if we examine the ecosystem of reading – at how the culture of reading is maintained – looking at the product won't necessarily tell us that much. We need to look at the human beings around it. All the publishers, readers, writers, agents, critics, booksellers, and printers – the 'book people', if you will – and how the books are affected by them. The people, more than the product, will tell us how books are kept alive. So, let's insert all the people into this book-creation process.

First, you have the writer, then the literary agent, the publishing house and production processes (which on their own have a slew of people), the booksellers (digital and bricks and mortar), the critics, and the readers.

This shows us that in fact the three phases we initially identified are complex and interrelated. They overlap in many places: an editor and an agent are certainly part of the writing process, but they are also definitely part of the publishing process; booksellers are often a book's first readers outside of the publishing house, but they are also an integral part of the industry. The lines blur (Figure 13.2).

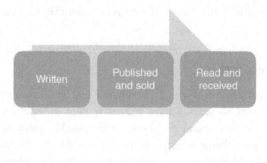

FIGURE 13.1 A basic analysis of book production

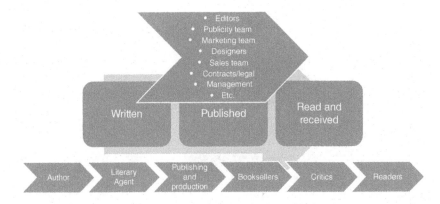

FIGURE 13.2 Book-production process with the 'book people' added

Now, in order to figure out how this ecosystem is perpetuated – how it continues year after year, decade after decade, generation after generation – we need to look at where the people fulfilling all these different roles are coming from.

There are many reasons that people become writers or get involved in publishing (though perhaps we can conjecture it isn't for the money). For the vast majority of us, however, I think it would be fair to say a love of books is key. Publisher James Spackman once commented that publishers are 'absolute freaks': we finish a book in one sitting and read more than one book a month – statistically, most people don't do that (Kirkbride, 2017c). There is something about books – for all of us – that makes us feel that they are worthwhile, even when we might be getting paid peanuts, or have dreadful managers, or miss the last free tote bag at the PRH London Book Fair stand. We publish because first we were readers.

Writers are also forever explaining that they were readers before they were writers. As Stephen King suggests, 'If you don't have time to read, you don't have the time (or the tools) to write. Simple as that' (King, 2012). The old adage that to be a good writer you must first be a good reader continues to be repeated by creative writing lecturers worldwide for a reason. Our writers too, then, emerge from being readers.

If we keep this view of the book-production process on a straight line it starts to look quite complicated and counter-intuitive once we add this in. That's because the ecosystem of reading isn't a conveyor-belt, it's a cycle; a complex network that continuously feeds bookish people through it (Figure 13.3).

It seems from this angle like a sustainable system, one that will keep feeding itself for many years to come without issue. That, unfortunately, is an illusion. Because of recent disruptions and the political climate in which we operate, I think we actually need to be careful and work hard to maintain this fertile soil from which books grow.

FIGURE 13.3 A basic reading ecosystem

Neoliberalism: a threat to the ecosystem

I have to preface this next section by saying that, as with all opinions on politics, what I am about to say is not the last word on the relationship between neoliberalism and publishing. At the end of the day, this is just a bunch of stuff I think, and it should not be exempt from scrutiny and questioning. My purpose here is not to tell you how things are, it is to make you think about one particular angle on how things might be, and perhaps through that to offer you something new and interesting.

I am not necessarily an ardent leftist or a socialist. I am not even against neoliberalism as such – politically, I can be quite agnostic – however, I do believe that if we engage in any political or economic ideology without objectivity, scrutiny, and self-awareness, it can only lead to turmoil. If we look at recent social upheavals such as the vote for Brexit or the election of Trump – and the accompanying growth in societal anger that must define both of these things as poorly-handled political messes whichever side of the fence you sit on – we can note that they arose in a large part because society was not self-aware enough. We stopped communicating with each other, and therefore ceased questioning ourselves and the status quo. In all systems, I believe that kind of apathy and stagnation are where danger is born.

So, with that caveat, I posit that some of the biggest threats to the reading ecosystem today may stem back to the advent of a neoliberal political culture.

Though many of you will have an extensive understanding of neoliberalism already, it is a complicated topic, so it is useful to give a quick definition, specifically within the context of publishing.

Incredibly simply, neoliberalism is a political and economic theory that encourages a freer spirit in how things are regulated, which sounds very nice but actually isn't always a good thing. It favours privatisation, unregulated free trade, and reductions in government spending. It prioritises GDP – that is, the basic growth of a country's economy in terms of profit – as a measurement of how 'well' a country is doing. Lorenzo Fioramonti explained the biggest flaw in this plan simply:

> If a country cuts and sells all its trees, it gets a boost in GDP. But nothing happens if it nurtures them... Preserving our infrastructure, making it durable, long-term and free adds nothing or only marginally to growth. Destroying it, rebuilding it and making people pay for using it gives the growth economy a bump forward.
>
> *Fioramonti, 2017*

Roughly, neoliberalism as an economic theory was first put forward in the 1930s and 1940s but gained traction only among the wealthy and elite of America and Europe. After the Second World War, neoliberalism was side-lined in favour of Keynesian economics. Keynesian economics has a pretty different agenda to neoliberalism: its goals include full employment and the relief of poverty, high taxation on the wealthy, and governments seeking social outcomes without shame, developing new public services and safety nets for poorer socio-economic groups.

However, during the 1970s, Keynesian economics fell into crisis in America and Europe – even the most well-meaning of economical ideologies can be riddled with flaws. It was replaced with neoliberalism, a change spearheaded by Margaret Thatcher and Ronald Reagan, though it is possible neither of them thought of the alteration in such conscious terms. 'Neoliberalism' rose without being referred to directly, which is one of the reasons it is so important now to scrutinise it: what have we been letting the silent ideology get away with right under our noses?

What followed this shift was tax cuts for the rich, the breaking of trade unions, deregulation, privatisation, outsourcing, and increased competition in public services.[1]

This shift in economic culture has been mixed for publishing, and it would be impossible to cover all the pros and cons comprehensively in an essay of this length.[2] However, many of the negative effects on the industry are still emerging, and some are even currently masquerading as positives. The issues I'm going to look at specifically in this essay are:

- an unsustainable growth-or-die attitude to business, resulting in increased corner-cutting in the publishing process;
- a 'more books, more money' philosophy that is resulting in a flooded market; and
- authorship as a career becoming financially unviable.

As we will see, these three issues all ultimately result in lower quality products and a breakdown in communication between these different sectors of the reading ecosystem, both of which will eventually result in dramatic discrepancies between what publishers create and what readers want to read. They will also destabilise the supply of raw materials from which the industry draws its strengths – ideas and stories.

So, let us examine these threats in closer detail.

Unsustainability of 'growth-or-die'

The 'growth-or-die' economic attitude actually has its roots in capitalism generally, but neoliberalism has taken the ideology to new extremes. 'Growth-or-die (or 'expand-or-die' or 'grow-or-die') is the theory that economic growth is inherently good, an adequate means by which to measure success of a company or country, and that economic growth must be achieved over other priorities.[3]

For a publishing house, this attitude means that they must aim to make more profit every year. For most, big, multi-national publishers, and also many independent ones, this is the goal of the company. Please note I said company, not individual. I think most people in publishing want to do well by their books and authors, but corporate culture is not detected in the individual, it is heard in the company's collective roar. This goal of making profit is one that was designed by an economic system that wishes to reward shareholders. *Not* employees or, in publishing's case, authors or even readers.

Since about 2007, publishing has been undergoing enormous disruption, mainly from influencers outside the industry.[4] In situations like this, where profits stagnate or even fall, it is a well-documented fact across all industries, that there are certain tricks you can use to artificially increase profits. It is hard to pin down evidence of these tricks being used, but when you've worked in publishing for a while, you start to see the patterns and you know what's going on under the surface. Though the following things are sometimes done for a good reason, I have also seen and reliably heard about all of them being done in multiple publishing houses for artificial profit-making purposes (Di Leo, 2014).

When a publishers' income doesn't rise year on year, artificial profits can be created by lowering outgoings. Technically, the amount of money a business is making in that year will go up, and shareholders will be satisfied, therefore maintaining the business' worth and kudos. This is done in a number of ways:

- Employ a lot of young people, who do not expect high wages.
- Squeeze employee benefits (such as training) where possible.
- Pay interns minimum wage or travel expenses only – if they are paid at all.
- Squeeze excess staff out of the system – fewer staff means fewer people to pay.
- Use freelancers wherever possible, prioritising those who will charge less over those who have more experience or qualifications.
- Cut corners in the publishing process – for instance, commission fewer edits on each book, or cut the number of cover redrafts and redesigns.
- Cut back on 'non-essential' departments – and it's amazing what some employers can find 'non-essential' when they really need to.

Publishing is not the only industry in which these kinds of shenanigans take place: it's an endemic result of neoliberal policies, which reward short-term profit over long-term sustainability. However, publishing is one of the industries where these kinds of cuts start to show in our products very quickly. Books end up with typos, dodgy covers, and storylines that just don't quite add up. What's more, these tactics lead to a stressed-out workforce that is not properly trained, and lacks mentorship from older employees; meaning legacy knowledge of the industry is lost.

None of this is good for a publisher's longevity: it does not attract new talent (certainly not diverse new talent); results in a higher than usual staff turnover (which annoys authors and agents); and drives the faithful of publishing to other industries (creating an industry 'brain-drain').

These cut corners also have an impact on books in another way: engagement with the text of the book within the publishing house is bound to diminish. Crucial decisions could even be made about the book – how it looks, how it should be marketed – by people who may not have had the time to read it. The more corners are cut and the more employees have on their plate, the less time they have to read. Then again, is it realistic to expect an employee to read every book they work on, when publishers are so focussed on publishing more books every year?

More books, more money...?

This leads us into the next big issue neoliberal ideologies have assisted in creating: the attitude that publishing more books will therefore make a publisher (or an author) more money. This attitude has its roots in neoliberal and capitalist thought, but it has been over-developed and taken advantage of by large internet retailers, who, I think it fair to say, perhaps do not always have the deepest understanding of how to preserve the book trade in the long term.

As I mentioned previously, publishing has been unrecognisably disrupted over the past decade, almost universally by influencers from outside the industry. The biggest disrupter has obviously been Amazon, but honestly, with the advent of the internet someone was inevitably going to come along and do what Amazon has done, it is just a shame it wasn't someone with an in-depth knowledge of the industry. And a shame, perhaps, that it happened under a loosely-regulated neoliberal agenda.

I'm going to say Amazon a lot over the next few lines, because it is the multi-national giant that happened to gain traction on our industry, but please in your heads think of it with just that flippancy – Amazon really could be anyone, and I don't particularly hold it against Jeff Bezos that this was the environment his business was birthed into. A lot of what has happened to Amazon is luck and chance, much as they would like us to believe otherwise.

Nevertheless, Amazon is now a fact of publishing and bookselling life, and it isn't going to go anywhere anytime soon. In some ways, it has been beneficial to publishing: it has re-opened the doors to out-of-print and backlist books,[5] given authors who can't get past the old-school gatekeepers of traditional publishing a chance to self-publish,[6] and almost single-handedly brought about the e-book revolution.

However, just because Amazon is here and we have to be friendly with the giant in order to sell books, doesn't mean that we can't level some constructive criticism at its business policies at the same time.

First and foremost, Amazon was at the centre of the drive to create an incredibly low price point for print and e-books, which has not been wholly beneficial for the publishing ecosystem. Before the 1990s, in the UK book prices were kept at particular rates by the Net Book Agreement (NBA). In 1995, the NBA was largely abandoned and deemed illegal, which led to supermarkets taking a chunk of the bookselling industry, and a culture of discounting books. Though some independent bookstores closed, it is uncertain whether or not they would have folded anyway, so it's hard to prove that this in itself was a problem. That is, until Amazon's release of the Kindle on 19 November 2007, which forever changed the face of publishing.[7]

The Kindle had been foreshadowed by lesser eReading devices for a few years, but because of Amazon's already strong hold on the book market, the Kindle really took off. One of the ways this was achieved was by selling e-books at such a low price that it made the cost of an eReader seem insignificant to the consumer. This is well known to have had a negative effect on the industry for a number of years, though now some balancing out has been achieved – rather than e-books having the price point of 99p-£1.99, as they did when the Kindle was first released,[8] by 2018, trade fiction e-books most commonly held a price point of about £3.99–£4.99. This is a low, but not insurmountably difficult, digital price for publishers to meet.

However, it remains true that the Kindle store still gives a high preference to books that discount deeply on a regular basis. This means that you have to sell *more* books for *less* money, to make the *same* profit. Or, to put it another way, more *sales* does not necessarily mean more *income*.

This fits into neoliberal economic policies because Amazon wants a low, low price for its books so that people buy more stuff on its site, therefore it is 'worth' more, and its shareholders are pleased. Obviously there are more complex economic cogs turning in the background there, but that's the basics. Note I said Amazon wants people to buy more 'stuff', not 'books', because it is important to remember that Amazon makes money not just through books but via many, many different revenue streams, which books contribute to. To scratch the surface, more books means a greater offering for the Kindle Unlimited (KU) subscription service, and more reasons to buy a Kindle over a Kobo, or a Fire tablet over an iPad. Books are a small part of a much wider picture for Amazon.

Moreover, the way internet algorithms (and particularly Amazon's) are currently programmed rewards the neoliberal ideal. Authors who produce more products rank higher, and therefore sell more books. Publishers have tried to replicate this technique in order to grab a bigger portion of the e-books pie, but I have actually never come across an instance when publishing more books was *necessarily* in the publisher's best interests, particularly if they are sold at a low price point.

This 'more books, more money' ideology bows down to that eternal growth scenario that neoliberalism upholds. Yet, it is completely irrational: you absolutely cannot grow every year, year on year, indefinitely. At some point you are going to hit that capitalist crash that the majority of economists understand perpetually waits in the wings.

For publishing, I also believe the inevitable crash is taking the form of a hugely flooded market. In 2017, Suzanne Baboneau, managing director of adult fiction at Simon & Schuster, said that there were too many books being published and that 'all of us in the industry are culpable' (Kirkbride, 2017a). Since then, we have seen a plateau in the e-book market – and with over 50,000 books published each year in the UK alone, who can blame consumers for being overwhelmed? Indeed, the UK publishes more books than any other country in the world (Flood, 2014). There are not an unlimited number of readers, and therefore a nigh on unlimited supply of books is bound to end in upset. Publishing fewer books, but doing it really well, offers both publishers and readers a more intellectually profitable (and therefore in the long term economically stable) scenario than publishing many books badly. More on this later.

However to me, the most dangerous part of this ideology is that Amazon – and even some publishers – doesn't seem to care whether books are *read* anymore, only if they *sell*. That cheap price point Amazon strives for might sell a book, but it by no means guarantees engagement with it. Indeed, with so many e-books being purchased on the attitude that 'gosh, at 99p it's basically free, why shouldn't I?' readers' devices are being flooded with books they will never even open.

This means that it's a short-lived success: yes, someone brought this author's first book, but if it isn't read, will they really bother buying the sequel? This method doesn't create a fanbase of readers, but a cult of purchasers, and these are two very different things.

Authorship: an unviable career?

On that note, let's take a look at how authors are faring under neoliberal publishing ideologies.

Not only does the 'more books, more money' ideal mean that authors are often not growing a genuine fanbase alongside their sales, there is an additional problem that a lower price point does not consistently work out in every authors' favour. Midlist authors, for instance, have by and large disappeared from traditional publishing, partly because at this lower price point, a mid-lister's 10,000 readers are no longer making their publishers enough profit, so the authors are being dropped.

Back in 2014 the Society of Authors' general secretary, Nicola Solomon, expressed what it feels like for many authors in the age of Amazon when she said that, 'Amazon are treating [authors and books] like they treat other commodities, but books are not like that. You can't switch authors like you switch washing powder' (Garside, 2014).

What's more, it isn't an attitude Amazon appears to have altered over the past few years. It has even aggrieved the self-published authors it works with by unleashing the KU subscription service. Using this service, which also requires the author to publish exclusively with Amazon, many self-published authors have found their revenues diminishing, and book sales plummeting in tandem. Many of the top self-published authors, who once advocated for Amazon-only publishing, have now aggregated their distribution base to include iBooks and GooglePlay: for example Mark Dawson ('Alli Admin', 2017).

Mark Coker, founder of Smashwords, spoke out about this in 2014, saying: 'Authors are in a difficult spot at Amazon. A few KU authors have publicly reported increased sales and readership, but that appears to be the exception rather than the norm... No other retailer makes authors play Russian Roulette with their books and careers like this' (Coker, 2012).

Yet, unfortunately, it seems this assumption that you can switch authors on and off can be found in publishing houses too – and it is a problem across the board. Every publishing house must be culpable in some way – how else do average author earnings drop by 42% in ten years, while publishers have reported growing profit margins? In 2016, Nicola Solomon reported that trade publishing was becoming more profitable, possibly by as much as third – a 'spookily similar' figure to the 29% by which author incomes had fallen at that time. Moreover, that same year, when publishers reported an average 13% profit margin, up from the 10% it once was, authors received only 3%–5% of publishers' turnover (Solomon, 2018).

Worse, in 2018, traditionally published authors' median income was £10,500 per year. It strikes me as poor long-term planning for publishers to reward their silent shareholders whilst starving those who create their natural resources of funds. Writers cannot become another commodity to be squeezed by neoliberal ideologies – yet, that is exactly what we appear to be seeing.

Of course, the Publishers Association and Amazon both offer competing viewpoints on this issue, and there are no doubt other sides to the story.[9] Nevertheless, there has clearly been a breakdown in communications here, as authors remain ardent they are not being paid fairly for their skills. Author and president of the Royal Literary Fund, Tracy Chevalier, spoke out on the matter in the summer of 2018, alongside many other authors, saying, 'I think writers starting out are getting less support from publishers – not just financial, but a commitment to develop them and see them through several books to build up a readership and steady sales' (Kean, 2018).

Writer and critic Philip Womack and author Joanne Harris agreed that publishers invest more in 'a shrinking pool of established writers and celebrities' rather than investing in the long-term careers of their authors as they used to (Kean, 2018). This is a devastating blow for the ecosystem of reading: if new authors are not nurtured and developed into established authors, this will undermine the long-term stability of the industry's supply of reliable, high-quality raw materials.

Indeed, we only have to look at Chevalier's closing words to feel the chill of what might be afoot if the industry does not treat its authors with more respect: 'Most writers cobble together a living from several sources: teaching, journalism, and odd jobs. Writing is just one shrinking source of income. Shrink it enough and people will stop writing altogether. It literally won't be worth it' (Kean, 2018).

That, we can all agree, would be a terrible – if not insurmountable – blow for publishing.

Combatting neoliberalism

I've tried to cover a lot of complicated ground here. I've probably made some vast generalisations, but hopefully I have also acted as a bit of a devil's advocate for some of the often-overlooked issues in publishing.

Ultimately, I am not calling for everyone to become idealistic publishers who don't give a fig for their profit margins. But there needs to be a tension between commercialism and intellectual idealism – one sells books and the other keeps them alive. Without one or the other element, the cycle will stop turning. To me, it seems that crucial tension is out of whack.

Before we finish though, let's go back to our cycle and insert a few of the topics we've talked about. First of all, authors are generally not making ends meet, which means that our raw materials are under threat. A blight on the harvest, if you will, but one that publishers are currently failing to treat. Publishers themselves are being squeezed, by Amazon's colossal share of the market on one side and shareholders on the other. (Not to mention the well-known side-effect these price squeezes are having on our bricks and mortar bookstores.) Meanwhile, the market is being flooded with books, which are deluging a finite audience, and this is resulting in a plateau we have yet to witness the full ramifications of.

In the wider view, answering to shareholders means publishers are also increasingly unable to justify 'risky' books, which is resulting in a lack of diverse publishing in every sense. This, in turn, leads to a lack of diverse publishers, which leads to even less diverse publishing, and so on.

This means that let alone seeing books that are increasingly compromised in terms of quality, readers are seeing the same kinds of books over and over again. Entire undiscovered markets are being missed because publishers feel unable to take the leap of faith required to try to discover them.

In the long run, these combined factors of a lack of diversity, compromised product quality, and passive reader engagement are likely to lead to a stagnant market, one that risks decreasing people's interest in reading generally. We might also conjecture that readers are buying more and reading less, meaning they are more engaged with the purchasing process than the actual ecosystem of books.

By digging these fault lines, we are, it seems, draining the pool our future authors and publishers would otherwise emerge from.

Of course, there are other factors at play in all this. Neoliberal politics cannot be blamed for all the world's sins, and I wouldn't want to try to form that argument. However, without examining the basic tenants on which we form our industry, how can we ever hope to effect any real change? And what would that change even look like? How should we go about trying to right the wrongs within the industry? To reconnect these dislocated parts? What is our role – individually and collectively – in the ecosystem?

First, and most obviously, we cannot turn neoliberalism on its head overnight. But we can be aware of the pressures that are exerted over us by forces outside of our control. Simply being aware of it, allows us to see those tiny steps we might be able to take that will eventually turn into a landslide of change.

My top tip for this is to develop mindful noticing habits. Keep a list of things about publishing you think aren't right, to remind yourself to work against them. Try to phrase it positively. The longer you are in publishing, the harder it will be to see the industry objectively, but it is never too late to start trying. I was recently reading through my own list and it includes notes on the mundanely simple to the very complex, such as:

- publishers should always provide milk, tea and snack budget – hungry people cannot work;
- never let 'to do differently would be difficult' stop you;
- design Excel sheets with Mail Merge in mind;
- always check lead times;
- pick up the damn phone;
- always get labels which fit the printer; and
- love the books, even the ones that don't love you.

This last point is my favourite. You have to love every book as if you were its midwife (or, in an author's case, its parent).

Once your internal noticing habits are up and running, break out some pleasantries: in an economic culture that is constantly squeezing all of us, civility and patience are often the first things to go – and that is inevitably followed by problematic breakdowns in communication. Here's a list of things you can do to combat this which are really simple:

- One day you might be the author, so don't badmouth them. One day you might be the publisher, so don't badmouth them either.
- Be honest, not cruel: constructive criticism should bruise, not stab.
- When you're an intern, make everyone tea. When you're the boss, still make everyone tea.
- Say good morning, good evening, and how are you. Then listen to the answer.

- In fact, listen to everyone all the time – even if it's the fifth call from this particular author/manager/bookseller in an hour. Listening is 90% of communication.
- Always follow up emails, even if it's been three months.

Yet, civility alone will not effect change. Once we have identified areas for change, we have to fight for them as well. And I have some top tips for that too:

- Fight like you're fighting your grandmother: be kind and polite, but firm and crystal clear. This will get more results than bull-in-a-china-shopping.
- If you are not sure, sleep on it. Giving your brain time to think is crucial to making balanced decisions. Similarly, uncomfortable issues with a project or situation do not always present themselves immediately: your feelings, like your intellect, can take time to process.
- On the other hand, if you are shaking with fury, breathe into your tummy, not your chest, and exhale to the internal count of five. This could save your career, and your plan of retaliation will be that much stronger (and objective) for the moment of thought.
- Wage your battles through bureaucratic violence, not insults. Paperwork is very powerful in an industry that runs on words. In any case if you're right, you should not need to fling barbs.
- Pick your fights. Some have more long-term effect than others. These are the ones to stick to your guns on.
- Pick your moments, too, you will know them when they appear, but as an example, it's probably best not to talk to a person you need money from directly after a Book Fair, a meeting with shareholders, or before they've had caffeine! Also, don't be afraid to contrive these moments yourself by organising a small meeting.
- If it needs doing and no one else wants to support you doing it, go out on your own and do it yourself. 'Become the change you want to see in the world' is a cliché for a reason. (Though you should also be aware of whose toes you might be stepping on and whether the project is worth it.)
- It's publishing, know that if you burn a bridge people will hear about it – don't be afraid of the gossip chain, but do be aware of it.
- Finally, be brave without becoming arrogant.

Conclusion: inhabiting the quantum state of bookishness

Ultimately, our place in publishing is defined by the moment and what it requires of us. Book people are simultaneously many things at once. Of course, everyone in publishing is also simultaneously a reader, whatever their job, title, or sector. But many of us exist in two or more different roles at once. For instance, I know book critics who are also literary agents, book-trade journalists who are also ghost writers, and every one of us knows at least one publisher who is also

FIGURE 13.4 We all exist within a quantum state of bookishness

an author. Many of us are writers by night, editors by day, and readers on our morning commutes. Critics by dusk and literary agents by dawn.

Each of us inhabits a kind of quantum state of 'bookishness' that is expressed by the job we are currently in, the readers and writers we are surrounded by, our moods and desires as we browse bookshelves.

What's more, publishing is one of those incredible industries where as you move through it, over the years, you will probably work in nearly every sector. By the time you retire (and bear in mind I have never actually met a retired book-person, I suspect we just keep booking about until we pop our clogs) you will probably have touched every aspect of the book ecosystem in some way. It's worth remembering this every day, because it helps us remain humane. Today you may be an author, tomorrow you could be a publisher. Next year, you might be a bookseller. Keeping the ecosystem going is not just keeping books alive for other people: it's keeping them alive for different aspects of ourselves, that we have been, are being, and have yet to be (Figure 13.4).

There is a theory of design principles in gardening called 'permaculture', which essentially tries to put into the soil as much as it takes out by harnessing the natural ecosystem. Our place as publishers – whatever we're doing, whichever hat we're wearing today – is at that metaphorical plough, putting in more than we can draw out in the current moment, tilling the earth and sowing seeds for the next generation of readers. And that, in these neoliberal times, is a very rebellious thought.

Notes

1 This is a vastly abridged overview of neoliberalism's history. For more in-depth analysis, I suggest the neutral definitions in Roy (2010) and the less politically agnostic but gripping analysis in Chomsky (2011).
2 For further reading, see the incisive insights and brutal honesty of Di Leo and Mehan (2014). I am deeply indebted to this work in my research, particularly Chapter 8 by Di Leo, 'Neoliberalism in Publishing: A Prolegomenon'.
3 For a history of the term, see Schmelzer (2014).

4 For an overview of specifically digital disruption, see Gilbert (2015).
5 For more, see Kirkbride (2017b).
6 For more, see Liu (2018).
7 See, for example, Fishwick (2008).
8 See, for example, Shaffi (2015).
9 For example, for the PA's response to Solomon, see Campbell (2018).

References

"Alli Admin". 2017. "Ask ALLi Self-Publishing Member Q&A with Orna Ross & Mark Dawson" in *Alliance of Independent Authors (ALLi)*: https://selfpublishingadvice.org/ask-alli-self-publishing-member-qa-with-orna-ross-mark-dawson/ (Web, accessed 23.01.19).Campbell, L. 2018. "Publishers Association Corrects Key Figure on Author Pay" in *The Bookseller*: www.thebookseller.com/news/pa-admits-figures-author-pay-were-wrong-847566 (Web, accessed 23.01.19).

Chomsky, N. 2011. *Profit Over People: Neoliberalism and Global Order* (New York: Seven Stories Press).

Coker, M. 2012. "Mark Coker's 2013 Book Publishing Industry Predictions – Indie Ebook Authors Take Charge" in *SmashWords*: http://blog.smashwords.com/2012/12/mark-cokers-2013-book-publishing.html (Web, accessed 23.01.19).

Di Leo, J. R. 2014. "Neoliberalism in Publishing: A Prolegomenon" in *Capital at the Brink: Overcoming the Destructive Legacies of Neoliberalism* (London: Open Humanities Press).

Di Leo, J. R. and Mehan, U. 2014. eds. *Capital at the Brink: Overcoming the Destructive Legacies of Neoliberalism* (London: Open Humanities Press).

Fioramonti, L. 2017. *Wellbeing Economy: Success in a World without Growth* (Johannesburg: Pan Macmillan SA).

Fishwick, F. 2008. "Book Prices in the UK Since the End of Resale Price Maintenance" in *International Journal of the Economics of Business*. Vol. 15, No. 3, pp. 359–377.

Flood, A. 2014. "UK Publishes More Books per Capita than Any Other Country, Report Shows" in *The Guardian*: www.theguardian.com/books/2014/oct/22/uk-publishes-more-books-per-capita-million-report (Web, accessed 24.01.19).

Garside, J. 2014. "Ebook Sales: Amazon Tells Hachette to Give Authors More, Charge Readers Less" in *The Guardian*: www.theguardian.com/books/2014/jul/30/amazon-hachette-ebook-sales-too-expensive (Web, accessed 23.01.19).

Gilbert, R. J. 2015. "E-books: A Tale of Digital Disruption" in *The Journal of Economic Perspectives*. Vol. 29, No. 3, pp. 165–184.

Kean, D. 2018. "Book Sales Boom but Authors Report Shrinking Incomes" in *The Guardian*: www.theguardian.com/books/2018/jul/19/book-sales-skyrocket-but-authors-report-shrinking-incomes (Web, accessed 22.01.19).

King, S. 2012. *On Writing: 10th Anniversary Edition: A Memoir of the Craft* (London: Hodder).

Kirkbride, J. 2017a. "The BookBrunch Interview: Suzanne Baboneau, Managing Director, Adult Publishing at Simon & Schuster" in *BookBrunch*: www.bookbrunch.co.uk/page/article-detail/the-bookbrunch-interview-suzanne-baboneau-managing-director-adult-publishing-at-simon-schuster/ (Web, accessed 24.01.19).

———. 2017b. "The Kindle -10 Years of Teaching Us Time Travel" in *BookBrunch*: http://bookbrunch.co.uk/page/free-article/the-kindle--10-years-of-teaching-us-time-travel/ (Web, accessed 24.01.19).

————. 2017c. "'Get over Yourselves' LBF Seminar Attendees Told" in *BookBrunch*: www.bookbrunch.co.uk/page/free-article/get-over-yourselves-lbf-seminar-attendees-told/ (Web, accessed 24.01.19).

Liu, A. 2018. "How Self-Publishing Is Diversifying The Book World" in *Thrive Global*: https://thriveglobal.com/stories/how-self-publishing-is-diversifying-the-book-world/ (Web, accessed 24.01.19).

Roy, R. K. 2010. *Neoliberalism: A Very Short Introduction* (Oxford: Oxford University Press).

Schmelzer, M. 2014. *'Expand or Die': The Historical Foundations of the Economic Growth Paradigm* (Leipzig: Degrowth Conference Leipzig).

Shaffi, S. 2015. "Authors Guild Warns Authors over Contributing Online Articles for Free" in *The Bookseller*: www.thebookseller.com/news/authors-guild-warns-authors-over-contributing-online-articles-free (Web, accessed 24.01.19).

Solomon, N. 2018. "The Profits from Publishing: Authors' Perspective" in *The Bookseller*: https://www.thebookseller.com/blogs/profits-publishing-authors-perspective-743226 (Web, accessed 23.01.19).

14

THE FOURTH FORMAT

How audiobooks have become a standard format for general publishers alongside hardback, paperback, and e-book

Nicholas W. N. Jones

Introduction

Until the late 1990s in the UK – perhaps a decade earlier in the US – audiobooks were seen as a specialist niche of the publishing industry, primarily a substitute for printed books for readers who were visually impaired or unable to manage a book physically. Yet by 2015, audiobooks had become a significant part (5%) of consumer digital publishing turnover in the UK, and have almost doubled (193.7%) between 2014 and 2018 (Publishers Association 2019), representing a total retail value estimated at £120 million.[1]

In the US, estimated consumer sales rose 41% from $1.77 to $2.5 billion in just two years to the end of 2017, and rose a further 24.5% in 2018; numbers of units sold in the US have more than doubled in the last four years to more than 100 million (Audiobook Publishers Association 2018, 2019a). By any standards, this is astonishing growth. What has happened? What moved audiobook publishing from backwater to mainstream?

It can take a surprisingly long time for a market to understand the potential of new technology and to appreciate how three key factors can make a new product become commercially viable: cost, price acceptable to a market, and consumer perception. Sometimes the stumbling blocks preventing development are not only the ultimate consumers, but those in the supply chain who fail to see the possibilities. This chapter will argue that this is what happened in the audiobook industry; whilst it might appear that the audiobook market has suddenly burst upon an unsuspecting publishing scene, it is actually one that has been in (largely latent) development ever since Edison demonstrated his phonograph more than 140 years ago. The idea of 'books that speak', perhaps surprisingly, is even older, pre-dating the existence of any technology that might make it a reality. French author Cyrano de Bergerac describes such a device in his *Voyage to the Moon*, published in 1656, and observes,

> When I since reflected on this Miraculous Invention, I no longer wondered that the Young Men of that Country were more knowing at Sixteen or Eighteen years Old, than the Gray-Beards of our Climate; for knowing how to Read as soon as Speak, they are never without Lectures, in their Chambers, their Walks, the Town, or Travelling; they may have in their Pockets, or at their Girdles, Thirty of these Books, … so that you never want the Company of all the great Men, Living and Dead, who entertain you with Living Voices.
>
> *Cyrano 1656*

What a brilliant exposition of the benefits of audiobooks! On that basis, the industry is more than 350 years old.

From the time publishing separated from bookselling as an independent trade, perhaps in the early 1800s, the hardback book has been by far the most usual format for presenting written works. Publishers needed time to recognise and establish other possible formats. Paperbacks were not added to publishers' output as a standard format until the 1930s. E-books became a consumer product not until the early 2000s. Those three formats are now usually issued by the same company. Although some children's titles were released in audio form by book publishers from about the mid-1970s, often only as book-and-audio sets, it is only very recently, in the teens of the twenty-first century, that audiobooks have been fully integrated into the regular output of general adult publishing companies for most titles rather than licenced to specialist audio-only companies. Audiobooks have now become 'The Fourth Format'.

The origins of spoken-word recordings

In the Victorian and Georgian eras, reading aloud was a widespread activity in many homes, and large crowds went to hear authors like Dickens and Thackeray, both of whom 'wrote in a way that works most effectively when read out loud'.[2] It could be argued that as the habit of reading aloud declined, so the view arose that reading was something always best done as a solitary mental activity, and that somehow it was impermissible to make it a shared activity or draw on someone else's wider knowledge of incidentals like accent or even correct pronunciation. As Matthew Rubery observes in his book that examines the relationship between the written and spoken word, 'This notion would hardly raise an eyebrow if applied to other media such as music or film, that we expect to be performed by professionals. Reading is exceptional among the arts in favouring the amateur' (Rubery 2016, p. 9).

The first known recording of spoken word was using a device called a 'phonautograph', devised in 1857 by the Frenchman Édouard-Léon Scott de Martinville – though it was at the time impossible to play it back,[3] and it was done solely as part of a scientific investigation into speech (soundrecordinghistory. net 2019). Prolific American inventor Thomas Edison was first to achieve a practical machine for both recording and playing back, and demonstrated his reading of 'Mary had a little lamb', played from a piece of tinfoil on his newly devised phonograph, sometime in December 1877. Incidentally, although there is a tendency to think of inventions happening in a neat linear way, Edison was probably not consciously developing the phonautograph concept, since his own account suggests the phonograph was almost a by-product of his work on automating the sending of telegraphic messages.[4]

With the tradition of reading aloud still entirely current, it was naturally expected that the phonograph would be used to record prose. Edison, a brilliant self-promoter, demonstrated his machine at many exhibitions in the following years, and it is clear that the inventor immediately perceived the possibilities of recorded readings: in 1878, he wrote an article in the *North American Review* (Edison 1878) that is astonishingly prescient in seeing how his audience would eventually come to regard audiobooks. He talks about the possibilities of 'electrotyping' recordings allowing them to be cheaply duplicated, then continues,

> The principal application of the phonograph in this direction is in the production of phonographic books. A book of 40,000 words upon a single metal plate ... becomes a strong probability.... Such books would be listened to where now none are [sic] read.
>
> *Edison 1878, p. 534*

The idea very soon appeared in popular culture: the *New York Daily Graphic* has in 1878 a cartoon showing a family seated around a table, with a large wind-up phonograph in the middle. The caption reads: 'The phonograph at home reading out a novel' (New York Daily Graphic 1878). However, the technology to achieve this was not to be available for some while yet.

Edison also anticipated the still-continuing discussion of whether authors should read their own works with, '[Recordings] would preserve more than the mental emanations of the brain of the author; and, as a bequest to future generations, they would be unequaled' (Edison 1878, p. 534). He also foresaw the possibilities for children's entertainment, adding that 'Every species of animal or mechanical toy — such as locomotives, etc. — may be supplied with their natural and characteristic sounds' and that his device would allow for the preservation of family memories: 'For the purpose of preserving the sayings, the voices, and the last words of the dying member of the family — as of great men — the phonograph will unquestionably outrank the photograph' (Edison 1878, p. 533).

Unfortunately, he was unable to make sound recording technology as simple or as cheap as photography, so as recently as December 2018, the London *Times* could report on a company offering a personal 'Desert Island Discs' service as a brilliant new idea (Moore 2018).

Awareness of, and concern for, blind people had become organised in Britain with the founding of the British and Foreign Society for Improving the Embossed Literature of the Blind (the forerunner of the Royal National Institute for Blind People) in 1868 (RNIB 2019) and the National Library for the Blind in 1882 (Wikipedia 2019a), which aimed to 'ensure that people with sight problems have the same access to library services as sighted people'. A similar organisation existed in the US from 1911 (Wikipedia 2019b). These organisations systematised support for creating tactile books, but none immediately considered the possibility of sound recordings as a means of providing blind people with access to literature. The potential remained unrealised.

The influence of the First World War and the first talking-book libraries

War, for all its horrors, can sometimes perversely bring benefits as a driver of innovation. It seems to have been the necessary stimulus for making recorded books a reality; it is hard to say why Edison's visions were unrealised for so long, given the rapid developments in commercial recording during the early 1900s (Centre for the History and Analysis of Recorded Music (CHARM) 2009). Perhaps it was only technology holding back the development of a market. It is certainly actually the case that the First World War concentrated the effort and resulted in the financial support. In retrospect, however, it can be seen that 'recorded' or 'talking' books became so strongly associated with disability that they were viewed only in that light by the population at large and by the industries – such as publishers – serving them. It was a further 80 or so years before 'ear-reading', as it has been termed, was not disparaged as somehow inferior to reading silently off the page.

The First World War resulted in many soldiers being blinded. One of the leading forces in rehabilitation was St Dunstan's, the British home for blinded soldiers and sailors. Captain Ian Fraser, blinded at the Somme in 1916, went to St Dunstan's, where from 1917 he was in charge of its after-care work and by 1924 was its Chairman (Blind Veterans 2019). He was inspired by his love of listening to music on gramophone to try to create 'books that could talk' early in the 1920s. He knew an engineer at the Gramophone Company (a predecessor of HMV), and they experimented with records rotating at less than the then-usual 78 rpm. However, achieving an acceptable reproduction quality took some while (Fraser 1961).

Fraser established a technical committee jointly between St Dunstan's and the National Institute for the Blind (NIB: the 'Royal' and 'of Blind People' came later, in 1953 and 2008) to determine what might be the most cost-effective way to create a library of recorded books (Rubery 2016, p. 136; Wilson 1935). They eventually settled on shellac records like consumer 78s but revolving at 24 rpm, so they could run for up to 25 minutes. The library first sent out discs in late 1935.

In the US, the American Foundation for the Blind (AFB) was lobbying in support of making recorded books for war-blinded veterans – once again, the First World War was the key catalyst, so in the US as well, talking books (as the US called them from the start) became associated in the public mind with disability. Helen Keller, under the auspices of the AFB, made a highly effective speech to Congress, and the National Library Service for the Blind was established as part of the Library of Congress in 1931. Unfortunately, for reasons valid at the time, the two organisations worked largely independently, although the NIB had been at work on the technical problems for some while before the AFB started, and the American service used a different standard (33 1/3 rpm, consequently running only about 15 minutes per side), which prevented ready exchange of recordings. The first US talking books were sent out in October 1934 (American Foundation for the Blind 2019).

One thing worthy of note is that there are estimated to have been only about 700 or 800 veterans in America with sight lost or severely impaired by the war, yet at the time there were approximately 120,000 blind people in the US (Koestler 1976). Comparable figures for the UK are 3,000 and perhaps 30,000.[5] It is, according to your point of view, frustrating or tragic that the added 'visibility' of war veterans should have been the necessary catalyst to make talking books a reality. But the awareness of the problem did result in the technology, the money and the resources finally being in place.

Making talking-book libraries a reality

What kind of books should be recorded? In America, the Library of Congress started with worthy and moral works – the Bible, Shakespeare, and patriotic documents like the Declaration of Independence – but soon broadened to reflect a range of tastes including popular fiction. In Britain, the NIB began with Agatha Christie's *The Murder of Roger Ackroyd*, Conrad's *Typhoon*, and the Gospel According to St John (Blind Veterans UK archives, quoted in Rubery 2016, p. 138). A novel by Thackeray soon joined these.

As long as talking books were being produced for a limited market – people unable to read by eye – and funded by grant or charity money, the output was inevitably very limited. There was ongoing concern from Braille readers that the creation of the talking-book libraries would divert funding from the maintenance of Braille libraries, and both the Library of Congress and the NIB had to reassure those concerned. However, by the end of 1945, the US talking-book library had a little over 1,000 titles, and the British one about 500.

It seems extraordinary that the distinction between 'books for the blind' and 'books for everyone' was to remain so deep for so long, but as recently as 2010, the Royal National Institute for the Blind reported that only 13% of the top 1,000 bestselling books in the UK (as listed in the Nielsen BookScan) were available in audio form, but once publishers serving the general market entered wholly into production, that figure rose astonishingly quickly, and by 2012 it was 49% (Publishers Association Audio Publishers Group 2013).

In the early days, a major question was not only what titles should be read, but *how* should they be read? Even the terms 'reading' and 'listening' are not without overtones, since for a sighted people listening is clearly a choice; blind people cannot read, so must listen, and may therefore refer to 'reading' an audiobook so that they are not drawing attention to the fact that they are necessarily absorbing the text in a different way.

Some users objected to the possibility that the reader might introduce an extra layer of interpretation, and wanted to be sure that the author's words were allowed to speak entirely for themselves. They thus demanded as neutral a reading as possible, without any kind of inflection or emphasis. Some blind people now prefer to use the text-to-speech facility on a computer rather than risk a human reader adding interpretation.

Users are clearly entitled to express their preferences, but it seems strange to object to the risk of 'reader contamination' for a book when no such similar objection is ever made about a play or film or music, which is clearly the work of performers and directors interpreting the script or score. That purist approach also overlooks the often considerable part played by an unseen editor in arriving in the first place at the final text of the printed book being recorded.

It is arguable that there is still, and probably always will be, a divide between the preferences of those who have a choice as to what format to read in – 'by eye' or 'by ear'– and those for whom 'by eye' is not an option. For those involved in creating audiobooks, however, the great change between the 1930s and now is that the sighted market is vastly larger than the vision-impaired, and for readers who have a choice, audiobooks must offer something preferential to reading off the page if they are to win an audience. For most of the time since talking books became a reality, the general public has not understood the pros and cons of ear-reading versus eye-reading, and has been led by the association with organisations for the visually impaired to presume that ear-reading is for those only.

Is listening the same as reading?

The first talking-book listeners, especially those unable to read Braille, were hugely appreciative, as letters in the Library of Congress National Library Service attest: 'You have no idea how much change these talking books have made to my life', and 'Just like listening to someone right in the room with me' (but, the correspondent adds, free of the sense of imposing obligation that many blind people feel when asking a friend or relative to read aloud to them). There was a general sense that most talking books were far better read than they would be by most volunteer readers, but from the start there was a vocal minority that considered listening to a book to be 'cheating'.[6] It was called 'lazy reading'. Using Braille (as with sighted readers reading printed text) requires effort and engagement: a Library of Congress report in 1933 even considered it 'an intellectual accomplishment' in its own right. This was contrasted with listening, where users could just allow the text to 'wash over them'. There is now physiological evidence that listening triggers the same parts of the brain as reading from print (Deniz et al. 2019; Hutton et al. 2015), and there is evidence that retention is as good or better by those who listen compared to those who read (Kintsch and Kozminsky 1977). However, the view that listening to books is somehow a poor substitute for reading them silently still continues.

In October 2018, the BBC Radio 4 programme *Front Row* had a debate on the matter then ran a survey (BBC Radio 4 2018). Sixty-nine per cent of responders said that they consider listening to a book to be as valid as reading it in text form. The comedian Jenny Eclair, herself recently suffering from a visual impairment, followed up the debate with a piece in the *Independent*:

> What I increasingly resent about the audiobook versus paper book debate is the idea that there's some moral high ground to be won from wading through every word of a literary classic and finding it really hard going but sticking with it, rather than listening to a few pages every night before you go to sleep.
>
> *Eclair 2018*

Storytelling, of course, is also accomplished in the modern multimedia world by film and television. Those who perceive listening as inferior to reading do not seem to attempt to make value comparisons between visual and written storytelling – perhaps they feel the conclusion is too obvious to warrant investigation. However, the audiobook retailer and publisher Audible commissioned a study by a team at University College London (UCL) that concludes that the spoken word is surprisingly powerful (Richardson, Griffin, et al. 2018). They played an extract from an audiobook, then showed a film clip dramatising the same scene, and recorded participants' heart rate, skin moisture, and body temperature, all of which are physiological indicators of engagement with perceived events. There was a consistently larger (though in this writer's opinion small) physiological response to the audiobook than to the film. The paper is yet to be peer-reviewed and published, but the conclusion garnered much press attention when released. The authors suggest the effect is because audiobooks demand that audience members engage their imagination in a way that film and television do not.

Some may be sceptical about this paper given that it is funded by Audible, but UCL is a highly respectable institution, and the writer of this chapter had already propounded much the same idea, albeit in a qualitative not quantitative way, in an article published in 2016, from which this is the key argument:

> Listening to an audiobook is not a passive process. It is all the better for the demands it makes on the listener. If one is adapting for a film it is necessary to specify things that are irrelevant to the story – such as the curtains in a Jane Austen period film. The very act of having to provide the 'furnishings' (in every sense) engages the reader in a way that deepens involvement and understanding, whereas a film version demands that every little detail is specified by the maker rather than the audience.
>
> *Jones 2016*

A similar argument has been made by Michael Morpurgo on the BBC Radio 4 *Today* programme on 12 March 2016: why has the film of *War Horse* been only a moderate success, whereas the stage version is a phenomenon? Having the horse be a puppet on stage, he said, not wholly realistic, prompts the audience to engage with the process of telling the story, whereas the definitive reality of the film leaves no room for the viewer to personalise the story to his or her own experience. The stage version, he concluded, 'leaves the audience room to imagine' (BBC Radio 4 2016).

The writer of this essay, having produced several hundred audiobooks, takes the view that ear-readers will usually benefit from the thought and care that goes into making a good audiobook. The reader of a printed book has either to look up the meaning and pronunciation of unfamiliar words or names, or may simply assume or not bother, but the production team will take great care to try to pronounce everything correctly. Further, a listener picks up meaning not just from vocabulary and grammar, but also from what is known technically as 'prosody', the pitch and intonation that communicate things like emotion, irony, sarcasm, emphasis, and urgency. A good reader will enhance understanding.

Writing for a general audience in *Forbes* magazine, Olga Khazan collated some research on reading versus listening: University of Memphis professor Arthur Graesser, who studies learning and cognition, told her,

> When the material is difficult … physical reading provides an advantage because the individual can re-read and look to surrounding words for context clues, [but] in some cases, listening offers major advantages over reading … because an audiobook pre-determines … prosody.
>
> *Khazan 2011*

Mary Beard, historian and experienced television presenter, has recorded two of her shorter books. She writes about the experience in the *Times Literary Supplement*:

> You learn about your own book simply by reading it out loud (and I would recommend anyone writing a book should try it). In general, when I am producing the text, I try to hear the sound and rhythm of the prose. And I like to think that I put store by euphony. But actually reading it out does reveal repetitions and awkward cadences, and in one case a tiny wee misprint, that I had never noticed.
>
> *Beard 2018*

There are other benefits too that although well appreciated have only recently been more academically identified. Danish social psychologists Iben Have and Birgitte Stougaard Pedersen remind us that, 'Reading audiobooks is timesaving, as you can do other things while reading; it promotes activity, because eyes and body are free to move; it is mentally engaging; it is convenient, inexpensive, etc.' and then suggest,

Rather than comparing audiobooks with printed books, we wish to advance a position that regards audiobook reading as a special instance of mobile listening (comparable to music, radio, audio guides, or audio therapy) – as a popular phenomenon that is part of the digital, mobile audio culture in a mixed-media environment.

Have and Pedersen 2013

They also suggest that listening to a recording produces the same physiological response, albeit to a lesser extent, as a conversation, so that listening can be of great benefit for isolated people: 'The voice in your ears produces effects of intimacy, as well as giving the user a sense of present social company'.

Moreover, 'we are more likely to stick with a book that we're listening to than one we're reading', according to Graesser (quoted in Khazan 2011),

which would also improve our chances of retaining what's in it.... The half-life for listening is much longer than for reading because we are pre-conditioned to listen to an entire conversation out of politeness. Generally, people keep listening until there is a pause in an idea, but (especially in today's information-overload age), we stop reading at the slightest suggestion that something more interesting might be going on elsewhere else.

These sorts of comments draw attention to one of the challenges that those foreseeing a general market for audiobooks faced for so long. Listening to text read aloud clearly engages the brain in a different way from reading silently, but it is actually less different than it appears. Few eye-readers realise the benefits of ear-reading until they experience it, so the wider adoption of audiobooks was limited by a vicious circle – potential listeners were unaware of the benefits of audiobooks until they tried listening, but would not try them since they did not perceive that it would be a desirable activity. This is why audiobooks seem to have appeared in the general market so suddenly – they were in effect an open secret, and came into plain view only once they had reached a critical mass.

Who should read, and how?

Like any activity, reading out loud improves with practice. It requires a specific set of skills: being able to interpret the grammar of a sentence on the fly so as to emphasise the right words and communicate the shape of a sentence; a good general knowledge of pronunciations; and, with fiction, a confidence at least to indicate, if not imitate, an appropriate voice for each character. A well-produced audiobook does the work for the listener and frees the imagination by painting aural pictures.

Imogen Church, a professional reader of audiobooks of more than one hundred titles, said in 2016 at a Library of Congress conference about the impact of digital technology on reading,

> Audiobook narration is a surprisingly arduous job, the levels of concentration required are immense and need to be sustained for a minimum of five hours in an average day; there is no lolling about between sentences, the flow is crucial....
>
> *Church 2016*

Mary Beard was also surprised:

> I spent a few hours this week recording the updated edition of *Women and Power* for an audiobook. Given that it originated in two 55-minute lectures, it seems amazing that it could take the few hours that it did (getting on for four).... Heaven knows what it would be like to record a 500-page doorstop... my *SPQR* was done by a professional! It is a learning experience in many ways.
>
> *Beard 2018*

There speaks someone who has given hundreds of university lectures and presented an international television series.

As an aside, it is fascinating to note that there was no way of editing early recordings, which were directly cut onto the disc from which the master stamper was to be made: this meant that readers had to read continuously for 20 minutes without making a serious error, or they would have to start the side again. Very few modern narrators can achieve that degree of fluency.

The first readers, working for the AFB and NIB, were usually asked to read with minimal inflection so as to follow the principle that the audiobook should be as close as possible to the printed book (the AFB initially suggested that errors and even misprints should be retained, such was the sanctity of the text). Gradually, it was recognised that some inflection and characterisation actually improved the listening experience. Imogen Church described her contemporary approach thus:

> An audiobook is a text book brought to life, brought off the page: a dramatisation. In my professional experience, the more successful audiobooks are narrated by people who bring drama to the story. My own narrating style is based (to the best of my ability) in truth and authenticity blended with enough drama to convey the story through only my voice.
>
> *Church 2016*

The very best audiobooks immerse the listener in the author's words such that those words appear to be delivered subconsciously into his or her mind. This requires that all those involved in the production understand the book, care about it, and can afford to care about it. The reader needs someone to perform to, who can provide feedback and encouragement. That person should be an informed producer, a first listener who is privileged to be able to intervene to make the most of the material. A good production will enhance the prosody so as to aid understanding and interpretation.

The artist Delacroix wrote in his *Journal* that: 'A picture is nothing but a bridge between the soul of the artist and that of the spectator' (Norton and Wellington 1995). That is analogous to the way in which an audiobook should connect author and listener.

Gradual growth from 1950s to 2000

What began this change towards a more universal appreciation of audiobooks?

In America, in 1952, two recent college graduates, Barbara Holdridge and Marianne Mantell, frustrated by their work in publishing and in the recording industry in New York, decided to establish their own record company, which they called Caedmon, after the poet. Their first recording was Dylan Thomas, whom they had seen reading his poems at the 92nd Street Y.[7] He agreed to perform a selection for a recording, but there was not enough for the B-side of the record, so Thomas suggested he read a story he had written a few years before for *Harper's Bazaar*. Thomas couldn't even remember the correct title – but it turned out to be 'A Child's Christmas in Wales'. This sold many thousands of copies as a vinyl long-playing record (LP). That chance event launched the company, which went on to record many poets including Eliot, Plath, Auden and Frost. With those discs and a wide range of plays including Shakespeare and George Bernard Shaw, Caedmon sowed the seeds of the audiobook industry in North America (National Public Radio 2002). They cautiously moved into prose readings – their catalogue includes, for example, Boris Karloff reading (rather well) *Just So Stories*, released in 1958 (Kipling 1958).

The British equivalent to Caedmon was Argo, founded by Harley Usill (who had worked with pioneering documentary filmmaker Humphrey Jennings) and Cyril Clarke. They started in 1951 to record British traditional music, but moved into spoken word, prompted by their experience in making field recordings of Indian music (Wikipedia 2019c). Their first spoken-word release was *Under Milk Wood*, also of course by Dylan Thomas, released in 1954, licenced from the BBC. Perhaps Thomas should be recognised as a co-founder of the audiobooks business? The Argo release was even more successful, reputedly selling two million copies, and is still available (Naxos AudioBooks 2019). Subsequent Argo releases included poems by John Betjeman, Willy Rushton reading *Thomas the Tank Engine*, a version of *Alice Through the Looking Glass* with Jane Asher, and 'Dr Who' stories starring Tom Baker (Children's Records 2019).

The success of these titles prompted the established music record companies to move into the field. HMV had its Junior Record Club, with titles including Vivien Leigh reading Beatrix Potter, Ian Carmichael reading *Winnie the Pooh*, and Richard Attenborough *Cinderella* – and, most improbably, in 1963, issued a record where Evelyn Laye and Susan Hampshire, among others, manage to tell the entire stories of Louisa May Alcott's *Little Women* and also its sequel *Little Men* in 15 minutes! A British label called Lantern has a recording of *Aladdin* read by Roger Moore in 1966.

In America, starting in the 1950s, as vinyl took over from shellac, Columbia Records released a series of 'Juveniles' and the 'Children's Library of Recorded Books'; Disney released audio adaptations of its animated films (it had released adapted film soundtracks as early as the 1930s); Mel Blanc performed audio-only versions of Bugs Bunny cartoons, and even Batman and Peanuts appeared in audiobook form (Children's Records 2019).

It is clear that at this point the market was seen as being primarily for children, but there are the first signs of adult releases other than poetry and drama: in Britain, the publisher Paul Hamlyn established the Listen for Pleasure spoken-word label when cassette players became standard in cars; it offered a range of books like James Herriot's 'Vet' series and classics like Jane Austen's books, abridged to three hours on two cassettes (Discogs 2019a).

The cassette was also to be responsible for developments in America, when in 1975, Duvall Hecht founded Books On Tape as a response to the tedium of his commute. His service was to provide unabridged titles for rental (Wikipedia 2019d). By 1979 it had been joined by Recorded Books (Recorded Books 2019). This was the turning point in the US, and by the time Bowker compiled its first catalogue of cassette books in 1985, it could list 22,000 titles from 250 companies (Rubery 2016, p. 219).

In the UK, the BBC recognised the value of its archives, and launched the BBC Radio Collection, which started with compilations of radio comedy shows in 1988, joined by detective stories and a few novels adapted from recordings made for radio. A few early releases appeared on vinyl discs (Discogs 2019b).

Because the BBC already had a book publishing arm, selling BBC Books (now part of Penguin Random House) into bookshops, it was a natural extension to sell Radio Collection cassettes into bookshops. Up to that point spoken-word recordings had been produced by record companies, so they were sold through the marketing channels those companies normally used: record shops. Visitors to record shops would be wanting to buy music, often very specific music; they were unlikely to buy information or stories. Once audiobooks were offered to a naturally book-reading public *in an appropriate context*, they sold. The appearance of audiobooks in bookshops was the start of their reaching a general public in Britain.

Mention should, of course, be made of audiobooks supplied to public libraries. Recorded Books and Books on Tape in America both offered their recordings to libraries, and in Britain companies like Ulverscroft (founded 1964) and Chivers (1979) saw audiobooks for libraries as a natural extension of their large-print book businesses (Ulverscroft 2019).

Few publishing areas escape the influence of Harry Potter: Stephen Fry's unabridged readings in Britain and Jim Dale's in America have undoubtedly played a part in raising awareness of audio as a valid form of storytelling for all ages. The first recording was released in 1999 and the rest of the series over the next eight years.

The Harry Potter books also demonstrated the viability of releasing unabridged titles for a general audience. Up to that point, books for the general market as opposed to libraries were almost invariably heavily abridged since publishers took the view that the prices necessitated by the cost of duplication of the full works would not be acceptable to consumers, since the primary sound-carrying medium was cassette, which had a maximum run time of 120 minutes. A typical unabridged book would run 10 or 15 hours, so would require many cassettes, making for an unwieldy and expensive product. The arrival of the compact disc (CD) into the market did not help much, since, although thinner, a CD maximum was even shorter, 80 minutes. That adult books were consequently heavily abridged added ammunition to those who still regarded ear-reading as a poor substitute for 'the real thing'.

After 2000: the internet, Audible, and online audiobooks

The groundwork for the current burgeoning of the audiobook market was laid in the 1990s with the arrival of the world wide web (1991, but growing rapidly after the first integrated graphic browser, Mosaic, in 1993), and the founding of Audible, 1995. The Web needs no explanation, but we should examine the Audible story in some detail.

The company was founded by former journalist Don Katz (American Reader 2013; WebTalk 2005; Wikipedia 2019e). In 1997, four years before the iPod, Audible created a portable player to which about two hours of audiobook could be downloaded in a proprietary file format that allowed it to protect content, something at the time considered essential by audiobook publishers. Audible had the only viable system at the time for providing that protection (known as Digital Rights Management, or DRM) on audiobook downloads. In the UK, publishers like Hachette, HarperCollins, and Random House would not licence content to retail sites without DRM. US publishers were equally reluctant to risk – as they saw it – widespread piracy.

Sites trying to compete with Audible were thus not able to offer certain key titles. Customers do not, by and large, care – or even notice – who publishes something: authors are much stronger brands than publishers. But they do notice if their favourite author is not available on a platform. In Britain, BBC Audiobooks, after privatisation as AudioGO, had both BBC Radio and Chivers catalogues (Chivers was purchased by BBC Audiobooks in 2001) and therefore a substantial range of sought-after content. It *was* willing to risk sales without DRM, and did launch an online shop, but the lack of many bestselling titles precluded success. AudioGO failed to appreciate that the change towards downloads could not support the overhead level of a company geared to the economics of physical product, and did not survive beyond 2013 (Page 2013).

The internet made downloadable files possible. Audiobooks need no longer be constrained in length by physical media, cassette, or CD. Although there had been players for mp3 files since 1997, it was the arrival of the iPod in 2001 that made portable sound playback an everyday occurrence. In 2002, Apple sold

325,000 iPods; in 2007, 51 million (Wikimedia Commons 2019). This laid the groundwork for the rapid growth of audiobook listening from portable players, and Audible achieved a coup in contracting with the Apple iTunes stores to be exclusive supplier of spoken-word content.

Downloads first overtook physical formats by 2008, but after that their uptake accelerated. In 2010, CDs accounted for 38.9% of US sales.[8] By 2015 it was still 15.3%, but by 2017, only 5.8% (Audiobook Publishers Association 2019b).

Amazon purchased Audible in early 2008, and as audiobook versions were linked on the Amazon website to the printed version, a vastly larger audience became aware of what was available. Furthermore, as Audible user numbers grew, Amazon could warrant substantial promotional budgets. In 2015 in Britain they ran a most effective campaign on television, in which Clare Balding, at the height of her fame as Olympic commentator, was seen reading alongside someone in a variety of everyday situations (Audible 2015).

The incorporation of mp3 players in smartphones – the first iPhone was released in June 2007, and Android phones followed in September 2008 – meant that a convenient player, crucially one likely to be kept near the user all the time, became available just at the time a viable catalogue of downloadable audiobooks was available. The 2012 remark by Don Katz at the London Book Fair is pertinent: '… if a member of Audible runs out of Science Fiction audio, we lose a member' (Kozlowski 2012).

The UK telecoms regulator Ofcom reports that in 2017, 76% of the UK population has access to a smartphone. The total UK digital audience is about 50 million, of whom 48% consider the smartphone to be the most important device for internet access (Ofcom 2019, p. 66, fig. 5.1). Since reading a book on the small screen of a phone is not an ideal experience, these figures suggest that audiobooks may be set for even greater growth.

The digital marketplace in both Britain and the US is now dominated by Audible. A well-funded viable competitor in both territories is audiobooks. com, part of Recorded Books, and Blackstone Audio is the largest independent, selling both to consumers (with a site branded as downpour.com) and to libraries. Two Scandinavian companies, Bonnier (with its streaming app BookBeat) and Storytel, have large customer bases in Europe, but have made little impact in Britain since they offer audiobooks on a monthly subscription basis allowing unrestricted listening, as opposed to selling individual titles, which means English language publishers are reluctant to licence title to them.

The library market is more diverse. W. F. Howes (RBDigital in the US), Overdrive (now owned by the Japanese company Rakuten), Bolinda (Australian, now very active also in the UK), and Ulverscroft (UK) and HoolaDigital (US) all have digital-loan platforms that allow library users to download recordings for a limited time.

It should be added that there are substantial markets for audiobooks in other languages than English, especially German, Spanish, and Italian, but that is outside the scope of this chapter.

The development of much more affordable recording equipment from the mid-1990s vastly reduced the entry costs of recording voice at reasonable quality.

There is now a move, encouraged by Audible with its ACX self-publishing platform and by companies like Bee Audio, towards audiobooks being recorded in home studios by one person. That will risk losing the polish that comes from having a sympathetically critical listener/producer who can advise not only on the prosody but also check and research pronunciations. Can a solo reader also pay due attention to the technical quality of a recording while concentrating on the performance? Audiobook production needs a team to achieve consistently good results.

The significance of podcasts

Listening to spoken stories and information as an activity in its own right, and not as a substitute for reading, was thus entering wider public perception from the 1990s onwards, but it was the ease of listening though dedicated apps on smartphones that took it to a new level. The term 'podcast' was coined in 2004 by *Guardian* journalist Ben Hammersley writing about the phenomenon of audio files to which listeners could 'subscribe', so that new episodes would be downloaded automatically; the word 'podcast' was the US Oxford Dictionaries 'word of the year' in 2005 (BBC Radio 4 2015; Oxford Dictionaries 2006).

Podcasts can be seen as a mid-point between radio and audiobooks. Some might be termed 'audiobooks for which there happens to be no book'; some are conversational and more informal, and closer to talk radio. But speech radio, such as BBC Radio 4, or American National Public Radio, draws on the same skills of research, careful writing, editorial expertise, and storytelling that book publishers would readily identify as *their* skills. The problem in the past was that radio has a very high barrier to entry, and also that it is still seen primarily as an ephemeral medium. Some radio programmes have been released as podcasts: the first BBC one was Melvyn Bragg's *In Our Time*, in 2004, and since then all episodes going back to the series start in 1998 have been made available (Wikipedia 2019f).

The BBC launched its iPlayerRadio in 2012, which gave a more visible longevity to much of its radio output, and in 2018 replaced it by BBC Sounds, which promotes podcasts, many specially produced, much more obviously. The distinction between catch-up radio and podcast is diminishing.

Launching the Sounds app, James Purnell, the BBC's Director, Radio and Education, said it was 'designed to reach younger listeners who did not tune into traditional radio output'. BBC Sounds is 'intended to look and feel more like other podcast sources, and will include other content not derived from broadcast output but specially created' (Thorpe 2019).

When podcasts do capture the public imagination, the results can be astonishing: the American true-crime series *Serial* was a cultural phenomenon of 2014, and by the end of 2018 had been downloaded over 175 million times (Serial 2019).

Audiobooks that closely follow printed books (some variation may be essential if a book is heavily illustrated) have a closely argued editorial line that follows the book, into which (usually) much care and thought has gone. That is equally true for radio programmes, which are increasingly seen as expensive. Podcasts offer an endearing and inviting informality that appeals to new audiences, and it is very likely that new listeners will be drawn to audiobooks as well. But, as Kate Chisholm writes in the *Spectator*, podcasts 'are not bound by time and the demands of a schedule. They can last for … as long as the story, the conversation, the facts require' (Chisholm 2019). Since the distinction between podcast and audiobook is ever diminishing in this audience's mind, this represents a very substantial opportunity for audiobook publishers. According to audience research organisation RAJAR, the number of UK adults who listen to a podcast each week increased from 3.2 million (7% of adults) in 2013 to 5.9 million in 2018 (11% of adults). This increase is across all age groups, but the steepest growth in the past year was among 15–34-year-olds, of whom about 18% listen; of those, 62% are male (Ofcom 2019, p. 45).

In early 2019, music streaming service Spotify announced it was to purchase two podcast companies, Gimlet Media and Anchor (Dean 2019). This indicates a new direction for Spotify, and the scale of the acquisition (Spotify paid $230 million) suggests that it sees a strong future in podcasting. Spotify CEO Daniel Ek has been quoted as saying that eventually more than 20% of listening on Spotify would come from non-music content (Duke 2019).

Given, in this writer's view, that podcasting was a key catalyst for the sharp growth of audiobooks post 2015, book publishers should take note. A book publisher is a company that communicates information from someone who has it to someone who wants to know it. Spotify knows its listeners: in January 2019, a student on a Publishing MA course, on work experience in the writer's recording studios, summarised the perception that the millennial audience has of audio material. 'Podcasts have normalised listening to content', she said. 'Everyone around me is listening – some of it will be to music, but a lot will now be to speech'. That correlates with a marked shift in audiobook listeners: in the 1990s the largest part of the market was historical or romantic fiction, and most listeners were women, usually older; the largest group of audiobook listeners now, according to Nielsen, is men from 18 to 35 – very closely reflecting the podcast profile (Watt 2018).

The growth potential is vast: 'It might feel like podcasts are ubiquitous, but, 83 per cent of Americans aren't yet listening to podcasts on a weekly basis, and a majority of them report that's because they simply don't know where to start', said Roger Lynch, Chief Executive Officer of the US streaming service Pandora. 'Making podcasts – both individual episodes and series – easy to discover and simple to experience is how we plan to greatly grow podcast listening while simultaneously creating new and more sustainable ways to monetize them' (Pandora 2019).

Current challenges

Just as for food suppliers to supermarkets, the link between cost of production and selling price has been broken. If dominant retailer Audible presents all audiobooks as being 'worth' the same price, £7.99, the standard member price, then all but the highest profile titles are going to be created at the lowest possible cost. As the number of titles produced rises (and it was more than 40,000 in the UK in 2017, up fourfold from 2011), so the sales of some titles will fall to a few hundred copies as the market saturates. One might argue that the industry does not do enough to educate the listening public about what good value audiobooks are. It takes six to eight times the running time of an audiobook to create one, more if you count the preparation by reader and producer. So a 12-hour production will have required 80–100 hours of work. Yet the total revenue to the publisher from some titles might be only £1,600 (400 sales, average revenue £4) if it is sold through Audible, who may remit as little as 20% to the publisher. Margins and therefore budgets are under pressure.

Audiobook producer May Wuthrich wrote in the February 2015 issue of US audiobook review magazine *Audiofile*:

> While there will always be 'platinum' productions for high-profile audiobooks, should these be reserved solely for a small percentage of books put into the market? I hope not. Put a great audiobook in the hands of a new listener and you have a fan for life; put an audiobook of lesser quality in those same hands and a precious opportunity might be missed.

Audible has for the last three or four years taken the view that in order to appeal to new markets it is beneficial to select as readers actors who are famous in other media - film and television. This has the immediate effect of driving up the expectations of actors' agents about fees payable for audiobooks, since Audible is willing to pay high rates, but it does not always produce good results. Reading an audiobook and acting are closely aligned, but there is one fundamental difference: when the characters in a story are being played one-actor-one-part on stage or film, the responsibility for the overall vision of the production lies with the director, who gives notes to each actor to meld the individual performances towards a coherent whole. That remains true for a play on radio. With an audiobook, responsibility shifts: performers who are going to create compelling listening in a single-voice reading have to have complete visions of the stories in their head, and then 'describe what they see'. An experienced reader will make characterisation decisions when preparing so as to ensure that it is as clear as possible in any dialogue scenes which character is talking. The capacity to create and remember many voices during the course of three or four days reading is one not given to all actors. There are some who are very good at taking notes from a director but apparently not capable of generating or remembering effective characterisations themselves.

As audiobooks have become such a substantial part of publishing – about 5% of the British general publishing market by 2018 (Publishers Association 2019) and 7.9% of US general trade publishing (Anderson 2019) – so there is increasing competition for the audio rights. For much of their history, audiobooks were produced by specialist companies, often the audio branch of a library book supplier. Once mainstream consumer publishers began to have audio lists of their own, so the contract departments would try to acquire the audio rights along with print rights. The print publishers could reasonably argue that their investment in the print book justified their also reaping the growing rewards of the audio market; they could rightly question why an independent audio publisher should benefit from the marketing campaign created and funded by the print publisher, so that in effect the audio publisher was riding on the print publisher's coat-tails. However, authors' agents saw this new competition as an opportunity to increase authors' earnings, and the entry of Audible into the origination of audiobooks has in some cases driven up the advances paid for audio rights to a point where earning out is unlikely.

A report from the media research company Enders, summarised in the *Bookseller* in August 2018, agrees:

> The growth of the audio market is "in no small part thanks to Audible, because the company has opened up the market to people who don't usually buy books, such as young men." However, it also dubbed Audible a "frenemy" for simultaneously "breathing new life" into the market and "putting publishers under pressure". It described its approach to bidding for audio rights and its investment in high-end productions as "aggressive", making it a player "more directly threatening to publishers in audio than Amazon publishing is in written books. While Amazon (e-book and print publishing) mostly picks up a long tail of genre fiction titles, Audible competes for the same [mainstream] authors and titles as incumbents. As a result, publishing audiobooks is more competitive and expensive than ever, prices are lower, and Audible [holds] more and more of the market."
>
> *Cowdrey 2018*

Publisher structure

There was relatively slow recognition within publishing companies that audiobooks could and should be part of their output, but starting in the early 1990s the main publishers started their own audio lists (Penguin UK in 1992, for example). In early years there was often no single audio commissioning editor in a company or group who took an overview, and it would be left to book editors to suggest titles that might work in audio. In this writer's view – observing sometimes at close quarters when producing titles for such companies – a dedicated audio publisher is essential. The skills required are related to print editing, but different.

Providing audio versions of books is increasingly demanded by authors and agents, and offering in-house audio publishing is seen as good author care. In 2014 HarperCollins took the brave step to embark on 'total audio', as they called it, guaranteeing to publish their entire general front list in audio form. HC's Audio Director at the time, Jo Forshaw, successfully argued to the company board that whilst it was inevitable that an appreciable proportion of titles would not break even in the short term, in the longer term sales would benefit from customers knowing that *every* title was available in audio form and it would reap benefits in the way that HarperCollins was perceived (Tivnan and Wood 2015).

This astute policy has been vindicated: in August 2019, the *Bookseller* reported, 'Digital sales [for HarperCollins] increased 7 per cent compared to the prior year, driven by the growth in downloadable audiobook sales, and represented 20 per cent of consumer revenues for the year' (Wood 2019).

It was an indication of how much and how rapidly audio entered the consciousness of senior management that in 2016 Penguin Random House UK established audiobooks as a separate division. Not much earlier it was sometimes necessary to raise awareness within a publishing house about the very existence of its own audio list. This writer knows of audio rights sold off to third-party publishers by rights departments that have not checked with the audio publisher, and it was common that advertising posters did not mention the existence of an audiobook. That has changed remarkably in the last two or three years. In 2018, Macmillan used Twitter to promote the publication of a new 'Shardlake' title by releasing clips from the audio version as the driving force of the campaign. Real integration between print and audio has become a reality, although even now not all senior management seems to appreciate the sometimes very different sales pattern of audio: backlist titles sell relatively far more strongly in audio form and it is not unusual for year 2 sales to be higher than year 1, which would be unusual for a print version.

Some publishers have adapted more than others to the new media landscape. Hachette is perhaps the boldest, having acquired since 2015 not only e-book publisher Bookouture, but also wider entertainment businesses such as the electronic games company, Neon in Britain in 2016, and a (physical) board games company, Gigamic in France in early 2019.

Hachette UK's Digital Director George Walkley talks cogently about the structural changes needed to make such developments work in an Economist Intelligence Unit podcast in January 2019 (Economist Intelligence Unit 2019). He observes (at about 10 min 30s), 'If you make it easy for someone to lay their hands on a product, the likelihood of them spending money on that product increases sharply'. That is why audio has grown so quickly: it has benefited from the perfect storm of new easy-to-use technology and a new podcast-aware audience.

Audio also serves as a bellwether for other digital products: in an interview with the *Bookseller* in February 2019, Madeline McIntosh, head of PRH US since mid-2018, comments: 'Everything we learned about what digital does to the business model – having to look afresh at retail, author compensation, consumer pricing – first happened with audio' (Feldman 2019).

The next major development will be control by smart speaker. Audible books can already be played on Amazon Alexa, and HarperCollins Children's Books have launched StoryCastle, a children's storytelling app available on Google Assistant (HarperCollins 2019). Ofcom observes that

> Beyond their use to access audio content and for ... search, some smart-speaker owners are using their devices to make purchases from online retailers. As the take-up of smart speakers grows, it may also further increase the shift in retail expenditure to online platforms, by shortening the time between the point of decision and the point of transaction. With 45 per cent of smart speaker owners having made at least one purchase via their devices, OC&C [a consultancy company] forecasts that voice-enabled e-commerce will account for £3.5bn, or 3 per cent of online spend in the UK by 2022, up from £0.2bn in 2017.
>
> *Ofcom 2019, p. 43*

Conclusion

For a while at the beginning of the 2010s it was assumed that e-books would displace physical books, a view encouraged by digital commentators like Nicholas Negroponte, who forecast confidently during a television interview subsequently reported on the CNN website in 2010 that '[physical books] will disappear in five years' (Combs 2010). What happened, though, is that after a sharp initial growth, probably due to novelty and better technology becoming available, e-book uptake levelled off. In January 2019, Lagardère (owner of Hachette) reported that e-books represented 7.9% of its revenue, almost the same as its previous year (Chandler 2019).

Despite all the technological changes, and after some uncertainties, the publishing industry has emerged from the last ten years stronger, with a clearer understanding of the relationships between the markets for different media. It also recognises that it has a role in fostering understanding among different groups in an increasingly diverse audience, and as a guardian of information quality in an era of fake news. Sales of print books fell back a little in 2018, to 2016 levels, but the *Publishers Association Yearbook 2018* reports that audiobooks (at publisher income level) rose by 43% over the year (Publishers Association 2019).

The industry has now recognised that it has an expertise in presenting and communicating information of all kinds in all formats ('information' is here used in a semi-technical sense to include fiction and pure entertainment as well as facts). Publishers are now comfortable with the idea that they can generate the expertise in house to create and manage audiobooks rather than thinking they are a distraction best left to others. By interacting astutely with the audience and refining the recordings offered, publishers may further strengthen and consolidate the interest in the medium.

Audiobooks have truly become the fourth format alongside the three textual ones.

Notes

1 It is difficult to give exact figures since in the UK the major retailer of audiobooks is Audible, an Amazon company that does not publish sales figures. The UK figures are compiled from publishers' invoice value.
2 'He wrote to be read aloud in the long Victorian family evenings, and his prose has the lucidity, spontaneity, and pace of good reading material' (Brander 2019).
3 This has since been achieved by optical means, and an 1860 recording of his singing 'Au Clair de la Lune' may be heard at www.firstsounds.org/sounds/Scott-Feaster-No-36.mp3. [Accessed 26 August 2019].
4 Whilst not directly relevant to the subject of this chapter, readers wishing to know more about the possible true origins of Edison's machine may like to read Patrick Feaster's study (Feaster 2007).
5 The figure of 3,000 comes from Rubery (2016); the 30,000 is the writer's estimate, extrapolating from the only exact figures available to him, those for Kent (Kent Association for the Blind 2019), and scaling up for the population of the UK at the time.
6 See Rubery (2016, pp. 75–78) for examples of appreciations and a much fuller discussion of the issues about reading style and the controversy of the legitimacy of 'ear-reading', as it was soon called.
7 A cultural centre founded in 1874, in full the 92nd Street Young Men's and Young Women's Hebrew Association.
8 Personal communication from Michele Cobb, Executive Director of US Audiobook Publishers Association, 4 February 2019.

References

American Foundation for the Blind (2019). 'AFB Talking Book Exhibit.' www.afb.org/about-afb/history/online-museums/afb-talking-book-exhibit [Accessed 27 August 2019].

American Reader (2013). 'Interview with Donald Katz, CEO & Founder of Audible.com by Uzoamaka Maduka.' *The American Reader*, August 2013. http://theamericanreader.com/interview-with-donald-katz-ceo-founder-of-audible-com/ [Accessed 29 August 2019].

Anderson, Porter (2019). 'AAP's StatShot Report for January to June of 2019.' *Publishing Perspectives*, 28 August 2019. https://publishingperspectives.com/2019/08/aap-statshot-report-for-january-to-june-2019-shows-6-billion-in-revenue/ [Accessed 29 August 2019].

Audible (2015). Television commercial. Available at: www.youtube.com/watch?v=T-qVtPN2qRo [Accessed 11 February 2019].

Audiobook Publishers Association [US] (2018). 'Audiobook Fact Sheet 2018.' www.audiopub.org/uploads/pdf/APA-FACT-SHEET-2018.pdf [Accessed 27 August 2019].

Audiobook Publishers Association [US] (2019a). 'Audiobook Fact Sheet 2019.' www.audiopub.org/uploads/pdf/APA-FACT-SHEET-2019.pdf [Accessed 27 August 2019].

Audiobook Publishers Association [US] (2019b). 'Audiobook Industry Sales Survey Key Points 2013–17.' www.audiopub.org/uploads/pdf/APA-Research-2013-2017.pdf [Accessed 28 August 2019].

BBC Radio 4 (2015). 'In Pod We Trust', ep. 3, First Transmitted Saturday 21 November 2015. www.bbc.co.uk/sounds/play/b06ppb2h [Accessed 20 January 2019].

BBC Radio 4 (2016). *Today*, 12 March 2016. Rebecca Jones talks to Michael Morpurgo in the 'Meet the Author' slot. The full interview is no longer available, but a clip is available at: www.bbc.co.uk/programmes/p03mfmmk [Accessed 3 February 2019].

BBC Radio 4 (2018). *Front Row*, 26 October 2018. Janina Ramirez discusses with Sarah Ditum and Sarah Shaffi whether listening to an audiobook counts the same as reading one. Discussion from 00:59 to 11:23 and result at 28:07. www.bbc.co.uk/programmes/m0000v9x [Accessed 1 February 2019].

Beard, Mary (2018). 'Talking Books.' *Times Literary Supplement*, 15 November 2018. Also accessible at: www.the-tls.co.uk/talking-books [Accessed 14 December 2018].

Blind Veterans UK (2019). 'Timeline of Blind Veterans UK.' www.blindveterans.org.uk/about-us/our-history/timeline [Accessed 27 August 2019].

Brander, Laurence (2019). 'Encyclopedia Britannica: William Makepeace Thackeray.' www.britannica.com/biography/William-Makepeace-Thackeray [Accessed 27 August 2019].

Chandler, Mark (2019). 'Hachette Hails "Very Strong" Fourth Quarter.' *The Bookseller*, 7 February 2019. www.thebookseller.com/news/hachette-hails-very-strong-fourth-quarter-lagard-re-reports-2018-decline-945121 [Accessed 29 August 2019].

CHARM [Centre for the History and Analysis of Recorded Music] (2009). 'A Brief History of Recording to ca. 1950.' https://charm.rhul.ac.uk/history/p20_4_1.html [Accessed 27 August 2019].

Children's Records (2019). https://childrensvinyl.wordpress.com [Accessed 28 August 2019].

Chisholm, Jane (2019). 'Out of Control.' *Spectator*, 5 January 2019, p. 36.

Church, Imogen (2016). 'The Explosion of the Audiobook in the Digital Age.' Paper presented at the International Summit of the Book in Limerick, Eire, November 2016. The paper is no longer available online; received by personal communication.

Combs, Cody (2010). 'Will Physical Books Be Gone in Five Years?' *CNN Edition*, 18 October 2010. http://edition.cnn.com/2010/TECH/innovation/10/17/negroponte.ebooks/ [Accessed 18 October 2010].

Cowdrey, Katherine (2018). 'Audible Revenue Soars 45%,' *The Bookseller*, 31 August 2018. www.thebookseller.com/news/audible-grows-revenue-45-over-97m-852751 [Accessed 29 August 2019].

Cyrano de Bergerac (1656). English Translation by Archibald Lovell, 1687. *The Voyage to the Moon*, Chapter 15. Edition of 1899 published by Doubleday, New York. Also available at: www.gutenberg.org/files/46547/46547-h/46547-h.htm [Accessed 27 August 2019].

Dean, James (2019). 'First Profit Hits Right Note at Spotify.' *The Times* [London], 7 February 2019. www.thetimes.co.uk/edition/business/first-profit-hits-right-note-at-spotify-jwcmhb3wv [Accessed 11 February 2019].

Deniz, Fatma, Anwar O. Nunez-Elizalde, Alexander G. Huth, and Jack L. Gallant (2019). 'The Representation of Semantic Information across Human Cerebral Cortex during Listening versus Reading Is Invariant to Stimulus Modality.' *Journal of Neuroscience* 19 August 2019, 0675-19. doi: 10.1523/JNEUROSCI.0675-19.2019 [Accessed 28 August 2019].

Discogs (2019a). 'Listen for Pleasure Label.' www.discogs.com/label/81721-Listen-For-Pleasure [Accessed 29 August 2019].

Discogs (2019b). 'BBC Radio Collection Label.' www.discogs.com/label/58734-BBC-Radio-Collection [Accessed 6 February 2019].

Duke, Simon (2019). 'Music Industry Forced to Change Its Tune.' *The Times* [London], 9 February 2019. www.thetimes.co.uk/article/music- industry-forced-to-change-its-tune-kdr3pb8gj [Accessed 12 February 2019].

Eclair, Jenny (2018). 'Stop the Intellectual Snobbery – Of Course Listening to a Book on Audible Counts as "Reading It".' *Independent*, Monday 29 October 2018.

www.independent.co.uk/voices/books-audible-kindle-listening-radio-4-literature-snobbery-curtis-sittenfeld-a8606476.html [Accessed 28 August 2019].

Economist Intelligence Unit (2019). 'Digital Economy Podcast: Why Digitisation Is Disrupting Your Business Model'. 24 January 2019. https://play.acast.com/s/eiudigitaleconomy/digitaleconomy-whydigitisationisdisruptingyourbusinessmodel [Accessed 8 February 2019].

Edison, Thomas A. (1878). 'The Phonograph and Its Future,' *North American Review*, vol. 126, pp. 527–536. Available from JStor at: https://archive.org/stream/jstor-25110210/25110210_djvu.txt [Accessed 10 January 2019].

Feaster, Patrick (2007). 'Speech Acoustics and the Keyboard Telephone: Rethinking Edison's Discovery of the Phonograph Principle,' *ARSC Journal*, vol. 38, no. 1, pp. 10–43. Accessible at: www.phonozoic.net/speech-acoustics-and-keyboard-telephone.pdf [Accessed 2 February 2019].

Feldman, Gayle (2019). 'McIntosh Begins to Make Her Mark at PRH US,' *The Bookseller*, 8 February 2019, p. 8; also at: www.thebookseller.com/insight/ten-months-after-taking-charge-prh-us-mcintosh-begins-make-her-mark-945221 [Accessed 30 August 2019].

Fraser, Ian (1961). *My Story of St Dunstan's*. London: George G. Harrap.

HarperCollins (2019). Press release: 'Harpercollins Childrens Books Launch Storycastle,' www.harpercollins.co.uk/corporate/press-releases/harpercollins-childrens-books-launch-storycastle-an-innovative-new-app-for-families-on-the-google-assistant [Accessed 7 February 2019].

Have, Iben and Birgitte Stougaard Pedersen (2013). 'Sonic Mediatization of the Book: Affordances of the Audiobook'. *MedieKultur*, vol. 29, no. 54, p. 18. Also available at: https://tidsskrift.dk/mediekultur/article/view/7284 [Accessed 27 August 2019].

Hutton, J. S., et al. (2015). 'Home Reading Environment and Brain Activation in Preschool Children Listening to Stories.' *Pediatrics*, vol. 136, no. 3, pp. 466–478.

Jones, Nicholas (2016). 'Jane Austen's Curtains.' *London Book Fair Daily (Publishers Weekly / BookBrunch)*, 12 April 2016, p. 20. Subsequently published on the BookBrunch website. www.bookbrunch.co.uk/page/free-article/jane-austens-curtains [Accessed: 30 January 2019].

Kent Association for the Blind (2019). 'History.' www.kab.org.uk/about-us/history.html [Accessed 28 August 2019].

Khazan, O. (2011). 'Is Listening to Audio Books Really the Same as Reading?' *Forbes*, 11 September 2011. www.forbes.com/sites/olgakhazan/2011/09/12/is-listening-to-audio-books-really-the-same-as-reading/#7ec40114167a [Accessed 28 August 2019].

Kintsch, W. and E. Kozminsky (1977). 'Summarizing Stories after Reading and Listening.' *Journal of Educational Psychology*, vol. 69, pp. 491–499.

Kipling, Rudyard (1958). *Just So Stories*. Read by Boris Karloff. Caedmon LP TC1139. 'How the First Letter Was Written' has been uploaded to You Tube and is at: https://youtu.be/up_dYmSEfGw [Accessed 27 August 2019].

Koestler, Frances A. (1976). *The Unseen Minority*. New York: David McKay. Figures quoted by Rubery (2016), p. 63.

Kozlowski, Michael (2012). 'Don Katz from Audible Talks about New Content Models.' *Good E-Reader*, April 15, 2012. https://goodereader.com/blog/e-book-news/don-katz-from-audible-talks-about-new-content-models [Accessed 28 August 2019].

Moore, Matthew (2018). 'Parents Become Castaways to Save Memories,' *The Times* (London), 17 December 2018. www.thetimes.co.uk/article/parents-become-radio-castaways-to-save-memories-lcpvtl38h [Accessed 27 January 2019].

National Public Radio [US] (2002). *Morning Edition*, 5 December 2002. Renee Montagne interviews Barbara Holdridge. 'Caedmon: Recreating the Moment of Inspiration.' www.npr.org/templates/story/story.php?storyId=866406 [Accessed 27 August 2019].

Naxos AudioBooks (2019). Sleeve notes to 'Under Milk Wood and other plays'. Also available at: www.naxosaudiobooks.com/under-milk-wood-and-other-plays-unabridged/ [Accessed 28 August 2019].

New York Daily Graphic (1878). 2 April 1878, p. 1. Reproduced in Rubery 2016.

Norton, Lucy and Hubert Wellington (1995). *The Journal of Eugène Delacroix* [English translation]. London: Phaidon Press.

Ofcom (2019). *Communications Market Report 2018*. London: Ofcom.

Oxford Dictionaries (2006). 'Words of the Year.' https://en.oxforddictionaries.com/word-of-the-year/word-of-the-year-faqs [Accessed 12 February 2019].

Page, Benedicte (2013). 'AudioGO Files for Administration.' *The Bookseller*, 28 October 2013. www.thebookseller.com/news/audiogo-files-administration [Accessed 29 August 2019].

Pandora (2019). Press Release: http://press.pandora.com/file/4247784/Index?KeyFile= 395749528 [Accessed 30 January 2019, but no longer available following the purchase of Pandora by Sirius XM].

Publishers Association (2019). *PA Publishing Yearbook 2018*, section 1.5. London: Publishers Association. Also at: www.publishers.org.uk/resources/yearbook/ [Accessed 27 August 2019].

Publishers Association Audio Publishers Group (2013). Minutes of a meeting of 2 July 2013 (attended by the writer) at which RNIB representative reported a survey carried out by Loughborough University.

Recorded Books (2019). 'Recorded Books – Our Story.' www.recordedbooks.com/Company/Our-Story [Accessed 28 August 2019].

Richardson, Daniel C., Nicole K. Griffin, et al. (2018). 'Measuring Narrative Engagement: The Heart Tells the Story.' *bioRxiv 351148*. doi: 10.1101/351148 [Accessed 27 August 2019].

RNIB [Royal National Institute for Blind People] (2019). 'Our History.' www.rnib.org.uk/who-we-are/history-rnib [Accessed 27 August 2019].

Rubery, Matthew (2016). *The Untold Story of the Talking Book*. Cambridge, MA and London: Harvard University Press.

Serial (2019). 'About Serial.' https://serialpodcast.org/about [Accessed 29 August 2019].

Soundrecordinghistory.net (2019). 'Phonautograph History.' www.soundrecordinghistory.net/history-of-sound-recording/phonautograph-history/ [Accessed 27 August 2019].

Thorpe, Vanessa (2019). 'Listeners and Stars Up in Arms as BBC Sounds App Backfires.' *Observer*, 20 January 2019. www.theguardian.com/media/2019/jan/20/bbc-sounds-app-angry-listeners-complaints [Accessed 28 August 2019].

Tivnan, Tom and Felicity Wood (2015). 'Audiobooks Making the Right Noises.' *The Bookseller*, 16 July 2015. Also accessible at: www.thebookseller.com/news/audiobooks-making-right-noises-307444 [Accessed 31 August 2019].

Ulverscroft (2019). 'Ulverscroft: Our History.' www.ulverscroft.com/history.php [Accessed 28 August 2019].

Watt, Jon (2018). 'Legacy of Success.' *Bookseller Online*, 16 November 2018. www.thebookseller.com/blogs/legacy-success-894006 [Accessed 29 August 2019].

WebTalk Radio (2005). 'Don Katz: Web Talk. Rob Greenlee Speaks with Don Katz, founder and CEO of Audible Inc.,' 9 May 2005. http://web.archive.org/web/20130729212538id_/http://itc.conversationsnetwork.org/shows/detail546.html [Accessed 3 February 2019].

Wikimedia Commons (2019). 'iPod Sales per Quarter.' https://commons.wikimedia. org/wiki/File:Ipod_sales_per_quarter.svg [Accessed 28 August 2019].

Wikipedia (2019a). 'National Library for the Blind.' https://en.wikipedia.org/wiki/ National_Library_for_the_Blind [Accessed 27 August 2019].

Wikipedia (2019b). 'National Library for the Blind (United States).' https://en.wikipedia.org/ wiki/National_Library_for_the_Blind_(United_States) [Accessed 27 August 2019].

Wikipedia (2019c). 'Argo Records (UK).' https://en.wikipedia.org/wiki/Argo_Records_ (UK) [Accessed 17 February 2019].

Wikipedia (2019d). 'Books on Tape (company).' https://en.wikipedia.org/wiki/Books_ on_Tape_(company) [Accessed 28 August 2019].

Wikipedia (2019e). 'Don Katz.' https://en.wikipedia.org/wiki/Don_Katz [Accessed 28 August 2019].

Wikipedia (2019f). *In Our Time* (radio series). https://en.wikipedia.org/wiki/In_Our_ Time_(radio_series) [Accessed 3 February 2019].

Wilson, P. (1935). 'Technical Talk: Talking Books.' *Gramophone*, vol. 13, no. 150, pp. 252–253.

Wood, Heloise (2019). 'HarperColins Sees Flat Annual Sales But Record EBITDA.' *The Bookseller*, 9 August 2019. www.thebookseller.com/news/harpercollins-sees-flat-annual-sales-1062356 [Accessed 30 August 2019].

15

FRENCH CHILDREN'S LITERATURE AND AUTISM

A case for more children's books on autism and for autistic children

Lucie Ducarre

Introduction: justification for research

The ability that books have to allow us to escape loneliness and to learn about ourselves and others has been a joyful relief to me since my early childhood. This is probably why I have read so much and so early and why, once grown up, I chose to study publishing. The power books have regarding our understanding of and relationship to the world is also probably why diversity in children's literature has become a growing issue in the last few years (Eyre, 2015; Johnson, 2016; Rosen, 2017). Indeed, studies have found that reading is a relevant tool to address social justice issues, including those within the school curriculum. Although books alone cannot fight against discrimination, they are indeed effective tools for parents and teachers to promote tolerance, prevent bullying, and educate children on human diversity (Artman-Meeker et al., 2016, p. 151). However, if recent improvements have been made regarding cultural or ethnic diversity (Smith-D'Arezzo, 2003), studies still point out a lack of children's books on disability or neuro-diversity (Brenna, 2009; Nasatir and Horn, 2003, p. 8).

I first realised how few French children's books there were on autism and for autistic children while I was searching for those types of books for a young autistic child I was volunteering with. Indeed, most of the available books were in English or originated from French Canada. I already knew that France was lagging behind most developed countries in its perceptions and treatment of autism and I realised that the lack of cultural resources on the subject was likely to perpetuate this situation. When looking at academic publications, I found several related studies on the issue of diversity in children's literature, including one examining the representations of autism in books for young adults, but I did not find any studies specifically researching the lack of children's literature on autism or studying this specific issue in relation to France. This dissertation will therefore address the following research question: is there a market for more children's books on autism and books for autistic children in France? Accordingly, the literature review will explain and support why and how these books could help autistic children in their development and inclusion. The primary research will investigate the available offer and the potential demand for more of these books. The dissertation starts with the recognition that other media can also play an important role in the development and inclusion of autistic children, and it is acknowledged that there are other urgent and important issues regarding autism in France and worldwide. However, publishing children's books on autism and for autistic children is what publishers can – and some might say should – do in order to improve autistic people's well-being.

Research scope, methods, and definitions

The aim of this paper is to explore the hypothesis that there is a market for more children's books on autism and for autistic children in France. To do so, it will present an inventory of the available books published by French publishers, a survey of parents of autistic children, a survey of parents in general, and interviews with professionals specialised in the fields of autism and/or publishing.

The research focusses on books for children aged 0–10 years old because this period, being this of pre-school and elementary school, is crucial for the socialisation of children. Indeed, studies show that children construct negative perceptions of their disabled peers at an early age and that the earliest interventions and education are undertaken to modify these constructions, the more likely they are to be effective (Nasatir and Horn, 2003, p. 10). Similarly, early interventions – which can be supported by the use of books – are also crucial for autistic children's development. It appears then essential to have books on autism and for autistic children aiming at this age range.

To categorise the books studied, I will use the terms Children's Books on Autism (CBoA), which includes fiction books and awareness books, and Books for Autistic Children (BfAC), which includes skills books and adapted books. These categories can be defined as follows:

- **Children's Books on Autism** (aimed at both autistic and non-autistic children):
  - **Fiction books** with characters identified as autistic (within the narration or in the blurb)
  - **Awareness books** aiming at explaining and informing about autism.
- **Books for Autistic Children:**
  - **Skills books** aiming at improving communicative, emotional, and social skills
  - **Adapted books** respectful of autistic children's sensory perceptual specificities. It is to be noted that adapted books are defined by their format, materials, and structure and can cover any subject (including skills learning, awareness, or fiction, whether on autism or not).

While many autistic people and specialists argue against it, in France as in many countries, autism is officially recognised as a disability and it will therefore be referred as such in this dissertation. While the latest appellation used by the Diagnostic and Statistical Manual of Mental Disorders (American Psychiatric Association, 2013) is now 'autism spectrum disorder' (ASD), the term 'autism' (encompassing all the continuum or spectrum) will be used in this study because it is better known from the general population and appears less nomenclatural. Finally, this paper will refer to 'autistic children' and 'autistic person' rather than 'children/person with autism' as it appears to be the terminology preferred by autistic people themselves (Couture and Penn, 2003, p. 19).

Contextualisation: autism and its perceptions

Autism is a neurodevelopmental disorder, impairing the sensory, cognitive, communicative, and social skills of an individual (Bogdashina, 2013; Center for Disease Control and Prevention, 2017b; Inserm, 2017; Vander Wiele, 2011). The causes of autism remain so far unknown, although most of the experts now agree on the neurobiological origin of the disorder (Markram and Markram, 2010). However, autism is still included in the Diagnostic and Statistical Manual of Mental Disorders (American Psychiatric Association, 2013), which in its latest version conceives autism as a continuum with different and evolving degrees of severity.

It appears important to highlight that intellectual disability is not a symptom of autism. However, the prevalence of intellectual disability in the autistic population seems higher than in the general population. Establishing the exact prevalence rate remains difficult. The Center for Autism Research estimates it at 38% of the autistic population (2017) but this rate can vary from 15% to 70% between different studies (Volkmar et al., 2005). This difficulty is exacerbated by the fact that autism symptoms may significantly impair autistic people's IQ score without actually corresponding to an intellectual deficiency.

The prevalence of autism is of about 1% of the world population (Brugha et al., 2016; Center for Disease Control and Prevention, 2017a). Studies highlight that this incidence has been increasingly accelerating since the last 10–20 years (Barillas, 2014; World Health Organisation, 2017). However, these variations can probably be explained by the better availability and effectiveness of diagnoses rather than by a real increase in the prevalence rate per se. Studies also forecast a crisis in the supply of education and support for autistic people (Moffat, 2003, p. 22; World Health Organisation, 2017). In France, it is estimated that there are currently 100,000 autistic youth aged under 20 years old, including 30,000 in early childhood (Inserm, 2017).

Main theories on autism

The term 'autistic' was first used in modern medicine by Dr Eugen Bleuler, in the beginning of the twentieth century, to describe schizophrenic patients displaying a total self-centred functioning. A few years later, Dr Leo Kanner (1943), who was working in Baltimore with allegedly deficient children, realised that these children were not clinically retarded but instead showed both areas of normal to high intellectual development and areas of great deficit. What is more, they displayed similar untypical behaviours and seemed especially impaired in the area of emotional development. At the same time, Dr Hans Asperger, an Austrian paediatrician, was reporting in the German journal *Archiv für Psychiatrie and Nervenkrankheiten* (1944) his work with young adults labelled as 'socially blind'. He described them as unable to express or react to emotional display, abnormally focussed on restrictive and repetitive behaviours and interests, and especially clumsy (Ritvo, 2006). Both of them borrowed the term 'autistic' from Bleuler and applied it to their patients, developing the first theories of autism. It took almost 50 years for the study of Asperger to be translated in English (Frith, 1991) and in the meantime, Kanner's analysis was altered and perverted, partly by restrictive psychoanalytic interpretations (Dachez, 2016). Consequently, for the major part of the twentieth century, the view of autism was of a non-communicative retarded patient. It is worth noting that, although the High Authority for Health[1] is encouraging developmental and behavioural therapies, and while other developed countries have been prioritising these approaches for years, psychoanalysis is still the main treatment offered to autistic children in France (Harris, 2016). The situation is so serious that, in December 2016, a hundred of deputies – unsuccessfully – submitted a legislative proposal to no longer reimburse psychoanalytic therapies for autistic children (Le Point, 2016).

Another example of the numerous past and present misbeliefs about autism may be found in its supposed link with vaccines. Indeed, in the late 1990s, Andrew Wakefield, a British medical researcher, and 12 of his colleagues published a study suggesting a link between vaccines and autism (Wakefield et al., 1998). Shortly after that, a number of theories emerged asserting that vaccines were causing autism (Taylor et al., 2014). Although the initial study was refuted by a number of its authors themselves (Murch et al., 2004), and their publisher (Eggertson, 2010), and subsequently exposed as a fraud (Sathyanarayana Rao and Andrade, 2011), and while these assertions have now been definitively contradicted by scientific studies (Center for Disease Control and Prevention, 2017c), they still remain present in people's minds (Stone, 2010).

Besides these damaging theories, different scientific concepts have been proposed to analyse and understand the specificities of the autistic functioning. As one example, Dr Simon Baron-Cohen introduced the concept of the deficit in Theory of Mind (ToM) in 1995. This concept argues that, for different possible reasons, autistic people struggle to acknowledge other people's mental states and to understand and treat other people's feelings, beliefs, and wishes, especially when they differ from their own (Morris, 2015, pp. 16–18). Another key concept of the autistic functioning, the theory of Weak Central Coherence (WCC), was developed by Uta Frith in the late 1980s (Frith, 1989). It maintains that autistic people would have a flawed perception of themselves and a fragmented perception of the world (Morris, 2015, p. 20) leading to a deficit in contextualisation and transferability.

In parallel, a number of theories focussing on an altered sensory and cognitive perception in autism have emerged over time. Indeed, Kanner (1943) and Asperger (1944) themselves had noticed sensory symptoms among the children they studied. Since then, a growing number of studies have regularly highlighted the relationship between sensory-integrative dysfunction and autism (Markram and Markram, 2010; Mottron et al., 2006). For some experts, autism might be a perceptual and sensorial disorder rather than a social disorder (Bogdashina, 2013, p. 33).

Finally, in recent years, Henry and Kamila Markram (2010) have offered a supplementary view of the autistic functioning through the Intense World Theory. This theory argues that due to a hyper-functioning of local neural microcircuits, autistic brains would experience 'hyper-reactivity' and 'hyper-plasticity' causing 'hyper-perception', 'hyper-attention', 'hyper-memory', and 'hyper-emotionality' leading to autism symptoms. In the same direction, Mottron et al. (2006) designed the Enhanced Perceptual Functioning model, relying on autistic brain's specificities and hyper-performance to explain autism symptoms.

School inclusion, and institutional and social perceptions of autism in France

Many international and European texts – such as The International Covenant on Economic, Social and Cultural Rights (UN, 1966), the Convention on the Rights of the Child (UN, 1989), the Convention of the Rights of Persons with Disabilities (UN, 2006), or the Resolution on the education and social inclusion of children and young people with autism spectrum disorders (Council of Europe, 2007) – stipulate the right of children with disability to education and to be protected against discrimination.

In line with these treaties, the French Constitution requires the state to 'provide free, non-religious public education at every level' (European Agency for Special Needs and Inclusive Education). In addition, French legislation, through the 2005 *Act on the equal rights and opportunities* and the Articles L112-1 to L112-5 of the Education Code, asserts the right for children with disability to schooling. The 2013 *Framework Act on the Reform of the Schools of the Republic* specifically mentions the principle of an inclusive school and recalls the right to every child to be schooled in his/her closest mainstream school.

However, despite its legislation and unlike most of other developed countries, France is regularly accused of violating the right to education of autistic children. Since 2004, France has been condemned five times by the Council of Europe for discrimination against autistic people, including violations of their educational rights (Alliance Autiste, 2015). In its Resolution of the 5 February 2014, the Committee of Ministers (Council of Europe) unanimously concluded that France was violating the right to education of autistic children because they were not educated primarily in mainstream schools, and because of the lack of educational work offered in specialised institutions (Council of Europe, 2014). Similarly, the UN's Committee on the Rights of Child has criticised France for massively institutionalising autistic children (Harris, 2016). French courts themselves have condemned the State to financially remedy to the moral prejudice its deficiency in providing a proper education has caused to numerous families of autistic children (AFP, 2015).

Indeed, studies report that only 20%–30% of autistic children are schooled in mainstream schools, whether full-time or part-time and within ordinary or specialised classes (Alliance Autiste, 2015, p. 4; Harris, 2016; Horiot, 2016). By comparison, this rate is around 70% in the UK (Ambitious about Autism, 2017) and around 80% in the US and Canada (Horiot, 2016). In France however, 70%–80% of autistic children are sent to medical institutions, receive home schooling, or have to leave France to seek a proper education (Alliance Autiste, 2015). What is more, studies also highlight that in a worrying number of cases, children are only registered to their mainstream school but do not actually attend classes there because of the ineffectiveness of the education provided or due to the unwelcoming attitude of the staff (Alliance Autiste, 2015). Studies also indicate that, regarding school inclusion, discrimination against autism is higher than discrimination against the disabled population in general. Indeed, the average rate of inclusion within mainstream schools for the general disabled population is of 70% (INSEE, 2017). Public institutes themselves recognise that school is less inclusive for autistic children than for disabled children in general (Compagnon et al., 2017, p. 47).

This worrying situation may result from a number of different factors. Associations regularly point out the lack of human support and resources as well as the lack of training and education about autism offered to teachers and schools' staff (Alliance Autiste, 2015). These deficiencies also illustrate how autism is perceived by the French institutions. Indeed, families support groups regularly denounce the oppression they suffer from public institutions. An illustration can be found in the scandals of the abusive placements in foster care of autistic children, regularly denounced by media and associations (Langloys, 2015).

Similarly, media often depict a very restrictive view of autism, oscillating between this of a non-verbal retarded children and this of a precocious gifted genius. Journalists also sometimes convey a very negative perception of autism (Dachez, 2016). As one example, during a very popular TV show in February 2017, one of the presenters V. Burggraf, in reference to a child character in a movie, stated that he was 'autistic'. When the film director answered that, no, he wasn't and asked why she would think that, she replied: 'Come on, he really isn't in a good shape {…} You don't want to say that he has a problem {…} but he is utterly dumb' (de Montalivet, 2017; Author's translation).

French society meanwhile seems to have a rather more informed perception of autism and predominantly recognises it as a neurological disorder (OpinionWay, 2012). However, studies show that a significant proportion of the French population (48%) considers that the place of autistic people is in medico-social establishments (OpinionWay, 2012). This can be partly explained by the general negative perception of diversity within the French culture. As highlighted by the Alliance Autiste (a French NGO encouraging mutual support and cooperation between autistic people), French society is not open to differences and diversity in general. 'It seems natural that someone "different" has to live apart (leave society to live in an institution), instead of changing the society to encourage the inclusion of all, each one with their own particularities' (2015, p. 5).

However, there seems to be a recent shift in this trend. Indeed, thanks to the launch of the 4th Autism Plan[2] (INS HEA, 2017) and the increasing involvement of autistic personalities (such as Hugo Horiot or Alexandra Reynaud, for example), autism is slowly becoming a subject of interest to the French society (Europe 1, 2017). This might represent a real opportunity to obtain better support from institutions and to educate the general population on autism. This might therefore also open a window for more books on autism or aimed at autistic people.

Children's literature and autism: books as a tool for autistic children's inclusion and development

The issue of diversity in children's books has been pointed out for several years now (Eyre, 2015; Johnson, 2016; Rosen, 2017) and recent improvements regarding cultural and ethnic diversity have proved to be useful to develop children's understanding and acceptance of other's culture (Smith-D'Arezzo, 2003). Indeed, studies report that narrative fiction positively impacts empathy and behaviour towards one another (Johnson et al., 2013, p. 306). Reading books with look-alike characters also help children develop their sense of belonging and their self-esteem (Shedlosky-Shoemaker et al., 2014).

After having focussed mainly on ethnic or cultural diversity, the debate now embraces more types of diversity, including special needs, disabilities, and mental illness (Smith-D'Arezzo, 2003). Stigma against people suffering from mental illness is common in Western societies (Couture and Penn, 2003). Although autism is now widely recognised as a neurological disorder, it is still included in the Diagnostic and Statistical Manual of Mental Disorders, and socially perceived both as a disability and as a mental illness (Dachez, 2016). Consequently, autistic people suffer from isolation and social stigma and studies have found that, from an early age, autistic people display a higher level of anxiety and a considerably lower self-esteem than the general population (Cooper et al., 2017, p. 3). Therefore, it appears that promoting CBoA might help changing future generations' attitude towards autism and reinforcing both autistic children's self-esteem and social inclusion.

The importance of books in building self-esteem, empathy, and inclusion: the need for children's books on autism

Different theories explain the mechanisms that allow readers to connect with fictional characters and to improve their acceptance of both themselves and others. The concept of parasocial relations, for example, was first proposed by Donald Horton and Richard Wohl in the 1950s (Giles, 2010, p. 3). It explains how an individual can develop emotional bonds with a fictional character. Indeed, Gallese and Lakoff have demonstrated that 'action, perception and imagination of the same action trigger the same neural networks' (in Park, 2008, p. 236). Therefore, imagining something through narration might have a similar neural impact than living it. Fictional characters theories relying on identification or empathy also demonstrate how an individual can share the emotions, challenges, and successes of a look-alike character or come to acknowledge, understand, and connect with an alien character (Hoorn and Konijn, 2003, p. 285). Studies show that self-identification – allowing sense of belonging – with fictional characters is likely to happen when these characters are representative of the 'individual actual self', whereas self-expansion – allowing to learn new understandings and knowledge – happens with characters representative of an 'individual ideal self' (Shedlosky-Shoemaker et al., 2014, p. 572). Parasocial relationships can also help developing positive individual and collective identifications and therefore compensate for social discrimination (*Ibid.*, p. 557). In addition, fictional characters, through their actions and successes, may increase the well-being of their readers and allow them to safely learn the appropriate behaviour in specific situations as well as exploring their own emotions (Hoorn and Konijn, 2003, p. 251).

Therefore, literature informing about autism or featuring autistic characters might help autistic children's self-esteem and identity. Authors have pointed out the importance for disabled children to feel that they are not alone (Brenna, 2009, p. 15). Conversely, studies underline that the lack of characters displaying their disability in mainstream literature could impact negatively the development of their self-identity and reinforce their feeling of isolation (Artman-Meeker et al., 2016, p. 155). These observations appear especially relevant to autistic children. Because of their difficulties regarding social situations and communication, autistic children often experience social rejection and isolation. This isolation then prevents them for developing social skills, entertaining a vicious circle, and hammering both their development and self-esteem. Awareness books informing them about autism would help them decrease their sense of guilt and understand their weaknesses and strengths. It would also allow them to realise that their difficulties are to some extent shared by thousands of other children and result from a condition rather than from their personal insufficiencies. In parallel, fiction books with autistic characters would allow them to experiment and gain skills related to social situations without being exposed to rejection or further stigmatisation (Shedlosky-Shoemaker et al., 2014, p. 557). Furthermore, through self-identification, autistic children would benefit from the successes achieved by their look-alike characters and share the pride for their specific strengths and resources. As Park states 'narrative as an imaginative practice may be integral to the healing and transformation of belonging for individuals facing the contingencies of chronic illness or lifelong disability' (2008, p. 248). Awareness books and fiction books with autistic characters can also allow autistic children to develop a positive autistic collective and social identity, which studies have found to positively impact autistic individuals' self-esteem (Cooper et al., 2017). It is important to underline that autistic children are a lot more than just autistic and can also identify themselves with non-autistic characters displaying other similarities – for example, interest for a specific sport, art, or subject, etc. However, considering the rejection they suffer specifically because of their autistic condition, it would appear important to provide them with examples and reassertions that autistic people can be successful and loved.

Similarly, awareness and fiction books on autism could help autistic children by promoting their inclusion. As demonstrated by Corrigan et al., 'individuals who are relatively more familiar with mental illness, either through school learning or experience with peers and family members are less likely to endorse prejudicial attitude about this group' (Corrigan et al., 2001, p. 223). Studies have found that indirect exposure – such as through books – to children with disabilities can enhance non-disabled children's perceptions and attitudes towards them (Nasatir and Horn, 2003, p. 3). Indeed, disability literature can inspire empathy (Yeager, 2010) and authors report that book characters may be used to introduce children to disability (Smith-D'Arezzo, 2003, p. 75). Disabled characters offer non-disabled children a way to engage with disability and thus to develop empathy, entrancement, and connectedness with disabled children (Brenna, 2009). Furthermore, reading plays a great part in building a diverse community and in enabling children to respect and understand others (Brenna, 2009, p. 16).

Although each reader responds to a book according to his/her own personal and cultural background (Smith-D'Arezzo, 2003), it then appears that children's books informing about autism or with autistic characters could indeed introduce children to autism. These books could then be used as a support for educational interventions (Couture and Penn, 2003), and help parents, educators, and teachers fighting against prejudice and promoting tolerance towards autistic children (Smith-D'Arezzo, 2003, p. 75). In parallel, these books could allow autistic children to have a better understanding and representation of their individual and collective identity, and to improve their self-esteem.

To be effective however, the anticipated books should represent quality literature (Smith-D'Arezzo, 2003, p. 76) with, for example, a real plot and realistic characterisations (Blaska and Lynch, 1998; Heim, 1994; Smith-D'Arezzo, 2003, p. 87). Indeed, children's literature has for a long time conveyed stereotypical individual and social constructions of children with disabilities (Brenna, 2009, p. 4). Stereotypes can here be defined as an 'oversimplified generalisation about a particular disability group or type that usually carries derogatory implications' (Nasatir and Horn, 2003, p. 6). These stereotypical representations of disabled children can prevent identification and reinforce discriminations (Smith-D'Arezzo, 2003, p. 88), and it appears crucial, when publishing CBoA, to avoid such stereotypes. Thus, disability must be represented in a realistic and appropriate manner while preserving a positive approach (Artman-Meeker et al., 2016, p. 152). Likewise, disabled characters should not have to display extraordinary skills to compensate for their disability (Nasatir and Horn, 2003, p. 7). They should be granted self-determination to the same extent that characters without disability would be (Artman-Meeker et al., 2016, p. 152; Flood, 2011). They should also be allowed not to be perfect and even sometimes bad or mean, without this being linked to their specific condition (Brenna, 2009, p. 14). A distinction should also be made between awareness books – potentially using fictional characters considering their targeted group age but focussing and informing on the disability – and fiction books displaying characters with disabilities while offering a disability-free plot (Brenna, 2009, p. 8; Hood, 2015). Finally, attention should be given to include cultural and gender diversity as well (Artman-Meeker et al., 2016, p. 152; Flood, 2011).

CBoA should therefore be cautious not to spread a stereotyped – even if positive – representation of autistic children. For example, while allowing a narrative approach to the autistic condition and underlining the specific strengths and abilities of autistic children, it should not systematically associate autism and giftedness. Likewise, it should allow autistic characters to be liked and included without being maths, languages, or music genius. There should also be a balance between awareness books addressing and informing about autism and fiction books with autistic characters focussing on a totally different plot. Finally, it appears that in any case, parents, teachers, or educators should be attentive to children's individual and collective reactions and should complete the reading with discussions (Artman-Meeker et al., 2016, p. 157).

Autistic children's communicative, social, cognitive, and sensory perceptual specificities and their possible implications for reading: the usefulness of books for autistic children

Every day autistic children experience social and communicative challenges. What would appear as a normal social situation to most children, potentially a stressful one for shy children, represents a chaotic, threatening event for autistic children. Indeed, while the causes and mechanisms involved are yet to be precisely determined, and though each child experiences these difficulties in a specific way, autistic children then face many challenges to make sense of the world surrounding them and to interact with others.

First of all, it is important to note that a part of autistic children are non or semi-verbal, meaning that they do not use verbal language to communicate (Wodka et al., 2013). Books or other printed material have proved to be a successful support to help these children to communicate and gradually acquire speaking (Hogan, 2017; Long, nd).

Partly because of their lack of ability in contextualisation and transferability, autistic children display a high rigidity, translating into specific interests, strict routines, and repetitive and stereotyped behaviours (Plimley et al., 2007). This rigidity can affect their communicative and social skill as well. For example, when they have found an activity that pleases them, autistic children might want to do it repetitively in the exact same way and sequence order, regardless of what their playmates may want or express. Similarly, they may be keen to talk endlessly about their subject of interest, even if their interlocutor is clearly non-responsive (Plimley et al., 2007). These types of behaviours may be really annoying to other children and may significantly impact autistic children's ability to maintain relationships with their peers or even with adults.

Similarly, autistic children also are in difficulty with social norms and interactions (Quinn and Malone, 2011, pp. 43–56; Shore and Rastelli, 2015, p. 274). For example, they do not know how to initiate or entertain a conversation, how to physically join a group, or leave it; they do not understand politeness conventions; they struggle to identify and handle their own and other people's emotions and to express their feelings (Shore and Rastelli, 2015, p. 288) – which is then often casted as a lack of empathy. These are so much other skills they thus need help to understand and learn.

Another specificity interfering with autistic children's communication and sociability is their literal understanding. Indeed, autistic children tend to understand sentences, words, or idioms literally (Shore and Rastelli, 2015). This then greatly disturbs their ability to communicate with others. Another consequence of their literal understanding is that autistic children cannot identify when a person is lying or exaggerating the same way a child of the same age would (Shore and Rastelli, 2015, p. 292). Conversely, they are alien to any form of 'little white lies' and can therefore appear as rude (Quinn and Malone, 2011, p. 115). Finally, this literal understanding, combined with their inability to seek comfort and help (Plimley et al., 2007), makes them especially vulnerable to any kind of abuses and abusers, ranging from bullies to sexual predators (Goldberg Edelson, 2010).

These challenges should be taken into account when establishing the content of BfAC. It indeed appears that it would be beneficial for autistic children to have access to dedicated skills books to help them in the language, emotional, and social areas. Although a lot of children's books focus on language and vocabulary acquisition and emotions management, they might not fit autistic children's requirements. Indeed, autistic children might need a deeper analysis an explanation, unravelling every communicative, emotional, or social component a lot more acutely than a classic children's book would do. In addition, because autistic children have difficulties transferring knowledge between similar but not identical situations, it might be helpful to offer a few blank pages at the end of each story where the child – with the help of the reader – could apply the story/lesson he/she has read to its own friends, teachers, or school, using pictures or photos if necessary. Blank spaces or removable illustrations could also be used to allow sticking photos of faces, places, or specific objects within the narration. This could be declined into an electronic format with e-books in which the user could upload its personal photos to create and/or replay the stories. Finally, considering the vulnerability of autistic children, it would be worth considering covering subjects as manipulation, bullying and inappropriate behaviours, including sexual ones, to allow them to identify these behaviours as such and to report them.

In Anglo-Saxon countries, experts have already acknowledged the specific needs of autistic children and the role that books and published materials may play in their language, emotional, and social learning. For example PECS (Picture Exchange Communication System), Power Cards, and Social Stories have been used to improved autistic children's communication and social skills (Kokina and Kern, 2010; Mancil et al., 2009; Tien, 2008; Xin and Sutman, 2011). Consequently, publishers directly provide customable PECS books, power cards, and social stories and publish guide books on the subject.

PECS has been developed by Andrew Bondy and Lori Frost in 1985 and consists in developing communication between a non-verbal or semi-verbal autistic child and a communicative partner by exchanging pictures. The system contains different and progressive phases that rely on initiating rather than responding, and mimics the logic and construction of spoken language in order to eventually acquire speech (Tien, 2008).

Power Cards are used to decrease social anxiety and inappropriate behaviours by capitalising on the child specific interest or favourite character. The aim is to allow the child to feel more comfortable and included, especially at home, school or in any kind of group (Gagnon, 2001). The SMSD ASD Support (2017), one major provider of Power Cards, described them as following:

> A brief text or story that is related to the special interest, person or character is combined with an illustration and made into a small, portable card, such as a bookmark or business card, that the child can carry with him and refer to whenever necessary.

Social Stories were first created by Carol Gray and are written to explain concepts, social situations, and expected and appropriate behaviours to autistic children (Kokina and Kern, 2010; Mancil et al., 2009). Studies have found them especially efficient in decreasing problematic behaviours (Kokina and Kern, 2010). Typically, a social story must include descriptive, perspective, directive, cooperative, affirmative, and control sentences with a recommended ratio of one directive sentence to at least two sentences of the other types by story (Kokina and Kern, 2010). It is also helpful to include pictures (*Ibid.*) and sometimes to personalise it, using photos of the child, of his/her peers and background. Electronic formats have also proved to be as efficient and favoured by autistic children for delivering social stories (Mancil et al., 2009), and they may likewise allow a more interactive use of the stories.

In addition to social and communicative difficulties, autistic children also experience cognitive and sensory perceptual disorders. These disorders may affect both their internal sensorial perception (that is, their proprioception – perception of stimuli within an organism, especially those connected with the position and movement of the body – and their vestibular abilities – sense of balance) and their external sensorial perception (that is, sight, hearing, smell, taste, and touch) (Shore and Rastelli, 2015, p. 224).

As for the other symptoms of autism, we can observe a continuum of sensory perceptual disorders in autistic people (Bogdashina, 2013, p. 236; Pellicano, 2013; Quinn and Malone, 2011, pp. 71–73). However, the main differences from a non-autistic functioning that have been observed include hyper or hypo sensibilities (Pellicano, 2013), fluctuation between different levels of perception (Pellicano, 2013; Rogers and Ozonoff, 2005), and difficulties to interpret and make sense of the data perceived (Bogdashina, 2013, p. 63). These differences may then lead to various responses. The first and very common is a sensorial mono-treatment (*Ibid.*, p. 116) leading to the impossibility to treat input from, and therefore use, two senses at the same time. For example a lot of autistic people explain that if they try to look at a person's eyes while she is talking to them, they cannot hear – or at least make sense of – what she is saying. Other responses might include a peripheral perception resulting from an avoidance of the direct perception that is too intense for the subject or, when the other strategies are not compensating enough a – temporary – sensorial shutdown (*Ibid.*, p. 115). On a cognitive level, this perceptual difference often leads to a delayed treatment of the information perceived (Bogdashina, 2013, p. 110) as well as to a fragmented perception and a focalisation on details rather than on the global information, especially regarding the conceptual area (Ozonof and coll., 1994 in Bogdashina, 2013, p. 68). Concerning the attention profile, autistic children are often also diagnosed with attention deficit hyperactivity disorder (ADHD). However, studies suggest that their attention specificities might result from an idiosyncratic focalisation – high focalisation on irrelevant information – and from slowness in moving their attention focus rather than from an actual deficit in attention or hyperactivity (Bogdashina, 2013, pp. 140–142).

As stated above, autistic children might experience sensory perceptual disorders with any of their senses. However, sight is one of the senses in which the disorders seem the most common and intense. As an example, a study carried out by Walker and Cantello (1994, in Bogdashina, 2013, p. 37) has showed that 81% of the autistic participants reported differences in visual perception. Another study conducted by Irlen revealed that at least 50% of autistic children might have a scotopic sensitivity (Shore and Rastelli, 2015, p. 228). Concerning their sight, the most current disorders that autistic people report is hyper or hypo sensitivity to light, a difficulty to differentiate background and foreground and to perceive contrasts and a difficulty to perceive a global picture, especially if made of different significant individual elements (Bogdashina, 2013). Autistic people also report difficulties to read non-verbal language and facial expressions and to recognise faces (Plimley et al., 2007; Quinn and Malone, 2011).

Notwithstanding these perceptual specificities, experts have found that autistic people seem to have a high reliance on vision and an enhanced visual functioning (Samson et al., 2012; Shore and Rastelli, 2015, p. 196). Studies consistently suggest that autistic children are mostly visual learners (West, 2008 in Morris, 2015; Vander Wiele, 2011; Xin and Sutman, 2011). A study conducted by Peterson (2002) has showed evidence for a high rate of 'pictorial' mind organisation using 'visual images' and 'nonlinguistic mental imagery' in autistic people (Peterson, 2002, p. 1457) and established that, 'although autistic children might demonstrate a deficit for narrative encoding, pictures might open routes to an awareness of mental states in children with autism' (*Ibid.*, p. 1444). Indeed, autistic people tend to show a better understanding of concepts if they are shown with images rather than orally or narratively described and experts therefore highlight the usefulness of books with illustrated scripts (Shore and Rastelli, 2015, p. 211).

Taking into account autistic children's sensory perceptual and cognitive specificities when designing adapted books might therefore lead to more pleasant and effective reading. A major point would be to pay a cautious attention to the light reflectivity generated by the books – especially when choosing paper and colour compositions – to make sure to keep it at the minimum. Indeed, a majority of autistic children display a specific sensitivity to light, whether it is a hyper-sensitivity, making reflectivity painful, or a hypo-sensibility, leading to a compulsive and alienating focus on reflection. Fragmented perception, hyper focalization on details, and contrast and background/foreground discrimination deficits should also be kept in mind when designing the illustrations. Combined to the attention specificities explained above, it would appear more effective to use sober and explicit illustrations and to keep the information conveyed on each page to the minimum. To deal with the mono-treatment and the delayed treatment of information, it might be worth considering systematically separating text pages from illustration pages so the oral/narrative and visual information are not offered at the same time. Similarly, it might be useful to divide the information to their thinnest possible component and to dedicate a text page and an illustration page to each piece of information given. Likewise, imagery seems to be an effective vector for autistic people. Though most of children's books rely on illustrations, it might be important to insist on that even more, giving every significant element of information its own illustration. Finally, to make older readers profit from this vector without ostracising them, comics format could be especially relevant.

Looking at the issue more deeply

The hypothesis behind this paper is that there would be a market for more children's books on autism or for autistic children in France. In order to assess the existence and the extent of the unfulfilled demand for CBoA and BfAC, three steps were undertaken:

The first was to inventory the existing offer already supplied by French publishers and to this end I conducted an inventory of the available books. The second was to investigate the demand from parents of autistic children and parents in general, since they represent one of the main categories of potential buyers. This was done through two surveys. Finally, to bring qualitative elements of context shading light on the quantitative results, I conducted a few interviews with people specialised in autism and/or publishing.

Research planning and data collection – how many children's books on autism or for autistic children exist?

There is no official database allowing researching for children's books on autism or for autistic children. In order to identify the existing books, I used the databases of 'Livres Access'[3] and 'Autisme France Diffusion'.[4] To add to my findings, I then researched the online catalogues and/or bibliographies of all the 'Autism Resources Centers'[5] (ARC) with an online access (20 out of 25) and/ or contacted their specialised librarians for further books recommendations. In order to focus my research on books, I only selected the items with an ISBN code. I then applied the following criteria to select the relevant books: Books aimed primarily at children (not parents or caretakers); Recommended age range from 0 to 10 years old; Books on autism or for autistic children; and Books published by French publishers. The first to third criteria were used to fit the dissertation scope. The third criterion was applied in a strict way. Consequently, although books aiming at a non-autistic primary audience may have been inventoried provided they presented characteristics especially relevant to autistic children – such as sign language books relying heavily on visual learning and therefore very useful for non-verbal autistic kids – books on disability in general were discarded. The last criterion, 'published by French publishers', was preferred to 'published in French language' because other French languages (such as French Canadian) may actually be very different from French. Though they might be understood to some extent, they are likely to impair the empathy and/or learning capacity conveyed by the books when read by French children. Books originally published by foreign publishers but translated and published by French publishers were included.

The main limitation regarding this inventory is that, since there are no official databases on the subject, it cannot be guaranteed that it is exhaustive. However, considering the systematic research I carried out with the ARCs and specialised online platforms and the time and energy it represented, it appears reasonable to consider that it is a fair representation of the offer available to potential buyers.

In total, I was able to identify just 64 books, published between 1993 and 2017. To give a comparison, in 2016 alone, 16,521 children's and young adult books titles were printed in France (SNE, 2017). I read the blurb and the description of the books I had identified, as offered by their publisher or the database they were referenced on, to extract more information. Figures 15.1–15.7 display their main characteristics.

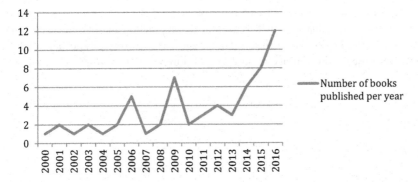

FIGURE 15.1 Number of CBoA and BfAC published per year

The timeline shows a relatively low production during the 2000s – around one or two books per year – with the exception of two peaks in 2006 and 2009. They might be linked to a renewed interest for the subject due to the two first governmental plans for autism (2005–2006; 2008–2010) and to the *Act on the equal rights and opportunities* (2005). From 2010, we can observe a steady increase that might however be weakened by the 2017 numbers. Indeed, at the time this research was conducted – May 2017 – only one book published in 2017 was identified. It is to be noted that only one book published before 2000 – in 1993 – was identified; however, it is possible that more books have been published during the 1990s but are no longer distributed nor referenced.

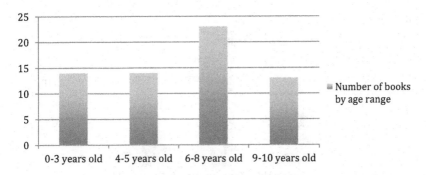

FIGURE 15.2 Number of CBoA and BfAC by age range

Concerning the repartition by age range, 14 books were aimed at readers up to 3 years old; 14 were aimed at readers aged 4–5 years old; 23 were aimed at readers from 6 to 8 years old and 11 at readers aged 9–10 years old. It is acknowledged that these categories do not cover the same number of years. However, they were designed to represent the different steps of child general and reading development. It is to be noted that the age used for this classification was the lowest on the recommended age scale. For example a book with a recommended age from 3 to 6 years old would be included in the 0–3 years old category. It is also important to note that the intellectual and developmental age of autistic children may significantly vary from their calendar age – in one way or another. We can however observe the scarcity of books for children aged 0–5 and 9–10 years old.

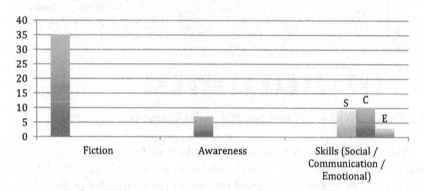

FIGURE 15.3 Number of CBoA and BfAC by category

When looking at the repartition of the books according to their categories, we can observe a predominance of fiction books over skills books and awareness books. It is to be noted that, among skills books, eight were to some extent adapted books (four in the sub-category of communication skills and four in the sub-category of social skills).

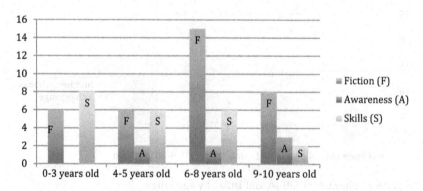

FIGURE 15.4 Number of CBoA and BfAC by age range and category

If we look at the repartition by age range and category we can see that, when spread across their intended group age, the lack of awareness and skills books is even more marked. The number of skills books is inversely proportional to the age progression. For the 9–10 years old category, there are only two skills books identified. Though children aged 9–10 years old with a lower level of development can use books aimed at a younger audience, the lack of skills books matching their peer age could be very detrimental as they progress and for other autistic children with a better level of development but who still need help to decode social norms.

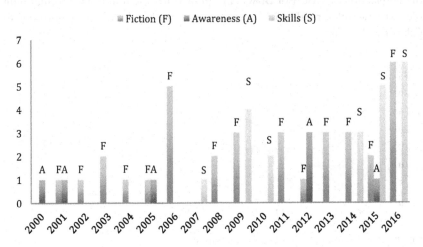

FIGURE 15.5 Evolution of books categories through time

The evolution of the categories of books published since 2000 shows a recent and steady progression of skills books, which may indicate a better acknowledgement of autism as a specific condition, therefore needing dedicated support. The evolution of the publication of fiction books fluctuates more, although generally increasing over the period. The publication of awareness books seems on the contrary completely random. Except for a slight peak in 2012, it can be seen that it has not increased over the period. It can also be seen that, although the *Act on the equal rights and opportunities* legally requiring disabled children to be schooled within mainstream schools was adopted in 2005, no new awareness book was published before 2012.

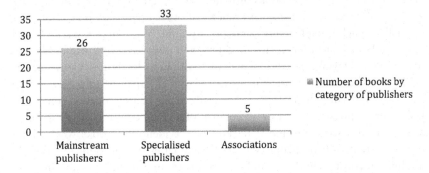

FIGURE 15.6 Number of books by type of publishers

When comparing the repartition of the books by type of publishers, it can be seen that, although specialised publishers are predominant, mainstream publishers still represent a significant part. On the contrary associations are a minority in the publication of CBoA or BfAC. This underlines the importance to highlight the existence of a market in order to encourage profits driven companies to publish such books.

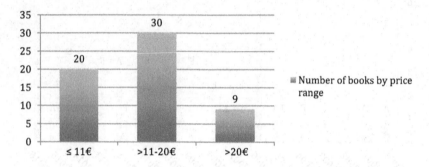

FIGURE 15.7 Number of books by price range

Finally, when looking at the repartition of CBoA and BfAC according to their price range, it can be observed that they tend to be more expansive than the average. Indeed, the average price for a book in France is around 11€ (SNE, 2014). It can be noted that 66% of CBoA and BfAC are above this price. Indeed, their average price is then of 14€ or around 30% more than the national average price. It is to be noted that five of the identified books were out of print and that therefore their price was not identified nor included in the chart.

Considering the results

Books from other French-speaking countries – especially French Canada – were referenced in all of the ARCs and databases consulted, therefore slightly increasing the number of books available. However, important language and cultural differences exist between France and other French-speaking countries, especially French Canada. For this reason, it is quite common to translate French Canadian books into French (Pépin, 2009), and most French Canadian movies, such as Xavier Dolan's, are released in France with French subtitles. Consequently, children's books written in these languages may not be appropriate to help autistic children improving their skills – especially their communication and social skills – or to promote a better acceptance of autism within their non-autistic peers. It is also worth noting that eight of the identified books were taking, to some extent, autistic people sensorial specificities into account – mainly by building on autistic children's high visual functioning to allow communication for non-verbal children or to enhance the comprehension of social concepts.

However, overall, this quantitative review shows that the number of CBoA or BfAC published by French publishers appears rather low.

In addition to this numeral scarcity, the quality of these books seems to be questionable too. Indeed, studies pointed out that in order to promote tolerance and inclusion, children's books on diversity should avoid stereotypes, bring quality literature, and should not require extraordinary skills from disabled characters in order to compensate for their disability (Blaska and Lynch, 1998; Heim, 1994; Nasatir and Horn, 2003; Smith-D'Arezzo, 2003). However, by looking at the titles and blurbs of the books identified and their overuse of some adjectives – such as 'amazing', 'extraordinary', or 'super' – it seems likely that a significant part of the fiction books do not meet these criteria. A further qualitative review of these books would then be needed to confirm or infirm this hypothesis and examine its implications.

Another issue may lie in the availability and the diffusion of these books. Indeed, there is no unique database that allows identifying children's books on autism or for autistic children. Researching these books then represents a significant time-consuming effort. What is more, ARCs do not offer the same catalogues and bibliographies and therefore induce inequality depending on autistic children's location. Besides, parents of non-autistic children are less likely to refer to these centres or to specialised databases when researching for new books and traditional research websites do not properly inventory these books. To give an example, when researching 'autism' on amazon.fr within the category of French-language children's books, only 24 results occur. Likewise, when applying similar criteria to the French National Library database, only six results occur.

As some elements of comparison, when doing the same research on amazon.co.uk within the category of English-language children's books, 1,224 results occur. The number of English-language children's books covering autism available on the British amazon website is then 51 times higher than this of the French-language books available on the French amazon website. In comparison, the number of English speakers worldwide is only seven times higher than this of French speakers (France Diplomatie, 2017; Saint Georges International, 2017; Statista, 2017). While this may also be partly explained by the difference in scale of French-language and English-language publishing markets, it nonetheless underlines the weak involvement of French publishers regarding autism in children's literature.

As another example, when applying the same three first criteria used for this inventory – Books aimed primarily at children; Recommended age range from 0 to 10 years old; and Children's books on autism or Books for autistic children – to the list of the British publisher Jessica Kingsley Publishing (JKP), I was able to identify 68 books published since 2000. This indicates that for the past 17 years, and although France and Britain have a similar population and a similar autism prevalence rate, one single British publisher has published more children's books on this subject than every French publishers gathered. Though JKP is acknowledged as the main British publisher on autism, and that therefore it is likely that other British publishers have issued lesser books on this subject, this gives an indication of how significantly the covering of autism differs between British and French publishers.

Seeking first-hand opinions on the availability of books on autism/featuring autistic characters

In order to evaluate the existence and characteristics of a market for more children's books on autism and for autistic children in France I conduced several surveys.

The first survey was aimed at parents of autistic children aged from 0 to 10 years old. Participants were asked to confirm that they were parents or legal guardians of an autistic child before completing the questionnaire. The second survey was aimed at parents of non-autistic children aged from 0 to 10 years old. Participants were asked to confirm this quality as well. To avoid numerical bias, participants were also asked to confirm that they were filling the survey for the first time.

Parents or legal guardians were chosen as the target population because they represent an important category of potential buyers of children's books. Other categories were also considered (such as schools or medical institutions) but were discarded due to practical reasons. In order to protect participants' privacy the surveys were completely anonymous and no personal details – other than those required to participate to the survey – were asked of them.

The first survey was available online on questenligne.com from 4 June to 4 August 2017. The online diffusion was preferred because it allowed an easier and potentially wider diffusion, as autism communities are highly involved online. This provider was chosen because it allowed all the type of questions involved in the questionnaire and provided interesting tools for exploiting the results. In order to share the survey, I e-mailed several French associations of autistic parents as well as French-speaking Facebook groups' administrators to ask them to relay it to their members.

The second survey was printed and distributed to parents at public children leisure centres (with the consent of their directors), libraries, and other shops. This type of distribution was chosen for practical considerations and because it allowed a good potential sociological and cultural diversity (except maybe for the wealthiest population). Printed forms were preferred to online forms because in this case it would have been harder to identify a specific community to contact by mailing.

Survey design

According to Swetnam, the most important aspect of a survey is that the 'respondent needs to understand what is required in the precise sense that the researcher meant it' (Swetnam, 2007, p. 60) and the surveys were therefore designed as simply and precisely as possible. To this end, both of the surveys were preceded by a short introduction explaining the context of the research and the terminology used. In addition, in the surveys forms, the category of BfAC was named 'Books specifically designed for autistic children' and the sub-category of Adapted books, 'Books adapted to autistic children's sensory perceptual specificities' in order to be more intelligible for the respondents. The surveys were written in French and I subsequently translated them in English, giving a particular attention to stick to the original meaning and not to alter the questions or responses in any way.

The first survey was made of 10 questions, the first one being a validation of the required criteria for participation. It used both dichotomous, multiple choices, and rating scale questions. Questions 2–5 were aimed at evaluating the current situation regarding books possession, their characteristics and purchase networks. Questions 6–10 were aimed at evaluating the level and characteristics of the demand for more CBoA and BfAC, with question 9 examining the interest in e-books and question 10 assessing the level of acceptance for higher than average prices. Questions 1 ('I confirm that I am the parent or legal guardian of an autistic child/autistic children aged from 0 to 10 years old and that I am filling this questionnaire for the first time'), 2 ('Do you currently own children's books on autism or specifically designed for autistic children?'), and 6 ('In general, would you like to have more children's books on autism or specifically designed for autistic children?') were made mandatory in order to complete the survey.

The second survey was made of 12 questions, using both dichotomous, multiple choices, and rating scale questions. Participants were also asked to confirm that they met the required criteria before answering the questions. Questions 1–3 were aimed at assessing the level of familiarity with autism. Questions 4–7 were aimed at assessing the current situation regarding the possession and uses of books. Questions 8–12 were aimed at evaluating the level and characteristics of the demand for more CBoA.

One limitation of these surveys could be the lack of background data regarding the participants. This was done on purpose because the aim was to evaluate the general demand for more books. This seemed to be a necessary preliminary step before more detailed surveys. However, such surveys would now be helpful in order to analyse further the sociological factors of this market with data such as parents' occupation, children's age, gender, and level of development.

Likewise, the surveys did not ask for participants' nationality or for the nationality of the publishers of the books they already possessed. This was considered at a stage, but was discarded both for practical and substantive reasons. The aim of the surveys being to assess the market it seems irrelevant to rule out international competition – from books published by publishers from other French-speaking countries or in other languages – nor international potential – from non-French respondents. However, due to the distribution networks used for both surveys, it appears very likely that a significant majority of participants were actually French or at least residing in France.

Another potential bias of the surveys could be that it is possible, due to their subject, that participants shared a pre-existing interest for books and reading. Therefore, the results might be more representative of books-friendly parents than parents in general – although a few participants actually stated their disinterest for books. However, this does not appear to be detrimental since market strategies generally focus on meeting their potential buyers' needs and expectations rather than on conquering a reluctant audience.

As every survey, an 'expectancy effect' and 'social desirability bias' – meaning that the responses given might have been influenced by the researcher's hypothesis or by what is perceived as more socially wanted (Grimm, 2010; Lewis-Beck et al., 2004) – might have also been present. It is to be noted that the second survey forms were distributed in or around my hometown, where my father works as a general practitioner. Though they were completely anonymous and I was not present and therefore not in contact with any of the respondents during this period, this could have nonetheless slightly increased these biases.

The main limitation of the first survey consists in the use of 'moderately interested' as a possible answer to questions 8 and 9. Indeed, with the phrasing of this answer it is difficult to establish whether respondents used it to show a limited interest, a neutral position or a polite disinterest. This is a flaw of this survey and I was careful not to reproduce it in the second survey. However, due to the small percentage of respondents choosing 'moderately interested' as their answer, the impact on the results was limited.

A final limitation might be found in the number of participants. In total, 65 respondents took part in the first survey and 36 in the second survey. Although these numbers are enough by research standards to allow quantitative interpretations (Dixon et al., 1987; Walliman, 2005), and while the very high pro or con response rate to most of the questions might allow careful generalisation, larger studies would be needed to confirm the present results.

Results and data

Survey 1 – Parents of autistic children

Below is presented a summary of the results for each question.

Question 1: I confirm that I am the parent or legal guardian of an autistic child/autistic children aged from 0 to 10 years old and that I am filling this questionnaire for the first time (mandatory in order to take part to the study).

Number of respondents: 65

All the respondents confirmed that they met the criteria to take part in the survey. It is to be noted that during the forms collection, I received one form completed by a respondent that had answered 'No' to this question. This form was therefore discarded.

Question 2: Do you currently own children's books on autism or specifically designed for autistic children?

FIGURE 15.8 Number of participants owning CBoA or BfAC

It is to be noted that three participants answered 'No' to this question then answered 'Skills Books' at question 4. The number of respondents already possessing CBoA or BfAC might therefore be slightly higher. We can observe that although they still represent a minority, a large proportion of respondents do not possess any CBoA or BfAC (Figure 15.8).

Question 3: If no, why (multiple answers allowed)?

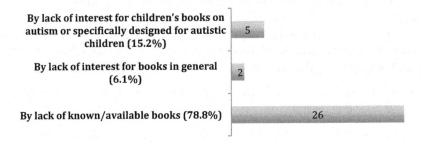

FIGURE 15.9 Reasons for not owning CBoA or BfAC

The high percentage of respondents declaring not owning any CBoA or BfAC because of a lack of known or available books tend to confirm an issue regarding these books' production and distribution rather than a disinterest for the subject (Figure 15.9).

Question 4: If yes, are they (multiple answers allowed):

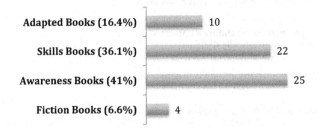

FIGURE 15.10 Types of CBoA and BfAC owned by participants

It is to be noted that three respondents answered 'No' to question 2 and then 'Skills Books' to this question. However, even when these responses are discarded, 'Skills Books' remains the second highest category (Figure 15.10).

Question 5: If yes, how did you come to know these books (multiple answers allowed)?

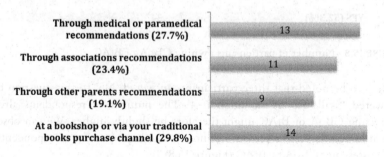

FIGURE 15.11 Purchase channels of CBoA and BfAC

It is to be noted that one respondent answered, 'Yes' to question 2 and did not respond to this question. Similarly, two respondents answered 'No' to question 2 and then answered this question ('Bookshop' for one and 'Association' for the other). We can nonetheless observe that only 1/3 of the respondents acquired their books through their traditional books purchase channel (Figure 15.11).

Question 6: In general, would you like to have more children's books on autism or specifically designed for autistic children?

FIGURE 15.12 Demand for CBoA and BfAC

Despite the low rate of current possession of such books, the high pro response rate to this question suggests a potential strong demand for more CBoA and BfAC (Figure 15.12).

Question 7: If no, why (multiple answers allowed)?

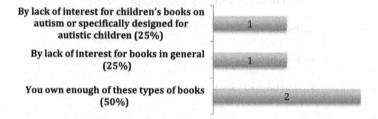

FIGURE 15.13 Reasons in case of absence of demand

It is to be noted that one respondent that has stated his/her interest for more books answered this question ('By lack of interest for books on autism'). He/she has also responded 'No' to question 2 but 'Skills books' and 'Association' to questions 4 and 5 (Figure 15.13).

Question 8: If yes, could you indicate your degree of interest regarding the different categories of books?

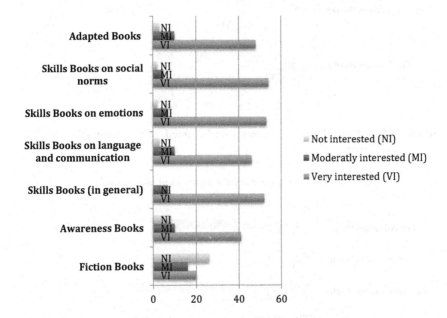

FIGURE 15.14 Demand for adapted, skills, awareness and fiction books

It is to be noted that among the respondents to this question, some did not respond for one or more category of books. This might indicate that they would have responded negatively. However, due to the really low number of respondents involved for each type of books this does not alter the general statistics of the results (three respondents did not answered for 'Awareness Books'; two for 'Skills Books in general'; one for 'Social Books in general'; three for 'Skills Books on language'; one for Skills Books on social norms' and one for 'Adapted Books') (Figure 15.14).

Question 9: If yes, would you also be interested by e-book versions?
It is interesting to note that, although the interest for e-books in France is rather low (Chrisafis, 2012; Hoffelder, 2015), a majority of the respondents did indicate a high interest for Awareness, Skills, and Adapted e-books. It is to be noted that among the respondents, one did not answered for 'Awareness Books' and two did not answered for 'Adapted Books' (Figure 15.15).

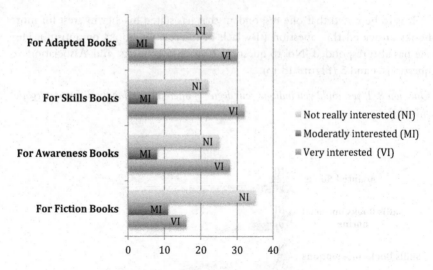

FIGURE 15.15 Demand for e-book versions of adapted, skills, awareness, and fiction books

Question 10: If yes, would you agree to a price higher than the average?

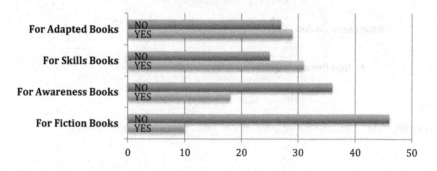

FIGURE 15.16 Price acceptance from parents with autistic children

Regarding fiction books and awareness books, more than the half of the respondents that were 'Very Interested' (for both formats) answered 'No' or didn't answer the question which might indicates a strong opposition to a higher price for these categories. On the opposite, for skills books and adapted books, 2/3 of those who were 'Very Interested' answered positively to a higher price for the e-book format and the majority of them answered also positively for the printed format. It can be noted that among the respondents two did not answered for 'Awareness Books' and that six of them who had answered 'Yes' to question 6 did not answer this question at all. This might indicate that the percentage of negative responses might have been slightly higher if they had (Figure 15.16).

Summary

There were a lot of discrepancies in the respondents' responses for this survey. It is possible that respondents gave insufficient attention to the introductory explanations or spent a limited amount of time answering the questions, resulting in mechanical errors.

Nonetheless, overall, the survey indicated a rather limited level of current CBoA or BfAC possession, induced mainly by a lack of known/available books, coupled with a high level of demand for more CBoA and BfAC, more especially for skills books, adapted books, and awareness books. Respondents also display a solid acceptance of higher than average prices for skills and adapted books, especially for e-books formats.

Survey 2 – Parents of non-autistic children

Below is presented a summary of the results for each question.

Question 1: How would you assess your knowledge about autism?

FIGURE 15.17   Level of participants' knowledge on autism

The responses to this question seem to reflect the state of the general population knowledge about autism (Figure 15.17).

Question 2: Have you ever been in contact with autistic people?

FIGURE 15.18   Level of participant's contact with autistic people

We can observe that 2/3 of the respondents have been in contact with autistic people, which might indicate a pre-existent interest for the subject (Figure 15.18).

Question 3: Has/have your child/children ever been in contact with autistic people?

No (69%)   25

Yes (31%)   11

FIGURE 15.19 Level of participants' children's contact with autistic people

Unlike the respondents themselves, most of their children have not been in contact with autistic people, which underlines the current poor (school) inclusion of autistic children (Figure 15.19).

Question 4: Have you ever used and/or would you be willing to use books in order to inform or familiarize your child/children on sensitive issues (disability, diversity, tolerance, etc.)?

No (0%)   0

Yes (100%)   36

FIGURE 15.20 Use of books as an informative support

All the respondents answered positively to this question, which indicates a high reliance on reading as a vector of information and tolerance (Figure 15.20).

Question 5: Do you currently own children's books on autism?

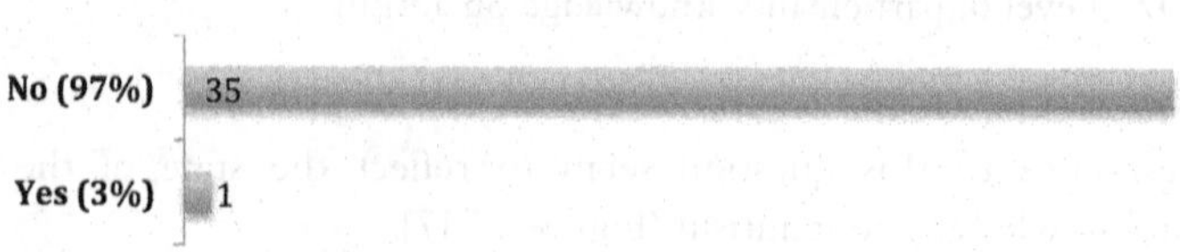

No (97%)   35

Yes (3%)   1

FIGURE 15.21 Participants' possession of CBoA

It can be seen that although all respondents declared using or being willing to use books to inform or familiarize their children on sensitive issues, and while the majority of them have been in contact with autistic people, only one of them currently own a CBoA (Figure 15.21).

Question 6: If no, why (please select the main reason why)?

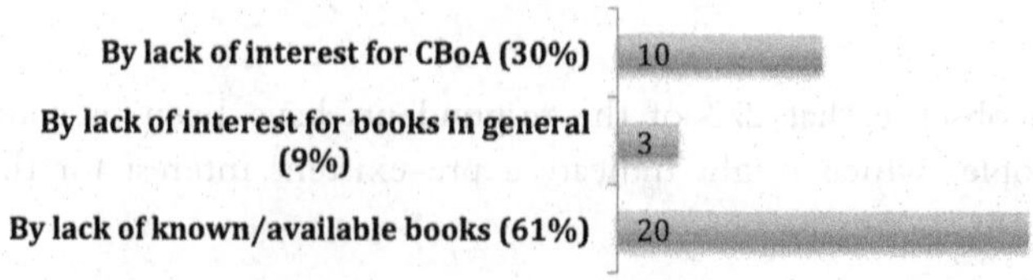

By lack of interest for CBoA (30%)   10

By lack of interest for books in general (9%)   3

By lack of known/available books (61%)   20

FIGURE 15.22 Reasons for the lack of possession of CBoA

The majority of respondents declared not owning any CBoA because of a lack of known or available books, which tends to confirm an issue regarding these books production and distribution rather than a disinterest for the subject. Moreover, eight of the respondents declaring not owning any CBoA by lack of interest for this kind of books did answered positively to questions 8, 10, 11, and/or 12 which might indicate a lack of spontaneous demand for these books rather than a real disinterest (Figure 15.22).

Question 7: If yes, are they (multiple answers allowed):
Number of respondents: 1

The only respondent having declared owning a CBoA said that it was a fiction book. It is to be noted that three respondents answered 'No' to question 5 but answered 'Awareness' to this question (these answers were therefore discarded).

Question 8: In general, would you be willing to acquire children's books on autism?

No (14%)	5
Yes (86%)	31

FIGURE 15.23 Participants' demand for CBoA

The high pro response rate to this answer suggests a potential strong demand for more CBoA matching the growing interest of the general population for the subject of autism. It is to be noted that one participant answered 'No' to this question but did answered questions 10 (Fiction: Interested; Awareness: Interested), 11 (Fiction: Not particularly interested; Awareness: Interested), and 12 (Fiction: No; Awareness: No) (Figure 15.23).

Question 9: If no, why (please select the main reason why)?
Number of respondents: 5

Two respondents indicated a lack of interest for books in general and the three others stated their disinterest for CBoA.

Question 10: If yes, could you indicate your degree of interest regarding these different categories of books?

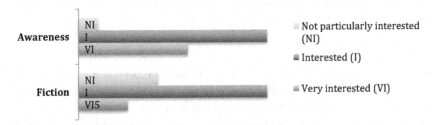

FIGURE 15.24 Demand for awareness and fiction books

Respondents displayed a strong interest for both categories of CBoA. 75% of them declared being 'interested' or 'very interested' by Fiction books. The interest was even higher for Awareness books with 93% of the respondents being interested or very interested (Figure 15.24).

Question 11: If yes, would you also be interested by e-book versions?

FIGURE 15.25 Demand for e-books versions of awareness and fiction books

The interest was however a lot lower for e-books formats, which echoes the general weakness of the e-books market in France (Chrisafis, 2012; Hoffelder, 2015). The positive responses rate was nonetheless slightly higher for Awareness books, which might reflect a highest general interest for this type of books (Figure 15.25).

Question 12: If yes, would you agree to a higher than average price?

FIGURE 15.26 Price acceptance from parents of non-autistic children

The majority of the respondents declared not to be willing to pay a higher than average price for fiction books (76%) or awareness books (58%). The higher pro response rate for Awareness books might nonetheless once again indicate a stronger interest for this category of books (Figure 15.26).

Summary

In summary, this survey indicates a solid demand for CBoA, and more especially for awareness books. Although the limited number of participants does not allow for a real generalisation, these results do seem to reflects the growing interest for autism from the broader population and suggest both a request and an opportunity to publish more children's books on the subject.

Discussion and analysis of surveys

The evaluation of the current rate of possession of CBoA and BfAC indicates a deficiency in production, distribution, and referencing of these books. The surveys suggest that there is a strong demand for these books coupled with a low current possession rate because of a lack of known/available books. This seems to show that there are not enough books published and that those which are published are not efficiently advertised, distributed, and referenced.

Looking at the subcategories, it is interesting to note that the results provided by the respondents of the surveys strongly differ from the data offered by the inventory of available books. Indeed, for Survey 1, respondents displayed a higher interest for skills and adapted books, whereas fiction books are majoritarian within the available books. Similarly, when examining the results of Survey 2 we can see that the general population would be highly interested by awareness books. However, it is the category with the fewest books currently published. This seems to indicate that the offer is not only rather poor in quantity but is also potentially unsuitable regarding the categories of the books published. The recent increase in the publications of skills books might however indicate that publishers have started to acknowledge this.

The results from both surveys regarding the level of acceptance for higher than average prices proved to be very informative. I chose not to indicate an average price in order to let people respond in regard to what they perceived to be the normal price, knowing that CBoA and BfAC are already consistently more expansive than the average. Retrospectively, it might have been interesting to state the national average price (11€) or the average price for these types of books (14€). However, the results clearly indicate a potential acceptance of higher prices for adapted and skills books, especially from those who are very interested in these books and therefore more likely to buy them. The negative answers given by the same and other respondents – even from those being very interested by these categories – for fiction and awareness books strengthen these results as they discard a possible expectancy effect or social desirability bias. These results appear to be very relevant from a publisher point of view since adapted and skills books – unlike fiction or awareness books – might have higher costs of production due to the need to collaborate with experts or to use specific material and designs.

Overall, the surveys suggest that there is a high potential demand for CBoA and BfAC, which is not currently met by the offer of available books. The demand is very high for skills books and adapted books, both in printed and e-books formats and including at a higher than average price. Likewise, the demand for more awareness books appears strong. In comparison, the demand for fiction books is lower but still existent.

Interviews

Whereas I was initially intending to consider the inventory of related titles and back this up with associated surveys, I decided to conduct some interviews with public librarians, including some working within Autism Research Centres (ARC). I was also able to interview a publisher of adapted books. Other potential interviewees – including publishers and representatives of associations – were approached but did not answer (or answered too late).

The librarians working within ARC were cautious on the subject of special resources to support autism, commenting generally that there was 'a lot to do' regarding the perception and attitudes towards disability or developmental and learning disorders in the French society, as well as for the perceptions of autism in particular. There was a general response that autism was less favourably perceived than other disorders and a general lack of knowledge and accurate information, even though there had been more recent media coverage of autism. There was similar general agreement among the librarians that reading and literature represent powerful tools for helping the development and inclusion of autistic children, but the opportunities for specific publishing to support autism were generally not taken up. The lack of a central resource providing information on all the titles available[6] was noted, as was a lack of training offered to librarians about disability and diversity.

In general, the interviews provided informative illustrations of the perceptions of autism in the French society. They illustrated how sensitive the subject can be and also highlighted the lack of accurate information on autism. The fact that France is lagging behind other developed countries in its treatment and perception of autism can partly explain why economic partners, such as publishers and booksellers, are also lagging behind in their coverage of the subject.

An interview with Mme de Vismes, president of the association TouPI,[7] offered some precious insights regarding how publishing BfAC. As identified by the literature review, autistic children have special needs regarding reading and books. Because mainstream children's books do not cover some subjects or do so inappropriately for an autistic audience, it appears that autistic children would benefit from more books specifically developed for them, regarding both their content and their format. Cooperation with child development specialists appears to be essential. In addition, when asked about books on other disabilities, Mme Vinson-Galy, public librarian at Le Chambon sur Lignon, indicated an upcoming collection published by a mainstream publisher (Belin) and aimed at 'dys-children' (children with dyslexia, dyspraxia, dyscalculia, etc.). She emphasised that an important aspect of these adapted books was that they would be written by established children's books authors. This highlights the importance to provide CBoA and BfAC matching the quality of other children's books and therefore the need for cooperation between autism specialists, authors, and publishers.[8] Considering concerns about the price of such books, it appears understandable to wish that families of autistic children could access books at the lowest cost. However, both the inventory and the surveys demonstrated that they were willing to pay – and were already paying – a higher than average price for skills books and adapted books, enabling publishers to finance the extra costs generated by the collaboration with specialists or by the use of specific materials.

The low involvement of French publishers in the publication of CBoA and BfAC may result from different and additional factors. One of these factors, which motivated this paper, could be that they are not aware of this potential market. Indeed, as Mme de Vismes and the Autism Alliance (2015) indicated, in France, disabilities or special needs are perceived more as liabilities than offering potential, and are therefore generally disregarded within conisation of market economics. In addition, for decades, autism was conceived in France as a psychosis or an untreatable intellectual deficiency, therefore preventing any behavioural or developmental interventions and the tools they might use, dividing the autistic community, and discouraging the general population to have any interest or involvement in the subject. However, recently, it seems that this context has begun to positively evolve. Indeed, surveys show that the general population is more and more aware and curious about autism (OpinionWay, 2010, 2011, 2012) and families of autistic children as autistic people themselves are gaining in visibility and coverage from both the politics and the media.[9] In parallel, economic actors appear to begin to understand the market potential of special needs (Charbonnier, 2017). This may be challenging for French economic actors, including publishers, as it necessitates new processes, such as collaborations with other fields and actors. It nonetheless represents strong enough opportunities to encourage publishers to follow their foreign fellows and start publishing books aiming at children with special needs – as showed by the two new imprints aiming at 'dys-children' recently developed by two French mainstream publishers Nathan and Belin (Develey, 2016; Fisne, 2017).

Overall, it therefore appears that the high levels of demand and price acceptance displayed by potential buyers combined to a favourable change in the socio-economic context represent a great opportunity for publishers to publish more CBoA and BfAC.

Recommendations for further research

The aim of this paper was to assess the hypothesis that there is a lack of children's books on autism and for autistic children in France. The research clearly indicated that the demand for such books was high and currently not met by the existing offer, both regarding its number, type, and diffusion. However, larger quantitative surveys collecting more detailed personal data would be needed to confirm and refine this demand. Additionally, it is to be noted that although general surveys can serve as good market indicators for economic actors, they cannot replace personalised and tailored companies' market studies.

Another important area of investigation would be this of the quality of CBoA and BfAC. Indeed, when looking at the books inventoried, some elements – such as the use of sensationalist vocabulary or the redundant structure of the stories – might suggest an issue regarding their quality. The need for quality appears however crucial in order to maintain the usefulness of these books and a lasting demand and market, and it would be interesting to further research this aspect.

Conclusion

The aim of this paper was to assess the hypothesis that there is a market for more children's books on autism and for autistic children in France. The literature review demonstrated how and why such books would be needed in order to support autistic children's development and to promote their self-esteem and inclusion. The primary research established a strong demand for such books, both from parents of autistic children and parents in general, which is not currently met by the existing offer. Available books are indeed insufficient and inefficiently distributed, advertised, and referenced. Issues regarding their quality might also be present. As explored throughout this essay, different historical and cultural factors might explain this discrepancy between demand and supply. These factors are nonetheless beginning to change, creating a more favourable context. It appears important that economic factors, in addition to the politics and media, take part in and advantage of this change. As this paper demonstrated, publishing more CBoA and BfAC is not only necessary to support autistic children's development and inclusion but may represent a financial opportunity for publishers. Likewise, not only autistic children deserved to be helped and included but their well-being and inclusion would be beneficial, culturally, and economically, to the whole of wider society.

Notes

1 The French national independent public institution in charge of regulating the health care system.
2 A governmental consultation aiming at designing a five-year plan in order to better address autistic people's needs in terms of diagnosis, therapies, and inclusion.
3 An online platform referencing books for readers with special needs. Available at: http://livres-acces.fr
4 An online platform and publisher created by the father of an autistic child to identify and produce resources about and for autistic children. Available at: www.autismediffusion.com/PBSCCatalog.asp?CatID=283256
5 Local public centres in charge of relaying information on autism, providing training to professionals and support to autistic people and their families. Each of them hosts a documentation centre.
6 This database could, for example, be created by the ARCs or by the state Secretary for Disability.
7 TouPI, tous pour l'inclusion, support association for the inclusion of people with cognitive disabilities, and publisher of adapted books (https://toupi.fr).
8 This compares well with the structures established by Quick Reads in the UK, part of The Reading Agency, to provide attractively produced materials for those with low literacy levels.
9 With, for example, the launch of the 4th Autism plan, the organisation of various sport events, the social media buzzes around autistic people, or the success of the Netflix show 'Atypical'.

References

AFP (2015). 'Autisme: l'Etat condamné à verser plus de 240 000 euros à sept familles'. *Libération*. Available at: www.liberation.fr/societe/2015/07/22/autisme-l-etat-condamne-a-verser-plus-de-240-000-euros-a-sept-familles_1352322 (Accessed: 10 September 2017).

Alliance Autiste (2015). *Submission about Education for Autistics in France for the Day of General Discussion (DGD) on the Right to Education for Persons with Disabilities.* Available at: http:// allianceautiste.org/wp/wp-content/uploads/2015/03/20150225_AllianceAutiste_ rapport_alternatif_France_CRC_en_6.pdf (Accessed: 10 September 2017).

Ambitious about Autism (2017). 'Stats and Facts'. Available at: www.ambitiousaboutautism. org.uk/stats-and-facts (Accessed: 10 September 2017).

American Psychiatric Association (2013). *Diagnostic and Statistical Manual of Mental Disorders, DSM-5.* 5th edition. Washington, DC: American Psychiatric Publishing.

Artman-Meeker K., Grant T.O. and Yang X. (2016). 'By the Book Using Literature to Discuss Disability with Children and Teens'. *TEACHING Exceptional Children,* January/February 2016, pp. 151–158.

Asperger, H. (1944). 'Autistic psychopathy in childhood'. In Frith U. (1991), *Autism and Asperger Syndrome.* Cambridge, UK: Cambridge University Press, pp. 37–92.

Auzanneau N. and et Chardron S. (2012). 'Autisme, clichés et préjugés'. *OpinionWay.* Available at: www.opinion-way.com/fr/sondage-d-opinion/sondages-publies/sante/ autisme-cliches-et-prejuges-pour-le-mouvement-pour-l-autisme.html (Accessed: 10 September 2017).

Auzanneau N. and Weidmann A. (2010). 'Connaissance et perception de l'autisme: etude miroir auprès des Français et des professionnels de santé'. *OpinionWay.* Available at: www.opinion-way.com/fr/sondage-d-opinion/sondages-publies/sante/connaissance- et-perception-de-l-autisme-etude-miroir-aupres-des-francais-et-des-professionnels- de-sante.html (Accessed: 10 September 2017).

Barillas R. (2014). '5 Reasons why everybody benefits from more diverse children's books'. *Huffington Post.* Available at: www.huffingtonpost.com/roxana-barillas/5- reasons-why-everybody-b_b_5529656.html (Accessed: 10 September 2017).

Baron-Cohen S. (1995). *Mindblindness: An Essay on Autism end Theory of Mind.* Cambridge, MA: MIT Press.

Blaska J.K. and Lynch E.C. (1998). 'Is everyone included? Using children's literature to facilitate the understanding of disabilities,' *Young Children,* 53, 36–38.

Bogdashina O. (2013). *Questions sensorielles et perceptives dans l'Autisme et le Syndrome d'Asperger.* Grasse: AFD Editions.

Brenna B. (2009). 'Creating characters with diversity in mind: Two Canadian authors discuss social constructs of disability in literature for children'. *Language and Literacy,* 11(1). doi: 10.20360/G2201G.

Brugha T.S. et al. (2016). 'Epidemiology of Autism in adults across age groups and ability levels'. *Journal of Psychiatry,* 209(6), 498–503.

Center for Autism Research (2017). 'Intellectual disability and ASD'. Available at: www. carautismroadmap.org/intellectual-disability-and-asd (Accessed: 10 September 2017).

Center for Disease Control and Prevention (2017a). 'Autism spectrum disorder. Data and statistics'. Available at: www.cdc.gov/ncbddd/autism/data.html (Accessed: 10 September 2017).

Center for Disease Control and Prevention (2017b). 'Diagnostic criteria for 299.00 Autism spectrum disorder'. Available at: www.cdc.gov/ncbddd/autism/hcp-dsm. html (Accessed: 10 September 2017).

Center for Disease Control and Prevention (2017c). 'Vaccines do not cause Autism'. Available at: www.cdc.gov/vaccinesafety/concerns/autism.html (Accessed: 10 September 2017).

Charbonnier R. (2017). 'Handicap, un business comme les autres?'. *La Tribune.* Available at: http://acteursdeleconomie.latribune.fr/strategie/management/2017-06-06/handicap- un-business-comme-les-autres-731835.html (Accessed: 10 September 2017).

Chrisafis A. (2012). 'Why France is shunning the e-book?'. *The Guardian*. Available at: www.theguardian.com/books/shortcuts/2012/jun/24/why-is-france-shunning-ebooks (Accessed: 10 September 2017).

Collectif Autisme (2011) 'Autisme et scolarisation'. *OpinionWay*. Available at: www.opinion-way.com/fr/sondage-d-opinion/sondages-publies/sante/ljcorp-autisme-et-scolarisation.html (Accessed: 10 September 2017).

Compagnon C., Corlay D. and Petreault G. (2017). 'Evaluation du 3^e plan autisme dans la perspective d'un 4^e plan'. Rapport IGAS no 2016–0946 / IGEN No 2017–031. Available at: www.igas.gouv.fr/spip.php?article606 (Accessed: 10 September 2017).

Cooper K., Smith L. and Russell A. (2017). *Social Identity, Self-Esteem, and Mental Health in Autism*. University of Bath. Available at: http://opus.bath.ac.uk/53727/ (Accessed: 10 September 2017).

Corrigan P.W., Backs E.A., Qreen A., Lickey Thwart S. and Perm D.L. (2001). 'Prejudice, social distance, and familiarity with mental illness'. *Schizophrenia Bulletin*, 27(2), 219–225.

Council of Europe (2007). 'Council of Europe Resolution on the education and social inclusion of children and young people with autism spectrum disorders'. Available at: www.autismeurope.org/main-fields-of-action/right-to-education/council-of-europe-resolution-on-the-education-and-social-inclusion-of-children-and-young-people-with.html (Accessed: 10 September 2017).

Council of Europe (2014). Resolution CM/ResChS(2014)2 *Action européenne des handicapés (AEH)* v. France, Complaint No. 81/2012. Available at: https://search.coe.int/cm/Pages/result_details.aspx?ObjectID=09000016805c66e8 (Accessed: 10 September 2017).

Couture S.M. and Penn D.L. (2003). 'Interpersonal contact and the stigma of mental illness: A review of the literature'. *Journal of Mental Health*, 12(3), 291–305.

Dachez J. (2016). 'Envisager l'autisme autrement: une approche psychosociale'. Thesis at Nantes University.

Develey A. (2016). '*La dyslexie, nouvel el dorado des éditeurs jeunesse*'. Le Figaro. Available at: www.lefigaro.fr/langue-francaise/actu-des-mots/2016/12/06/37002-20161206ARTFIG00070-la-dyslexie-nouvel-eldorado-des-editeurs-jeunesse.php (Accessed: 10 September 2017).

Dixon B.R., Bouma G.D. and Atkinson G.B.J. (1987). *A Handbook of Social Sciences Research*. Oxford: Oxford University Press.

Eggertson L. (2010). 'Lancet retracts 12-year-old article linking autism to MMR vaccines'. *CMAJ*, 182, E199–E200.

Europe1(2017)'Autisme:despersonnalitéssoutiennent10mesurespourchangerlequotidian'. Available at: www.europe1.fr/societe/autisme-des-personnalites-soutiennent-10-mesures-pour-changer-le-quotidien-3218051 (Accessed: 10 September 2017).

European Agency for Special Needs and Inclusive Education. 'Country information, France'. Available at: www.european-agency.org/country-information/france/national-overview/complete-national-overview (Accessed: 10 September 2017).

Eyre C. (2015). 'Children's book industry discusses diversity charter'. *The Bookseller*. Available at: www.thebookseller.com/news/children-s-book-industry-discusses-diversity-charter (Accessed: 10 September 2017).

Fisne A. (2017). 'Education: ces livres numériques qui aident les enfants dys à lire'. *La Tribune*. Available at: www.latribune.fr/technos-medias/education-ces-livres-numeriques-qui-aident-les-enfants-dys-a-lire-746066.html (Accessed: 10 September 2017).

Flood A. (2011). 'Study finds huge gender imbalance in children's literature'. *The Guardian*. Available at: www.theguardian.com/books/2011/may/06/gender-imbalance-children-s-literature (Accessed: 10 September 2017).

France Diplomatie (2017). 'The status of French in the world'. Available at: www.diplomatie.gouv.fr/en/french-foreign-policy/francophony-and-the-french-language/the-status-of-french-in-the-world/ (Accessed: 10 September 2017).

Frith, U. (1989). *Autism: Explaining the Enigma*. Oxford, UK: Blackwell.

Frith, U. (1991). *Autism and Asperger Syndrome*. Cambridge, UK: Cambridge University Press.

Gagnon E. (2001). *Power Cards: Using Special Interests to Motivate Children and Youth with Asperger Syndrome and Autism*. Shawnee, Kansas, USA: APC.

Giles D.C. (2010). 'Parasocial relationships' in Eder J., Jannidis F. and Schneider R. (eds.), *Characters in Fictional Worlds: Understanding Imaginary Beings in Literature, Film, and Other Media*. Berlin: de Gruyter Editors, pp. 442–458.

Goldberg Edelson M. (2010). 'Sexual abuse of children with Autism: Factors that increase risk and interfere with recognition of abuse'. *Disability Studies Quarterly*, 30(1), 2–21.

Grimm P. (2010). *Social Desirability Bias*. Wiley International Encyclopedia of marketing, vol. 2.

Harris C. (2016). 'France lags behind the rest of Europe when it comes to autism with around just one fifth of children getting the support they need, it's been claimed'. *Euronews*. Available at: www.euronews.com/2016/03/30/children-losing-out-as-france-lags-rest-of-europe-on-autism-vision (Accessed: 10 September 2017).

Heim, A.B. (1994). 'Beyond the stereotypes: Characters with mental disabilities in children's books'. *School Library Journal*, 40, 39–42.

Hoffelder N. (2015). 'eBooks Made up 6.4% of France's Book Market in 2014'. *The Digital Reader*. Available at: https://the-digital-reader.com/2015/06/29/ebooks-now-make-up-6-4-of-frances-book-market/ (Accessed: 10 September 2017).

Hogan K. (2017). 'Nonverbal thinking, communication, imitation, and play skills with some things to remember'. *UNC School of Medicine*. Available at: http://teacch.com/communication-approaches-2/nonverbal-thinking-communication-imitation-and-play-skills-with-some-things-to-remember (Accessed: 10 September 2017).

Hood J. (2015). 'Why diversity in children's literature really matters'. *Huffington Post*. Available at: www.huffingtonpost.com/jacob-hood/why-diversity-in-children_b_7718510.html (Accessed: 10 September 2017).

Hoorn J.F. and Konijn E.A. (2003). 'Perceiving and experiencing fictional characters: An integrative account'. *Japanese Psychological Research*, 45(4), 250–268.

Horiot H. (2016). 'Scolarisation des enfants autistes: les réponses de la France ont de quoi inquiéter'. *L'Obs*. Available at: http://leplus.nouvelobs.com/contribution/1471830-scolarisation-des-enfants-autistes-les-reponses-de-la-france-ont-de-quoi-inquieter.html (Accessed: 10 September 2017).

INSEE (2017). '9.4 Personnes handicapées. Tableau de l'économie française'. Available at: https://insee.fr/fr/statistiques/2569386?sommaire=2587886&q=enfants+handicapés (Accessed: 10 September 2017).

Inserm (2017). 'Autisme'. Available at: www.inserm.fr/thematiques/neurosciences-sciences-cognitives-neurologie-psychiatrie/dossiers-d-information/autisme (Accessed: 10 September 2017).

INS HEA (2017). 'Lancement du 4e plan autism'. Available at: www.inshea.fr/fr/content/lancement-du-4e-plan-autisme (Accessed: 10 September 2017).

Johnson C. (2016). 'The books world is a massive diversity fail – here's how we change it'. *The Guardian*. Available at: www.theguardian.com/childrens-books-site/2016/jun/17/childrens-books-diversity-change-inclusive-minds (Accessed: 10 September 2017).

Johnson D.R., Cushman G.K., Broden L.A. and McCune M.S. (2013). 'Potentiating empathic growth: Generating imagery while reading fiction increase empathy and prosocial behavior'. *Psychology of Aesthetics, Creativity & the Arts*, 7(3), 306–3012, August 2013.

Kanner, L. (1943). 'Autistic disturbances of affective contact'. *Nervous Child*, 2, 217–250.

Kokina A. and Kern L. (2010). 'Social Story™ Interventions for Students with Autism Spectrum Disorders: A Meta-Analysis'. *Journal of Autism and Developmental Disorder*, 40, 812–826.

Langloys D. (2015). 'L'aide sociale à l'enfance: une impitoyable machine à broyer les familles d'enfants autistes. Rapport de l'association Autisme France sur les vilations des droits et dysfonctionnements de l'aide sociale à l'enfance'. *Autisme France*. Available at: http://anae-revue.over-blog.com/2015/08/rapport-autisme-france-sur-les-dysfontionnements-de-l-ase.html (Accessed: 10 September 2017).

Lewis-Beck M.S., Bryman A. and Liao T.F. (2004). 'The sage Encyclopedia of social science research methods'. Available at: http://methods.sagepub.com/Reference/the-sage-encyclopedia-of-social-science-research-methods (Accessed: 10 September 2017).

Lindsay J. Vander Wiele, (2011). 'The pros and cons of inclusion for children with Autism spectrum disorders: What constitutes the least restrictive environment?'. Thesis, Liberty University.

Long B. (nd) 'Using picture books to support the development of language in young children with Autism'. *Diagnostic Center Central California*. Available at: www.dcc-cde.ca.gov/af/Autism%20Presentations/B.%20Long%20-%20Using%20Picture%20 Books.pdf (Accessed: 10 September 2017).

Mancil G.R., Haydon T. and Whitby P. (2009). 'Differentiated effects of paper and computer-assisted social stories™ on inappropriate behavior in children with Autism'. *Focus on Autism and Other Developmental Disabilities*, 24(4), 205–215.

Markram K. and Markram H. (2010). 'The intense world theory: A unifying theory of the neurobiology of autism'. *Frontier*. doi: 10.3389/fnhum.2010.00224.

Moffat C. (2003). 'The human right that the north won't name: Education for Autistic children'. *Fortnight*, 420, 22–23.

De Montalivet (2017). 'Les associations d'autisme furieuses contre Vanessa Burggraf après ses propos dans ONPC'. *Huffington Post*. Available at: www.huffingtonpost.fr/2017/02/28/ les-associations-dautisme-furieuses-contre-vanessa-burggraf-apr_a_21838162/ (Accessed: 11 September 2017).

Morris S. (2015). *Social Narratives*. London: Jessica Kingsley Publisher.

Mottron L., Dawson M., Soulières I., Hubert B. and Burck J. (2006). 'Enhanced perceptual functioning in Autism: An update, and eight principles of Autistic perception'. *Journal of Autism and Developmental Disorders*, 36(1), 27–43.

Murch S.H., Anthony A., Casson D.H., Malik M., Berelowitz M., Dhillon A.P., et al. (2004). 'Retraction of an interpretation'. *Lancet*, 363, 750.

Nasatir D. and Horn E. (2003). 'Addressing disability as a part of diversity. Through classroom children's literature'. *Young Exceptional Children*, 6(4), 2–10.

Park M. (2008). 'Making scenes: Imaginative practices of a child with Autism in a sensory integration-based therapy session'. *Medical Anthropology Quarterly, New Series*, 22(3), 234–256.

Pellicano E. (2013). 'Sensory symptoms in Autism: A blooming, buzzing confusion?' *Child Development Perspectives*, 7(3), 143–148.

Pépin E. (2009). 'De l'Hexagone au monde entier, une conquête du livre québécois'. *Les libraires*. Available at: http://revue.leslibraires.ca/articles/sur-le-livre/de-l-hexagone-au-monde-entier-une-conquete-du-livre-quebecois (Accessed: 10 September 2017).

Peterson C.C. (2002). 'Drawing insight from pictures: The development of concepts of false drawing and false belief in children with deafness, normal hearing, and Autism'. *Child Development*, 73(5), 1442–1459.

Plimley L., Bowen M. and Morgan H. (2007). *Social Skills and Autistic Spectrum Disorder.* Chapters 1 and 2, edited by Plimley L. et al., London: SAGE Publications.

Le Point (2016). 'Autisme: un texte anti-psychanalyse rejeté par l'Assemblée'. *Le Point. fr* Available at: www.lepoint.fr/politique/autisme-un-texte-anti-psychanalyse-rejete-par-l-assemblee-08-12-2016-2088978_20.php# (Accessed: 10 September 2017).

Quinn B. and Malone A. (2011). *Autism, Asperger Syndrome and Pervasive Development Disorder: An Altered Perspective.* London: Jessica Kingsley Publishers.

Ritvo E. (2006). *Understanding the Nature of Autism and Asperger's Disorder. Forty Years of Clinical Practice and Pioneering Research.* London: Jessica Kingsley Publishers.

Rogers S.J. and Ozonoff S. (2005). 'Annotation: What do we know about sensory dysfunction in autism? A critical review of the empirical evidence'. *Journal of Child Psychology and Psychiatry*, 46(12), 1255–1268.

Rosen J. (2017). 'Young writers call for diverse books at Children's Institute'. *Publishers Weekly.* Available at: www.publishersweekly.com/pw/by-topic/industry-news/bookselling/article/73300-a-new-generation-of-writers-calls-for-diverse-books-at-children-s-institute.html (Accessed: 10 September 2017).

Saint Georges International (2017). 'How many people in the world speak English'. Available at: www.stgeorges.co.uk/blog/learn-english/how-many-people-in-the-world-speak-english (Accessed: 10 September 2017).

Samson F., Mottron L., Soulières I. and Zeffiro T.A. (2012). 'Enhanced visual functioning in Autism: An ALE meta-analysis'. *Human Brain Mapping*, 33, 1553–1581.

Sathyanarayana Rao T.S. and Andrade C. (2011). 'The MMR vaccine and autism: Sensation, refutation, retraction and fraud'. *Indian Journal of Psychiatry*, 53(2), 95–96.

Shedlosky-Shoemaker R., Costabile K.A. and Arkin R.M. (2014). 'Self-expansion through fictional characters', *Self and Identity*, 13(5), 556–578.

Shore S.M. and Rastelli L.G. (2015). *Comprendre l'autisme pour les nuls.* French adaptation by Schovanec J. and Glorion G. Paris: Editions First.

Smith-D'Arezzo W.M. (2003). 'Diversity in children's literature: Not just a black and white issue'. *Children's Literature in Education*, 34(1), 75–94.

SMSD ASD (2017). 'Power cards'. Available at: www4.smsd.org/autism/html12764.htm (Accessed: 10 September 2017).

SNE (2014). 'Accès au livre et prix du livre'. Available at: www.sne.fr/acces-au-livre-et-prix-du-livre/ (Accessed: 10 September 2017).

SNE (2017) 'L'Edition jeunesse'. Available at: www.sne.fr/app/uploads/2017/11/SNE_Chiffres_EditionJeunesse_VOK.pdf (Accessed: 16 August 2019).Statista (2017). 'The most spoken languages worldwide (speakers and native speaker in millions)'. Available at: www.statista.com/statistics/266808/the-most-spoken-languages-worldwide/ (Accessed: 10 September 2017).

Stone M. (2010). 'Vaccines cause autism'. *Yale Scientific.* Available at: www.yalescientific.org/2010/04/mythbusters-vaccines-cause-autism/ (Accessed: 10 September 2017).

Swetnam D. (2007). *Writing your Dissertation.* Oxford: How to Book.

Taylor L.E., Swerdfeger A.L. and Eslick G.D. (2014). 'Vaccines are not associated with autism: An evidence-basedmeta-analysis of case-control and cohort studies'. *Vaccine*, 32, pp. 3623–3629.

Tien K.C. (2008). 'Effectiveness of the picture exchange communication system as a functional communication intervention for individuals with Autism spectrum disorders: A practice-based research synthesis'. *Education and Training in Developmental Disabilities*, 43(1), 61–76.

The United Nations (1966). 'The international covenant on economic, social and cultural rights'. Available at: www.ohchr.org/en/professionalinterest/pages/cescr.aspx (Accessed: 11 November 2019).

The United Nations (1989). 'The convention on the rights of the child'. Available at: www.ohchr.org/en/professionalinterest/pages/crc.aspx (Accessed: 11 November 2019).

The United Nations (2006). 'The convention on the rights of persons with disabilities'. Available at: www.un.org/development/desa/disabilities/convention-on-the-rights-of-persons-with-disabilities.html (Accessed: 11 November 2019).

Volkmar F.R., Paul R., Rogers S.J. and Pelphrey K.A. (2005). *Handbook of Autism and Pervasive Developmental Disorders.* Volume 2, 3rd edition. Hoboken, New Jersey, USA: Wiley.

Wakefield A.J., Murch S.H., Anthony A., Linnell J., Casson D.M., Malik M., et al. (1998) 'Ileal-lymphoid-nodular hyperplasia, non-specific colitis, and pervasive developmental disorder in children'. *Lancet*, 351, 637–641.

Walliman N. (2005). *Your Research Project.* London: Sage.

Wodka E.L., Mathy P. and Kalb L. (2013). 'Predictors of phrase and fluent speech in children with Autism and severe language delay'. *Pediatrics*, 131(4), 1128–1134.

World Health Organisation, Media Center (2017). 'Autism spectrum disorders'. Available at: www.who.int/mediacentre/factsheets/autism-spectrum-disorders/en/ (Accessed: 10 September 2017).

Xin J.F. and Sutman F.X. (2011). 'Using the smart board in teaching social stories to students with Autism'. *TEACHING Exceptional Children*, 43(4), 18–24.

Yeager L. (2010). 'Disability literature can inspire empathy'. *Reading Today*, 28(3), 44.

INDEX

Note: **Bold** page numbers refer to tables; *italic* page numbers refer to figures and page numbers followed by "n" denote endnotes.